# Pablo Casals

*Music advisor to Northeastern University Press*

GUNTHER SCHULLER

# Pablo Casals

## ROBERT BALDOCK

*Northeastern University Press*

BOSTON

Copyright © 1992 by Robert Baldock

First published in Great Britain in 1992. Published in the United States of America in 1993 by Northeastern University Press, Boston, in arrangement with Victor Gollancz, Ltd.

*Library of Congress Cataloging-in-Publication Data*

Baldock, Robert, 1950–
Pablo Casals / Robert Baldock.
p.   cm.
Discography: p.
Includes bibliographical references and index.
ISBN 1-55553-176-8 (cloth : acid-free paper)
1. Casals, Pablo, 1876–1973. 2. Violoncellists—Biography.
I. Title.
ML418.C4B28   1993
787.4'092—dc20
[B]          93–10115

MANUFACTURED IN GREAT BRITAIN
97  96  95  94  93   5  4  3  2  1

Music must serve a purpose, it must be
something larger than itself, a part of humanity, and that, indeed, is at the core of my
argument with music of today – its lack of
humanity. A musician is also a man, and
more important than his music is his attitude
to life. Nor can the two be separated.

*Pablo Casals*

# Contents

# List of Illustrations

Acknowledgement is made to the following individuals and institutions for their generosity in supplying photographs. For the cases in which it has not proved possible to ascertain accurate provenance, a general acknowledgement and apology is given.

Fundació Pau Casals, San Salvador, Spain: 2–5, 8, 10, 13; Museo Pablo Casals, San Juan, Puerto Rico: 17, 18, 24; the United Nations: 20; the Reid Music Library, the University of Edinburgh: 7, 12; Hélène Jeanbrau, Prades: 15, 16, 19; the Fred and Rose Plaut Collection, Yale University Music Library: 23, 26; the John Fitzgerald Kennedy Library, Boston: 22; Mário Cláudio and Imprensa Nacional/Casa da Moeda, Lisbon: 6; Edm. Joaillier, Paris: 11; Fritz Henle, by kind gift of Rosa Cueto Coll: 25; Michael Berry, London: 21, 27; Dennis Stock, Magnum Photos Ltd, New York and London: 9; author's collection: 14.

# Acknowledgements

This book was researched on two continents, and written, at times, on three. I have received advice, support, stimulus, friendship, boosts of morale and generous hospitality from very many people, and acknowledge a real contribution which can scarcely be honoured in a brief list.

My thanks are due first to Marta Casals Istomin, for permission to study the papers in her own possession and in the collection of the Fundació Pau Casals, for the time she put aside to recall her own life with Casals, and above all for her consideration in permitting a stranger to traverse memories which are more precious to her than to anyone. To Eugene Istomin I am grateful for vivid access to his long friendship with Casals, and for his enormous perception, intellectual vigour and candour.

I am conscious of my debt to all those who have written about Casals before me, whether or not I have followed their approach. The benchmark work is H. L. Kirk's magisterial *Pablo Casals*, completed and in page proof at the moment of Casals' death in November 1973. The more I have learned about Casals, the more respect I have had for Mr Kirk's book. Mine is a different work, but he has been unfailingly wise and encouraging in my attempt to master, as he did, this huge life.

Crucial help with details of research was provided by Señor Macià Alavedra, Vice-President of the Generalitat in Barcelona, José Alfaro, Christopher Bunting, Rosa Cueto Coll, Pablo and Helen Eisenberg, Amaryllis Fleming, Pilar Casals Frizzoni, Sylvia Fuhrman, Bernard Greenhouse, Señorita Mercèdes Guarro i Tapis (of the Casa Museu Pau Casals in San Salvador), Pamela Hind O'Malley, Mary Jordan, Rui Paes, Professor Paul Preston, Alexander Schneider, Milly Stanfield, and Sándor and Alice Végh.

In addition, I acknowledge important assistance, in Britain, from Dr John and Pauline Anderson, Margaret Campbell, Catharine Carver, Kenneth Harris, Ronald Hayman, Dr Werner Kilian, the late Nelly Kromwell, Rhys Lewis, Professor Isabel de Madariaga, James Methuen-Campbell, Paolo lo Rito, Dr Eric Sams, Anthony Sattin, Wilfred Stiff (of Ibbs and Tillett), Philippa Stockley, and Jeremy Upton (of the Reid Music Library at the University of Edinburgh).

For friendship, advice, connections, hospitality and much more while in the United States, I thank in particular Gladys Topkis, Richard Coe, Judy Turner-Meyer and Dr Pat Romero. For help in many ways I am indebted to Dr Debórah Dwork, Harry Haskell, Professor Jaroslav Pelikan, Kate Rivers and Kevin Levine (of the Music Division of the Library of Congress in Washington, DC), John G. Ryden, Harvey Sachs, Harold E. Samuel (the Librarian, Yale University Music Library), and Teri Noel Towe.

In Barcelona I was particularly assisted by Señor Juan Maragall of the Fundació Pau Casals, and by Dr Jon Arrizabalaga, Dr Francesc Bonastre, Montserrat Cabre, Señora Joana Crespi (Biblioteca Nacional de Catalunya), Professor Emili Giralt, Dr José Vicente Gonzalez del Valle, Dr Ramon Balius i Juli, Francesc Pollés Farré, Henry Sire, Amelia Trueta de Strubell and Dolores Vives.

For generous help in Prades, I thank Françoise Anglade, Mme André Four, Mme Dolores Gouzy, Christine Hicks, Pierrette and Nannou Hostelrich, Hélène Jeanbrau and Enriquetta Casals Touron.

For their welcome, invaluable assistance, and friendship to me in Puerto Rico, I am grateful to Aníbal Ramírez, of the Museo Pablo Casals in San Juan, Vincente Aguirre, Jack Delano, Luz Hernandez, Señora Angélica Montañez, Dr Amaury Rosa Silva, and Emilia Vallecillo.

I am grateful to the staff of the Westminster Music Library, London, the Wren Library, Trinity College, Cambridge, and the John F. Kennedy Library, Boston. I acknowledge the gracious permission of Her Majesty The Queen to publish an extract from the journals of HRH Queen Victoria, at The Royal Archives, Windsor.

I have received indispensable help and support from my literary agents, Caroline Davidson and Robert Ducas. I am grateful to Livia Gollancz for her early encouragement of the project, to Richard Wigmore, my editor at Victor Gollancz, for patience, persistence and wise counsel, to Helen Dore, for her skilled editing, warm good humour and remarkable speed, and to Katrina Whone, Kate Hordern and their colleagues at Gollancz for unflappable professionalism under duress.

For several happy weeks in the summer of 1991 I was fortunate enough to be invited to join a BBC Television team filming, on location in France and Spain, an 'Omnibus' documentary, first broadcast in September 1991 as 'Song of the Birds: A Portrait of Pablo Casals'. For their invigorating companionship and fresh perspectives I thank the director, Anna Benson Gyles, and her colleagues, Tricia Chacon, Colin Waldeck, Bruce Gallaway, Pilar Cortes, Kelvin Billing and Kath Bedford. Colin Spector, who originated the idea for the programme, has supported and challenged me throughout the project.

Writing a book is both a pain and a pleasure. Those close to the author have only the pain. For their forbearance, tolerance and support I thank, deeply, Joan and John Baldock, Sophie Baldock, Marion and Robin Adam, Michael Berry, Dr Ann Geneva, Rolf and Jenny Hangartner, Christopher Warwick, Brian Auld and Ethna Clifford. My greatest debt is to my father, Frank Baldock, whose quiet knowledge and profound love of music inspired this endeavour, more perhaps than he knew. He died while the writing was in progress. I dedicate the book to my mother, with love, and to my father, in his memory.

# *Prelude*

Arriving at Barcelona's stylish marble and glass international airport – constructed at El Prat de Llobregat as the gateway to Catalonia in Olympics year – the traveller can transfer effortlessly to a sleek double-decker railway connection. If, instead of taking the fast train to the city, one heads south, the old nineteenth-century line shadows the coastline all the way, eventually, to Valencia. From Llobregat, it first passes Sitges, then Catalan place-names roll by – Castelldefels, Vilanova i la Geltrú, Cunit . . . until, 70 kilometres on, the train halts at the small station of San Vicens.

A short walk from the station finds the main coast road. First one encounters the new resort of Comarugga, with its modern hotels and apartment complexes constructed for Swiss and German tourists. Further on, the road becomes the Avinguda Palfuriana, and enters the village of San Salvador. Here – other than a few low apartment blocks – the houses along the seafront have been standing for most of the century.

The Casa Museu Pau Casals abuts the beach. Photographs reveal that, fifty years ago, it stood in relative isolation, secluded and protected by its own land. Now all around is built up. From the road one can see a tiled rooftop emerging from tall, deep-reddish-coloured walls. Through heavy iron gates one glimpses a formal, Italianate garden – a pond, terraces, statues and paths, with pines and fir trees, pampas grass, succulents and red tubular cannas. At the main entrance a dog barks at the gatekeeper's lodge. Stepping inside, one is immediately away from the noise of the holiday environment.

Inside, the villa – as its name suggests – is a mixture of museum and private house. The first rooms are full of display cases, exhibiting documents, photographs, certificates, medals and letters. Further along the central passage one finds the bedrooms, furnished with personal ornaments, a wash-bowl, an old piano. Suddenly it feels like a house that has been abandoned, as if the occupant has departed suddenly without having quite enough time to arrange things. Though the house has since been occupied by other members of the family, that is precisely what did happen. In January 1939, with Franco's propagandist, the savage General Queipo de Lano, threatening to sever his arms at the elbow, Casals left. He was sixty-two. Before he could return the Nationalist victory had been completed, Madrid fell, and the Republic was over. Except briefly – when he returned in 1955 to bury his longtime companion and second wife in the neighbouring cemetery at El Vendrell – Pablo Casals did not see his home again.

Here is the house he built and lovingly extended over a period of thirty years, his possessions still inside it. Because he would not set foot in Franco's Spain, it was lost to him for almost thirty-four years. For seventeen of those he was not 300 kilometres away – a five-hour car ride across the Pyrenees – in the French Catalan town of Prades. But he might as well have been at the other end of the earth.

With a jolt one begins to appreciate what exile means, and understand the strength of Casals' resolve: to be able to breathe the same air, but not to see one's own home. Being so close it would have been easy to weaken, and make the concession that Franco needed. But Casals did not. This is the central fact, the tragedy of his life. This is where one understands the kind of man one is dealing with.

Casals has not of course been ignored. There are books about his life and books about his music: I have identified some seventy-five separate books and articles devoted exclusively to the man or his performance. But in a sense he eludes all of them, and will always do so. Casals himself did not have time for autobiography, just as he had no time for an edition of the Bach Unaccompanied Suites, nor indeed very much for a recording of them. Life was to be lived, for the moment, as Bach was to be played, in a different way at a different time. Nothing was frozen. But he did co-operate with others, who re-created his story from recollections late in life. Biographical works have tended to feed off each other: myths and distortions have perpetuated themselves, and anecdotes have been transformed into narrative, as a life viewed retrospectively tends to recast its own trajectory. What has often been presented is a sanitized, reverential account. But Casals is diminished by reverence and awe. He was full-blooded, a man of passion. His powerful character, likes and dislikes, moods and temperament, were all vital elements of his genius. We know a great deal about what happened during this colossal life, the facts, actions and statements. But we know relatively little about feelings, motives and emotions. Casals possessed a severe nineteenth-century discretion: emotion was not on display. And because he had several lives, he tended to disremember one in order to avoid pain to another. The loss of significant portions of his archive – the destruction of early papers during the war, and of others to keep them from falling into Nationalist or Nazi hands, has helped to keep the story uncorroborated. But there is still a lot to go on, and through the generosity of Casals' family and the Fundació Pau Casals I have been able to examine a good proportion of it.

Casals' emotional reticence ceased the moment he began to play. While he sought to influence the perception of himself in print, his musical performance was predicated on the principle of total honesty, total truth, total revelation. The source of the most powerfully emotional string playing of the twentieth century – possibly of all musical performance – is known largely through the facts of his life. Exploring deeper sources is a treacherous business, both in itself and to the man. But Casals does not need protecting from himself: his was substantially an heroically selfless life. The intention of this book is to link facts to feelings, where they can be plausibly inferred, in order to show the human source of the most exquisite sounds anyone has ever obtained from the violoncello.

There are few lives that can have spanned so dramatic a period. Casals was born before the motor-car, and died three years after man had first walked upon the moon. At the age of twenty-two he performed for Queen Victoria. Sixty years later, when he played for John F. Kennedy, he still had twelve years to live. His century was the century of total war, and he witnessed all of it. Casals outplayed time at its own game: he had several lives. Towards the end it must have seemed that some had been lived by another man.

Working on Casals one is confronted by a wall of love. It is not a sentimental worship, but a deep and honest affection for a man who, on any level of analysis, possessed a substantial streak of saintliness – with both its inspiration and its blindnesses. Not having known him personally – the first biographer to be in this position – is both a loss and a liberation. It is a loss in the sense that Casals so enhanced and charged the lives of all who knew him, that many felt it the most important relationship of their lives. And it is a liberation because his presence and charm were so powerful as to disarm the capacity for dispassionate evaluation. I offer here an evaluation which I trust honours what I was told by those who loved Casals, as well as what I found, an account perhaps of a life as it might have appeared as it was lived, not as it seemed to a great man looking back.

Almost inevitably, some of those who helped most will like it least: a study of an individual in fresh living memory is almost by definition an act of betrayal. One man's memory is not another's. The value of the life as it appears twenty years on is not as it appeared then. The world today is a different one. It may not be a world that Casals could have handled especially well. The brutality, the speed with which we learn of it, and the immediacy with which we witness it, would have caused him ceaseless agony. Casals had standards of morality and reason so severe that they sometimes made him appear unreasonable. But the world needs its heroes, however painful it is for them, and it needs them now.

This is primarily an account of Casals' life, not an analysis of his music. But music was intrinsic to his life, and he cannot be comprehended without it. Life and music happened together, not apart. What he played, and how he played, reflected what he did and how he felt. Fortunately Casals recorded copiously. We have a lot, if not everything. A comprehensive discography of performances by Casals which are available on compact disc is provided at the end of the text, to encourage the discovery.

# PART I

## *The Student*

# 1

## The Quiet Birth of a Genius, 1876–1890

If it hadn't been for my mother's conviction and determination that music was my destiny, it is quite conceivable that I'd have become a carpenter. But I do not think I would have made a very good one.

*Pablo Casals*

Pablo Casals very nearly did not have a life at all. The infant born to Doña Pilar Defilló i Amiguet and her husband Carlos Casals in the late afternoon of Friday, 29 December 1876[1] emerged with its umbilical cord twisted round its neck, its face turning blue from the constriction. The midwife – who was married to the local coal merchant – acted swiftly to avoid asphyxiation and after some anxious moments the child, a boy, began breathing normally.[2] The small Tarragonese town of El Vendrell, where the delivery took place in the parents' own home, had nothing in the way of medical facilities, even by the standards of the time, and problems at birth or soon afterwards normally led to the death of the infant. Pilar Casals knew this better than most: her first child, born the previous year, had died of lockjaw after only a few months. Over the next seventeen years she would have a further nine children. Of the total of eleven, only three survived beyond their first few years: most died within days of their birth. The three that lived were all boys, and each survived to be nearly 100. Pablo Casals was the eldest, and his continued existence became his mother's central preoccupation.

In 1876, El Vendrell was a busy provincial market town of about 4000 inhabitants. Four kilometres inland from the sea, it stands alongside the old Roman highway which stretches from Barcelona, 70 kilometres to the east, to the provincial capital of Tarragona, about 30 kilometres further west. The soil of the surrounding coastal plain is not rich, but it is well drained and supports excellent vineyards which for several centuries have produced the wines of the Penedès, a good quality *cava*, and the blended *Priorato* which is drunk in households throughout the region.

The town itself is built on a gentle slope, and its narrow, winding streets are as unsuitable for the cars that crowd them today as they must have been for the horse-drawn *tartañas* a century ago. The focal points of the town are its several tree-lined squares, in the shade of which the townspeople gather to talk, drink, or set up their market stalls. In the principal square is the surprisingly spacious, dark and ornate Church of Santa Anna, with its substantial Renaissance bell-tower. Off the square leads the carrer Santa Anna; immediately on the right-hand side, as you walk down it, is the house in which Casals was born.

Number 2 carrer Santa Anna is a tall, narrow, terraced building, comprising three floors and an attic. Carlos Casals and his wife took the main two floors as their home upon their marriage on 16 July 1874. He was not yet twenty-two, and she just twenty, and they had known each other for not much longer than a year. Neither was a native of the town, and the circumstances by which they came to be there were very different. Carlos Casals i Riba had been born in 1852, in a working-class area of Barcelona known as Sants. *Casals*, in Catalan, means small castle, or large country house, and indeed for eight generations the family had been involved in the relatively prosperous activity of manufacturing paper: the occupation is mentioned as much as eight generations before, in 1693, on the marriage certificate of Bernard Casals and Mariangela Elias.[3] Almost 200 years later, the direct line of ownership had passed to a different side of the family, and whereas his elder brother had gone into the business, Carlos himself was encouraged to follow instead his natural talent for both music and mechanics. He joined a Barcelona piano factory as an apprentice repairman, continuing, in his spare time, to study the piano and organ and sing in a local choral group. Sometime after his eighteenth birthday he chose to follow a friend, a barber called Peret Simó, to El Vendrell, where he found work repairing the baroque organ in the town's parish church. When the organist and choir-master died in 1872, Carlos took over his job.

Casals' mother, Pilar Ursula Defilló i Amiguet, came from much more adventurous stock. At the age of eighteen she had experienced a good deal more and travelled a great distance further than Carlos Casals. Pilar was one of eight children of a young Catalan couple who had emigrated from Barcelona to the Spanish Caribbean in the 1840s, settling first in Cuba, and then making their home in Puerto Rico. Pilar had been born in Mayagüez, on the eastern side of the island, at the end of 1853. As her father, José Defilló, grew more wealthy and successful, the family enjoyed the typically comfortable life-style of the nineteenth-century colonial expatriate. For reasons that are not clear, but perhaps had to do with official reaction to his outspoken criticism of the extreme harshness of the Spanish colonial regime, Defilló killed himself sometime in the late 1860s, his death being closely followed by the suicide of his eldest son. After these tragedies, his wife Raimunda, a determined and resourceful woman, returned with her two youngest children to Spain, settling with her sister in El Vendrell. Pilar enrolled at the local school and began to take piano lessons with the young organist at the Church of Santa Anna.

By the time Pilar Defilló married Carlos Casals, her mother Raimunda was dead, her younger brother had returned to the Caribbean, and the inheritance left by her father was virtually extinguished. Within the limited horizons of El Vendrell Pilar appeared educated, well-spoken, sophisticated and, to those around her – including her husband – rather grand. And to an extent she must have felt it. She was an imposing woman, not tall, but elegant and serious, her long dark hair coiled in neat braids around her head. Her manner was reserved, perhaps even censorious, and she did not fall into easy intimacy with the young women of the town. Early in her twenties she seemed naturally to command the title of *Doña*, usually applied to married women much later in their lives. But as a woman with no money and no immediate family, several thousand miles from her home, Pilar's options were decidedly few. She put aside, for the moment, any unrealizable ambitions and devoted herself to Carlos and to the succession of babies she bore – one almost every year – over the following decade. And as if in mourning for the identity she was putting behind her, Pilar Defilló wore black for the rest of her life.

Pablo Casals' childhood is highly susceptible to myth. Documentary sources for his early years are few and relatively unrevealing – formal certificates, school notices, the odd press clipping, are all that survive. Yet accounts of his youth are thick with anecdote and incident, and stories which have been perpetuated from one biography to another have acquired the status of verifiable truth. Casals' brother Enrique (Enric, in the Catalan form), in his own collection of what he termed 'unedited biographical data', published in 1979, includes an appendix which warns against this kind of factual cannibalism.[4] Enrique's account of Casals' youth is conspicuously brief, though he mentions some of the old stories and introduces several that are new. Much of the evidence for the early period, however, comes direct from Casals himself, via recollections given much later in his life to interviewers, and edited by them into book form.[5] These accounts are intriguing, plausible and doubtless substantially accurate, although since no individual is an unselfconscious witness to his own immaturity, the images which have been handed down do need to be handled with caution.

Casals' youth was not, except in romantic accounts, a carefree period of happiness and security. Life for the family was tough. His parents were young, poor and very largely alone: unusually, they did not have a wide network of family support. Pilar herself had, in recent years, lost her father, mother and one of her brothers, and her remaining siblings were effectively inaccessible in Puerto Rico: she never saw them again. Carlos came from a Barcelona family, not a local one, and there is little evidence that he received much assistance from it. There is no mention in Casals' 'memoirs' of grandparents, and little of uncles, aunts or cousins. It was not until 1955 that, at eighty, he made his first visit to Puerto Rico and encountered, in his Defilló relatives, the family he had always lacked. At his christening in January 1877 he was named Pablo after Pablo Palau, a pupil of his father but not a relative, Carlos after his father, and Salvador after the priest who baptized him. Pilar's first cousin, Fidèlia, became a godparent, along with Palau, but otherwise the little family was on its own. The young Pablo – or Pau, as the name was designated in Catalan – grew up tightly bonded to his father and his mother and influenced almost exclusively by them.

Carlos Casals was a strikingly good-looking man with dark eyes and a full beard. He maintained his interest in physics and mechanics as well as music, subscribing to scientific journals and, for years, experimenting with technical inventions. But his passion was political republicanism, and his hero Francesc Pi i Margall, founder of the Spanish Democratic party and briefly, in 1873, President of Spain's First Republic. Pi i Margall was a republican federalist, who favoured a Spain made up of a union of semi-independent states and governed on broadly socialist principles with strict controls over the power of both the Church and the military. Republicanism found its main following in the cities, however: in rural Catalonia the conservative peasantry was more solidly behind the Carlists, seeking to reinstate the monarchy and install a Bourbon pretender. As the Carlist guerrillas swept through El Vendrell in March 1874, Carlos Casals had joined a small group of republican enthusiasts in an unsuccessful attempt to defend the town, risking his life for a hopeless cause. Later in the year a constitutional monarchy was restored to Spain, with the young Alfonso XII as king, and the republic was defeated. As a child Pablo Casals learned from his father that what the Catalans needed was not what they had: separatism was in his blood even before he knew what there was to separate from.

As well as being church organist and training the choir, Carlos formed and led a men's chorus – La Lira – in the town and, with other local musicians, performed for fiestas and other secular celebrations in El Vendrell and neighbouring villages. To supplement his income further he took private pupils for piano and singing lessons in his first-floor studio at carrer Santa Anna. From his earliest consciousness, the infant Pablo was surrounded by music. Stories abound of the young child sitting with his head pressed to the upright piano, absorbing the resonances as his father played, or mimicking the solo lines of the voice pupils, though rather more finely in tune. What is certainly true is that he displayed early signs of an amazing gift, a conspicuous sensitivity to sound, and an inexhaustible musical curiosity. Casals sang before he could speak, and the moment any kind of musical instrument came within his grasp, he obtained from it sequential tones which were musically recognizable. Carlos gave his son his first lessons on the piano at the age of four, and in April 1882 Pablo was permitted to join the trebles in the church choir. Growing familiarity with the rhythm of Gregorian chant, with psalms, hymns and anthems, served only to make the young boy impatient to play the organ, and on occasions his father would allow him to join him in the organ loft and pull and push the stops as requested. But Pablo was firmly informed that there would be no organ lessons until his feet could comfortably reach the pedals.

Although his father held the key to the secret world of music, Pablo's strongest relationship – probably of his life – was with his mother. Until he began school at the age of six the two were inseparable; while Carlos was working, Doña Pilar would often take her son the 4 kilometres to the neighbouring seaside village of San Salvador, where they would play on the beach or visit the ancient Romanesque hermitage, the Ermita, next to which they occasionally stayed overnight in an inexpensive guest-house. But, repeatedly pregnant, Pilar was experiencing her own trauma. Her third child, Arturo, was born in 1879, when Pablo was two, fol-lowed the year after by José, who survived for only a few days. The next year, Enrique was born, but he too died painfully soon (Pilar would name her youngest child after him). The birth of Ricardo in 1883 was especially difficult. The baby died, and Pilar herself was very ill. Despite this she was pregnant again by Christmas, and the infant Carlos – the name of the first child being revived for the seventh – was born in 1884. The happiness brought by his survival was, however, shattered by the death soon afterwards of Arturo who, at almost five, had been a real companion for his brother and shown a similarly remarkable early musi-cal talent. Arturo had contracted cerebral meningitis and died on Three Kings' Day.

Each death made Pablo the more precious to his mother, and she the more focused upon him. From an early age he was made to feel the centre of the world he inhabited: in a real sense he never knew a world in which that was not so. Pilar, though not physically affectionate, was the source of all his self-confidence. 'I have never known anyone like my mother,' Casals wrote later. 'She dominates the memory of my childhood and youth, and her presence has remained with me throughout the years. Under all sorts of circumstances, in times of difficulty . . . I have asked myself what she would do, and I have acted accordingly.'6 Pilar held a radically independent view of life: she had learned to rely on no one, and to be obliged to nobody, and she communicated this to her son. Having seen the consequences of violence in her own early life, she was totally opposed to war. Years later, rather than see her youngest child called up to serve in the Spanish army, she dispatched him to Argentina where, for eleven years, he remained cut off from his family. Pilar's almost ruthless self-reliance extended to her view that man's primary responsibility was not to the law, or to the Church, but to his own conscience. Although Casals' early life was intimately bound up with the Church, neither his father nor mother suggested he need belong to, or believe in, a routine or institutionalized faith. Instead, he absorbed his mother's absolute trust in nature and in the beauty and simplicity of the natural order. It meant that, like her, he could not comprehend the possibility of natural *disorder* nor, if perfection proved unachievable, take a philosophic view of failure. The consequence was that life, despite its joys, was almost bound to be a disappointment.

By the time Pablo was old enough to attend the local community school in the carrer Montserrat near his home, he already had command of a piano repertoire which included the more straightforward works of Beethoven, Chopin and Mendelssohn, as well as the preludes and fugues from Bach's *The Well-Tempered Clavier*. But he was by no means fixated on the instrument; he did not spend every hour practising. He seemed rather to want to explore different areas of musical expression, and to master a broader range of instruments. When the boy heard villagers playing the *gralla* – a reed instrument of North African origin with a bitingly raucous tone – he insisted on trying it, quickly succeeding in reproducing whatever traditional melody the musicians had performed. Finding a *fluviol* – a crude version of a piccolo – in his father's studio, he taught himself to play until he was good enough to take his place in town processions on saints' days. And at the age of seven Pablo began to learn the violin, taught by Carlos who had, along with everything else, a basic grasp of the rudiments of string playing. Within a year Pablo was giving a solo performance as part of a local recital, and earning his first press review.

Sometime in 1885 a group of itinerant musicians arrived in El Vendrell and set up their equipment for a number of street performances. Los Tres Bemoles ('The Three Flats') played a colourful combination of instruments including an upturned wash-tub, makeshift guitars constructed from wooden boxes, and a series of drinking glasses to be struck with a spoon. What particularly intrigued Pablo was a bent broomhandle, strung with a single cord, and plucked or bowed from a standing position. He described the contraption to his father, who, with his friend Peret the barber, fabricated an altogether superior version out of a dried and hollowed gourd. With a rough scroll and fingerboard attached, the instrument, though primitive, resonated sufficiently for a tune to be picked out on it. Within hours, Pablo was performing a version of Gounod's 'Ave Maria', to the intense emotion of his father and his friends.[7]

For a young boy with an acutely musical ear – Pablo had apparently already taken to correcting his fellow choristers when their pitch went astray – the experience of these clumsy and makeshift instruments must have been frustrating and could have been pernicious. It highlights the extent to which Casals' boyhood was simultaneously very rich in musical stimulus and very deprived of musical opportunity. That his father was a full-time musician, and a skilled and versatile teacher, ensured that music was a central element of everyday life. By the age of nine, Pablo was familiar with a range of wind, string and keyboard instruments, and was extraordinarily adept at playing them. Carlos had taught him the basic principles of music theory, and encouraged him, from the age of six or seven, to compose short pieces – songs or melodies for the piano. By his tenth birthday he had grown sufficiently to begin his longed-for instruction on the organ, and within several months was of a standard to substitute for his father at selected points during mass.

At the same time, the young Casals had no opportunity to hear good music from any other source. Before the era of radio or recorded sound, people heard only what they encountered, and Pablo encountered very little beyond his father and the church across the square. El Vendrell was a musical vacuum. Until Pablo was eleven he heard no orchestral or chamber playing, nor much of a repertoire beyond the conventional range for which Carlos possessed the score. And nothing prepared him for the shock, in 1888, of hearing a professional chamber trio which had come from Barcelona for a concert at the El Vendrell Catholic Centre. Pablo was thunderstruck: it was the first occasion he had seen a real violoncello, let alone heard it played by an expert performer: the cellist was José García, a teacher at the Escuela Municipal de Música (Municipal School of Music) in Barcelona. Casals recalled the event:

. . . the moment I heard the first notes I was overwhelmed. I felt
as if I could not breathe. There was something so tender, beautiful
and human – yes, so very human – about the sound. I had never
heard such a beautiful sound before.[8]

Pablo returned home and announced to his father, 'That is what I want to
play'; from that point he proceeded to play his violin with the instrument
upright on his knees.[9] Somehow Carlos managed to locate a small cello
and began to give his son a few preliminary lessons. The instrument
became the focus and obsession of Pablo's life, and remained so for the
next eighty-five years.

The arrival of a cello in the house at carrer Santa Anna brought a decisive
change in the relationship between Carlos Casals and his wife, and signalled the end of a chapter in the life of the family. For Carlos Casals it
had seemed unexceptional that his son should be highly talented: he was
himself, after all, musically gifted and versatile, but all his abilities had
brought him was a tenuous and unpromising career in El Vendrell. He
saw no reason to encourage his son to emulate him, and secured instead
an opening for Pablo as apprentice carpenter in a neighbouring
workshop.

Doña Pilar, however, knew there was another world outside El Vendrell, for she had seen it. She also recognized that what children achieve
is circumscribed, in most cases, by their parents' expectations, unless
pre-empted by some external stimulus. No such stimulus would come
in El Vendrell, and Pilar knew she had to get Pablo away from it, in
order that her only living son might have the possibility of a greater
horizon. Perhaps, too, she saw an opportunity to get away herself. The
last two years had been devastating for her. Early in 1887 her seventh
son, little Carlos, had died aged three, of diphtheria triggered by a heart
deficiency.[10] In May she had given birth to a daughter, Antonia, who
choked to death after six days. Pilar had barely recovered when Pablo
himself was bitten by a rabid dog, an eventuality everyone knew was
almost certainly fatal. In desperation Carlos rushed his son to Barcelona,
where a hospital had begun experimenting with Louis Pasteur's hydro-
phobia serum. In a ward crowded with patients in various stages of
delirium, Pablo underwent an excruciating series of injections by which
progressively stronger solutions of the rabies virus in hot liquid were
administered.

Pablo survived, but for his mother it was enough. She demanded that
he should transfer to Barcelona to begin serious musical study with
García at the Municipal School of Music, and that she should accompany

him. Carlos opposed such a radical idea: they could not afford the fees, and there would be nowhere to live. Pablo overheard his parents in intense argument, and knew he was the source. But Pilar was determined and Carlos, ultimately, submissive. He wrote to enquire about enrolment at the school and, late in August 1888, his wife and son boarded a third-class compartment at the nearby station of San Vicens, and set off on the two-hour journey to Barcelona. Pilar was pregnant for the ninth time, and knew she would need to return to El Vendrell for the birth. But one child at least, she knew, had a chance of a successful future.

Doña Pilar and Pablo Casals arrived in Barcelona in the middle of the thirty-five-week Universal Exposition of 1888. Like the Olympic Games a century later, the Exposition was a conscientious attempt to give an economically stricken city a degree of self-esteem. The 'Glorious Revolution' of September 1868 had rid Spain of the Bourbon monarchy for a brief six years, and the First Republic had survived for barely two. But even after the Restoration things were never the same. Catalanism, in particular, became a political as well as an emotional movement in the 1880s, and in promoting the idea of a world's fair in 1888, Rius i Taulet, the colourful Mayor of Barcelona, sought to capture for Catalonia the confidence and spirit of the 'New Spain'.[11] The problem was that the city was actually in deep recession. The commercial and industrial boom of the 1870s, based largely on credit and on a capital influx from Cuba, Puerto Rico and the other Spanish colonies, had been devastated by *phylloxera vastatrix*, the aphid that destroys the vine. By 1887 the vine-yards of Penedès were dead, and the Catalan wine industry almost completely wrecked. So the grand gestures of Catalan self-confidence – the construction of the 187-foot-high Columbus monument overlooking the waterfront, and the transformation of the Parc de la Ciutadella – were set against the context of financial collapse.

The Universal Exposition attracted a million and a half visitors, and closed with a deficit of 6 million pesetas. But the scramble to get it ready, together with the effort to take it down, created hundreds of jobs and masked the effect of the general slump on Barcelona's labour force. And, in the end, the contrived orgy of Catalan optimism did succeed in boosting the city's self-image, even if it was based on a sham. The bourgeois paradise of Barcelona, with its population of half a million, was busy, exciting and colourful, and represented for Casals, 'in more senses than one, the gateway to the world'.[12] His arrival at a time of conspicuous Catalan self-aggrandisement had a strong and permanent impact on his sense of who he was and where he belonged.

After a successful audition at the Municipal School of Music, Pablo

Casals became, at twelve, one of its youngest students. The plan was that he should follow a full five-year programme of advanced study in harmony and counterpoint, composition, musical theory, piano and cello, in addition to the standard subjects of the conventional educational syllabus. Pablo was, at first, intimidated by the erudition of the professors and the social ease of his fellow-students. He had never had an opportunity to compare himself with other young musicians, but intense application brought him top prize in the class – and the chance of a recital – at the close of his first year. Throughout his five years at the school José García was his cello instructor. Indeed, unlike most very talented cello pupils who migrate from teacher to teacher in a routine of apprenticeship and, to an extent, of obeisance, Casals only ever had one, García. For within months of beginning serious study of the instrument, Pablo was questioning the central principles of cello technique. He was, in effect, teaching himself.

In music as in life, Casals never encountered a law he did not regard as open to question. It was what his mother had taught him. Conventional cello practice was to keep both arms stiff, with elbows tight to the sides of the body. Pupils would play with a book wedged in their armpit to ensure their bowing arm did not leave its ordained position. Casals could not see the logic of it: 'certain things are obvious even to children', he wrote later.[13] The cello seemed difficult enough without imposing unnecessary restrictions on the player. Casals began to lift his right arm, bringing his elbow up into the air if it seemed appropriate in order to obtain the sound which the music demanded. Nor did he see any merit in consistently using the full length of the bow: a waste of effort, he thought, 'a stupid idea'.[14] Music seemed to demand many categories of bow-stroke, and there was no reason to withhold them.

As well as freeing the bow arm, Casals looked at restrictive practices in relation to fingering. The left hand was generally kept tight, the entire hand moving up the fingerboard as the music called for higher positions. Casals opened the hand and extended the fingers, reaching for notes rather than shifting the hand unnecessarily backwards and forwards. A century on, these technical revisions seem simple and obvious. At the time, they amounted to subversion. They did not happen suddenly, and indeed with some teachers they would not have happened at all. But José García was a tolerant man: 'he came to see there was a method in my seeming madness'.[15] Madness or not, he could see that his new young pupil was making startlingly rapid progress, and later conceded that, at Barcelona, Casals learned a good deal more about the cello than he had been able to teach him.

Pilar Casals had lodged her son with a distant relative, Benet Boixados, the brother-in-law of her cousin Fidèlia. Boixados was a gentle and charitable man who lived with his wife in the old quarter of the city, and helped the boy through the double ordeal of separation from his parents and attendance at the new school. Pilar returned from El Vendrell after the birth of her ninth child and second daughter – baptized Pilar but dead in a week from tetanus. She found rooms not far from Boixados, in the carrer de l'Hospital, intersecting with the Ramblas. The problem was how to pay for them. In the spring of 1889 Pablo found a part-time job as cellist in a café trio, paying 4 pesetas a day. Cafés had sprung up throughout the city, being places of some style to which professional men, in the main, went for relaxation. They were, in the description of Barcelona's contemporary chronicler, Josep Pla, 'grand, commodious, with large mirrors and ample banquettes . . . places of relaxation, stock exchanges and information centres . . . [their] decline signified the twilight of an entire civilization'.[16]

The Café Tost was at the north end of the Passeig de Gràcia, beyond the Plaça de Catalunya, and on the way towards the industrial suburbs. Casals was hired to perform for three hours a night, seven nights a week, to leisured patrons drinking coffee, chocolate or liqueurs. The performance constituted something between a formal recital and crush-bar background music, but standards were often very high. Amongst the popular tunes, *zarzuela* selections and waltzes, Casals and his fellow-players inserted more serious pieces. Eventually they convinced the proprietor, Señor Tost, to devote one full evening each week to a classical programme. Word spread, and patrons began to atttend that evening specifically: indeed they came to hear *El Niño del Tost*, 'the Tost boy-wonder'. Most evenings, Doña Pilar sat quietly with her coffee at a corner table.

Days spent at the school, and nights at the café, represented a heavy schedule. But even in the summer holidays, when Casals returned with his mother to El Vendrell and spent time at San Salvador, he would earn extra money by joining a travelling orchestra and performing at country fairs and festivals throughout Tarragona and Gerona. Back in Barcelona, he would resume his job at the Café, supplementing it with performances at weddings and funerals, just one of which paid rather more than an evening at the Tost. It was a strenuous life and not a glamorous one. The regular practice was useful for its own sake, of course, and the performances of folk music and popular songs extended Casals' repertoire and provided the source for many of his later compositions. And the habit of relentless performance meant, at least, that when he began his solo career ten years later, the element of grinding repetition was not wholly unfamiliar. But there were other compensations too. Señor Tost would occasionally take his protégé to concerts at the Teatro Lírico, where they heard the virtuoso Spanish violinist Pablo de Sarasate – Casals recalled that he did not play in tune – and the young Richard Strauss conducting his own *Don Juan*.

At the start of his second year at the Municipal School, Pablo and his mother moved to rooms in the carrer Valencia, more convenient for the Café Tost. Carlos Casals would travel from El Vendrell whenever he could, especially for school concerts and ceremonies at which his son would invariably feature prominently. On one occasion in 1890, before he was fourteen, Pablo and his father were strolling in the little streets near the harbour, and entered a small music shop in the carrer Ancha to look for new pieces to perform at the Café. Browsing among the manuscripts, they came across several Beethoven Sonatas for Piano and Cello, and then a battered Grützmacher edition of Bach's Six Suites for Unaccompanied Violoncello. It was the crucial musical discovery of Casals' life. García had not spoken to him of them; he had heard no one perform them. But when he got the score home and began to work through the Suites, he realized he had found the music that was closest to his soul:

> I began playing them with indescribable excitement. They became my most cherished music. . . . I was thirteen at the time, but for the following eighty years the wonder of my discovery has continued to grow on me. Those suites opened up a whole new world.[17]

Casals discovered that, if they were played at all, the Bach Suites had been used as academic, technical exercises. After Bach's death they had been neglected for a century, until Robert Schumann recast them in an edited form with piano accompaniment. Cellists might offer a single section as a concert encore – a sarabande, minuet or gigue, for example – but a suite in its totality was seen as too demanding, and frankly too dull, for a recital audience. For Casals, however, they were fascinating and complex pieces. For the next twelve years he worked on them in seclusion, practising several each day, in full, with all their repeats. Around the turn of the century, at the beginning of his solo career, he began to introduce them into his recital programmes. But although the Suites became Casals' hallmark, and he performed them on many hundreds of occasions, he never approached them without reverence, humility – and even fear. He declined to publish his own edition, and recorded the Suites only once, and then after heavy pressure, in sessions between 1936 and 1939. For Casals, the music of Bach was a chromosomal fit. Emotionally and intellectually it encapsulated his sense of the world:

Bach is the supreme genius of music. . . . This man, who knows everything and feels everything, cannot write one note, however unimportant it may appear, which is anything but transcendent. He has reached the heart of every noble thought, and has done it in the most perfect way.[18]

Performing a Bach Suite was an act of intense self-revelation. This was the difficulty. As an adult, Casals guarded his privacy and concealed his emotion. Playing Bach, however, he felt he could hide nothing: the truth came flooding out. It was a dichotomy which caused him great pain and which resulted in his finest music: the dilemma between the urge to communicate and the fear of exposure was one he never resolved.

Casals had given solo performances in Tarragona during the summer of 1889, and in Barcelona in November 1890, and received strong newspaper commendation for each.[19] But his major Barcelona debut came on 23 February 1891, when he performed two works at the Teatro de Novedades as part of a benefit concert for an aged comic actress, Concepción Palá. Before the performance he was struck by appalling nervousness, and Carlos, who was with him for the concert, had to propel him on to the stage. He played his pieces, including an *Allegro Appassionato* by Tusquets, without mishap, however, and his reviews in both the Catalan and Castilian papers referred to the confidence and security of his performance.[20] But Casals never conquered his pre-performance terror, and admitted in the late 1960s that: 'It is always an ordeal. Before I go onstage, I have a pain in my chest. . . . The thought of a public performance is still a nightmare.'[21]

During 1891 Casals left his job at the Café Tost and joined an orchestra which was rehearsing for a season of performances of *Carmen* at the Teatro Tívoli. It was his first experience of an adult orchestra, and of opera in performance. Two years earlier an acquaintance at the Café Tost had lent him scores of *Parsifal, Tristan* and the *Ring*, and he now perceived resonances of Wagner's style in Bizet's writing. At the same time he found work at a new and highly fashionable café in the Plaça de Catalunya, La Pajarera, which, built of glass in a circular structure, resembled the 'bird-cage' its name described. There he joined an ensemble of seven musicians which, as well as the popular selections, played movements from chamber works by Schumann, Schubert and Mendelssohn. But most importantly, it paid well.

One evening La Pajarera was visited by a leading Spanish musician who came to investigate the rumours he had heard about *el nen*, the brilliant boy cellist. Isaac Albéniz was the country's best-known pianist:

as a six-year-old prodigy he had entered the Paris Conservatoire, and at eight the Conservatory at Madrid, studying later with Liszt in Leipzig and Rome. Performing trios in Barcelona with Enrique Fernández Arbós and Augustín Rubio, he and his colleagues approached Casals after the café performance to suggest that he return with them to London, where all were working, for advanced study with Rubio and a range of greater opportunities. Doña Pilar was far from inclined to see her fourteen-year-old son disappear from Spain, and insisted he would complete his course at the School of Music in Barcelona. Albéniz, though a Catalan himself, argued that Casals should at least escape the provincialism of Barcelona by moving to study in Madrid, and gave Pilar a letter of recommendation to the Count of Morphy, private secretary to the Queen Regent, María Cristina, and one of Spain's most influential music patrons. Three years later, Doña Pilar used it.

# 2

## Patronage and Discovery, 1890–1899

Everybody has an epoch of distress. I had it very young.
*Pablo Casals*[1]

In the spring of 1893, four months after his sixteenth birthday, Casals graduated from the Municipal School of Music in Barcelona, taking highest honours in cello, piano and composition. On the advice of his teacher, José García, he entered a competition for a scholarship provided by the City Council to meet the costs of further advanced study in Paris. To the great surprise of his teacher, the local musical press, and indeed himself, he did not win. The scholarship was awarded to another young cellist called Pujal.[2]

It was the first time Casals had failed at anything, and the experience inflamed feelings of self-doubt and uncertainty that had preoccupied him for several months. Casals' high intelligence and musical ability were matched by a growing sensitivity to the world around him, and he did not like what he saw. Squalor, poverty and human degradation, all of which were readily evident in the Barcelona of the early 1890s, made him question the fundamental usefulness of his continued absorption in the study of music:

> I could not understand why there was such evil in the world, why men should do such things to one another, or what, indeed, was the purpose of life under such conditions. . . . I could no longer lose myself in my music. I did not feel then – nor have I ever felt – that music, or any form of art, can be an answer in itself.[3]

What Casals was feeling was in part of course the normal anxieties of adolescence. But soon there was evidence of something more serious. Returning home after a day at the School of Music, he would sometimes turn down the carrer de Ferran, sit in deep gloom in the Church of Sant Jaume and, according to his own subsequent admission, consider the possibility of killing himself. Casals himself later identified the root of his depression in metaphysical terms: 'I felt at loggerheads with a world where there was no justice, selfishness was rampant and charity non-existent.'[4] But it is much more likely that the source of his unhappiness was, in a precise sense, closer to home.

For Casals had not been permitted to be young for long. At the age of eleven he had left his home and his boyhood friends to enter what was almost wholly an adult environment, and by twelve his job at the Café Tost denied him almost any opportunity for leisure. He was never apart from his self-denying and somewhat lugubrious mother, and had to face each day the consequences of what his talent had done to his family. At the beginning of Casals' third year in Barcelona, his mother had given birth to her tenth child, Luis. Carlos took the opportunity to ask his wife to return home permanently, but Pilar refused, placing her new son to board with a family in El Vendrell before returning to Barcelona as soon as she could. In June 1892, when the eleventh child – a son, again called Enrique – was born, Carlos gave up his position in El Vendrell and joined his wife and now three sons in Barcelona. The family rented an apartment in the carrer de Paleyo, not far from Pablo's workplace in the Plaça de Catalunya, and Carlos began to take music students. But he continued to oppose the idea that his son should follow a musical career, putting Pablo in the position of having, effectively, to choose between his parents. 'My greatest wish was to get them to agree,' he remembered, sixty years later. 'But how could I do it? . . . my father could not understand me and did not realize how near I was to a fatal crisis.'[5]

Pablo Casals' only means of escape would have been as a musical prodigy, displaying his instrumental brilliance to an excited and grateful world. But though his talent was clearly prodigious, there was in fact never a chance that he would be one. For one thing, his musical interests were too diffuse. For another, his serious study of the cello had begun too late. But most decisively, Casals' mother would not let him. The suggestion of Albéniz and his colleagues – just after the boy's fourteenth birthday – that he come to London for privileged cello tuition at an advanced level, would almost certainly have led to celebrity and public acclaim, if not to the gifted-infant routine of sailor suit and velvet breeches. And it would undoubtedly have prolonged his youth. Doña Pilar's preference for Albéniz's alternative recommendation – a period of stimulation and study in Madrid – very probably postponed the start of her son's virtuoso career for as much as ten years, while providing the opportunity for a more complete and rounded musical education. But what it also meant, as the family set out for Madrid early in May 1893 – the recommendation to the Count of Morphy their sole security – was that Pablo, at the age of only sixteen, had effectively taken over from his father full responsibility for Doña Pilar and his two infant brothers. Carlos Casals returned, bewildered and abandoned, to El Vendrell.

The 800-kilometre railway journey to Madrid took a day and a half. On arrival, and presumably by appointment, Pilar – with her three sons, luggage, and a cello – went immediately to the home of the Count of Morphy in the suburb of Argüelles in the north-west of the city. The Count welcomed them, asked to see some of Pablo's compositions, and then listened to him play. Immediately impressed, he invited Casals back the following day, and then announced that he had arranged for the boy to play for the Infanta Isabel, elder sister of the late Alfonso XII and sister-in-law to the Queen Regent. A day later, in the Infanta's apartment in the royal palace, Casals performed some of his own compositions on both piano and cello. Pilar had accompanied her son to the palace, bringing with her Luis and eleven-month-old Enrique; during the recital, she calmly settled her fractious baby by unfastening her dress and feeding him.

A week later a further concert was arranged at the palace, this time for the Queen Regent, María Cristina, herself, and an audience of about thirty of Madrid's senior musical figures. Casals played a string quartet of his own composition, with Enrique Fernández Arbós as first violin, and several smaller pieces on both piano and cello. The next day the Count of Morphy informed Casals that the Queen Regent had awarded him a monthly allowance of 250 pesetas, enough for the family to take a small apartment in the calle de San Quintín, not far from the palace gardens, and live in modest but tolerable comfort. It was the first of many favours María Cristina would bestow on Casals over the next thirty-five years, and Spain's Queen Regent was the first of many monarchs with whom he would establish a personal friendship.

The Count of Morphy – Guillermo Morphy y Férriz de Guzmán – was the grandson of Irish emigrants (called Murphy), but had himself been born in Spain. After graduating in law and music, he was appointed tutor to the Infante Alfonso, the seven-year-old son of Isabel II, accompanying him into exile in 1868, and returning as the King's private secretary when Alfonso was restored to the Bourbon throne in 1875. After the King's death ten years later, Morphy remained as private secretary to his second wife, the Hapsburg Archduchess María Cristina, who became Regent during the minority of her own son, the future Alfonso XIII. Morphy was an instinctive tutor and patron, and for more than two years became Casals' mentor, guide and example. 'I have had two sons,' he would say, 'Alfonso XII and Pablo Casals.'[6]

Access to Morphy's sophisticated and cultured mind exposed the deficiencies in Casals' own modest Catalan education. An intensive regime of compensatory instruction was begun, with Morphy himself in charge of general subjects, art, literature and language, while tuition in musical composition was placed in the hands of Madrid's leading chamber music and *zarzuela* composer, Tomás Bretón. What Casals received, in effect, was the style of education appropriate to an heir to the throne: civilized learning across the humanities, wide acquaintance – if not full comprehension – of the scientific and philosophic problems of the age, a privileged intimacy with the arts, and a heavy emphasis on foreign languages. It provided a disciplinary foundation of immense usefulness as Casals, years later, assumed the status of an international humanitarian and 'monarch of the human spirit'. What it did not provide was the conviviality of Casals' own age-group. The loneliness and isolation he had experienced in Barcelona persisted in Madrid, until he himself reached the intellectual level of the adults with whom he was continuously surrounded. For Casals, throughout his life, children and childhood would be 'a vacuum in his psyche'.[7] Though he had none of his own, he loved children, and made instant contact with them without artifice or embarrassment. Disappointed by adults, he attributed to the innocence of young people all the hopes and aspirations of the world, an over-estimation of the child that can come only from someone who was not one for very long.

Casals would report each morning to the Count of Morphy's home, where for three hours he would receive intensive tuition in individual subjects, and explore the Count's vast library. Back in the family's apartment each evening, Pilar would attempt to discover what he had learned, in the hope that an intellectual gap would not open between them. Once a week Morphy would dispatch Casals to the Spanish Cortes, where he would witness debates between the leading politicians of the day, including his father's former hero, Pi i Margall, and relate them to his tutor. Each week, too, Casals would be instructed to make a visit to the Prado to study, and write a response to, an individual painting. It instilled in him a love of French and Italian painting of the seventeenth and eighteenth centuries, but most of all for the great Spanish works of Velásquez, Murillo and Goya. On tour later in countries around the world, Casals would explore galleries and museums, developing a taste in art which came to mirror his preference in music. His own collection of drawings and paintings would be dominated by Catalan painters of his own generation – Ramon Casas and Santiago Rusiñol, for example – though it conspicuously excluded the Post-Impressionist experimentation of fellow Catalans Pablo Picasso, Joan Miró or Salvador Dali.[8] When, much later,

Casals himself was interestingly painted by Oskar Kokoschka, he furiously repudiated the painter's powerful but distorted image.

In September 1893, at the start of the autumn term of the royal Madrid Conservatory – the Conservatorio de Música i Declamación – Casals enrolled – in addition to his existing schedule – for the classes in chamber music taught by its director, Jesús de Monasterio. Monasterio was a superb teacher of style and interpretation, and his classes represented one of the most profound influences on Casals' developing musical personality. Casals at this stage was no longer amenable to straightforward instruction, but looked for experienced musicians on whom he could test his own artistic principles. In Monasterio he encountered a wholly compatible sensibility, and one that reinforced, rather than challenged, his ideas, in particular his growing obsession with accuracy of intonation and 'musical accentuation': 'all my personal tendencies, and my artistic doubts, found in his well-tried convictions an admirable anchorage'.[9] Jesús de Monasterio had himself been a violin prodigy, and a student of François Gevaërt at the Brussels Conservatoire, before returning to Madrid to become violinist of the royal chapel and professor at the Conservatory. Now, at sixty, his approach to music was intensely serious, and from him Casals acquired his fundamental dislike of showmanship and gratuitous musical display. What Casals did not study at the Conservatory was the cello, Monasterio having established that there was no one in the city from whom he could learn anything. Casals continued to teach himself, practising for hours each day between his other commitments. His two years in Madrid provided him – between the ages of sixteen and eighteen – with an intellectual grounding and a philosophy of music that would remain substantially unchanged throughout his life. Monasterio not only taught Casals how to interpret music, he taught him how to think about it.

As well as providing for his education, Queen María Cristina took a genuine personal interest in Casals himself. At least once a week the boy would visit the Queen Regent in her private suite within the vast Palacio de Oriente. She would question him about his family, about his work and his latest compositions, and he would play his cello for her: sometimes they would play duets – four hands on one piano – generally Mozart. On other occasions he would entertain the seven-year-old Alfonso XIII, but more often it was toy soldiers they played rather than music. This astonishingly sudden intimacy with the Spanish royal family was probably only possible because Casals appeared unimpressed, and remained unaffected, by it. He admitted that he did not care for what he saw of court life:

That was a world to which I felt I did not belong and which I did not like. There was much affectation among the nobility, with their airs and pretensions; and there was constant court intrigue. I had grown up among the common people, and I continued to identify myself with them. I was by upbringing and inclination a Republican.[10]

And so, looking back seventy years after the event, it may indeed have appeared. At the time, however, his position was rather less clearly drawn. Deeply loyal to the political views he had learned from his father, and strongly conditioned against snobbery and social affectation by his mother, Casals at seventeen must have been aware of the absurdity of the situation in which he found himself. Twenty years earlier Carlos Casals, the ardent Catalan republican, had risked his life in skirmishes with the forces of the Carlist pretender. Now his son spent leisurely hours performing for the Castilian Queen Regent in private, and playing schoolboy games with the heir to the restored male Bourbon line. What was going on, in fact, was patronage at a deliberate and serious level, the object of which would soon become clear.

By the end of 1894 the young Pablo Casals was by general consensus the most outstanding musical talent in Spain. In September he had been dispatched, along with the pick of the Conservatory's student violinists, pianists and singers, on a concert tour of the provinces, with performances in Vigo, Bilbao, Santiago de Compostela and other large towns outside Madrid. Of all the young artists, Casals won the best – and most florid – notices. For the Santiago paper *El Pensamiento*, Casals was 'a violoncellist of such extraordinary merit that, hearing him play, one seeks to examine his instrument to discover if there lurks inside it a gathering of spirits responsible for producing such an outpouring of art'. For the critic of *El Alcance*, he deserved a paragraph to himself: '[Señor Casals] is a true celebrity . . . at barely eighteen years old he can proclaim himself *Maestro* and create true beauty with the violoncello.'[11]

Back in Madrid, Casals was chosen to join a prestigious new chamber ensemble, created by Monasterio to replace the Sociedad de Cuartetos he himself had led for thirty years. The Quartet Francés, named after its leader and first violin, Julio Francés, began rehearsing in October – meeting sometimes in the studio of the painter Ordóñez – and gave its debut performance on 30 November in the Salón Romero in Madrid.[12] The concert, which took place on a particularly icy winter evening, elicited eight highly enthusiastic reviews in the city's newspapers – and gave Casals double pneumonia. After a second concert by the Quartet, early in December, he was sent to bed and, attended by the Queen's physician as well as his own mother, remained there, at times very seriously ill, until his birthday on 29 December.

Slowly but conscientiously, Jesús de Monasterio was grooming Casals for a career as a solo instrumentalist, and creating opportunities for him to play. The Count of Morphy, however, with Queen María Cristina, had other plans. From Casals' first arrival in Madrid, Morphy's attention had been focused on the boy's gift for composition. That was what had most impressed him at his first hearing, and that was what Casals was required to exhibit to the Queen during their regular encounters. Morphy's prime interest was the music of Spain. He was himself the composer of a cantata, a mass and three operas, and had written the definitive scholarly accounts of Iberian music of the sixteenth century and of Spanish folk traditions. The preoccupation of *El Músico*, as Morphy was nicknamed by other Madrid functionaries, was to broaden the corpus of indigenous Spanish opera, and he saw in Casals an ideal accomplice.

It was Italian opera that filled Madrid's major theatres in the 1890s, as indeed it always had been. Elsewhere, in the playhouses, the vulgar *zarzuela*, the Spanish version of light operetta, was the national craze. What Morphy sought was to liberate high culture from the Italian yoke, and create a genuine Spanish grand opera, with Spanish themes and Spanish music. His own early compositions had not had great success, any more than had those of his colleagues Tomás Bretón – Casals' tutor – and the distinguished Castilian musicologist, Felipe Pedrell. Strenuous expectations were placed on Casals, and for a while he more than fulfilled them: in terms of composing, the years 1893–5 were among the most fecund of his life. He produced about a dozen separate finished pieces, including a romance on a text by Heinrich Heine, and several songs based on traditional Catalan themes.[13] Queen María Cristina rewarded him with the cross of the Order of Isabel la Católica and, early in spring 1895, invited the eighteen-year-old Catalan to join the court as a musician of the royal chapel.

But by now it was clear to Casals, as it was to the concert reviewers, that what he was best at was precisely what Madrid had not taught him – playing the cello. Strongly backed by Monasterio, and indeed by his mother, Casals informed Morphy that his preference was to concentrate on the cello and the performance of its solo and chamber repertoire. The decision caused a tumult. Heavy pressure was brought on him to change his mind. To gain leverage over the boy, Morphy himself deliberately engineered a quarrel with Monasterio which threatened to end Casals' career at the Conservatory.[14] After several weeks, depressed by the continued haggling over his future, Casals and his mother announced that they would simply leave Madrid and return to Barcelona. Faced with the possible loss of his protégé, Morphy contrived a deal: Casals would transfer to the Conservatory in Brussels to study composition with the Count's friend and former colleague, François Gevaërt, in return for which the Queen Regent's allowance would continue. So in the middle of July 1895 the family gave up their calle de San Quintín apartment and prepared to leave for Brussels, returning to San Salvador for the summer – and to a bemused Carlos Casals who had, over the last two years, seen his children only once. On 10 August Casals performed in Tarragona, and on 1 September gave a concert in El Vendrell, accompanied by his father and the La Lira chorus, the proceeds going to local charities. Several days later Doña Pilar set off again with her three sons, this time for Paris en route to Brussels. Carlos was desperate. 'What is this woman thinking of?' was all he could say.[15]

Casals' first visit outside Spain was a disaster, and resulted in one of the worst years of his life. The plan for him to study with François Gevaërt had not been well considered, nor, apparently, had Gevaërt himself been consulted in advance. When the family reached Brussels, Pilar Casals quickly settled her family into a cheap *pension* and accompanied her son to the royal Conservatoire de Musique et de Déclamation. Gevaërt was indeed one of Europe's most distinguished musical scholars, and Casals came with an unequivocal endorsement from the Count of Morphy. But the professor was now almost seventy and not prepared to take on new students. After a long conversation with Casals and a careful examination of his recent compositions, Gevaërt declared that there seemed little, in any case, he could teach him, and advised Casals to move to Paris to benefit from the incomparably rich and exciting musical atmosphere which he promised the French capital would provide. But since the Brussels Conservatoire was acknowledged as Europe's leading centre for string playing, Gevaërt referred Casals to the school's professor of cello, Edouard Jacobs. Their meeting the following day provides one of the most celebrated incidents of Casals' career. It also confirms the view that, four months short of his nineteenth birthday, Casals knew exactly what he did not want.

The pedigree of cello teachers at the Brussels Conservatoire was immensely distinguished. At its foundation in 1831, Joseph Platel, a pupil of Jean-Louis Duport, had been appointed first professor. He was succeeded by his pupil, the dazzling Adrien François Servais, known in his time as the 'Paganini of the cello', who in turn was succeeded by his own son, Joseph.[16] Edouard Jacobs, who had also studied with the great

Servais, became first professor in 1885. During his career, Jacobs taught many notable pupils, including the English cellist Felix Salmond, but Casals was not to be one of them. On his second day in the country, and speaking very halting French, Casals was plainly not equipped to deal with the patronizing sarcasm that he discovered to be Jacobs' natural style. Casals was invited to sit in on a cello class. After ignoring him for the first part of the lesson, Jacobs – referring to Casals as 'the little Spaniard' – asked him what he would care to play for the class:

> Without conceit or even thinking what I was saying, I replied, 'Anything you like.' I had said the wrong thing; the professor smiled sarcastically and remarked that I must be remarkable! The class tittered, the professor amused himself with further ironical remarks, and I began to feel more and more awkward.[17]

Jacobs challenged Casals to play a virtuoso piece by the Conservatoire's own Adrien Servais, *Souvenir de Spa*. Casals knew it, and he played it, on a cello which had been lent to him by one of the other students. Despite his superior manner, Jacobs recognized Casals' outstanding quality. Changing his tone, he accepted him immediately for the Conservatoire, and ingratiatingly guaranteed him the school's first prize. Almost speechless with anger, Casals refused the offer and left. Two days later the family was on its way back to Paris.

There must be a suspicion that the whole Brussels fiasco was to an extent stage-managed from Madrid: the Count of Morphy had relaxed his grasp on his brilliant protégé, but he had not let him go. If Casals had remained at the Conservatoire and been able to study with Gevaërt, the effect would have been to deepen his involvement in musical composition. When he left, the assumption must have been that he would return to the post kept open for him at the royal chapel. It was never Morphy's intention that Casals should remain in Brussels simply to study the cello.

But there was a third option, and to Morphy's surprise Casals took it. Upon reaching Paris, he wrote to explain that the opportunity to study with Gevaërt had turned out not to be feasible. Tightening the net, Morphy insisted that Casals return to Brussels or forfeit his allowance, confident that he would not do so. Casals, exhibiting the honourable self-destructive obstinacy of principle that would distinguish his entire life, chose to lose the allowance. For the first time, but not for the last, he demonstrated that he was content to accept patronage, but only so far as it enabled him to do what he wanted. There were to be no compromises.

But the price was high. Paris was hard for a young man supporting a mother and two young brothers, without an income. The family found very basic accommodation near the Porte St-Denis, and Pilar went out each day to take in small pieces of sewing. Casals himself heard about a vacancy for a cellist in the orchestra of the Folies-Marigny, a second-rank music-hall off the Champs-Elysées. At the audition each candidate was required, bizarrely, to play the first movement of the Saint-Saëns A Minor Cello Concerto. Casals got the job, which – for 4 francs a day – necessitated two round-trips across the city, on foot, from where the family was living. But the winter began severely and Casals fell ill with dysentery and enteritis; he was compelled to give up his job. Carlos sent what little money he could afford from Spain, but the position was desperate. Pilar returned home one day having sold her own hair to a wigmaker to raise a small extra sum.[18]

For seven years Doña Pilar had devoted herself to her son, caring for him, protecting him and supporting him at every stage of his career. For the last two years, joined by the two younger boys, they had seemed an almost perfect family unit, with little sign of stress or impatience. But as Casals reached his nineteenth birthday, his mother and brothers had become, quite plainly, an encumbrance, even if his deep affection for his mother prevented him from acknowledging the fact. Paris was by no means an impossible challenge for the most talented cellist in Europe, as Casals would himself discover when he returned to the city – alone – three and a half years later. But in the final months of 1895 his burden of responsibility was simply too great, and the musical opportunities Gevaërt had described failed to manifest themselves. Pilar decided to take her sons home, and Carlos Casals recovered his family.

As swiftly as Paris had destroyed Casals' expectations, Barcelona fulfilled them. Back in the city – and on his own – at the beginning of 1896, he began to accept cello pupils; one of the earliest, who came for her first lesson on 2 January, was Franchisca Vidal, the seventeen-year-old daughter of a wealthy local furniture manufacturer and later a substantial figure in Casals' life. By March he was performing at discreet society recitals, and by May had been appointed to the faculty of the Municipal School of Music. José García had absconded precipitately, but conveniently, to the Argentine, following a scandal involving another man's wife, and Casals took over most of his former teacher's professional commitments, including private pupils and orchestral engagements. And at the beginning of the new opera season he became, in addition, principal cellist of the orchestra at the Gran Teatro del Liceu.

Teaching absorbed much of his time, as it would throughout his life. Casals became one of the great cello teachers of the twentieth century, and this is perhaps his most permanent legacy. He saw teaching, for seventy-five years, as an integral part of the process of learning: 'A teacher, of course, should know more than his pupil. But for me, to teach is to learn.'[19] And as he taught, he continued to develop his own technique:

> I was determined not to be hampered by any of the restrictions of the past – to learn from the past but not to be shackled by it. My aim was to achieve the best possible effects on the cello. . . . One must, of course, master technique; at the same time one must not be enslaved by it. . . . The most perfect technique is that which is not noticed at all.[20]

The income from teaching and performing enabled Casals to take a house in the centre of Barcelona, and to buy himself out of military service. He established himself, his parents and his two brothers in number 6, Plaça de Catalunya, and became the main provider for the rest of all their lives. He soon became, too, a figure in the musical society of the city, performing, for example, in December 1896, at an exclusive private concert in honour of Camille Saint-Saëns. Casals had first met the great French composer five years earlier when Saint-Saëns, on a visit to Barcelona, had been brought to the Café Tost to hear the fourteen-year-old boy-wonder. On that occasion he had performed the A Minor Cello Concerto, and in December 1896 he played it again – with Saint-Saëns again accompanying him on the piano. Later, joined by the violinist José Rocabruna, they played the composer's E Minor Piano Trio.

In breaks from teaching, Casals joined friends for chamber recitals in Barcelona and elsewhere. In spring 1897 he agreed to become cellist in a regular quartet formed by Mathieu Crickboom, the Belgian violinist and pupil of Eugène Ysaÿe, now living in Barcelona.[21] In August he travelled with Crickboom, and the pianist–composer Enrique Granados, to perform trios at the Gran Casino in San Sebastián, the fashionable holiday resort in northern Spain. The San Sebastián papers described Casals as 'without doubt the foremost Spanish cellist', even though he was slightly built and, they noted, scarcely taller than his cello. At almost twenty-one, Casals had reached his full height, a modest 5 feet 3 inches, and had lost the roundness of face that had marked his early adolescence. In his student years at Barcelona and Madrid he had worn his hair closely cropped. Now he let it grow, and sported a full moustache in the fashion of the time. Middle-class Catalans were as expansively hirsute as they were constricted in dress. 'Donde hay pel hay alegria', went the contemporary proverb: 'Where there is hair, there is happiness'.[22]

Casals and Granados had first met in 1891. Also a Catalan, Granados had settled in Barcelona after a period of study in Paris. Tall, diffident, and highly gifted as a composer, he more nearly filled the role of saviour of Spanish grand opera than Casals could ever have done. Ten years Casals' senior, he became his closest musical friend and, in personal terms, a kind of elder brother. For twenty years the two men met and performed together in Spain, France and the United States until Granados' tragically early death in 1916.

Casals celebrated his twenty-first birthday – on 29 December 1897 – in Bilbao, on tour with Granados and Crickboom. Professionally he seemed to have achieved everything he had sought: professor at Barcelona's leading music school, lead cellist in the city opera, member of several nationally recognized chamber ensembles, and frequent soloist in towns and cities throughout Spain. He was, as one newspaper had described him, 'a national glory'.[23] For many this would have been enough. But Casals wanted more, and felt he was capable of it. In personal terms he knew his life was just beginning. He had colleagues, admirers and acquaintances throughout Europe, but the major disruptive relocations of his early life – first to Madrid, then Paris, then back to Barcelona – had destroyed any chance of permanent close friendships. The constant presence and possessiveness of Pilar had clearly been an inhibition, particularly in terms of relationships with women. As a boy in El Vendrell, Casals had established a friendship with Rosina Valls, daughter of the local doctor. Neither Rosina's family nor Casals' mother had encouraged the relationship, and it faded before he left for Madrid in 1893. The girl, severely tubercular, died later at the age of twenty-four.[24]

As Casals reached the age of majority, Pilar discreetly but formally relinquished her intimate involvement in his life.[25] Within little over a year he had left for Paris and a different kind of existence. Soon he was involved in a pleasant but unimportant flirtation with Andrea Huré, sister of the French composer Jean Huré.[26] Shortly afterwards he began the first major romantic relationship of his life.

But it was not for love that Casals needed to get away. The Barcelona of the 1890s was no place for a young man at the start of his career, particularly one whose loyalties remained with the poor while his success lay determinedly in the hands of the rich. Socially it was, at the end of the century, the most polarized city in Europe. The Catalan economic miracle had been achieved through the exploitation of slave labour on the Cuban sugar plantations and cheap labour in the cloth factories of Barcelona: 'Grinding the workers was almost a patriotic act.'[27] It bred resentment and led to violence. Anarchist bombings had begun in 1891, the most celebrated being the attempt of Santiago Salvador to blow up the Liceu theatre during a performance of *William Tell*. He partially succeeded, killing twenty-four patrons. In June 1896 someone threw a bomb at a religious procession, headed by the Bishop of Barcelona, as it moved along the carrer dels Canvis Nous. The perpetrators were caught, tried at the military prison on Montjuïc, and garrotted.

The violence, and the repression that followed it, did nothing good for social cohesion. Nor did the defeat of Spain's pacific fleet in May 1898 and the loss to the United States of the country's Caribbean empire. Remnants of the 200,000-strong Spanish army trickled back to Barcelona, adding to the unemployment and fuelling the despair. Spain had suffered its worst military humiliation in history. And Catalonia had lost its colonial markets. Catalanism was in a depression and it was time to leave.

Before he went, however, Casals needed to mend his fractured relations with Madrid. Since the episode in Brussels, he had heard nothing from the Count of Morphy or the Queen Regent. Returning to Barcelona from San Sebastián in August 1897, Casals planned to break his journey in the capital, and wrote in advance to Tomás Bretón. The welcome far exceeded his expectation: Morphy received him with relief and affection, and Queen María Cristina commanded a concert at the palace, rewarding him with a sapphire which in due course he had mounted on his bow. Three months later Casals was invited to perform with the Madrid Symphony Orchestra – playing the Lalo D Minor Concerto under Bretón – and again was requested to give a royal recital. This time the Queen Regent honoured him with the award of the Order of Carlos III, and presented him with funds to purchase a fine Gagliano instrument, his first important cello.

By his early twenties, Casals was the most well-connected republican in Europe. In September 1898 he was invited to Holland to play for the inauguration of the eighteen-year-old Queen Wilhelmina. Later in the month he had an engagement at the Portuguese resort of Espinho and, at the season's end, received an invitation to perform in Lisbon for King Carlos I and Queen Amélia. By the time he reached Barcelona in November, Casals was ready to tell his parents of his intention to return to Paris and seek the opportunities François Gevaërt had forecast but which had eluded him three years before. The family was securely established in the Plaça de Catalunya, with Carlos, now weakened by chronic asthma, attending to his son's business affairs. After Christmas Casals travelled to Madrid to discuss his plans with the Count of Morphy, who gave him a letter to deliver to Charles Lamoureux, and wished his pupil well. 'Once more,' Casals wrote, 'I determined to brave Paris.'[28]

PART 2

*The Professional*

# 3

## Touring the World, 1899–1906

[He] travels through Europe, and always I have my heart
on a string.

Pilar Casals i Defilló[1]

For almost six years, Casals had no permanent address. His life was
spent in concert-halls or hotels, trains, trams and steamships. He
travelled, practised, performed and earned ferociously. In a way there
was nothing else for him to do. He had stretched to the limit the
opportunities offered him at home. He had accepted, profited by and
now relinquished the highest patronage of Spain, that of the King and
Queen. He had studied in Barcelona and Madrid until there was nothing
more he could be taught, and established his family in comfort and
security. He now needed stimulation and experience, in music and in
life, and the optimism of a new century provided as good an occasion
as any to go and look for it.

Casals turned twenty-three in the final month of the nineteenth century. Neither as a child nor an adolescent had he been forced into the
precocious role of a prodigy, and there were no unrealistic expectations
to disappoint. His musical education had been gradual, solid and
thorough. Until 1899 he had not played a major solo concert outside
Spain: it was a late start for a player of his extraordinary talent. But by
the early summer of 1899 he was ready for a solo career. His technique
was flawless and he had mastered virtually the entire solo repertoire for
his instrument: he knew there was no musical trial he could fail. But
talent alone was no guarantee of a career. It required social and professional connections, of which Casals had almost none, and ruthless
determination, which he had not yet had reason to test. Carrying introductions from his reinvigorated Madrid patron, the Count of Morphy,
Casals travelled to Paris at the beginning of May.

*Belle époque* Paris was the cultural centre of Europe, arguably of anywhere: it was, as Gertrude Stein, who settled there in 1903, remarked,

'where the twentieth century was'.[2] But Paris had also been where the nineteenth century was, and the elegant architectural grid established by Baron Haussmann fifty years before was already being restructured to meet the requirements of a new era. In the ten years before and after 1900, commemorated in Paris by the Universal Exposition – a great commercial fair – the vast, sprawling capital of the Third Republic underwent both a physical revolution to cope with the arrival of the railway, the automobile and the omnibus, and a social revolution to cope with the masses that used them. The Paris Casals encountered in 1899 was in the process of being dug up to construct the Métro, and built upon to provide housing for its expanding population. And the *époque* was not self-evidently *belle*, but merely appeared so when viewed later from the miserable perspective of world war and depression.[3] Culture, too, was predominantly of a popular variety, with an abundance of music-halls, cinemas, circuses and fun-fairs. Serious music, in fact, was relatively neglected in Paris, in comparison with Berlin, Vienna or London. There were few adequate concert-halls: the Salle Erard and the Salle Pleyel held three or four hundred, the Salle des Agriculteurs even fewer, giving recitals the atmosphere of a private salon. And symphony concerts, given by the three major orchestras – the Société des Concerts du Conservatoire, the Colonne and the Lamoureux – took place only on Sundays, their musicians being employed more routinely on weekdays, when the large theatres were busy with more popular entertainment.[4] But as a centre where musicians were based, composers worked and students studied, Paris matched any city in Europe. And it was certainly more fun to live in.

Casals arrived in Paris with an invitation from the American soprano, Emma Nevada, whom he had first met through Count Morphy at the royal palace in Madrid. Nevada and her English husband, Dr Raymond Palmer, welcomed Casals to their imposing house in the Avenue Wagram. Since they were about to leave for England, where Madame Nevada was booked for two concerts in London on 20 and 27 May, it was arranged that Casals should join the excursion. It was his first visit to the country, and he spoke only a few words of English. His name was wholly unknown to the English public. But within three months Casals was performing for the Sovereign. The Nevada connection was clearly critical, for at her first performance, at Crystal Palace on 20 May, she enabled Casals to make his London debut, playing the Lalo Concerto in D Minor accompanied by the Crystal Palace Band, under the nonagenarian conductor August Manns. Manns's Saturday Concerts had been a regular, though not especially sophisticated, feature of London's musical life for over forty years, and took place in the extraordinary metal and glass hall in the south-east of London erected for the Great Exhibition of 1851.

The Crystal Palace performance was a respectable success: it did not cause a commotion – Casals was in any case billed as the secondary artist of the evening – but it did lead to other invitations. Rather more useful was the social network to which the Palmers provided access. The couple had rented Lady Low's home in Kensington for the London Season, an aristocratic agenda of parties, dinners and sporting functions which ran from late May until the start of game-shooting in the country in the middle of August. One institution of the Season was the At Home, the equivalent of the European salon, at which upper-class hostesses entertained guests, often to a musical accompaniment. As a protégé of the Queen Regent of Spain, and a favourite of other European monarchs, Casals was immediately in demand both as a guest and a performer. Rarely were such performances remunerated, the pay-off being in social connections; it was more a question of what an artist might lose if he refused. Casals had no objection to being used in this way: he was in any case accustomed to performing for wealthy patrons in Spain. And from an early age he discovered that he held a particular appeal for women of rank, generally but not invariably older than he. He retained this appeal, a combination doubtless of his intelligence, his formal charm and his ability to entertain, throughout his life, his patronesses becoming younger as he grew older.

During June and July, Casals played small recitals in the homes of several society families – the Layards, the Meyers and the Rothschilds among them.[5] The ultimate social 'invitation', a command to play for HRH Queen Victoria, resulted from Casals' friendship with three women, Constance Eliot, Enid Layard and Blanche Ponsonby, daughters of the Welsh iron magnate, Sir Josiah Guest. Constance Eliot, whom Casals later called 'my English mother', was the wife of Colonel the Honourable Charles G. C. Eliot, a member of Queen Victoria's Royal Household. Edward Ponsonby, the husband of Constance's sister Blanche, was brother to the Queen's private secretary.[6] The recital itself took place on Wednesday, 2 August, at Osborne House on the Isle of Wight, the Queen's favourite residence in which she spent much of her widowhood and where she was to die seventeen months later. Casals, accompanied by a young English pianist, Ernest Walker, travelled from London by train and ferry to Cowes, where they dined at a local hotel before being taken by royal carriage to Osborne. The whole experience was one of formal courtesy, rather different from the relaxed atmosphere Casals was used to at the royal palace in Madrid.[7] There was an air of 'hushed solemnity' in the room in which the concert was to take place, and Casals and Walker were not formally greeted by the Sovereign before the recital began. Casals later recalled the Queen, then eighty years old, as:

> a small stout woman with soft wrinkled cheeks and prominent eyes. She wore a headdress of white lace that came down to her shoulders. While she chatted with a British admiral, the rest of the guests stood about in respectful silence. An Indian servant in a green silk dress and yellow turban placed a stool under her feet, and she raised a small plump hand as a signal for the concert to begin.[8]

It was not a long recital. Casals played Fauré's *Elégie*, an Italian sonata and the Allegro from the Saint-Saëns A Minor Concerto, all received in total silence. After the concert, 'two six-foot Indians came and grasped the Queen's arms, and helped her slowly, inch by inch . . . from her chair'.[9] The Queen congratulated Casals in French, and wished him well with his career. The musicians were given supper, which they ate alone, and gifts – Casals received a set of gold cuff-links – before leaving; there was no formal farewell. That evening Queen Victoria wrote in her journal:

> After dinner a young Spaniard Señor Casals played on the violon-cello most beautifully. He is a very modest young man, whom the Queen of Spain has had educated, and from whom he received his fine instrument. He has a splendid tone and plays with much execution and feeling.[10]

At the end of the London tour, Casals returned to Paris to face one of the most difficult and critical encounters of his career. The Count of Morphy, as one of his final acts of beneficence – he died on 28 August – had provided Casals with a letter of recommendation to Charles Lamoureux, the most important conductor in Paris. Lamoureux had his own orchestra, had established a famous series of weekly concerts, and he was an unquestionable route to musical success. A recommendation, however, was one thing; Lamoureux's acceptance of it was quite another. The venerable conductor, sixty-five and rheumatic, was celebrated for his bad temper. After years promoting Wagner to a culture resistant to anything Teutonic, he was now preoccupied with plans for the first com-plete concert performance in Paris of *Tristan und Isolde*. When Casals entered his room, Lamoureux ignored him, complaining of incessant interruptions from ambitious young musicians. Casals was accustomed to patronage, but not to being patronized. He explained that he had come simply to deliver a letter entrusted to him, turned, and withdrew.

Lamoureux called him back, read the Count's letter, and asked Casals to return with his cello the following day. At the audition Lamoureux feigned a similar lack of interest until Casals played the opening bars of the first movement of the Lalo Concerto. The conductor, a friend and patron of Edouard Lalo, put down his pen and listened intently, then laboriously and painfully got to his feet and remained standing until Casals finished the movement. With tears in his eyes – according to the only witness to the moment, Charles Chevillard, Lamoureux's son-in-law – the great conductor embraced him. 'Mon petit,' he exclaimed, 'tu es prédestiné!'[11]

The Lamoureux connection provided Casals with a Paris debut, and with a job. The conductor not only offered to adjust the programme of the first concert of his nineteenth season to include the Lalo Concerto, but agreed to Casals' suggestion that he join the cello desk of the full orchestra for its performance of *Tristan*. That was an astringent experience. Lamoureux was known for brutalizing his orchestra, honing and brow-beating it into clarity and precision, rehearsing over and over until he obtained the results he sought. Casals kept his head down, learned and observed. The performance of *Tristan*, a major Paris event, was on 28 October. Fifteen days later, at the Sunday matinée concert in the Théâtre de la République on 12 November, Casals was soloist with the Lalo Concerto. It was the perfect piece for a Spaniard's debut in Paris. Lalo was French, but his family origins were Spanish. His Cello Concerto, written only twenty years earlier, is rhythmic and uncomplicated. The opening prelude is deceptively subdued, the cello line played principally on the C-string. But within a few bars the sonorous and dramatic Allegro maestoso bursts out, powerful runs of the cello solo answered by swipes of noise from the orchestral accompaniment. It was an ideal vehicle for Casals, allowing him to display both his luscious singing tone and his impatient, physical, attacking technique.[12] The critics did not know what to say, and the notices were respectful, if a little formal: *Le Figaro* observed that 'the public did not stint its bravos'. The music critic of *Le Temps* happened to be the composer's son, Pierre Lalo; he commented on 'an enchanting sound and a beautiful virtuosity'. But Casals' strongest impact was on his French counterparts. The young cellist Joseph Salmon, later one of Casals' closest Paris friends, attended the debut with several colleagues, all somewhat irritated that an unknown foreigner should have been selected over them. They emerged dazed from the performance: the Lalo Concerto had been part of their repertoire for years, yet Casals' highly personal interpretation exposed facets of the work that were entirely new to them.[13]

The major breakthrough came when, on 17 December, Casals

appeared for the second time with Lamoureux and his orchestra, on this occasion playing the Saint-Saëns A Minor. The reception was tumultuous, and Lamoureux himself was visibly moved. On 22 December Casals left Paris to return, via Madrid, to Barcelona for the New Year. It was some time before he received the news that the conductor had died the day before his departure. In the final concert of his own life, Lamoureux had given Casals the key to a new career.

For a cellist, there was no precedent for the kind of musical life Casals embarked upon in 1900 – that of the travelling virtuoso. But for Casals, the absence of a precedent was never any kind of inhibition: even at this early age he was an innovator, original and untrammelled by others' assumptions of what was acceptable, or indeed possible. His experience so far in life had shown that there was virtually no obstacle that could not be surmounted. In the case of even the greatest of the nineteenth-century cello virtuosi, solo performance was a supplement to a career, not the essence of it. The very greatest contemporary violinists and pianists could and did pursue individual careers, Joseph Joachim and Jan Paderewski being contemporary examples. But the convention for even the most gifted cellist was to join an orchestra, play in an established trio or quartet, or teach – or all three. The Russian maestro, Karl Davidov (1838–89), for example, gave concerts throughout Europe, but only in breaks from his principal employment at first the Leipzig and subsequently the St Petersburg Conservatoires.[14] The Hungarian cellist and composer, David Popper (1843–1913), toured Europe and Russia, but again in intervals between standing commitments with the Vienna Opera Orchestra and the Royal Hungarian Academy of Music. The leading nineteenth-century German players, Julius Klengel (1859–1933) and Hugo Becker (1864–1941), played regularly within orchestras and were outstanding teachers, but they were not much heard outside their own country.

The reasons are clear. Up to the end of the nineteenth century, the cello was by no means a popular solo instrument. The concerto repertoire was small: there was not much to play. And of what there was, relatively little was of the first rank. Apart from Haydn and Boccherini, the eighteenth-century composers wrote little specifically for the cello. Vivaldi produced twenty-seven concertos, which are mainly student exercises or occasional pieces, and not significant solo works. Beethoven wrote five superb sonatas, the first genuine duo sonatas in which the cello part was equal in importance to the piano, three sets of variations and a Triple Concerto, but he wrote no individual cello concerto. Mozart left no finished work for the cello. The Romantic period produced many concertos, but few of special distinction other than Schumann's lyrical

Concerto in A Minor, written comparatively recently in 1850, Camille
Saint-Saëns' First Cello Concerto, also in A Minor (1873), and Antonín
Dvořák's Second Cello Concerto, in B Minor, written in 1895 when
Casals was nineteen and already established as a professional cellist.[15]
Mendelssohn, Chopin, Brahms, Grieg and Strauss all wrote solo pieces
or chamber music for the cello, and Brahms even a Double Concerto for
Cello and Violin, but there is not a concerto for cello solo between them.
Before 1900 the credibility of the cello as a solo instrument had not been
established. Bluntly, it did not fill concert-halls. And it did not support
solo careers.

Casals broke the mould. In retrospect his career appears a steady progression towards success. But as he set out there were no certainties
or guarantees. Plainly it was a risk, and called for a large measure of
self-confidence. The easier course for a twenty-three-year-old cellist,
returning to Paris in January 1900, would have been to continue with
the Lamoureux, or audition for another Paris orchestra, and supplement
his income by giving private lessons. But that, as the future revealed,
was not Casals' temperament. He did not join orchestras, he founded
them. He taught very sparsely and reluctantly until, when he found
himself in exile after 1940, there was little else for him to do. And though
he played some of the most legendary chamber music of the century, he
was never part of a permanently constituted full-time chamber ensemble.
Other cellists of Casals' generation and that which followed, such as
Emanuel Feuermann, Guilhermina Suggia, Paul Grummer and Gregor
Piatigorsky, became full-time, internationally known performers; but
they were following the pattern Casals had established. No cellist before
him had so effectively brought the sound of the cello to a mass audience:
no cellist after him needed to do so. From his earliest career Casals was
a solo player, musically and indeed personally, to a degree that seemed
almost congenital. He acknowledged no frontiers nor limitations, and
was in that sense, if not in others, profoundly modern. 'In reality,' said
Marcel Dupré, 'the cello dates from him.'

The career was not instantaneous, however, and Casals' life was not
immediately easy. Despite the acclaim following his debut, he faced a
tough and lonely winter. Early in 1900 he returned to Paris, booking
into a cheap, cold Montmartre hotel. Within three days he was ill. Within
several more he was rescued by another in the long line of benefactors
who arrived at critical moments to ease his life. Mrs Betina (Abel) Ram
was a wealthy British widow and amateur pianist, living in Paris. Along
with other gifted young musicians in the city, Casals had played at
several of her musical soirées the previous autumn. For several months
that spring, Casals lived at Mrs Ram's home, before moving to a respect-

able *pension* in the rue Leon Cognet. It was what he needed: a quiet, convenient base from which to launch his career. The young Casals was highly disciplined. Each day he read scores and practised for three or four hours. And he was equally meticulous about organization, listing carefully in separate notebooks the names and details of musical and social contacts in Spain, Britain, France and Belgium and in Germany, Austria and Russia.[16] As yet the list of engagements was modest – several recitals in the Salle Pleyel and elsewhere – and Casals had to supplement his earnings by playing at the Café Suez.[17]

What the Ram household provided, in addition to comfortable lodging, was an entrée into a very useful social and professional network. For *belle époque* Paris offered virtually limitless opportunities for artistic encounters and a general cultural education. Casals began to make up for the sacrifices and isolation of his childhood and adolescence. He attended the theatre, seeing Sarah Bernhardt, Eleonora Duse and Isadora Duncan. He met again Camille Saint-Saëns and was introduced to Arnold Schönberg, and at a concert in the Salle Erard made the acquaintance of the great Paderewski. And among those whom Casals met casually were many who would become major figures, such as the twenty-four-year-old Maurice Ravel, then a student of composition at the Paris Conservatoire, studying with Gabriel Fauré. Through Emma Nevada, Casals was introduced to the household of Mathilde Marchesi, the doyenne of singing teachers who, as a young woman in Germany, had been a friend of Brahms, Verdi, Wagner and Rossini. Madame Marchesi became an influential promoter of Casals' interests, inviting him to perform – the only instrumentalist so selected – at the concert marking her golden jubilee as a teacher of voice. Among other fashionable salons at which Casals became a regular guest was that of Aline Ménard-Dorian, the leading hostess of the political Left in Paris. Here he encountered major political figures and statesmen such as Georges Clemenceau, Aristide Briand and Léon Blum, painters and writers such as Degas, Eugène Carrière, Romain Rolland and Marcel Proust, and the philosopher Henri Bergson.[18]

It is not especially surprising that Casals, having made a spectacular musical arrival in Paris, should have been sought after as a guest at its society musical functions, or become acquainted with the leading musical figures of the time. But it is remarkable that, as a young man of twenty-three and newly settled in Paris, he should have taken himself so seriously and devoted himself so single-mindedly to the business of acquiring intellectual and social acquaintances. Casals' own accounts of his life at the time focus on the distinguished personalities he met and the importance of the issues to which he was exposed. He spoke, for example, of his encounter at the Ménard-Dorian home with Colonel Georges Pic-quart, a central figure in the Dreyfus affair, whose account of the details of the anti-Dreyfusard campaign introduced Casals to the prevalence of anti-Semitism in France and alerted him to its consequences.[19] And he wrote of the impact of discussions with Bergson about the decisive role of intuition in artistic creativity; Casals' fundamental conviction, crucial to him throughout his life, of the supremacy of musical instinct over both intelligence and technical competence received from Bergson a sort of higher philosophic validation.[20] It may have been simply in retrospect that these intellectual encounters, rather than the more conventional plea-sures and routine activities of a successful young man in a large and exciting city, appeared as the highlights of his life. But the evidence is indeed that, even in his early twenties, Casals took a sober view of life, made serious and intelligent friends, and did adult things. It was as if he had been released from a long period of cerebral slumber and sensed he had a great deal of catching-up to do. Casals threw himself urgently, intensively and determinedly into adult life.

The primary need was to make music, and Casals looked for musicians with whom to make it. At one of Mrs Ram's gatherings he had met the pianist Harold Bauer. Bauer came from a musical Jewish family in Hampstead, London, and was three years older than Casals. He was adventurous, enthusiastic and effortlessly talented. Having set out on a career as a violinist, Bauer, at nineteen and on the advice of Paderewski, took the radical decision to switch to the piano, his second instrument: soon he was touring internationally and performing an immense reper-toire on the piano as he had on the violin. During the summer he and Casals played a few modest recitals in Paris. Between engagements they became friends and began to spend time together, playing tennis and exploring the main works for piano and cello. In August they set out on a short recital tour to Spain. The following month, after Bauer had honoured solo commitments in Switzerland, the two met again for some joint concerts in Holland. By November, when Casals left for solo book-ings in England and Bauer for a concert tour of the United States, they had resolved to play together on a regular basis. The 'regular basis' lasted for fourteen years, until the outbreak of war in 1914.

Back from their separate tours at the beginning of 1901, Casals and Bauer gave a series of joint recitals in Paris, before travelling again to Holland. In the autumn they returned to Spain, their tour ending on 26 October with a concert at the Teatro de la Comedia in Madrid. Two weeks later Casals left Cherbourg on the steamship *St Paul* for his first visit to the United States. North America was by no means a fashionable or sophisticated destination at that time, and for an artist who had not yet performed in Berlin, Vienna, Rome or St Petersburg, it was perhaps a surprising choice. But if America was not exactly regarded as a leading cultural centre, it had at least made a lively impact on French popular imagination. Late in 1899 Buffalo Bill brought his Wild West show to Neuilly, stimulating the French fascination with American movies during the early years of the new century. The Barnum and Bailey circus, 'the greatest show on earth', came to Paris for a five-month stint in November 1901.[21] For Casals the catalyst was once again Emma Nevada, who had invited him to join her American tour as an 'assisting instrumental artist', alongside his friend the pianist Léon Moreau, and the flautist Daniel Marquarre. Encouraged by Bauer, whose visit the previous year had been a financial success, if not a critical one, Casals accepted.[22] Nevada's party, which included her husband, Raymond Palmer, and her secretary, Raymond Duncan, brother of the dancer Isadora Duncan, docked at New York on 16 November, after a rough and lengthy crossing. Between then and 4 June 1902, when he left America, Casals entered sixty-one different tour stops in his concert log. When he returned to Barcelona in early August 1902, he had been away for nearly ten months.

The tour was very much a vehicle for Emma Nevada's talents, and Casals and the other assisting artists were decidedly secondary acts. Nevada had been born Emma Wixom in 1859, in the Californian mining town of Alpha, near Nevada City. She had acquired her stage-name from Mathilde Marchesi, just as a fellow pupil, Helen Mitchell Armstrong from Melbourne, Australia, had become Nellie Melba. Her strengths were the flamboyant coloratura roles of nineteenth-century grand opera, and her major triumphs had been in Europe, where she spent most of her career. Her tours home to America, as the girl-from-Nevada-made-good, were showy and sentimental occasions, and she took full advantage of every emotional opportunity. Casals was not entirely in his element, and the story goes that he did not altogether care for Nevada's voice or style of singing. Another story has it that he began an affair with her during the tour. But there is no firm evidence for either suggestion, and they remain stories. The Paris years between 1899 and 1906 were in fact the only period of Casals' life in which he did not have close female companionship.

The role of the supporting artist, then as now, was to entertain the audience while the lead performer rested between sections of her programme. It was emphatically not to steal the show. Moreau and Marquarre contributed the occasional solo piece, but were primarily billed as Nevada's accompanists, Marquarre playing flute obbligato to such show-stoppers as the 'Bell Song' from Delibes' *Lakmé* and the mad scene from *Lucia di Lammermoor*. Local artists occasionally joined the tour for several performances, but Casals was the only regular soloist, doubtless selected partly because he was not an excessively demonstrative crowd-pleaser. In publicity photographs of the time he affected a severe, even stern expression; there was never a trace of a smile. Some years later the Chicago *Journal* observed that he looked neither Spanish nor like a musician but, 'in outline, costume and demeanor, is strongly suggestive of the English solicitor'.[23] Being only of modest height and already balding, the young Casals was not America's conventional idea of a European virtuoso: the memory of Paderewski's dramatic tours of the mid-1890s was still very much alive. On a subsequent tour one impresario even suggested that a flowing wig might help fill the halls. But Casals was never a platform exhibitionist and preferred to let his sound, not his appearance, make the impact. And it worked. There was something about Casals, his biographer H. L. Kirk noted, that 'drove journalists of the time to romantic superlatives in the attempt to explain the fact that so unpretentious a man should produce art so great'.[24]

The American tour opened in Worcester, Massachusetts, on 25 November 1901, and then moved from Rhode Island through New York State, Pennsylvania, Maryland and Virginia southwards to Florida, Louisiana and on to the ranch lands of the American South-West. Apart from occasional guest performances by local artists, the programme was relentlessly repetitious. In the first half of the concert Casals would play the Fauré *Elégie* and Saint-Saëns' *Allegro Appassionato*. In the second he played a Locatelli sonata and, if necessary, an encore, often the Popper cello transcription of Chopin's E flat Nocturne. The arduous progression across America taught Casals that the sheer physical effort of travel left no energy for a varied and adventurous touring repertoire, and the lack of opportunity for serious practice left no possibility of it. For the next forty years Casals repeated concerts and programmes, night after night, across the world.

The concerts were not always well attended, but the itinerary – playing in small towns, school halls – gave Casals a clear sense of the massive size and variety of the country. It made a strong impression on him: 'for me, at the age of twenty-four, America was an emancipation'.[25] And so, many years later, it turned out to be, in a much more permanent sense. But then, like many European visitors before and after, Casals was struck by the 'newness' of the country, and by its openness. If, outside the main cities, it was not culturally sophisticated, Casals was impressed by the provision of schools, libraries and theatres, and by a sense of opportunity unhampered by class-consciousness. He compared the continent to a great symphony in rehearsal: 'one sensed a nation still in the process of coming into being . . . that man could accomplish anything and that everything for his happiness was possible here'.[26]

Outside the recitals and the travelling, there was time to explore. Léon Moreau had an adventurous spirit and the two young men investigated everything of interest. They went down a coal-mine in Wilkes-Barre, Pennsylvania, played poker with cowboys in Texas and went hiking in the New Mexico desert. The company performed in El Paso on 4 February 1902 and travelled on through Arizona to southern California and a concert in Los Angeles on 11 February. Then they proceeded north and arrived in San Francisco at the beginning of March. There Emma Nevada's local popularity ensured a successful series of concerts. On Saturday, 8 March, the venue was Metropolitan Hall, at Fifth and Market Streets, and Casals played Boellmann's *Variations Symphoniques*, his regular Locatelli sonata and, as an encore, the Bach–Gounod 'Ave Maria'. His performance stole the show, the *San Francisco Chronicle* conceding it was established 'beyond doubt' that 'first honors . . . go to Pablo Casals'.[27] If Emma Nevada felt any pique, it need only have been temporary, for a week later Casals had an accident which removed him from the remainder of the tour. On Sunday, 16 March, while climbing with friends on Mount Tamalpais, overlooking the San Francisco Bay, a tumbling boulder, loosened by winter erosion, hit and smashed his left hand. Looking at his mangled fingers, Casals' first thought, as he later recalled, was 'Thank God, I'll never have to play the cello again!'[28] The truth was that a mere few inches probably saved Casals from a much more serious accident or indeed from being killed.

As it was, the injury might well have ended Casals' solo career. With a permanently damaged left hand he might have been restricted to conducting and composition – a scenario which held some attractions – but he would have lost the digital dexterity essential for performance. Momentary elation soon turned to depression when the local physician, Dr Oscar Mayer, warned of the possibility of nerve and bone damage. A press conference was held and, when the news reached Paris, plans were laid for a European specialist to travel to California. As it turned out, the worst was avoided, aided by skilful bone resetting, rest, and subsequent regular massage therapy. The tour party continued its itinerary, while Casals remained for two months as a guest in the home of Sarah Solomons Stein and her husband Michael, director of the Bay Area cable-car company. The Steins had lived in Europe and were a cosmopolitan family, and Casals' convalescence was spent in the agreeable company of new young friends, American, Spanish and French. Michael Stein's younger sister, Gertrude, was at that time completing her medical studies at Johns Hopkins University, having studied psychology with William James at Radcliffe College. Casals was later to know Gertrude and her brother Leo in Paris, but it is not clear whether they met in California. At any rate the enforced break gave Casals the opportunity to do some composition, something for which he had not found time since his early months in Paris in 1899. To a text by Matthew Arnold he wrote a song appropriately entitled 'Absence'. It turned out to be a rare pleasure, for he was not to find the time or conditions to compose again for the next quarter of a century. This period of leisure was brief, however, for early in May the restrictive cast around his hand was removed; Casals was able to give a modest informal recital before travelling by train to New York for the return passage via London to Paris.

By the time Casals reached Barcelona on 3 August, all that remained of his injury was a scar. After a short holiday with his family in San Salvador, he travelled to Portugal for a recital in Porto with the violinist and pianist Bernardo Valentin Moreira de Sá, whom Casals had first met in 1898 at the time of his performance at the Espinho Casino. Moreira de Sá was a man of energy and musical enthusiasms. Casals liked him and accepted an invitation to join him on a six-week tour of Brazil the following summer. Meanwhile he and Bauer resumed their recital engagements in Spain and Holland during the last months of 1902. In Madrid they were invited to the royal palace to play for Queen María Cristina and the Infanta Isabel. By Christmas they were back in Paris.

During 1902 Casals had spent a total of perhaps four weeks in Paris. During 1903 he would be in a different country each month. The pattern of his peripatetic existence was set. The physical demands of the relentless travelling were considerable: in the early years of the century, before motor vehicles or aeroplanes, it very often meant night after night in trains, disturbed sleep in a *wagon-lit*, a constant progression with luggage and a heavy cello case. There is no comparison with the burdens of even the most energetic of modern travelling virtuosi. And Casals did not find it an appealing life-style:

> Even for a young man, full of energy and curiosity, the excitement of travel wears off; and to spend a night here, a weekend there, and to hurry on – to have to rush to catch trains after concerts when your clothing is still drenched with perspiration, and to travel all night and have a rehearsal the following morning – becomes fatiguing and frustrating. . . . Regardless of how successful my concert tours were, I was always glad when they were over and I returned to Paris.[29]

Physically Casals was unusually vigorous. Though small and compact, he was solidly built, with immense stamina developed through regular exercise. Since boyhood he had been an excellent swimmer. The terrace of the family's small rented villa at San Salvador led directly on to a beach which stretched in a straight line for several miles along the coast to neighbouring Calafel in the north and Comarruga in the south. Casals swam rather than bathed, walked for miles each day, and rode his horse on the beach at sunset. His enthusiasm for tennis arose out of his highly developed competitive instinct. In all games and sports Casals, quite frankly, liked to win, and showed relatively bad grace when he did not. The royal palaces and aristocratic mansions he had frequented as a student invariably provided access to tennis courts, and one of his first personal indulgences was to construct, in 1915, a full-sized court in the grounds of the family home at San Salvador.[30] That summer he competed in the Espluga de Francoli tennis tournament, a Catalan competition of a not insignificant standard, reaching the semi-finals of both singles and mixed doubles.[31] In subsequent years he invited to his home, and played matches with, several of Spain's national champions, including Eduard Flaquer, Carles Sindreu and the great woman player, Panchita Subirana. The balance and muscular co-ordination developed in tennis is not unrelated to that required for the playing of stringed instruments. Consciously acquired or not, the strength and control gained from serious engagement in sport helped Casals master techniques of muscular relaxation that played a fundamental part in the longevity of his musical performance.[32]

Tiring or not, tours were unavoidable. Casals had chosen the life of a solo artist, and needed to play wherever engagements were offered. Taking the cello to places where it had not before been heard as a solo concert instrument meant, on occasions, small audiences and unresponsive critics. But there were compensations. By the age of thirty, Casals had travelled throughout Europe – including Russia – and North and South America: he was a genuinely international figure. He had made friendships and professional contacts across the northern hemisphere, and learned seven languages. And by the nature of his instrument, he generally travelled with an accompanist, rarely alone. On the ambitious first trip to South America, for example, he had the company of Bauer and of Moreira de Sá. The trio left Lisbon on 3 May 1903 and docked in Rio de Janeiro on the 21st. They played eleven recitals in five cities before returning in August. Despite a sea voyage of four weeks out of a total tour-length of ten, and a sequence of depressing, cockroach-infested hotels, Casals enjoyed the trip and was booked for a return visit the following year. What made the early tours bearable was the companionship of Harold Bauer. The two men had very similar tastes, musically and personally. They travelled well, enjoyed the same sport and diversions, and appreciated each other's sense of humour. Most importantly, they shared complete musical confidence and trust. Bauer, like Casals, took a broad view of interpretation and felt under no pressure to reproduce the exact intentions of the composer, even if they could be ascertained. In his memoirs he wrote of 'the futility of blind respect to the text'.[33] In rehearsal he and Casals agreed an overall conception of a work, but left details of interpretation free so that, in performance, each could respond to the precise mood and temperament of the other; since they repeated the same works many hundreds of times on tour, the technique helped prevent staleness.[34] The mental collusion between the two men was so acute that they contrived a 'telepathic' parlour trick in which one would identify a playing-card shown in secrecy to the other by means of an agreed composition silently counted to a prearranged tempo.[35]

Following the return from South America, Casals and Bauer played concerts in France, Spain, Switzerland and Holland before leaving for the United States on the day after Christmas. This first solo US tour lasted until the beginning of May 1904 and was largely confined to engagements on the East coast. The opening performance was on 12 January in New York, when Casals played the Haydn D Major Concerto with Sam Franko's American Symphony Orchestra at the New Lyceum Theater. Three days later, on 15 January, Casals performed at the White House as one of three soloists invited by Mrs Theodore Roosevelt, the President's wife. Since the Spanish–American war was still a recent memory, it was clearly something of a diplomatic coup, possibly engineered by the Spanish embassy, that a twenty-seven-year-old Catalan cellist was invited at all; the standard history of music and patronage at the White House rates the concert as 'historically' most distinctive.[36] Advice on the selection of musicians to perform at the White House musical evenings, a regular feature since Roosevelt's inauguration in 1901, was given by the piano-makers Steinway and Sons. The evening was one of stiff formality and protocol, but the President, whose interest in music was probably fairly limited, made a friendly impression. Casals played a light programme including a Boccherini sonata and Saint-Saëns' *Le Cygne*. The 400 guests in the East Room of the White House represented the social elite of Washington. Casals' introduction to the leading families of America – the Smiths, Coolidges and Roosevelts, for example – echoed his remarkable access to the aristocracy of Europe and led to similarly useful connections in later years: at crucial points in his life he was rescued by American initiatives and American money. Some connections were more significant than others, however, and one such was anticipated during the 1904 tour when, on 8 March, Casals played the Bach C Major Suite during a recital at the Mendelssohn Hall in New

York. A fellow artist that evening was a twenty-four-year-old soprano and New Jersey socialite, Susan Metcalfe. Casals and Metcalfe met again almost ten years later, in Berlin, and shortly afterwards they were married.

The intervening decade, however, was full. The day after meeting Susan Metcalfe, Casals made his first appearance at the Carnegie Hall, playing the solo cello part in Richard Strauss's tone-poem *Don Quixote*, with Strauss himself conducting. The North American tour continued until 5 May, when Casals and Bauer sailed direct for Rio de Janeiro to begin three months of concerts in Brazil, Argentina and Uruguay. Though financially rewarding, the South American tour was not a memorable event for the two musicians. Without Moreira da Sá, Rio was not as much fun, and Buenos Aires and Montevideo disappointed Casals in the disparity between the high elegance of the concert audiences and their apparent lack of musical awareness. Casals was always sensitive to the mood and nature of those who came to hear him. He preferred the feel of a mixed audience, rich and poor, young and old, that revealed a genuine enthusiasm for the music performed. He disliked concerts that were explicitly social and fashionable events. Invited to give his impressions of Buenos Aires in a local English-language periodical, Casals entitled his article 'Conservatropolis' and commented on the slightness of musical culture in the city. He was never invited to return to Argentina.

After a sixteen-day passage from Rio, Casals and Bauer landed at Lisbon on 3 September. They had been travelling for close on nine months, and Casals was anxious to return to San Salvador for a break with his family. As often happened when Casals was travelling through a country, however, his presence in Lisbon was discovered: an invitation from Queen Amélia to perform at the Palacio dos Necesidades delayed him and Bauer for two further weeks. On 22 September Casals reached Madrid, travelling on to Barcelona and El Vendrell. By mid-October he was back in Paris, but only briefly: he and Bauer had engagements in Switzerland, Spain, Holland and Belgium. He was in Amsterdam for Christmas, a guest of the Dutch composer Julius Röntgen, by then a close friend, and returned to Paris on 29 December, his twenty-eighth birthday, to see in the New Year.

It had been an invigorating but exhausting year, and Casals knew he needed more stability, a place to store his growing collection of books, music, paintings and furniture, and a home. At the start of January 1905 he found and rented a modest two-bedroom house in a little side-street off the rue Molitor, in the Auteuil district of Paris. The Villa Molitor was, and is, not a single dwelling, as it appears, but a group of twenty-five small houses; Casals took number 20, which had a small garden and stood at the end of the street. The Auteuil district, which lies within the 16th arrondissement, in the south-west of Paris, was at that time an unostentatious residential area, quiet, and with good access to the centre of the city. Auteuil and the neighbouring suburb of Passy had been popular with literary figures – Voltaire, Diderot, Chateaubriand, Balzac had lived there – since the eighteenth century. Nearby at St-Cloud were tennis courts, where Casals liked to play, and further north the Bois de Boulogne. The area had, in effect, more benefits than it had social standing. The house itself was on three levels: a dining-room and studio-living-room on the main floor, bedrooms and bathroom above and a kitchen below. It was to be Casals' base for the next eight-and-a-half years.

The rent at the Villa Molitor was 325 francs a quarter, a sum Casals could easily afford.[37] At this stage in his career a single concert could bring in upwards of 500 francs, less perhaps than the leading music-hall singers of the time – Yvette Guilbert commanded 1000 francs a performance – but a substantial sum none the less.[38] For a recital at Ostende, Belgium, on 20 July 1906, for example, Casals received 700 francs. In March 1908, for three concerts with the Lamoureux Orchestra, and rehearsals, he was paid a total of 8566 francs.[39] During the years he was based at the Villa Molitor, Casals was giving between 150 and 200 concerts each year. (By comparison, some eighty years later, the contemporary virtuoso Yo-Yo Ma was reported as giving about 100 performances each year – if travelling rather further to do so.[40]) Casals' total earnings were considerable: a rough present-day equivalent would be over $300,000 [£160,000] a year. And he was not yet thirty. From his first years as a professional, Casals did not believe in undercharging. He knew the value of money, even if he disliked handling it or discussing it. And he knew his own worth. He soon learned that requesting too high a fee was generally more likely to intrigue and impress an impresario or concert manager than lose the booking. Until 1913 Casals did not use a solo international agent, but employed a series of local managers in different countries. When, during the 1904 American tour, he discovered that his New York representative was misappropriating a proportion of the fees, Casals ordered the man to his hotel, angrily confronted him with his suspicions, and ejected him with such force that the hotel's revolving door was spun off its axle.[41] Casals' priority, then as on many subsequent occasions in his life, was not so much to recover the money as to make a moral point.

If Casals' fees were high, so were his expenses. As well as the costs of travel and accommodation while on tour, he was, throughout the Paris years, substantially supporting both his parents and his brothers. In 1905

Doña Pilar was living with Luis, then fourteen, and Enrique, twelve, principally in Barcelona. Carlos had developed chronic asthma, and Casals had bought him a house in Bonastre, a mountain village north-east of Barcelona, to which Pilar and the brothers came from time to time. Carlos died in June 1908, prematurely old at only fifty-five. For several years he had largely been an absence in his son's life, and Casals in his. At the time of the death, Casals was in Basel for a performance of Bach's *St John Passion*. Casals subsequently revealed that he had sensed his father's death, at its precise moment, during the performance of the *Passion*. Without waiting for news, he returned immediately to El Vendrell, arriving just hours after the burial.[42]

At the time of Casal's Carnegie Hall debut in March 1904, another Paris musician was in New York at the start of his own first American tour. The French violinist Jacques Thibaud had been part of Casals' circle of young musicians since late 1902, along with the pianists Alfred Cortot and Alberto Casella, the cellist Joseph Salmon and the composers Jean Huré and Florent Schmitt. By late 1904 members of this group were meeting informally in one another's houses to play chamber music, joined by others – Ferruccio Busoni, Eugène Ysaÿe, Fritz Kreisler, for example – when their solo schedules brought them to Paris. Out of this private music-making came the most famous chamber trio of the twentieth century, that of Casals, Cortot and Thibaud. Sometime in late 1905, or early 1906, after a particularly pleasurable evening of music at the Villa Molitor, Cortot suggested to his two colleagues that they might – when their schedules permitted – perform together in public as well as for their own pleasure. They rehearsed when they could during the summer and early autumn, and gave their first concert in Lille on 18 December 1906.[43]

The association was based, as Casals put it, 'on music and friendship':[44] the three musicians were much the same age, and each was already firmly established in a successful solo career. There was no excessive pressure to perform, professionally or financially: they did it because they enjoyed it. They began to arrange concerts for about a month a year, usually in May or June, fitting rehearsals around their individual solo commitments. Cortot, the pianist, was Swiss by birth, a year younger than Casals, and a man of great energy and intellectual power. His early ambition had been to conduct, and after winning first prize at the Paris Conservatoire in 1896, he had been sponsored by the Pleyel company to visit Bayreuth. He remained for several seasons as musical assistant, and at the age of twenty-four, in May 1902, conducted the first Paris production of *Die Götterdämmerung*.[45] Jacques Thibaud was also a graduate of the Paris Conservatoire. At eighteen, when playing at the Café

Rouge, he had been 'discovered' by the conductor Edouard Colonne, and offered a debut which led to fifty-four solo bookings in the same season.

The 'Holy Trinity', as the Cortot–Thibaud–Casals Trio became known, was a brilliant and high-spirited combination, and Casals was determined that it should be a success. Although at that time chamber music was rarely a viable proposition in the concert-halls, he subsidized the Trio from his own funds until it became celebrated and highly in demand. Before long there were up to twenty engagements during the month – in 1908 there were twenty-two – and the Trio was able to turn down invitations that offered less than 4500 francs a concert.[46] Cortot, Thibaud and Casals played together regularly until 1933, not only as a trio but in other chamber and orchestral combinations as well; the only long-term separation occurred during the First World War. Their greatest successes came in the late 1920s, with international tours and pioneering chamber recordings on gramophone record, some of which, like the Beethoven 'Archduke' Trio and Schubert's Trio No. 1 in B Flat Major, remain classics of the repertoire.[47] The Trio survived precisely because its partnership was intermittent rather than permanent. The three men had quite different temperaments, and the creative tension that resulted was clearly a factor in the brilliance of their performances.

1905 was Casals' busiest year. Though he took over the tenancy of the Villa Molitor house in January, he spent little of the rest of the year in it. His itinerary explains everything. Before engagements in England and Scotland beginning on 18 January, he had given concerts in Berlin and Brussels.[48] On 25 January he was back in Paris, leaving for Frankfurt on 3 February. March saw concerts in Switzerland and Italy, and a return trip to London on the 28th. During April he was in Holland, and back in London at the beginning of June. July gave him some weeks at home in Paris, before travelling to San Salvador for his customary summer holiday. He left again for London on 22 October, returning to Paris in time to proceed to Barcelona on the 27th. Early in November he had bookings in Switzerland, before travelling via Berlin to St Petersburg, where he began his first Russian visit with a concert on Saturday, 18 November. From Russia he travelled via Vilna and Warsaw to London, then on to Paris. In December he fulfilled engagements in Switzerland before travelling to Holland where he was booked for ten concerts with Julius Röntgen in January 1906. It was a frenetic existence, and one that began to suggest that Casals could not bear to be still, could not face being in one place for more than a few days. What he needed was a reason to stay at home. In 1906 he found one.

# 4

## Paris, 1906–1910

The difficulty of playing the cello is knowing how to get from
one note to the next.

*Pablo Casals*[1]

Guilhermina Suggia was ten years old when she first encountered Casals,
and he was twenty-one. It was the late summer of 1898, and Casals had
come to fulfil his engagement at Espinho, the highly fashionable casino
resort 10 miles south of Porto. Casals was contracted to play nightly as
part of a septet, and Guilhermina, encouraged by her teacher – her father,
Augusto – travelled each week by train from her home village of Matos-
inhos to hear the performance. During the season Casals heard the young
girl play, as he heard many gifted children, and was sufficiently
impressed to give her a number of impromptu lessons. Certainly Casals
detected real talent, and apparently he saw Guilhermina again when he
played in Porto the following March. For Suggia was no precocious
schoolgirl cellist; she was well on the way to becoming one of Portugal's
leading players, and had a personality to match. She had given her Porto
debut, at the Palácio de Cristal, in May 1896, at the age of seven.[2] When
she was twelve, two years after her first encounter with Casals, she
became leader of the cello section of the Porto City Symphony Orchestra. At thirteen she joined one of Europe's leading chamber ensembles,
Bernardo Moreira de Sá's Quartet, with which she gave over fifty public
performances before leaving, early in 1902, to study with Julius Klengel
in Leipzig, on a scholarship personally provided by the Portuguese King
and Queen, Carlos and Amélia.

Guilhermina and her sister Virgínia, a pianist, had been indulgently
raised and doted upon by their Portuguese–Italian parents. From an
early age Guilhermina had taken against authority and rigidity: the lessons with her father had been tempestuous, and she had developed her
own exaggerated style of performance, linked to a fastidious concern for
dress which remained a hallmark throughout her life. Augustus John's

superbly evocative – and accurate – portrait of Suggia, painted in London in 1923 and now in the Tate Gallery, depicted her as dramatic and haughty in a sumptuous geranium gown. Suggia was unquestionably striking: slim, dark, olive-skinned and graceful. Her habit, when playing, of sitting firmly erect and thrusting out her jaw, turned her large nose into a dramatic accessory. Augustus John's painting dealt conclusively with the suggestion that the cello was not an elegant instrument for women.[3] Suggia herself dealt with the idea that a woman could not make a career as a cello virtuoso.

It was entirely in character that Suggia, having won a royal scholarship to study with Klengel, should soon forfeit it as punishment for accepting a fee to appear with the Gewandhaus orchestra on 26 February 1902.[4] Despite the transgression she remained in Leipzig, joining the orchestra and continuing to study with Klengel. In 1905 she gave her solo debut with the Gewandhaus, conducted by Artur Nikisch. It led to a European tour which took her to Paris, Budapest, London, Warsaw and Karlsbad: an account of a performance of the Dvořák Concerto at this time related that 'not only was her technique remarkable, but her tone was of a masculine power seldom heard from a lady violoncellist'.[5] In Karlsbad Suggia met and befriended the great cellist and composer David Popper, but it was doubtless through Julius Klengel that Casals, on visits to Leipzig, again encountered her. Though twenty-five years Casals' senior, Klengel was a great champion of the younger man and of his developing style. He shared Casals' passion for the Bach Suites, having taught them to his own students since the 1880s, and defended Casals' performance of them against the bitter criticism of his Frankfurt contemporary, Hugo Becker.[6] Sometime during 1906 Suggia came to Paris, apparently in straitened circumstances, her father having died. Once again she played for Casals, who agreed to take her as a student. And he did more than that: he took care of her. Early in 1907, friends visiting Villa Molitor became aware that Casals and Suggia were sharing the home.

Guilhermina Suggia is an absence in the autobiographical literature on Casals. In *Conversations with Casals*, recorded with José Maria Corredor in the 1950s, she is mentioned only once, not by Casals but by his interlocutor.[7] In *Joys and Sorrows*, Casals' 'own story as told to Albert E. Kahn', she appears not at all. There seem to be several reasons for the omission. Casals was the product of a Victorian sensibility and felt very strongly that personal matters should be private; he never responded to repeated invitations to write his own full autobiography, and insisted on the considerable discretion of those, like Corredor and Kahn, through whom a version of his story was told. Later biographers, such as Juan Alavedra and H. L. Kirk, were requested to remove some intimate passages when their typescripts were read by Casals: for Kirk this led to undeservedly critical reviews, including one which identified that he had not gone 'beyond his subject's prejudices'.[8] In large part, of course, Casals' reticence about Suggia was intended to lessen the pain, or the shame, for himself and for others, of remembering what he claimed to be 'the most cruelly unhappy episode of my life'.[9] Later in life Casals revealed himself capable of wiping from memory whole segments of his past, while at the same time recalling happier circumstances with extraordinary precision.

It is not difficult to sympathize with the subject of a biography who seeks to direct the account of his life towards happiness and success. And there are many critics who would argue – as Casals did, though not for the same reasons – that the private experience of a creative artist is entirely superfluous to an understanding of his art. The biographer tackling the issue of his personal relationships is plainly going into areas Casals preferred to remain closed, and the inquisitiveness should be justified. On one level it is simply to do with the search for accuracy. But on another it stems from a recognition that relationships were pivotal to Casals' life, and to his music. Though strong, he was a highly sensitive man, physically and emotionally. He was deeply affected by extremes, whether of temperature or mood, and profoundly influenced by close relationships. An artist's creativity is closely linked to his character, sensibility and perception of life, and one cannot comprehend Casals as a musician if one does not attempt to understand the way he viewed the world.

It would be easier to be precise on personal matters if the documentation were thorough. In the case of the relationship between Casals and Guilhermina Suggia, little has survived. The Casals archive is rich and well preserved across a broad front, but only a small proportion of papers relating to the Paris years, stored in France during Casals' absences in the United States during the First World War, has survived.[10] And there is almost nothing on Casals' early relationships with women, though there are impressive sequences of correspondence with other close musical friends. On Suggia's side there is little more than a few isolated letters, for she requested in her will that the correspondence with Casals be destroyed.[11] What evidence there is comes largely from third parties, and needs to be handled with caution. The full story is probably irretrievable. What we do know is that Suggia played a large part in reconciling Casals to Paris, in adding an element of domesticity to his life, and in making the Villa Molitor a place he could regard as home.

At first the relationship seemed entirely unlikely. No two personalities could have been more different. Suggia was volcanic, capricious, dissipated. Casals was organized, disciplined and serious. What they had in common was a passion for music, for the cello and, very soon, for each other. By March 1907 Casals was including greetings from 'Mademoiselle Suggia' in his letters to friends. Less than a year later, on 7 February 1908, the programme for Casals' debut performance as a conductor in Paris, at the Salle Gaveau, announced the soloist as 'Madame P. Casals–Suggia'.[12] On 18 February, according to her Portuguese biographer, Suggia wrote from Rome to friends in Porto: 'I think my friends know by now that I am getting married in April, but only regret it will not be in Oporto. I shall marry in Paris.'[13]

Though Casals and Suggia were indeed both in Paris during April 1908, there is no clear evidence that they did marry. Nor is there any indication that a divorce was required before Casals could marry Susan Metcalfe six years later. Some stories had it that Casals proposed marriage, but that Suggia was reluctant to risk surrendering her professional independence, and prevaricated. Even in the first decade of the twentieth century the fact of two celebrated public figures, both from strictly Catholic countries, living together openly and indefinitely would have caused comment, if not offence. The likelihood is that Casals and Suggia did not marry, but encouraged the view that they had, if only for the sake of their mothers: in correspondence through to the summer of 1913, their closest personal friends certainly addressed them as husband and wife. Either way it did not really matter; for almost seven years their lives were closely connected, musically and personally, initially for good but eventually at profound cost to them both.

Casals and Suggia toured and performed both separately and together, but Casals was in Paris more often and for longer periods than before. The home of the most talented musical couple in Paris was the centre for a wide range of interesting and intelligent guests. The young friends of the early Paris years, Cortot, Thibaud, Bauer were regularly there, to talk or to play chamber music, together with some of the society acquaintances. Soon they were joined by older musicians or foreign performers on visits to Paris – and extraordinary musical evenings resulted. In late spring or early summer, at the close of the concert season, players returning from their tours would meet at the Villa Molitor or, if more space was needed, at Thibaud's home, for long evenings of music. Diran Alexanian, later Paris's leading cello professor, would come, perhaps with violinists Fritz Kreisler or Georges Enesco, the pianists Ferruccio Busoni and Raoul Pugno, or violist Pierre Monteux. During summer weekends, 'the band of thieves', as they referred to themselves, with their wives, might visit the great Belgian virtuoso, Eugène Ysaÿe, at La Chanterelle, his rented country house on the banks of the Meuse near Namur. There they walked, played tennis, went fishing, and, each evening, made music, sometimes well into the early hours of the morning.[14] Combinations of artists that no concert hall could ever afford played together at La Chanterelle and at the Villa Molitor: quartets, for example, with Kreisler, Thibaud, Casals and Ysaÿe – Ysaÿe, though one of the greatest violinists of the time, would often elect to play the viola part. They played together, as Casals later remembered, 'for the sheer love of playing, without thought of concert programs or time schedules, of impresarios, box-office sales, audiences, music critics. Just ourselves and the music!'[15]

In between concert tours, Casals was able to teach, though the necessary irregularity of the lessons did not suit everyone. In terms of long-term individual pupils, there were, apart from Suggia, only two. Charles Kiesgen came in 1903, after military service, and continued until a heart condition put an end to his hopes of a performing career in 1909. He married a grand-daughter of Charles Lamoureux – Casals attended the wedding on 29 June 1909 – and began an alternative career as a theatrical and musical agent. Kiesgen represented Casals from 1913 until 1937 and indeed, despite his early affliction, was still at work when he was ninety, and Casals ninety-five.[16] The second pupil was Gaspar Cassadó, after Casals the most prominent Spanish cellist of the early twentieth century. Cassadó's origins echoed those of his teacher – perhaps too closely. Born in Barcelona in 1897, Cassadó began taking lessons from his father, an organist and choir-master. Making phenomenal progress, he won, at the age of nine, a scholarship from the Barcelona municipality to study in Paris. Cassadó's six years with Casals, 1906–12, were critical, and turned him into a deeply accomplished composer as well as a distinguished cellist. A solo career did not, however, happen at once: in a sense Europe was not large enough for three virtuoso cellists, particularly when one was Casals and the second Suggia.[17] Cassadó returned to Spain during the war, and after 1918 performed largely in South America and then Italy, where he eventually settled. Though he withdrew from performance in fascist Italy, he continued to live in Florence, a decision Casals never wholly forgave.

But touring and performing continued to occupy the bulk of each year, and had to, for it provided the income. Casals would be available for concert tours between mid-September and the end of April, with only a brief break at Christmas, and often not even then. He sought to remain in Paris during May and June, giving concerts, rehearsing, teaching and planning his forward itineraries. Two months each summer were set aside for visits to the family in Barcelona, and for a holiday in San Salvador. There Casals would entertain close friends and receive streams of Catalan dignitaries coming to pay their respects. Inevitably he would be persuaded to play some local concerts and attend rural fêtes and festivals. And by late August he would have bookings for recitals in Madrid or San Sebastián, before returning to Paris by the second week of September. During the years he shared with Guilhermina Suggia, the overall pattern of touring remained, but the detail altered perceptibly. Gone were the major tours, which involved his absence for three to six months. Between 1905 and 1913 Casals made no trip to the United States, nor to South America. His regular tours were to Holland, Belgium, Germany, and Switzerland, all of which could be reached by an overnight train from Paris. England, too, was accessible, and Casals would contentedly play a couple of concerts in London, followed by one in Liverpool, and be back in Paris the following evening. Italy was less convenient, with Rome and even Milan well out of a single day's travelling range, and Casals' diary for these years logs very few Italian appearances. So it was rare that Casals and Suggia were apart for more than a few days, or two weeks at worst. If a longer absence was in prospect, Suggia would travel with him when free from her own engagements. In November 1905 Casals played his first concert in St Petersburg, and for the next eight years his annual visits to Russia became the main events of his winter tour. On the fourth of these visits, Suggia accompanied him, and together in Moscow they performed Emanuel Moór's Concerto for Two Cellos.

By pure chance, Casals' first encounter with Russia occurred at a moment of acute political crisis in the country. The Revolution which culminated in 1917 had effectively begun: in Lenin's own words, 1905 was 'the general rehearsal'.[18] Nicholas II's government, impoverished, dispirited and threatened by emerging revolutionary activism, was rocked in May 1905 by defeat at the hands of the Japanese after fifteen months of a foolish and unwinnable war. This ignominy followed soon after 'Bloody Sunday' – 22 January 1905 – when a huge but essentially peaceful workers' demonstration, led by an idealistic young priest, Father Gapon, was fired upon by the Tsar's troops outside his Winter Palace. Several hundred silent protesters were killed. The two events set off a wave of strikes and demonstrations throughout the Empire, compounded by mutinies among the demoralized armed forces, the first and most famous being on the battleship *Potemkin*. By September strikes had become endemic, the biggest coming late in October when the entire railway network of the empire shut down.

This was the moment at which Casals arrived. Having played several concerts in Berlin at the beginning of November, he had set out on the thirty-hour rail journey to St Petersburg, en route for an engagement in Moscow. The train got as far as Vilna, just inside the Lithuanian border, where it halted, and the passengers and their luggage were unloaded in pandemonium on to the station platform. As he contemplated the prospect of a 1500-kilometre return journey to Paris, Casals was recognized by a fellow passenger, a Russian general who had attended one of his recent Berlin performances. Arrangements were made for Casals to join an emergency train carrying officials to St Petersburg: Moscow was out of the question. Arriving in the darkened capital, his schedule in disarray and his luggage abandoned in Vilna, Casals made contact with Alexander Siloti, the great Russian conductor and pianist whose early encouragement had led him to make the Russian tour. It proved a highly fortuitous contact. Siloti was anxiously awaiting the arrival of Eugène Ysaÿe, booked to play the Glazunov Violin Concerto within his series of concerts with the Maryinski Theatre orchestra, but stranded in Warsaw by the general transport strike. Siloti invited Casals to take Ysaÿe's place as guest artist.

Casals' first performance in Russia hence took place on Saturday, 18 November,[19] in St Petersburg's Hall of the Nobility, a substantial auditorium on the Nevsky Prospekt. Among the audience of 2000 were the composers Nikolai Rimsky-Korsakov, Alexander Glazunov and Anatol Liadov – whose works were featured on the programme – together with a notable proportion of the musical establishment of the city. The occasion, however, contained strong elements of farce. The distinguished audience, in formal attire, sat in candle-light, the city's power plants having failed again that evening. The audience, dismayed at the announced substitution of a young and unknown Spanish cellist for the spectacular and famous Belgian violinist, broke into impatient laughter as Siloti ushered on to the platform a short, bald, stooped figure in a business-suit. Casals, however, seemed oblivious to both his missing evening dress and the discourteous reception. Within bars of the opening of Saint-Saëns' A Minor Concerto he had the full attention of the audience, just as he had captured that of the orchestra at that morning's rehearsal. At the end of the first movement the auditorium was on its feet, clapping and cheering. Andrei Borisiak, later a leading Russian cellist but then still a student at the St Petersburg Conservatoire, was present at the performance, and recorded the impression made by Casals:

> instead of Ysaÿe whom we expected, an unknown cellist appeared on the stage, a short man with a childlike smile. His face subsequently took on the expression of a powerful concentration that at once riveted the attention of the audience. The interpretation that then came forth was so convincing that at every phrase one had to think: 'Yes, indeed, this is how it should be played!'[20]

That the concert should have taken place at all was remarkable. St Petersburg was in a state not simply of disorder, but of genuine anarchy: the political priorities were highly confused. One evening, returning in their carriage after a concert, Siloti and Casals heard shots and sounds of serious rioting, and took a diversion to investigate. As protesters raced past, they could make out the slogan: 'Long live the Republic of the Tsars!'[21] The Tsar himself, isolated in Peterhof, his palace outside the city, had on 30 October issued an Imperial Manifesto, promising a fundamental transformation of the political system, the essentials of which had remained unchanged since Peter the Great. Within the city, the Petersburg Soviet of Workers' Deputies, masterminded by the young Leon Trotsky, sought to paralyze the economic life of the capital. These were, briefly, 'days of freedom', and Rimsky-Korsakov at least felt it. Earlier in the year, after protesting against 'Bloody Sunday', he had been dismissed from his post as director of the St Petersburg Conservatoire and his compositions banned. Now, at the 18 November concert, his symphonic work based on the revolutionary song 'Dubinushka' received its first performance. But by 16 December it was all over, the army and police having marshalled their forces and crushed the Workers' Soviet. A limited form of representative government emerged in the early months of 1906, increasingly weak parliaments (the Duma) dominated by increasingly ruthless prime ministers.

On 22 November Casals was able to perform again, this time a recital, accompanied by Siloti, the programme being works by Bach and Léon Boellmann. The response of one reviewer was conclusive: 'big tone, pure sound, fine phrasing and temperament – everything is combined in this artist. It is astounding!'[22] The following day Casals left St Petersburg, travelling via Vilna and Warsaw to London. The tour as planned had been totally disrupted. But Casals had found it an exhilarating experience, and he returned to Russia the following year and indeed each year until 1913. For even in decline Moscow and St Petersburg were centres of social sophistication and cultural excellence and offered appreciative audiences and impressive social networks. The standard of musical performance in the conservatories and orchestras of Imperial Russia was among Europe's highest, and the audience for it considerable. Four Russian cities sustained permanent opera companies, attracting the leading European soloists. Visiting instrumentalists such as Ysaÿe, and soon Casals, repeatedly filled auditoriums seating several thousand. The Deutsche Grammophon Company had constructed a pressing plant solely to service the Russian demand for gramophone discs.[23]

The circles in which Casals moved insulated him from real contact with the process of political change in Russia. His hosts were wealthy liberal intellectuals, relatively untouched by the convulsions around them. For them, the years between the first two revolutions were deceptively congenial. Adam Ulam has observed that 'never before or since has Russia come as close to being an open society, to achieving both freedom and stability' as during those years, 1907 to 1914'.[24] Alexander Siloti came from an aristocratic landed family, and had married a daughter of the art collector and gallery owner Tretiakov. In their apartment overlooking the river Neva Casals encountered the artistic elite of the country. Siloti himself had studied with Tchaikovsky and Nicholas Rubinstein, and at twenty had been a favourite pupil of Liszt, to whom, Casals reckoned, he bore an uncanny likeness, down to the wart on his face.[25] He introduced Casals to the big musical names – Rimsky-Korsakov, Glazunov (later to write a cello concerto for him), César Cui and Mikhail Glinka. In Moscow Casals encountered the unconventionally talented Alexander Scriabin, and during his 1909 tour began an association with Sergei Rachmaninov which survived for many years within Russia and beyond. On the periphery of the Siloti circle, too, Casals met the new generation of Russian musicians, including Stravinsky and the teenage Prokofiev.

Casals' Russian tours occupied two or three weeks each December or January. The focus was Moscow and St Petersburg but he gave occasional additional performances in Kiev, Riga, Lódz or Lvov.[26] For his Moscow debut in 1906 he played the Dvořák Concerto with the conductor Emil Mlynarsky.[27] Gradually, and sensitively, he added some Russian works to his regular repertoire, Glazunov's *Melody* or *Spanish Serenade*, for example, or – in recitals – a Rachmaninov sonata, or a piece by Mikhail Gnesin. During his 1912–13 tour Casals performed, with Rachmaninov conducting, the Second Cello Concerto of Karl Davidov, Tchaikovsky's contemporary, who was popularly regarded within Russia as the king of the cello – before the arrival of Casals.

Though protected from the harsher discomforts of Russian life, Casals was by no means oblivious to them. He later recalled a feeling of suffocation each time he crossed the Russian border, the sense of entering a prison. 'There was ample evidence of the heavy hand of the rulers. On all sides one felt apprehension, suspicion, fear. Everyone was spied on.'[28] He also experienced the staggering inequalities. One evening, leaving a prince's palace after giving a recital, he encountered a double line of servants, prostrate in his path. 'Walk over them,' his host observed, 'that is why they are there.'[29] Casals' last performance in Russia was on 14 December 1913. A tour was arranged for December 1914, but the war intervened. And after 1917 Casals did not care to return. He was fully aware of both the scandalous corruption of the system and the inevitability of change. But when the Revolution came, its impact on his Russian friends and acquaintances was more than he could bear. The Siloti wealth was confiscated, and for two years the family shared its spacious home with a contingent of the revolutionary establishment. In 1919, aided by British Intelligence, the family escaped to Belgium. Casals went to them immediately, provided emergency funds, and explored the possibility of a musical position for Siloti in the west. In 1922 Siloti joined the faculty of the Juilliard School of Music in New York, where he taught until 1944. The money loaned was returned by one of Siloti's daughters in the late 1930s, when Casals himself had been forced into exile. And Casals never set foot in Soviet Russia. There were aspects of the socialist system he admired, but personal loyalty to his friends took precedence. 'No ends and no achievement,' he wrote, 'can justify such means.'[30]

Despite years of touring and hundreds of performances, there was a notable gap in Casals' log: Vienna. To an extent this was accidental, a consequence of schedules and itineraries. But for a virtuoso at the height of his career, Vienna was hard to miss, and there is another explanation. What Casals felt for music – all his life – was an intense reverence. The nervousness he felt before any performance came not from fear of public reaction, but from a fear of not playing his best, of – by his own standards – risking dishonour to the music. Vienna was the city of the great composers, the 'temple of music', the place in which his reverence was most powerfully engaged. For there was in this reverence an element of superstition, indeed of ghoulishness, stemming perhaps from Casals' Catalan catholicism. Some of his most treasured possessions were relics – Beethoven's birth certificate, a copy of the violin method written for Mozart by his father, a lock of Mendelssohn's hair. A piece of stone from the room in which Beethoven died remains prominently displayed at the Villa Casals in San Salvador today. These fragments held great emotional and symbolic importance for Casals, and so did Vienna. At the beginning of 1910, aged thirty-three, he finally accepted an engagement there.[31] The prospect almost made him ill:

> I have never known such apprehension before a concert. I wandered through the streets with my heart pounding – I had the feeling that any moment I might come face to face with Mozart or Schubert, that suddenly Beethoven would stand before me, looking at me silently and with immeasurable sadness, as over the years I had seen him in my dreams.[32]

His debut concert took place in the Great Hall of the Vienna Musik-verein. Deliberately, one suspects, he had chosen to play a new work by a living composer, Emanuel Moór's Concerto in C Sharp Minor, and had persuaded Franz Schalk and the Vienna Philharmonic Orchestra to accept this manifestly unconventional selection.[1] Even so, his nervousness overcame him. The solo entrance in the Concerto is abrupt, and at that point Casals' bow slipped from his grasp and shot nine rows into the audience. As it was retrieved and passed back, from row to row, by the shaken and silent audience, Casals recovered his composure and began the Concerto again, without mishap. The young Arthur Rubinstein was in the audience and recorded that 'the concerto proved to be insignificant, but Casals played it with his inimitable tone and such a deep concentration that it was impossible to resist him'.[33] A second concert, a recital with Bruno Walter, took place several days later, and Vienna became a regular destination in Casals' diary, and the scene of some of his most historic performances. There, two years later, on 4 March 1912, he and Ysaÿe played what is generally remembered as their greatest performance of the Brahms Double Concerto. It was possibly the height of his travelling career. The only regret is that the development of the phonograph was not at an equivalent stage. At Casals' next concert in the city, later that year, he played the Haydn D Major and Boccherini B Flat Concertos. The performance had a seismic impact on a ten-year-old Austrian boy-cellist in the audience. Emanuel Feuermann had heard other great cellists, like Popper and Klengel, but Casals' performance convinced the young 'Munio' that what he wanted was a solo career.[34]

By his early thirties, from about the end of 1906, Casals found that his position and status had subtly but noticeably changed. In the six years since his Paris debut, he had become an established musical presence, no longer the recipient of favour and patronage, but the dispenser of it. It was a position in which he was altogether more comfortable, and it is revealing to see how he handled it. After several years of repeated performances of a number of cello showpieces, Casals was as interested in discovering composers capable of adding to the concerto repertoire as he found himself a magnet to them. Over the next few years he encountered, supported and to a large extent indulged three composers in particular – Emanuel Moór, Julius Röntgen and Donald Francis Tovey – all of whom were to write cello concertos and remain devoted to him throughout their lives. None survives as a regularly performed composer today.

Emanuel Moór was the most energetic, persistent and difficult of the three. Born of a Jewish family in Hungary in 1863, he had been a boy-wonder pianist, studying in Budapest, Prague and Vienna as well as with Franz Liszt in Eisenstadt. At the age of twenty-two, Moór travelled to the United States with his father, who was to take up a position as cantor to a New York congregation. In New York he met Anita Burke, daughter of a wealthy Irish–American family, married her in London in February 1888, and became a British citizen. Supported by his wife, Moór began to compose – instrumental pieces, concertos and operas – winning performances in Germany and Austria during the early 1900s. Casals encountered Moór in March 1905, introduced by the Russian cellist Anatol Brandoukov, while on tour in Lausanne, Switzerland. Attracted by Moór's blazing intensity, Casals invited the composer to visit him in Paris and bring some of his music. Soon afterwards, Moór arrived at the Villa Molitor with a caseful of music, sat down at the piano and played through his First Cello Concerto (Op. 61), recently written for the young French cellist, Marguerite Caponsacchi.[35] Moór's music was moody and lyrical, yet highly structured, and Casals was immediately impressed. Incautiously he declared, as Lamoureux had to him, that Moór was a 'genius', and the Hungarian, though twelve years Casals' senior, became a passionate disciple virtually instantaneously.[36] For the next few years Moór returned almost monthly to see Casals in Paris, when he was not on tour, and to bring him quantities of new compositions.

Throughout his career, Moór won admiration for his obvious musical gifts and repelled it, equally, through his uncontrolled and boorish personal behaviour. Casals recalled that he had never known a man 'with a greater capacity for offending people and making enemies . . . he was peremptory, short-tempered, violently opinionated'.[37] On several occasions in his company, Casals was deeply embarrassed by Moór's outbursts: Moór's powerful *sotto voce* was often employed to strategic effect in the quiet movements of performances by rival composers. In Casals' own home Moór would abuse and deride other guests, including, once, the Hungarian pianist and transcriber of Bach, Tivador Szántó. Some years later Moór accompanied Casals to the home of the English pianist, Leonard Borwick, a pupil and favourite of Clara Schumann, to rehearse a programme for a Classical Concert Society performance in London. As Borwick began a Beethoven sonata, Casals noticed Moór working himself into a rage, and signalled to him – unsuccessfully – to remain calm:

> We began playing the next work – a Bach sonata – when Moór suddenly strode to the piano, seized Borwick by the shoulders and thrust him violently off the bench, shouting, 'Let me show you how to play Bach!' Borwick – who was very much of an English gentleman – simply said to Moór, very quietly, 'Thank you, sir, I shall play to the best of my ability.'[38]

Even though Casals was a man of considerable decorum, these out-bursts did not shake his confidence in Moór's abilities. Casals viewed eccentricity neither as a sign of artistic genius nor as a disqualification from it. Nor did the antagonism of other musicians dissuade him from performing and championing Moór's compositions. He organized and personally financed performances of Moór's chamber music, conducted some of his works for full orchestra, and encouraged other conductors, like Nikisch, Willem Mengelberg in Amsterdam and Fritz Steinbach in Cologne, to include Moór's works in their programmes. It did not make Casals popular. Cortot, Thibaud, Kreisler and others were persuaded to play Moór's works, but without enthusiasm: 'they did it out of respect for my convictions'.[39] Casals himself included a Moór sonata in the programme of his first tour to Russia, in November 1905, playing it also in Geneva, Paris and Lausanne on his return. Moór, however, was congenitally impatient, every performance fuelling his ambition rather than satisfying it. By December he had completed his Second Cello Concerto, inscribing the title-page of the manuscript score with a dedi-cation to 'my dear friend Pablo Casals, in admiration for his playing of Bach, without which I never would have written this work. Long live Casals!!'.[40]

The C Sharp Minor Cello Concerto had its first performance on 24 October 1906, in Amsterdam, Casals playing with the Concertgebouw under Mengelberg. Moór was in the audience. Casals performed it again the following day, and two days later repeated the performance in The Hague. A month later he played it in St Petersburg. It was not simply an act of gratitude; the Concerto was very much the sort of music Casals liked to play. The solo part was highly demanding and spectacular, and the work as a whole combined lyrical passages with sections of densely written counterpoint. It came to be rated as one of Moór's more impor-tant works but, at the time, earned slight critical enthusiasm. Undaunted, Moór spent the winter of 1906–7 composing a triple concerto for piano, violin and cello, intended for the 1907 autumn tour of the Casals–Thibaud–Cortot Trio. Cortot rented a country house in Switzerland where the three men began rehearsing trios by Schumann and César Franck as well as the Moór Concerto. Cortot soon declared the piano part unplayable, and proposed substantial emendations which Moór, to Casals' surprise, accepted.[41] Jacques Thibaud was less hostile to Moór's work, and later that year gave a performance of the G Major Violin Concerto in Leipzig, Berlin and Geneva. Persuaded by Casals, Eugène Ysaÿe also adopted the G Major Concerto, playing it in Belgium, France and, on 30 November, at the Queen's Hall, London, under Henry Wood. The following April, Harold Bauer gave the first American performance of Moór's D Flat Piano Concerto, with the Boston Symphony Orchestra.

The years 1907–9 were Moór's heyday. His works were performed throughout Europe, by some of the greatest soloists of the time, and each new soloist stimulated a rush of new compositions. Everything could be traced back to Casals: no composer could have received more powerful or continuous support. It was paradoxically Moór's ultimate work of piety – a Double Cello Concerto written for and dedicated to Casals and Suggia – that began the unravelling of his career, and contributed to growing domestic dissent between the two cellists themselves.

The Concerto for Two Cellos and Orchestra received its first performance in Brussels on 19 January 1908, Casals and Suggia being conducted by Ysaÿe. Two weeks later they played it again, at the first of three Paris concerts for which Casals had himself hired the Lamoureux orchestra and booked the Salle Gaveau. For the Paris correspondent of *Musical America* these were 'the most important concerts of the year'.[42] The critic of *Le Monde Musical* was less effusive, suggesting that Moór's compositions were rushed and not fully finished.[43] By the end of the year Casals and Suggia had performed the Concerto in France, Germany, Switzerland and Russia, and on 7 February 1909 returned with it to Paris. This time the response was less polite, *L'Eclair* asking rumbustiously, 'Why the devil do M. and Mme. Casals play such routine music?'[44]

Until then the French critics had generally indulged Casals in his championing of Moór, concentrating more on the performances than on the works themselves. Stylistically Moór was rootless, appearing to compose without reference to any external musical tradition. His work was too austere and intellectual to be identified as a development of nineteenth-century romanticism, and too formal to fit the avant-garde experimentation embraced by his fellow-countrymen, Bartók and Kodály. Moór was of course a foreigner, and the growing hostility to his over-exposure in France may have been substantially a function of that. Dented but not crushed, he threw himself into yet more work: during 1909 he composed at least fifteen major pieces. Casals, meanwhile, took on the critics. He introduced Moór to a new virtuoso, the brilliant young Polish pianist Mieczyslaw Horszowski, and engineered an extraordinary concert of Moór's works in the Salle Pleyel on 15 June 1909, at which he performed a new Quartet for Four Cellos with Joseph Salmon, André Hekking and Diran Alexanian.[45] More spectacularly, at the concert marking his long-delayed Vienna debut, in January 1910, Casals chose to play Moór's Second Cello Concerto.

The basis of the relationship with Moór was Casals' deep admiration for this startlingly gifted man. Moór was extravagantly talented, with excessive creative energy, and he excelled at almost any activity which caught his attention. As well as a pianist and composer he was an accomplished painter, a voracious reader and scholar, and an inventor. Much later in his life he invented a double-keyboard piano, an instrument intended to simplify the performance of rapid sequences of octaves – common in Liszt, for example – which was put into production by the Aeolian and Pleyel–Wolff companies, and for a time considered for manufacture by Bechstein and Steinway.[46] Casals was fascinated by Moór's intellectual energy and found him invigorating and challenging on a musical level. For it was during these early years of stability in Paris that Casals became not merely a musical virtuoso, but a musical scholar. He returned constantly to the scores not only of the repertoire for solo cello but of chamber, orchestral and vocal music, exploring them microscopically; he studied the lives of the great composers, read their correspondence, evaluated their style and technique. For most virtuosi performance was an end in itself. For Casals it was a means to the understanding of a composer's work, a process which was never complete. Whenever players demonstrated impatience with a piece, or boredom through repetition, which was not uncommon, Casals was mystified, and often angry. Along with the gifts of a performer, he had the temperament of a musicologist: his conviction, often repeated, that he would be 'satisfied with perfection' guaranteed that there was always more to be done, and greater depths to be explored. He sought the company of those who shared his reverence for music and total absorption in it, and minds that could enlighten, educate and stimulate his own. It became increasingly difficult to find them, at least among individuals who could at the same time operate at some normal level of human communication.

Emanuel Moór's creative frenzy was rooted in self-doubt and damaged self-esteem. He needed ratification, and Casals was able to provide it. The friendship was mutually rewarding, Moór gaining performance and Casals gaining music to perform. But there was something else. Casals' musical relationships, as indeed his personal ones, always involved an element of submission: he connected best with those he could teach, promote or assist. Artists already successfully established, or individuals with clear sexual or professional self-confidence, did not win his attention. The Paris music world of the early 1900s was full of confident egos, and was sharply divided. On one side were the admirers of Ravel and of the developing style of impressionist composition associated with him. On the other were the critics who accused him of plagiarizing Debussy and making free with the older composer's innovations. Others, exemplified by César Franck, continued to honour the austere, disciplined style of Germanic tradition.[47] Fauré, Ravel's composition teacher, often seemed alone in maintaining an open-minded approach to musical evolution. Suggia relished the rivalry, engaged with it and favoured the Debussy camp. Casals did not, and avoided the dispute, privately expressing scepticism and dismay at what he saw as the undisciplined experimentation of the impressionists. Though acquainted with all the major figures – Saint-Saëns, Debussy, Fauré and Ravel – his closest musical allegiances were with composers he could influence. Casals flourished in relationships which involved dependency and called for nurture. Throughout his life he generated apparently inexhaustible reserves of knowledge and energy, and felt most comfortable in circumstances in which he could share them.

Casals' relationship with the Dutch pianist and composer, Julius Röntgen, was as important as that with Moór, and much less tormenting. From 1903 until the outbreak of war in 1914, Röntgen was a stable and sustaining influence in Casals' frenetic existence. Röntgen's father Englebert had been leader of the Gewandhaus Orchestra (and cousin of the scientist who discovered the X-ray), and Julius had been born in Leipzig in 1855. From the age of twenty-two he lived in Amsterdam where he became a professor at the Conservatory and performed, composed and conducted. With his second wife and a total of five children, Röntgen established a warm and hospitable home on the city's Vondel Park, to which Casals would come each time he had engagements in Holland. In 1905 Röntgen wrote a sonata for cello and piano, dedicating it to Casals, followed by a second in 1907 and finally a full cello concerto in 1909. Casals was consistently polite about Röntgen's compositions, later declaring him a highly underrated composer, and included them in his performances around Europe, if less frequently than the compositions of Moór. Röntgen's particular performing accomplishment was chamber music, and as a young man he had played with Joachim, Brahms and Clara Schumann. Through him Casals met some of Europe's leading musicians, including the Norwegian composer Edvard Grieg in the final years of his life. Röntgen's wife, Amorie van der Hoeven, was the sister of the wife of the English writer Robert Trevelyan, and through that connection Casals was introduced to a whole generation of English musical life.

Julius Röntgen was also valuable on a personal level. Casals addressed him in correspondence as 'my very dear elder brother' and shared with him, if in a limited and sometimes oblique way, some of the strains and anxieties of his developing relationship with Guilhermina Suggia, as well as some of the happiness. Suggia accompanied Casals on a visit to the Röntgens during a tour of The Netherlands in November 1907, and joined the family, Casals and Bauer in chamber music – including one of Grieg's quartets – at their home. The visit ended precipitately and in distress: after an argument Suggia left the house on 8 December and returned to London. Casals continued on his tour in very low spirits. The relationship was taking its toll of both of them, and with the demands and fatigues of the relentless travelling schedule, Casals entered the first serious depression of his adulthood.

The root of the problems during the first years of Casals' relationship with Suggia had to do with age, rather than temperament. Casals was now over thirty, established, famous and in demand throughout Europe. Suggia was nineteen and had still to make her musical mark. Effecting the transition from Casals' pupil to his lover involved a leap into adult society. For Casals had never been frivolous, and his friendships were now very often with those older than himself. Suggia was cast in the role of the junior partner, musically and socially, and it was not a state that came easily to her. She wanted professional opportunities, to travel and to perform as a solo virtuoso. She began to make a serious success of her career at a time when Portuguese women rarely made a career at all. Casals could not accept it, however much he appreciated her talent, just as in the future he would never be comfortable when women close to him sought professional success independent of his own. Suggia resented his jealousy and confronted it with moods, challenges and petulant dares. The tension began to affect both their careers, and Casals found it difficult to perform at all. Suggia's mother Eliza, who came to stay when Casals was on tour, made clumsy attempts to conciliate, pointing out to Guilhermina that with domestic security, three fur coats and a little dog, her sacrifice was not without its advantages.[48]

The circumstance of two talented cellists living together could never be easy. They both needed to practise for hours each day, and there was inevitable comparison between their performances, their reviews and their popularity. The music-going public in Paris came to know of their rivalry, or imagined it, and rumours circulated that Casals had put Suggia's cellos away, for example, or that one or other had the superior vibrato. And it was exacerbated, doubtless unintentionally, by Moór, who was captivated by Suggia, flattered her and, in his Double Concerto, indulged her with the more spectacular solo line. This was harmless enough mischief, but Casals could not see the point of it. What never faltered, however, was Suggia's belief in Casals' genius, and her admiration for his music. Of the Bach Suites she would say that only two, those in G and C, were hers to play. The rest were Casals', 'until the angels took over'.[49]

The final weeks of 1907 and the first few of 1908 represented a kind of emotional peak. Just before Christmas Suggia was in a clinic for minor surgery, and Casals was intensely anxious. Their relationship had ceased to be a casual affair. Though disruptive, it was clearly serious, and permanent. Amidst the first signals of incompatibility, they began to speak about the possibility and implications of marriage. Casals was restless and distracted. Indeed, the tension made him ill. For several months he could not concentrate on his music and sensed his playing was lacklustre. He travelled to Russia in January, and made short visits to Holland in February and England in March. But compared to the schedules of the previous six years, it was a very light spring.

By early summer the atmosphere at the Villa Molitor seemed less strained: Casals and Suggia appeared to have found, for a while, a *modus vivendi*. Visiting the house in June 1908, bringing his new cello sonata, Julius Röntgen found Casals 'stretched out on the sofa in dressing-gown and Suggia playing cello nearby. . . . After playing we went into the garden, Casals turned on the fountain, Suggia brought out Spanish wine, the blackbirds were singing, [it was] the most beautiful summer afternoon.'[50] As if to acknowledge the rise in their spirits, Casals had bought a new cello in May. The instrument, located through the Paris dealers Caressa & Français, 'Luthiers du Conservatoire', was a Matteo Gofriller, made in Venice around 1700, but bearing the inscription of Carlo Bergonzi in whose workshop Gofriller had been an apprentice. The quality and reputation of Gofriller's individual work was only then being rediscovered, his cellos having hitherto been ascribed to Bergonzi (as was this one), to Guarneri or to Stradivarius.[51] The 'Bergonzi–Gofriller' instrument had been owned by a collector in Lille, a M. van de Weghe, and on 15 May Casals agreed a price of 18,000 francs, roughly his earnings for five concerts.[52]

In the course of his life Casals owned a number of fine instruments, including the Gagliano presented by Queen María Cristina, a Ruggeri given him by the American philanthropist, Isabella Stewart Gardner, and a Carlo Tononi which he bought in 1910,[53] but the Gofriller remained his favourite instrument for over sixty years and in a real sense his life-time companion. When the instrument later developed a fault, Casals had the French *luthier* Laberte construct a cello of identical proportions which he used for over two years until the Gofriller had been fully restored.[54] For most great cellists, owning a Stradivarius is so powerful an ambition as to be almost commonplace. Casals, typically, rejected the possibility. Once offered the 'Piatti' Stradivarius of Robert van Mendelssohn for 150,000 marks, he refused, sensing that the instrument's personality might overwhelm his own.[55] It would also have been uncomfortably large. Casals, at his height, preferred a smaller cello: the Gofriller was 74 centimetres in height, the Tononi 73.7.

In July Casals and Suggia left for San Salvador. That year Casals allowed himself an extended summer break: they were not back in Paris until October, and then spent much of the autumn together. Casals' schedule was light, and Suggia accompanied him to Switzerland in October, and to Germany and Russia during December, performing Moór's Double Concerto in each country. And they were back home at the Villa Molitor for Christmas.

With his strength and confidence returned, Casals took up his 1909 concert programme with a vengeance. At the end of February he was in Hamburg, travelling in early March to Manchester, to play the Dvořák Concerto with Hans Richter and the Hallé Orchestra. He returned via Brussels, continuing on to Spain for several concerts to mark the anniversary of the Musical Association of Barcelona. Again Suggia travelled with him, and Moór's Concerto was performed. By the end of the month, Casals was in Holland to play Boccherini and Saint-Saëns with the Utrecht Symphony Orchestra. He was bursting with energy and enthusiasm, keen to welcome Röntgen to Paris to play sonatas and, in June, to try out the new Cello Concerto. These few months mark the high point of Casals' life with Guilhermina Suggia.

# 5

## The English Connection, 1910–1914

You are perfectly right about the English superiority complex
concerning themselves and 'foreigners'. They certainly are a con-
ceited race.

*Maurice Eisenberg to Casals, 1932*[1]

Since his Osborne recital for Queen Victoria in 1899, Casals had visited
England about a dozen times, but he was far from a familiar name there,
and far from comfortable either. Between the autumn of 1909 and the
outbreak of war in 1914, his connections with the country increased
considerably, and he began to find English friends with whom, for the
first time, he could relax.

The agency at first, significantly, was a German. Edward Speyer, an
amateur musician and member of a wealthy Frankfurt banking family,
had acquired 200 acres of Hertfordshire in 1893 and transformed himself
into an English gentleman. Speyer's father had been a friend of Beethoven, and of Mozart's eldest son, and he himself had known Clara
Schumann, Max Bruch and Brahms.[2] Edward Speyer was in a sense a
collector of musical experiences as well as musical manuscripts, and used
his substantial wealth to maximize the opportunities for doing so; his
wife Antonia would sometimes hire the London Symphony Orchestra
to entertain dinner guests at their country home, Ridgehurst, near Shen-
ley. A close friend of Joachim since 1856, Speyer established the Joachim
Quartet Society in 1901, to bring the great violinist and his Quartet to
London for six concerts each year. After Joachim's death in 1907, Speyer
launched the Classical Concert Society over which he maintained a similarly exclusive control. But without the powerful attraction of Joachim
himself, the new Society was only moderately successful. To establish its
reputation in London it needed to present artists of international calibre,
capable of filling the recital hall, and Speyer set out to recruit them.
Having received reports of Casals' 'sensational success', but never having
heard him perform, Speyer dispatched an invitation. Casals' debut with

the Society was on 20 October 1909, at the Bechstein Hall. He played a Bach Suite, followed by the Brahms C Minor and Schubert B Flat Major Trios, with the violinist Marie Soldat and pianist Leonard Borwick. The reception was outstanding. 'Casals had for the first time obtained the ear of an English audience,' Speyer announced, inaccurately.[3] What Casals had done was win the favour of a generously self-indulgent musical patron.

Accepting Speyer's patronage was no more difficult than accepting the support that had come from many sources in the past. What it required was performances for Speyer's Classical Concert Society and regular visits to Ridgehurst. The recitals became less congenial as their popularity waned, damaged by Speyer's conservatism – nothing later than Brahms could be performed – and the fact that there were so many other opportunities for music in London at the time. But Casals enjoyed the visits to Ridgehurst, where he could browse amongst Speyer's musical memorabilia, make up chamber ensembles with other guests, or play a game of tennis. A well-worn story from Speyer's memoirs has Casals arriving one summer morning to announce: 'Now, six sets of tennis first and then the two Brahms Sextets!'[4] The highlight of Casals' first visit to Ridgehurst was his meeting with the English pianist and composer Donald Francis Tovey, then attempting to advise Speyer on his choice of concert programmes. Tovey was almost exactly Casals' age, and a freakishly brilliant musician. They found they had much in common – their musical taste, their approach to the performance of Bach, their fastidious scholarly knowledge of the chamber repertoire. Within days, and before Casals' London recital in October, they had set up two small recitals together and given the first performance of Tovey's *Elegiac Variations*, written for cello and piano in memory of Robert Hausmann, cellist of the Joachim Quartet. Joachim had been Tovey's youthful idol: aged eighteen and at the start of three dazzlingly wayward years at Balliol College, Oxford, Tovey had performed with the great violinist in 1894. The relationship had intensified, Joachim providing the ultimate accolade by mentioning to a friend that of all the younger musicians he knew, Tovey was 'the one that would most have interested Brahms'.[5] On Joachim's death, Tovey was left without a musical hero and influential musical patron. Casals came dangerously close to filling the gap.

Donald Tovey was the child of a clergyman–schoolmaster at Eton, who entrusted the education of his evidently gifted son to a nearby private school – Northlands – at Englefield Green, run by a young German woman of means, Sophie Weisse. Weisse was not herself a music specialist, but recognized the prodigious early abilities of her pupil and sought to develop them by providing the finest teachers and unlimited musical opportunities. By the age of twelve Tovey's life was a regime of piano practice, lessons in composition, visits to concerts and the opera, and virtually total seclusion from children of his own age – to all of which he submitted with benign tolerance. As an adolescent he was highly precocious, a technically brilliant pianist with a staggering capacity for profound and detailed musical analysis. By his early twenties he had mastered sixty-five piano concertos as well as a vast corpus of chamber and orchestral music. He read full scores like a book and memorized them almost instantaneously; and he could perform phenomenal intellectual tricks such as playing complex piano works on request, from memory, and backwards.

Tovey became – and remains – the supreme English musical analyst. His academic writing, collected in the 1930s as *Essays in Musical Analysis*, together with his articles for the eleventh edition of the *Encyclopaedia Britannica*, effectively established a British musical orthodoxy. Sixty years on, Tovey can be challenged on detail, but in the estimation of the critic Andrew Porter, 'essentially what he says about the making and meaning of western music remains true'.[6] For all his brilliance, and probably because of it, Tovey was incapable of normal human communication. He was disorganized, impractical and unreliable, with 'a perfect genius for failing to turn his opportunities to worldly advantage'.[7] Much of the blame must fall on Sophie Weisse, who colonized his mind and refused ever to release him, even to the women he attempted to marry. Through her gifted pupil Weisse lived a life which she, as a woman and a foreigner, perhaps sensed had been denied to her. Increasingly embittered and brutal as Tovey struggled to make some kind of connection with other people – the full horror will not be known until a thorough biography of Tovey is written – she ultimately savaged the talent she had sought to engender.[8]

What interested Casals, of course, was not Tovey's social incompetence, but his extraordinary musical mind. Tovey, like Moór, not only performed music but understood its nature and structure; and he could compose it. His musical taste owed more to Henri Bergson's neo-Romantic concept of 'creative evolution' than to the purist intellectual dogmatism of late-nineteenth-century scientific rationalism, and as such was highly congenial to Casals.[9] The two men enjoyed performing together, and Casals was happy to play Tovey's own compositions. After the success of the October 1909 recitals, they arranged two further concerts, later extended to three, for Casals' London visit the following year. At the first concert, in the Aeolian Hall on 2 June 1910, they played Bach, Brahms and sonatas by both Tovey and Röntgen, *The Times* critic commenting on the Tovey work that 'even the dull parts were infused with life by Señor Casals' wonderful playing'. That October Casals returned for a further concert in Speyer's series, this time sharing the billing with Tovey. *The Times* again noted the dominance of the cello, contrasting it with 'Mr Tovey's rather limp treatment'.[10] Despite Tovey's spectacular gifts, it was Casals who was in control. And this was what they both wanted.

Although 1910 and 1911 were among the busiest performing years of Casals' career, visits to England featured regularly and prominently in his diary.[11] The principal attraction was Tovey, and the opportunity to be with him and perform with him. But through Tovey, and indeed through Speyer, Casals quickly made a wide circle of English musical friends with whom he could be genuinely comfortable rather than, as before in England, simply obliged. At the beginning of January 1911, Casals brought Moór to London for a Classical Concert Society performance at which he had persuaded Speyer to include a Moór cello sonata alongside works by Bach and Beethoven. Moór remained in London for performances of two of his operas at the Savoy Theatre while Casals travelled to Budapest for concerts with Ysaÿe and Pugno, returning to London for his Promenade Concert debut with Sir Henry Wood on 18 March. The concerto that evening was the Dvořák, the conductor being careful to reduce the orchestral accompaniment to a double quartet of strings and two basses during the solo passages for fear of Casals' habit at rehearsals 'of turning round to the orchestra and hissing them down if they dare to make too strong a *crescendo*'. Sir Henry later learned to warn the orchestra in advance:

> You know what an intensely light orchestral accompaniment he demands – no colour at all. So I beg of you Strings to try to play on one hair of your bow; perhaps two – sometimes three – but never more. Thus you will save endless stoppages and many scowlings and hisses.[12]

In May Casals gave two performances as part of the Chelsea Concerts series organized by Tovey himself. Between the concerts he joined Tovey as house-guest at Sophie Weisse's Northlands School, almost a family occasion attended by Röntgen and his wife, their relatives Robert and Elizabeth Trevelyan, and two great-nieces of Joachim, Adila Fachiri and Jelly d'Aranyi, themselves both accomplished violinists. Robert Trevelyan had written the libretto to the opera *The Bride of Dionysus*, which Tovey was then struggling to complete. Northlands had now become Casals' home-base while on tour in England: he had spent some time there during May and October the previous year, and now again took part in the informal, but high-quality, concerts Miss Weisse arranged in the school music-room. The evenings at which Casals performed were often attended by several royal princesses from Windsor Castle, a twenty-minute carriage-ride away.[13]

Casals had always made a clear distinction between public performances, for which he expected to be paid, and private musical occasions which were given for pleasure. Once, in Brussels, he abruptly stopped a rehearsal upon learning that the promoter had sold tickets to it as well as to the final performance, while he himself was receiving a single fee.[14] Early in his career he accepted invitations to unpaid private soirées if he stood to benefit in terms of professional connections. Later he had no such need. The violinist Pablo de Sarasate once responded to a London dinner invitation which requested he bring his Stradivarius with the information that 'my Stradivarius does not dine'.[15] Casals, too, attended At Homes only if he cared for the hosts. Apart from Northlands, the home he visited most often in London in the years before 1914 was that of the American singer Paul Draper and his wife Muriel. The Drapers were not ostentatious society figures, but young musicians who enjoyed entertaining and had a lot of friends. After moving to London from Italy in 1911, they first took a house in Holland Street, Kensington, and then moved to 19 Edith Grove, Chelsea, near the Brompton Cemetery, where Muriel Draper transformed a decrepit adjoining studio into 'a magnificent, spacious, square, noble music room', with bare brick walls, a large fireplace, comfortable chairs and a Bechstein concert grand piano.[16] There friends such as Ysaÿe, Thibaud, Bauer, Cortot, Rubinstein, Albert Sammons, Eugene Goossens and Lionel Tertis used to come for chamber evenings – with excellent food sent in from the Savoy – or simply to unwind at a late-night supper after their concerts. Casals was introduced by his Spanish colleague, the cellist Augustín Rubio, a particular friend of Muriel Draper, and at that time teaching at the Royal Academy of Music. Among many great performances recalled by Muriel Draper in her memoirs were Schubert's 'Trout' Quintet played by Thibaud, Tertis, Rubinstein, Casals and Felix Salmond, and the Brahms B Minor Piano Trio with Thibaud, Casals and Rubinstein.[17] Rubinstein described the enchanted evenings of music at Edith Grove as 'the supreme musical euphoria of my life'.

Rubinstein's own introduction to London had been engineered by Casals. At their first meeting, in Vienna, at the beginning of 1910, Casals had offered to incorporate the young pianist into one of his Queen's Hall matinée concerts that June. Casals' reputation ensured that the concert was a sell-out, and the linking of their names in the notices led to further contacts and engagements for Rubinstein in a city that was notoriously tough on unknown European artists. But the concert also led to a misunderstanding which the two men never fully resolved. Rubinstein expected, and indeed badly needed, a share of the Queen's Hall receipts, but none was forthcoming. To remind Casals of the omission, Rubinstein requested – and obtained – a loan of £10. Several months later Casals was reported as refusing invitations that would bring him into contact with Rubinstein, explaining that friends who do not pay their debts 'cease to be friends'. Rubio eventually smoothed over the differences and brought the two men together, but for Rubinstein the charm was broken: 'we did not look at life with the same eyes'.[18]

At the beginning of September 1911 Casals and Suggia invited Tovey to join them at San Salvador for a holiday. But the visit was pre-empted by a sudden outbreak of cholera in Catalonia, and instead the three arranged a rendezvous in Paris at the beginning of October. Suggia wrote to reassure Sophie Weisse that although they could not put Tovey up at the Villa Molitor – the house was 'toute minuscule' – they would take good care of him by day. She reported that 'her husband' was planning concerts with Tovey in Barcelona, Vienna and Paris next season.[19] Casals was indeed promoting Tovey – as he had promoted Moór and Röntgen – both as pianist and composer, and encouraging his friends to recognize the Englishman's brilliance. Casals' schedule precluded the venues he initially had in mind, but after two further joint recitals in London in November, he and Tovey arranged to meet the following February for a performance in Budapest. For Tovey the patronage was perfectly timed: having exasperated several leading London concert promoters through his awkwardness and unreliability, the prospect of a European booking pulled him 'out of the dumps'.[20]

1912 proved to be a devastating year in Casals' life. It began powerfully, with triumphant performances of the Brahms Double Concerto – with Ysaÿe – in Moscow and St Petersburg in early February, and in Vienna on 4 March.[21] The mid-February recital with Tovey in Budapest led to a second concert there on 2 March at which, with Enesco, they performed the Beethoven Triple Concerto; the remainder of the demanding programme that same evening included the Brahms Double Concerto and the Schumann Cello Concerto.[22] After further concerts in Leipzig and Frankfurt, Casals travelled to England where, on 21 March, he received the Gold Medal of the Philharmonic Society of London, an award commemorating the Society's links with Beethoven, and previously awarded to Brahms, Joachim and Anton Rubinstein among others. It was an extraordinary honour for an artist aged thirty-five, and reflected the esteem in which Casals, barely three years after Speyer's initial invitation, had come to be held in the country.

But whatever England thought of Casals, he himself still viewed England as a distinctly alien culture. Edwardian London was a thriving and wealthy artistic metropolis which could afford to hire the best European talent, and did so. Casals permitted himself to be afforded, following the advice of a fellow Spaniard with long experience of music in London – his old friend the violinist and conductor Enrique Fernández Arbós – that the best way to succeed in a city where there were at least eight concerts each evening was to double one's fee.[23] In October 1910, Casals charged a total of $4100 for seven concerts, six in England and one in Belfast. For a single evening at Englefield Green his fee (calculated in American dollars by his French agent) was $525.[24] Given the sizes of the venues, these charges were high, though they were not conspicuously greater than the fees Casals obtained elsewhere in Europe. During that full season, from October 1910 to May 1911, Casals earned a total of just over $45,000, a sum which should be multiplied by fifteen to get a sense of its comparable value today.[25]

In relation to Casals' personal connections in England, what is interesting is that they were, in the main, not with the English. Ridgehurst and Northlands, for example, were the homes of German émigrés, while Edith Grove was that of an American couple. The musicians who performed for pleasure at the Drapers' studio were largely European – with Tertis, Sammons and Goossens the occasional exceptions. Harold Bauer and his sister Gertrude were first-generation Britons, as indeed were most of the close friends Casals made in England in the future. His strongest English connection was with Donald Tovey, though it was not Tovey's Englishness that was of primary interest to him. Between Casals' Latin experience and the English temperament there was a chasm which defied every earnest attempt to overcome it, a mutual impenetrability that left Casals intermittently puzzled and pained at different points in his life. The truth is that Casals never really cared for the English, because the English – particularly its musical establishment – never took the trouble to understand him. He continued to admire what he took to be the English commitment to political freedom until, following the Second World War, he came up against its limitations. Profoundly betrayed, he visited the country only once again, in October 1963, when he conducted *El Pessebre*, his oratorio for peace.

Casals returned to England in both April and early May 1912 to perform in two of Tovey's five Chelsea Concerts, and was back for other London bookings later in May and in June. So frequent were his visits that he opened a London bank account, at the City and Midland Bank in Charing Cross. On at least one of his English visits – there were six in a half-year – Casals brought Suggia to London, introducing her generally as his wife. She performed informally at one of the Northlands concert evenings and joined Casals' friends for musical occasions at Edith Grove. Twelve-year-old Milly Stanfield met Casals for the first time in the artist's room before one of this season's concerts; a gifted student-cellist herself, she later became his English secretary and followed his career closely for the rest of his life.[26] For Guilhermina Suggia, it was her last tour with Casals.

In September 1912, Tovey joined Casals and Suggia at San Salvador for the holiday he had missed the previous year. Casals' villa, built on land bought in 1908, stood right on the beach at Playa San Salvador. From its veranda, framed by three tall arches, one stepped on to the sand; 30 yards away was the sea, clear, shallow and excellent for bathing. The house itself, white with painted shutters, was on two storeys. The two rooms on the upper floor led on to a terrace overlooking the sea. The ground floor extended back from the double-storey section and contained two large reception rooms, a kitchen and several bedrooms. This modest beachfront home formed the core of the spacious mansion which, over the next twenty years, would be constructed round it, paid for out of the proceeds of Casals' increasingly remunerative concert tours. Doña Pilar lived in the house and, until her death in 1931, supervised the seemingly endless extensions and improvements, the gardens, terraces, fountains and walkways. Luis Casals farmed the surrounding 14 acres of land and later, with his wife Teresina, brought up his own young family under the benign shadow of his world-famous and often absent brother.

In 1912, however, the house was a pleasant and comfortable base for a summer vacation. In addition to Tovey, the house-guests included Enrique Granados, his wife Amparo, and the Polish pianist, Mieczyslaw Horszowski. Horszowski and his mother had been introduced to Doña Pilar and Enrique Casals in 1905, when, as a thirteen-year-old prodigy, he had given a concert in Barcelona.[27] He first met Casals – and played for him – in Milan in February 1906, though the two did not become close friends until Horszowski settled in Paris as a student in 1910, at the age of seventeen. 'Meicio' became a regular visitor to the Villa Molitor, and Casals later played a key role in persuading him back to the concert career he had interrupted to gain a wider university education. Horszowski had been the archetypal sailor-suited prodigy. His Vienna debut recital, at the age of eight, led to concert tours in Europe and America, and presentations to the great figures of music – Joachim, Ravel, Toscanini. His first Carnegie Hall performance took place in 1905, when he was thirteen. Brilliant but shy, laconic, prickly and sometimes impenetrable, Horszowski became Casals' closest friend, and certainly his oldest: at Casals' death they had known each other intimately for over

*Pablo Casals aged about five.*

*Casals' father, Carlos* (at the harmonium), *with musical colleagues in El Vendrell.*

*Casals aged about twenty.*

*Pablo Casals* (seated) *with Enrique Granados* (second from right) *and friends in Paris.*

Below *The Crickboom Quartet (Mathieu Crickboom and Josep Rocabruna, violins, Rafael Gálvez, viola, and Pablo Casals), 1897.*

*Casals and Guilhermina Suggia*
*in Paris, c. 1909.*

*A publicity photograph, New York, 1914.*

Below *At Northlands, May 1911.* Left to right: *Robert Trevelyan, Donald Francis Tovey, Elizabeth Trevelyan, Jelly D'Aranyi, Sophie Weisse, Casals, Adila Fachiri* (front), *Julius Röntgen, Amorie Röntgen.*

*Casals on the tennis court, San Salvador, c. 1912.*

*Albert Schweitzer, Casals and Donald Tovey,
Edinburgh, November 1934.*

*Alfred Cortot, Casals, Gabriel
Fauré and Jacques Thibaud, Paris,
1922.*

*Casals and Frasquita Capdevila,
on the balcony of Villa Colette,
Prades, c. 1947.*

'El Cant dels Ocells', *Casals* *home in Prades, 1949–57.*

*Prades: Casals in rehearsal with Isaac Stern, Alexander* *Schneider and the Festival Orchestra, 1952.*

sixty years. They lived very separate lives, met sporadically and corresponded irregularly, but shared a personal and musical intuition that seemed to require little upkeep and no prolonged discussion. The relationship was built on total mutual trust and a complete absence of fawning or obeisance.

In September 1912, however, Horszowski was only just twenty, and somewhat in awe of his celebrated companions: the only known photograph of the group shows him boyish and awkward at Tovey's feet, ducking shyly from the camera as his friends relax around him. September was a perfect month: the searing heat of midsummer was over, yet the sea was warm and ideal for bathing. 'Exercise consists of disturbing the waters of the Mediterranean,' Tovey noted, though not everyone shared his enthusiasm: 'I,' he wrote, 'who suffered the tortures of the damned when I learned to swim, never in my worst moments dreamed of such terror as Horszowski has of lifting his feet off the bottom, even when supported by two people! Yet he has been up the Matterhorn!'[28]

Casals and his youthful house-guests entertained themselves by swimming, walking, playing tennis or making up different chamber-music combinations, using one or more of the three pianos in the house, all of which were out of tune. 'In spite of the heat,' Tovey reported, 'I never felt better in my life.'[29] In fact Tovey threw himself into leisure much as he threw himself into everything – with excessive fervour: 'I am getting quite my top speed,' he wrote to Weisse, 'without the slightest fatigue.'[30] For several intensive hours each day he worked on his opera, dispatching repeated progress reports to Robert Trevelyan. Soon he had presented his hosts with an embarrassingly contrived Sonata for Two Cellos – based on a Catalan folk melody – which they were constrained to try out.[31] And in breaks from composition he imposed vigorous routines and activities on the other members of the party.

Towards the middle of the month Tovey received news that his father was seriously ill (the Rev. Duncan Crookes Tovey died on 29 September) and the news seemed to derange him further. Somehow he managed to precipitate a bitter emotional incident that severed Casals' relationship with Suggia, suddenly and, after an uncertain reconciliation, permanently. 'Malheureusement nous touchons à la fin,' Casals had written in a letter to Sophie Weisse on 16 September.[32] He was in fact referring to his own and his guests' summer holiday, but it may as well have been a terminal comment on the friendships that were about to be blown apart.

The precise cause and course of the quarrel is probably irretrievable. But its effect was to bring to a head the tension between Casals, Suggia and their conflicting expectations, held in check for years but always susceptible to explosion. The catalyst, undoubtedly, was Tovey, a man whose eerily spectacular intelligence was matched by a quite remarkable opacity to human feeling. Seeking, plainly from the best of motives, to ease the tension between Casals and Suggia, he touched some painful sexual vulnerability and triggered in Casals an explosive jealousy. The holiday ended abruptly. Tovey returned to London, hurt and confused. Guilhermina Suggia left for Portugal, soon afterwards travelling on to England. She was twenty-four years old.

Casals himself was due back in England a few days later, for a tour scheduled to open, as luck would have it, with a recital at Northlands on 3 October. He was committed to an especially crowded schedule of concert obligations that autumn, culminating in a particularly ambitious tour of Russia at the end of the year. He had no option but to try to get through it. The evening at Northlands was cancelled, as were several Classical Concert Society recitals he was due to have given with Tovey. But Casals continued with the remainder of the English tour, giving concerts in Birmingham – where he was soloist in Richard Strauss's *Don Quixote* under Sir Henry Wood – Chester and Liverpool.

The view in most published accounts, including Casals' own, is that he put this painful episode behind him, wiped it from memory after a period of healing, and continued with his career. On Suggia's death, almost forty years later, he was reported to observe that he had not thought of her for years.[33] In fact it was far from a clean break. In the short term there was a flurry of letters between the parties, with Weisse, the Trevelyans and Röntgen all being drawn into the recriminations. Sometime during October Casals and Suggia were reconciled, and were together again in Paris. Earlier confidences were broken, and Tovey – probably inevitably – was cast as the villain of the piece.[34] Feeling humili-ated and now betrayed by each of his former friends, he travelled to Liverpool at the end of October, in the hope of a meeting with Casals. Losing his nerve at the last minute, however, Tovey merely sent a lengthy letter of explanation and apology, the wording of which – it was written in French – had been discussed in advance with Sophie Weisse and Elizabeth Trevelyan. Casals responded in a brief and formal note, seeking to close the incident.[35] Several days later, Robert Trevelyan attempted to intervene on Tovey's behalf. Again Casals responded politely but terminally: 'I now need peace, complete tranquillity and the opportunity perhaps to forget.'[36] The friendship with Tovey was spoiled, he agreed, though 'a good sentiment' remained. It was almost fifteen years before the two men could be friends again.

The reconciliation between Casals and Suggia was disruptive, imprac-tical and ultimately fruitless. Casals was travelling throughout the autumn, and they had little time together; by the end of the year they were apart again, this time for ever. For both of them the relationship, and the manner of its end, remained a severe and continuing trauma which affected their lives and decisions for years afterwards. On 31 December, back in Paris after an exhausting Russian tour, Casals wired Suggia a New Year greeting in which he could not conceal his loneliness and pain: 'At the moment the clock strikes midnight I shall be alone, and thinking of you with all my heart. Perhaps you will think of me too.'[37] That telegram, along with a few photographs, was all Suggia preserved of the relationship.

In a state of depression, Guilhermina Suggia spent part of the following two years with her sister in Brive, near Périgord, before moving to England in 1914. There, as Milly Stanfield later reported, her long-standing association with Casals led many to regard her as his musical representative at a time when, during the war years, he himself was absent from England.[38] There is, however, no indication that Suggia either wished or attempted to capitalize on Casals' name, although she did pay clear if somewhat leaden tribute to his inspiration in three articles on cello performance and technique published in the newly established journal *Music and Letters* during 1920 and 1921:

> If the 17th century had Domenico Gabrieli followed by Domenico Galli, if the 18th century had Luigi Boccherini and later on Romberg, Dotzauer and Duport – the last perhaps the most famous of all – the end of the 19th and the beginning of the 20th century has in Pablo Casals the greatest of all . . . and it will be due to him that the cello will take rank, not only by the side of the violin, but as the first bow instrument there is.[39]

After the war Suggia became engaged to a wealthy English magazine publisher who reputedly presented her with a Stradivarius cello and an island off Scotland as engagement gifts. Breaking off the association, Suggia returned the island.[40] In 1923 she married a Portuguese radiologist, Dr José Carteado Mena, but continued to live principally in London until 1939. After 1917 she was a regular guest of the Speyers at Ridgehurst, and performed with Tovey at Northlands in the autumn of 1919. Her presence in London undoubtedly discouraged Casals from returning to England during and soon after the First World War. When he did return after 1920, Suggia regularly attended his concerts. One evening in 1926, at a concert in the Albert Hall conducted by Felix Weingartner, she found herself seated unusually conspicuously in the front row of the audience. During his performance of the Haydn C Major Concerto, Casals developed a cramp in one hand and had to stop, sit out the symphony, and begin the piece a second time. He claimed later that he had not noticed Suggia.[41] Casals and Suggia both appeared with the Hallé Orchestra during the same three seasons in the 1920s, but reportedly met only once, at St Pancras railway station, in 1923. They shared a compartment with the English composer Herbert Howells on the journey to Leicester, Casals travelling on to Manchester. They said little, but Suggia, who was engaged to play a concerto with Malcolm Sargent that evening, informed Howells that she would 'play like a goddess'.[42]

The break with Suggia also involved a break with that part of Casals' life that reminded him of her. It meant an end to several important friendships and a cooling in others. Of the guests at San Salvador in September 1912, none remained wholly unaffected, though Horszowski was too young to be closely embroiled in the fracas. In any case, he took some time to realize that anything permanent had occurred, continuing to address cards and messages of courteous greeting to 'Monsieur et Madame Casals', and only in July 1913 did he cease to refer to Suggia directly.[43]

Although they were not directly involved, continued regular contact with both Julius Röntgen and Emanuel Moór seemed more than Casals could bear, at least for the time being. Röntgen wrote kindly, but Casals did not seem able to accept sympathy: knowing that Röntgen remained in touch with Tovey, he dared not risk fresh contact 'unless I were to feel on your part more comprehension of what has happened or, better, until time and new developments in my life have come to efface the memories that do not cease to torment'.[44] After a few brief further letters, their correspondence ceased for seventeen years, resuming only in 1931, less than a year before Röntgen's death.

The friendship between Casals and Moór had survived the hostility of the critics and the indifference of their fellow artists, but it could not survive the war, Moór himself, and the collapse of Casals' private world. Moór's Double Concerto, perhaps his most successful work, could never again be performed by the combination for which it was written. And his Suite in E Minor for Two Cellos, dedicated jointly to Casals and Suggia, was never performed at all. For a man whose enthusiasm for composition was a direct response to the stimulus of performance, it was a crushing blow. After 1912 Moór wrote only one further cello piece, a Ballade in E Major for Cello and Orchestra. After 1914 he wrote almost nothing at all. The war eliminated the possibility of performance in Germany and Austria, where he had previously found strong support, while France and Belgium were closed to all music. Moór and his wife withdrew in despair to Switzerland, where in April 1916 their spirits were further crushed by the death in action of their stepson and nephew,

Laurence Burke. A requiem in his memory was Moór's last significant composition.

Casals and Moór rarely met again, though Casals remained fiercely loyal to Moór's music, often performing his songs in public – with Susan Metcalfe – and his *Improvisations for Orchestra* during the first season of the Orquestra Pau Casals in November 1920. Years later he persuaded Bernard Greenhouse and the Beaux Arts Trio to perform Moór's Triple Concerto, against their better judgement and once only, in Milwaukee.[45] As Moór's obsessive focus shifted to the competing distractions of painting and invention, Casals sought to retrieve him for music. 'I think of you more than you realize,' he wrote in 1920, 'composez, composez!'[46] But it was too late: Moór was enmeshed in the development of his Duplex-Coupler Pianoforte. Tovey, predictably, became fascinated by the double-keyboard piano, buying a prototype of the instrument and demonstrating its possibilities by performing formidably difficult duets with himself.[47]

Emanuel Moór's second wife was English, and he spent the last years of his life in England. Röntgen, too, through the Trevelyan connection, was a regular visitor to that country, and maintained a close connection with both Tovey and Suggia. Partly for that reason, Casals stayed away. At the start of the war he had thought to settle in London, and in November 1914 shipped his furniture and bulky effects to a warehouse in Redcliffe Mews, adjoining the Drapers' home in Edith Grove.[48] But it could not happen. To the lives of those friends closest to him during the Paris years, Casals was effectively lost for a decade, and only the friendship with Tovey was recovered in any real sense. For Casals the price was high: he forfeited his closest musical relationships and the stimulus of a stream of fresh compositions. But Röntgen, Moór and Tovey were the real casualties: they lost their most effective and influential champion, and their careers either declined or perceptibly changed direction as a result. Each died without a recording to his name, and none was widely performed subsequently. Even Tovey's Cello Concerto, the fruit of his renewed friendship with Casals in the 1930s, was not issued in a commercial recording until fifty-two years after his death.[49] For Casals, none of this would have been a surprise. 'Only the mediocre are impatient,' he observed. 'The great know how to wait.'[50]

For Casals' biographers, 1913 is a missing year. After the late autumn of 1912 his concert log is blank and his regular correspondence is silenced. Early in spring 1913 he was in Paris, and to cheer him Cortot and Thibaud, on tour in the provinces, wrote lighthearted letters from small hotels in remote locations.[51] In July he closed the Villa Molitor, stored his papers and belongings in a local warehouse, and returned to San

Salvador for the summer. The autumn brought his last visit to what he described, in a note to Enrique Granados, as 'the sad land that is Russia'.[52] It turned out to be an exhausting tour, and the final concert, conducted by Rachmaninov, was in Moscow on 14 December. As if to mark his premature farewell to the country, Casals played three complete concertos, the Dvořák, the Saint-Saëns A Minor, and Davidov's Second Cello Concerto.[53] At the start of 1914 Casals was in London, giving what would be his last group of English recitals before the war; in mid-February he travelled to Bucharest for several performances both there and in Budapest. But his world seemed to have collapsed. He had given up his home, his friends and his routine. Everything was out of kilter, and he was wretchedly thrown by it. He sailed for New York in March, his first visit for ten years, in a state of private panic.

# 6

## An American Refuge, 1914–1918

Mr Casals does indeed feel with his head and think with his heart;
and is not the man who does that greater in deed than he who
takes a city?

Olin Downes, March 1915[1]

Barely ten days after reaching New York, Casals married the American
soprano, Susan Scott Metcalfe. The marriage was an immense shock for
his family and friends. It may indeed have been something of a surprise
for Casals and Metcalfe themselves. Clearly it had not been extensively
premeditated. The ceremony, on 4 April, took place in front of a large
open fireplace in the New Rochelle Courtroom of State Supreme Court
Justice Martin Keogh. It was the first marriage at which Keogh had
officiated, and the certificate was afterwards sent for approval to the
Spanish Consul of New York City. Only a handful of Metcalfe's relatives
witnessed the ceremony, and there was little attempt at a reception. The
married couple made a brief honeymoon visit to Washington and set off
almost immediately for Europe.

The marriage was reported in the New York papers on 5 April, but
most of Casals' friends and colleagues were informed through an elegant
engraved wedding announcement dispatched after the event. The
announcement bore the addresses of Villa Casals, San Salvador, Spain,
and 105 Neptune Avenue, New Rochelle, a New York suburb north
of Manhattan, and displayed parallel announcements by the mothers of
both bride and groom. The elegance of the typography and thickness of
the card were the only conventional elements of the occasion. For anyone
who had known Casals during the first thirty-seven years of his life,
the event was entirely out of character, and the conjunction wholly
improbable.

Susan Metcalfe was one of four children of an American father and an
Italian–Swiss mother. Frank J. Metcalfe, himself the son of a wealthy
New York physician, had established himself in medical practice in

Florence in the 1860s, married and raised his family in Italy. After Metcalfe's death the family had returned to New York where in 1897, and aged about eighteen, Susan made her debut as a mezzo-soprano.[2] She and Casals had shared the programme at the Mendelssohn Hall in New York in March 1904, and may possibly have met earlier, during Casals' first American visit. Though Susan Metcalfe was a serious musician, she was financially secure and had no need to perform more frequently than she wished. Until 1908 she gave two or three solo recitals each year in New York, and made occasional smaller appearances outside the city. She sang in Europe after 1905, and made her London debut at the Bechstein Hall in 1908. Casals could have encountered her when she appeared on the programme of one of Speyer's Classical Concert Society evenings in London, or indeed in Amsterdam, where she sang with the Concertgebouw Orchestra, but there is no clear trace. We do know they met in Berlin late in 1913 when Metcalfe came backstage after a performance by Casals.

Casals and Metcalfe remained married for forty-three years, though they lived separately after 1928. Despite fifteen years in which their lives, and to an extent their careers, were closely connected, Metcalfe is mentioned only once in Casals' memoirs, as told to Albert E. Kahn, and not at all in his volume of autobiographical 'conversations' with José Maria Corredor, published in 1954. Early biographers handled the marriage with discreet inattention, largely at Casals' request: Lillian Littlehales, though herself a friend of Metcalfe, mentioned her only in passing in the account of Casals' life she published in 1929 and reissued in 1948.[3] It was, once again, a relationship Casals did not care to remember. Despite the years in which 'Susie' was mentioned in his correspondence and appeared on his concert programmes, his own account says simply that 'we were, however, ill-suited to one another, and our relationship was short-lived. . . . Our life together was not a happy one.'[4]

There is nothing like reticence to provoke conjecture, especially in connection with a failed marriage, and the relationship between Casals and Susan Metcalfe has engendered its quota of speculation. The indisputable fact is that it was an ill-considered association. When Casals met Metcalfe in Berlin at the end of 1913, he was alone, depressed and bereft of the supports of his earlier years. They talked and reminisced, and she cheered him. He offered to help her prepare some Spanish songs for her repertoire, and by the end of that first evening – according to Juan Alavedra, Casals' Catalan friend, colleague and biographer – they had agreed to marry.[5] The few friends with whom Casals shared his plans tried to dissuade him. It would be, they knew, a *malaurança* – an unhappiness and a misfortune. Casals ignored them. In his mood of emotional desperation, he made a 7000-mile round-trip to New York to collect Metcalfe, marry her and return with her to his home. Neither could have given serious consideration to the consequences, and their haste led to great anguish which ruined her life and severely mauled his own.

On the surface each had something which might plausibly appeal to the other. Susan Metcalfe was a refined and cultured woman, born in Italy and familiar with Europe, but with a firm family base and wide-spread connections, both private and musical, in East Coast society. She was unmistakably attractive, petite, dark and birdlike, if a little cool and reserved in her manner. As a singer she was comfortable in Casals' professional world, and as an American had the advantage of absolutely no connection at all with the life he was seeking to put behind him. In 1914 Susan Metcalfe was thirty-five, two years younger than Casals, and she was unmarried. If New York society had not provided her with a husband, marriage to a European virtuoso of world rank called for no apology.

At first all went well. Casals and his new wife arrived in Europe at the end of April 1914, and travelled at once to Italy where Casals was booked for a recital tour. Their plan was to set up home in London and transfer Casals' furnishings and possessions from Paris. By late May they were in England, and Casals was in a very positive mood. 'A new life begins indeed for me,' he wrote to Röntgen. 'This happiness that has invaded me has helped every trace of past sufferings to disappear and has given me the calm to repair so many of the important things of my life.'[6] But the cheerfulness was short-lived. The war was beginning, and options were closing. As the German army threatened first Belgium and then France, opportunities for musical performance were gradually extinguished across Europe, and the appropriateness of a permanent winter home in London appeared doubtful. After two months in San Salvador during September and October – Susan Metcalfe's first introduction to Casals' home and family – the Casals sailed again for New York in mid-November. Aboard the RMS *Adriatic*, Casals wrote to Röntgen that they planned to spend the winter in America – the scheduled January tour of Russia was of course impossible – and return, if feasible, the following March: 'We are so dispirited that we can neither think nor do anything. . . . God grant that we shall be able to see you soon and that all these horrors will end.'[7]

Spain had adopted a neutral status at the outbreak of war and Casals was, in theory, in an easier position than many of his friends and colleagues who lived in Germany, France and England. But there was no music to be played, and Casals could see no point in remaining in Europe while the lives of those who meant most to him were wrecked and distorted. In any case he now had an American wife, and it seemed logical to remain at her home until, as many imagined would happen, the war was resolved and life could resume in a number of months. Indeed, North America became a refuge for many of Europe's leading performers: in a sense the musical life of pre-war Paris was systematically packed up and relocated in New York. Fritz Kreisler arrived late in 1914 after having been conscripted into the Austrian army and wounded on the Russian front. Thibaud was employed for a time as a military driver in France, but found his way before long to the United States, together with Harold Bauer, Leopold Stokowski, Jan Paderewski and, rather later, Eugène Ysaÿe. For some, trapped behind German lines, like Adolf Busch and Bruno Walter, there was no possibility of escape.

There is no question but that Casals was powerfully disturbed by the war, and immensely depressed as it stretched out from months to years without end. In Paris when war was declared, he had been appalled at the demonstrations of indiscriminate nationalist fervour: 'Bands playing martial music, flags flying from every window, bombastic speeches about glory and patriotism! What a macabre masquerade!'[8] And what he felt compelled to do, in the face of such turmoil and human misery, was perform with enhanced intensity and purpose:

> During the War, when some were so blinded by hatred they sought to ban German music, I felt it all the more necessary to play the works of Bach, Beethoven and Mozart . . . perhaps at such a time, when evil and ugliness are rampant, it is more important than ever to cherish what is noble in man.[9]

But it is also fair to observe that, if war had to happen, its timing, for Casals, was fortuitous. He had broken decisively with his past and, by marrying Susan Metcalfe, had made striking claims on a new country, new activities, new friends and a new life. The First World War coincided with a caesura in his life; it did not create it. For over half of each of the following five years, America provided Casals with both a musical and a personal refuge.

On his return to New York in December 1914, Casals threw himself into a heavy performing schedule. His new managing agents, the Metropolitan Musical Bureau, had set up about fifty concert engagements for the three-month period to March 1915. It was almost ten years since Casals had last been heard in the United States, and he needed to reinstate his name and his reputation. He did so swiftly and with aplomb. At a Sunday-night concert on 13 December, he opened his season with dramatic performances of a Saint-Saëns concerto and Bruch's *Kol Nidrei* at the Metropolitan Opera House, playing with the Opera orchestra and the Dutch conductor, Richard Hageman. In February he returned to Boston, where he had last played in 1901, giving first a recital with Harold Bauer and then a performance of the Lalo Concerto with the Boston Symphony Orchestra under Dr Karl Muck. Neither the soloist nor the Concerto itself was well known to the otherwise self-confident and knowledgeable Boston audience, and a full line-up of the city's music critics, which included some of the most distinguished in America, was present to hear the performance. The Concerto was a huge success, Casals being called back again and again to the platform. Henry T. Parker of the *Transcript* compared the concert with the best Boston appearances of Paderewski and Kreisler, while Louis C. Elson of the *Globe* referred to 'a beautiful tone, a technique beyond anything that we have heard, and an absolute purity of intonation'. The startlingly bright twenty-nine-year-old music critic of the Boston *Post*, Olin Downes, described the constituents of the performance as 'annihilation, oblivion of technical difficulties, and the superb balance of head and hand and heart that only the great of the great artists achieve'.[10]

Between the Boston concerts and his departure for Europe on 29 May, Casals played a demanding sequence of performances within and outside New York – evening, morning and matinée engagements, in large venues and small. Of greater long-term significance, even if it did not appear so at the time, was his agreement during this season to make recordings for the Columbia Graphophone Company. In 1915 the United States led the world in gramophone technology, and competition between the three large recording companies was fierce, and litigious. The rivalry was plainly a function of the large potential rewards: that year Columbia made a profit of $2 million on turnover of $14 million, while the Victor Talking Machine Company showed an enormous surplus of $14 million on assets of $21 million, $7 million of which represented cash in the bank. Both those companies were dealing in lateral discs, while Thomas A. Edison Inc., still faithful to the cylinders it had pioneered in the 1890s, had a turnover of only $9 million.[11]

The dominance of the Victor Company was very largely the result of the extraordinary success of its Red Seal series of celebrity recordings. The early enterprise of the Gaisberg brothers, Fred and Will, had secured exclusive contracts with a whole swathe of leading European operatic performers and transformed them into artists of mass appeal before they even set foot in the United States.[12] The most conspicuous example was Enrico Caruso, recorded by Fred Gaisberg in Milan in 1901 and, in consequence, heard and hired by the New York Metropolitan Opera the following season. Caruso's long-term commitment to Victor was worth millions to the company in succeeding years, and provoked an almost desperate struggle among its competitors to sign other leading artistic performers. Casals was persuaded into Columbia's New York recording studio on 15 January 1915, and for the rest of his life – and indeed after it – was linked, in North America, to the Columbia label, its subsidiaries and its successors.[13]

Recording by the early acoustic process was by no means easy, nor fast. It involved performing in front of a large extended horn, before which endless adjustments of position were required to regulate balance and volume. On his first day in the studio Casals recorded Elgar's *Salut d'Amour*, the Largo 'Ombra mai fù' from Handel's *Xerxes*, an arrangement for cello of Anton Rubinstein's Melody in F Major (Op. 3, No. 1) and the second movement (Adagio) from Tartini's Cello Concerto in D Minor. For each piece he was given the accompaniment of a small orchestra, a clear indication of the value Columbia placed on its new solo artist. For while contemporary phonograph recording techniques worked well with a single voice or instrument, ensemble or orchestral recordings were highly problematic technically. As the number of instruments was increased, the proportional volume of each was decreased, and surface noise became more pronounced.[14]

An orchestra was again provided when Casals returned to the studio, three days later, to record Bruch's *Kol Nidrei*, but very rarely thereafter. Until the early 1920s, a piano accompaniment produced a clearly superior result. On 24 and 27 January the pianist Charles A. Baker joined Casals for recordings of Popper's Spanish Dance No. 2, 'The Swan' from Saint-Saëns' *Carnival of the Animals*, and a romance by Campagnoli.[15] In March, April and early May Casals recorded further pieces, including the Prelude, Bourrée and Sarabande from Bach's Suite No. 3 in C Major. Over eight days he recorded seventeen pieces in all, of which only one, the *Variations Symphoniques*, was rejected as unsuitable for release.

Casals' 1915 recordings were first issued – on nine separate discs – between April that year and April 1916. Thirty-eight years later they were reissued on long-playing record, as a premium offer to accompany recordings of the 1953 Prades Festival. These early recordings are marked by a brisk self-confidence: Casals was already thirty-eight and a veteran of concerts around the world. The repertoire was relatively superficial: the popular demand was for short romantic pieces, performed with heavy sentiment. In April 1916 Casals spent four more days in Columbia's New York studio, recording fourteen more items, including Bach's arrangements of *Air on the G String*, Schumann's *Abendlied* and Goltermann's Cantilena from the Cello Concerto in A Minor (Op. 14), all performed with indulgent *portamenti* and *glissandi*. Between 1915 and 1924 he recorded over fifty different shorter works for Columbia, during more than thirty days in the studio. This was Casals performing his Café Tost selection, and it was not until 1926 that Fred Gaisberg, by then working for HMV, convinced him to record substantial items from the cello repertoire. Casals was content to record when asked, but was never ambitious for a recording career. He saw recording as a marginal activity – a good deal less important than live performance – and he was fifty before he made, with Cortot and Thibaud, his first serious full-length recordings. The irony, however, is that Casals' global reputation (and indeed his income) owed more in the long term to his studio recordings, and the vast market they served, than they did to his platform performances.

Casals had had, so far, a fairly easy war. In New York, the conflict in Europe appeared a distant tragedy. At San Salvador it seemed closer, but not yet an immediate threat. Early in 1916, however, the war became a sudden and violent reality in Casals' life. After spending the summer and autumn of 1915 in Spain, he and Susan were back in America by mid-December. Casals resumed his concert appearances, cheered by the presence in New York of his friends Enrique and Amparo Granados. In 1914 Granados had been commissioned by the Paris Opéra to adapt a set of his piano compositions, inspired by the painter Goya, into an opera. After the start of the war, the Metropolitan Opera took over the project, and *Goyescas* was set to open in New York on 28 January 1916. Granados spoke little English, and was innocent of American theatrical practice; Casals steered him through the rehearsals, the press interviews and the general razzmatazz that accompanied the premiere of New York's first grand opera to be sung in Spanish. The occasion was a highly fashionable success, and Granados was invited to play for President Woodrow Wilson at the White House on 9 March. Two days later he and his wife sailed for England en route for Spain. On 24 March, crossing the English Channel from Folkestone to Dieppe, their vessel, the *Sussex*, was torpedoed by a German submarine. At the age of forty-eight, Granados had been on the verge of an international breakthrough. His death had removed, in Casals' words, 'the purest musical expression of the Spanish soul'.[16]

Casals was godfather to one of the six Granados orphans, and organized a memorial concert in their benefit which raised the very substantial sum of $11,000.[17] The evening, at the Metropolitan Opera House on 7 May, turned into a legendary occasion. The centrepiece of the concert was a performance of Beethoven's 'Archduke' Trio by Paderewski, Kreisler and Casals – the last time Casals and Paderewski were to meet. Each also played solo works and accompanied the singers John McCormack, María Barrientos and Julia Culp. The concert closed with the funeral march from Chopin's B Flat Minor Sonata. The lights in the opera house were extinguished: a single candle flickered on the piano as Paderewski played.[18]

After the shock of Granados' death, and the news, that July, of the death of Emanuel Moór's nephew, Casals delayed until August his departure for his now customary summer visit to Europe. When he did sail, via London, on board the *Touraine*, Susan Metcalfe Casals was not with him. On the thin pretext of needing to prepare for her coming season of recitals, she remained at the Metcalfes' summer home at Stockbridge, in the Berkshires, Massachusetts, for the rest of the season, and spent the fall in New York. Casals was away for five months, returning only in January 1917. Until then they had rarely been apart. It was a clear sign that something was going wrong with their relationship.

Susan Metcalfe was by no means an artist of the first rank, though her singing was fastidious and her concerts impeccably presented. For the first two years of their marriage, Casals had given her firm professional support, appearing in joint recitals and providing cello obbligato, or accompanying her on the piano during private musical evenings at the homes of New York friends. He broadened her repertoire to include, among other items, about a dozen songs of Moór, and doubtless provided useful hints on interpretation and delivery. It seemed to work. Earlier in her career, Metcalfe's reviewers had praised her 'slender' voice, but deplored the techniques she employed to expand it. The *New York Telegraph* had observed in 1907 that 'her voice, while sledge-hammered and ultra-decisive, is a remarkably good one, while her method is a remarkably bad one. She sacrifices everything to a good single note.'[19] Almost ten years later, at a concert in the Aeolian Hall on 8 January 1916, Casals conducted his wife in a programme of Handel and Mozart arias, accompanied by the New York Symphony Orchestra. It was a booking Metcalfe could not have achieved on her own. This time the *New York Times* reported that 'Mrs Casals sings with riper and more finished art', and praised her improved intonation and surer overall control.[20]

The priority within the family was of course Casals' own career, though it became increasingly clear that Susan did not fully comprehend quite what that involved, or meant. What she provided initially was a social base in New York and valuable musical connections. The couple's movements – from their New York apartment on East 96th Street, to Stockbridge, San Salvador or the Casals' Barcelona base, 440 Diagonal – were tracked in the *New York Social Register*, listed under the entry for Susan's mother. It was through Susan that Casals made a connection with the American philanthropist and musical patron, Mrs Elizabeth

Sprague Coolidge, whose financial support and artistic encouragement were very real factors in his American tours of the early 1920s, and who remained both friend and benefactor until her death in 1953.[21]

But what Susan quite clearly did not relish were the long summers spent in Spain: there was a whole world of difference between New York's upper East Side, the fashionable Berkshires, and a seaside village some miles outside Barcelona. Though the Metcalfes were an unusually cosmopolitan family, and Susan a fluent Italian speaker, it did not especially ease the transition to rural Catalonia. She found the climate at San Salvador difficult and, speaking no Catalan, had no chance of direct communication with her powerful mother-in-law and the rest of Casals' family. Tovey had written of his visit in 1912 that:

> this place and house are most simple and straight and touching . . . These dear people . . . don't know very much French. Madame mère Casals is a very quiet little old lady with Pablo's nose projecting from the blue goggles that conceal the rest of her; Luis, the brother . . . is a very nice boy, and makes himself extremely useful in all manner of practical ways: but most of the conversation goes on in Catalan.[22]

Two summers later, Susan Metcalfe's introduction as the new wife of the revered son of Catalonia was something of a cultural trauma. Though she returned the following year and, with the exception of 1916, was in Spain for a substantial part of each year until 1929, she was never comfortable in Casals' home and, in consequence, never popular with his family and his Catalan friends. Enrique Casals summarized the problem generously but accurately in his memoirs of his brother: 'Susan, like Casals,' he wrote, 'rated her family and her country above everything. While Casals wanted to be in Catalonia with his mother and brothers, so she wanted to be with hers.'[23] The schism between his wife and his family should not have been difficult to foresee, but Casals did not foresee it. For him it became a source of mental torment and physical illness which was alleviated only by their separation more than a decade later. During the years in between, such evidence as survives suggests real tenderness and a shared respect between Casals and Metcalfe, wrecked by the contrast in their backgrounds and the incompatibility of their expectations.

Returning to New York in January 1917, Casals threw himself into a demanding programme of concerts and recitals: 'in the midst of the war's madness, it was perhaps mainly through music that I maintained my sanity'.[24] But, as in Europe ten years before, he seemed almost to volunteer for an excessively punishing schedule of engagements at great distances, leading to relentless travel and night after night spent in hotels. And, just as before, the experience drove him close to physical and mental exhaustion. It was, again, a sign of unhappiness, this time of frustration at a war which continued to separate him from his family and from the career he had made in Europe, and to which there seemed no end. It was four years since he had last performed with Cortot and Thibaud, and more than three since he had toured anywhere in Europe other than Spain. And after spending, since 1914, the larger part of each year in North America, that was no longer an adventure.

Late that summer Casals travelled again to San Salvador, performing in Switzerland and giving two concerts in Madrid before returning to New York in December.[25] Early in 1918 he toured with his old friend Harold Bauer and, later that spring, as soloist with the New York Philharmonic. When the United States formally entered the war in 1918, Casals readily performed in benefit concerts to aid the Red Cross and other humanitarian charities and, with Bauer, Kreisler and John McCormack, founded the Beethoven Association in New York in calculated opposition to growing calls for the boycott of German music. Late in spring 1918, Casals and Susan returned once more to Europe to spend the summer at San Salvador, and when they returned to New York – docking on Armistice Day, 11 November 1918 – the war was over.

PART 3

*The Hero*

# 7

## Barcelona, 1919–1931

> If I have been so happy scratching a violoncello, how shall I feel
> when I can possess the greatest of all instruments – the orchestra?
> *Pablo Casals*[1]

The war had given Casals an opportunity to escape the past. When it
was over he found he did not want to resume the life he had lost. For
twenty years he had travelled and performed to exhaustion: in the previous five years alone he had crossed the Atlantic eleven times, in addition
to his regular tours within America. At forty-two he needed more
stability, and a permanent home. Paris held too many memories: 'it
belonged, I knew, to a past that could not be recovered'.[2] London, too,
had uncomfortable connotations. Casals decided to return to Spain, and
to set up home in Barcelona.

But first he had to fulfil his remaining American engagements. At the
beginning of January 1919 he and Susan Metcalfe travelled to Mexico, a
country which was to become important to him much later in his life.
Both were scheduled to perform during a visit lasting four weeks. The
first of fourteen concerts took place on 10 January, in Mexico City,
where the City Symphony Orchestra was directed by José Rocabruna,
second violinist with the Crickboom Quartet when Casals had joined it
twenty-five years earlier. Mexico was in a state of acute political
upheaval, but Casals was in confident and inquisitive mood, and insisted
on a dangerous trip into the forest of the Sierra Leone until stopped and
turned back by Zapata's guerrillas. Casals' tour happened to coincide
with a visit to the city by Anna Pavlova. During her performance of
'The Dying Swan' at the Teatro Arbeu in February, Casals crept backstage and, by prior arrangement with the first cellist, took over the solo
part of Saint-Saëns' famous accompaniment – to the startled delight of
both Pavlova and the company's manager, Diaghilev.[3] Returning to
New York, Casals gave his final concerts of the season, including a
performance with Rachmaninov of the composer's own Cello Sonata at
the Bohemian Club on 14 April, before sailing for Europe.[4]

The Barcelona Casals returned to in 1919 was very different from the one he had lived in twenty years before. It was larger, richer, more populous, and politically far more volatile. Above all, it offered a very different artistic and cultural environment. What Catalonia had discovered, in the last years of the nineteenth century, was *modernisme*, the cultural expression of a new, national, Catalan renaissance. At first it was preponderantly a literary and artistic manifestation. But the crisis in the central Spanish state which followed defeat at the hands of the United States in 1898, and the humiliating loss of its empire at a time when the rest of Europe was busy acquiring one, made it possible for Barcelona's commercial middle class to adopt *modernisme* without appearing ridiculous. *Modernisme*, as explained by Manuel Vázquez Montalbán, 'not only embraced architecture, sculpture and painting but defined a specific perspective of life and history which was fundamentally bourgeois and quintessentially Catalan'.[5] So effectively did Barcelona's prosperous middle class embrace modernist design in particular that, within a period of some twenty years, the architectural face of the city had been conspicuously altered.

Clearly *modernisme* had not happened suddenly while Casals was not looking; indeed some of its early exponents, like the painters Ramón Casas and Santiago Rusinyol, had been his friends, and he had sat for them. But it did have its greatest physical manifestation in the years between about 1900 and 1912, precisely the period during which Casals had been most frenetically engaged upon his musical tours around the world. The Barcelona he returned to displayed striking new evidence of the work of the three greatest architects of Catalan *modernisme*, such as Lluís Domènech i Montaner's Hospital de Sant Pau, Josep Puig i Cadafalch's Casa Amatller and the staggering masterpieces of Antoni Gaudí, the Palau Güell, the Casa Milà and – most intestinal of all – the looming but still unfinished Cathedral of the Sagrada Família. The most obvious characteristic of these remarkable modernist constructions was their solid, heavy and rational structure, upon which an excess of neo–Gothic ornamentation, with strong Arab influence, seemed to have been deposited. Visually it was a witty parody of medievalism, but emotionally it was an acknowledgement of Catalonia's historical roots, and a clear display of cultural separatism.[6] Catalan modernist architecture was powerfully distinct from that of Granada or Seville, and was meant to be so.

By 1919 the style of *modernisme* had peaked. Gaudí, for example, no longer saw himself as part of that tradition. But its quality of energy and élan remained, as did its nationalist message, and Casals could not avoid it. Indeed he was surrounded by it. Only yards from his home, in Barcelona's principal street, the Diagonal, was Puig i Cadafalch's Casa Terrades, 'the House of Points', a profusely ornamented high gothic structure, on a gable of which the architect had inscribed the legend: 'Holy patron of Catalunya, give us back our freedom'.[7] But by far the most important architectural influence on Casals was to be the Palau de la Música Catalana (the Palace of Catalan Music). This Wagnerian auditorium, along with Gaudí's Casa Milà the ultimate celebration of Catalan *modernisme*, was built by Domènech for the Orfeó Català, and completed in 1908. The Orfeó was a choral society, established in 1891 by two musicians in their early twenties, Lluís Millet and Amadeu Vives, to continue the work of the great figure of the Catalan musical revival of the 1860s, Josep Anselmo Clavé. The aim of Millet and Vives was to use traditional song and folk music as a way to introduce working people to classical music. The Orfeó had an explicitly socialist agenda and a hatred of elitism and condescension. Like most 'improving' socialist programmes, however, it managed to be, in parts, both elitist and condescending. Domènech's Palau, commissioned by the Orfeó, was its most heroic and intimidating manifestation. And this was the auditorium in which Casals was to spend a large part of the next seventeen years.

The Palau de la Música Catalana was constructed as a monument to Clavé and to his ambitions for Catalan culture. Robert Hughes has described it as 'encrusted with allegory, inside and out: a text on which the cultural values of Catalanism are written and rewritten'.[8] It encapsulates the core features of the high gothic revival – height, colour, extravagant and didactic ornamentation and, above all, cascades of light. Using huge expanses of stained glass, Domènech created 'essentially a glass box permeated by daylight'. Within this brilliant space, and beneath the Palau's spectacular proscenium, Casals conducted the greatest performances of his forties and fifties and experienced the part of his career which he later described as 'the most fruitful of my life'.[9] The symbolism is dense but accurate: Casals had been away for two decades, but he returned to inherit, perhaps indeed to head, the full panoply of Catalan cultural nationalism, just at the moment *modernisme* was beginning to decline. By the late 1920s there was talk of demolishing the Palau, and locals had renamed it the Palau de la Quincalleria Catalana (the Palace of Catalan Junk). But Casals loved the place. (Eventually, in 1971, and with justice, it was declared a national monument.) Even if the terminology was foreign to him, Casals remained, throughout his life, loyal to the core values of turn-of-the-century *modernisme* – and did not stray far beyond it. His interpretation of Bach or of Beethoven, for example, was based upon an almost puritan mastery of formal structure, embellished by a sense of ornamentation that came straight from this cultural heritage. 'Freedom with order . . . fantasy with order' was how, very often, he would describe his objectives, in life as in music. It encapsulated the Catalan view of the world.

Like many great cellists, Casals came at times to feel the limitations of his instrument: 'the cello,' he somewhat surprisingly confessed in his memoirs, 'had never given me full satisfaction'.[10] The reason, in part, was simply the restricted repertoire for the solo cello, and in part the sheer repetitious physical effort of solo performance. Re-established in Barcelona after an international career of twenty years, Casals began to search for an additional musical outlet. Within a year he had founded his own orchestra. His plan initially had been to give his support to the two existing Barcelona orchestras – the government-subsidized Municipal Band and the orchestra of the opera house, the Gran Teatre del Liceu – to create at least one full-time, professional symphony orchestra worthy of the Catalan capital. To his innocent surprise he found the city's musical establishment defensive and hostile, with Lluís Millet of the Orfeó Català especially resistant: there was not enough talent, the argument went, nor popular demand for good music, and a new initiative would damage those institutions that already existed.

Stung by the rebuff, Casals set out to create the Orquestra Pau Casals. He contacted the musicians' union, established what players earned within the existing orchestras, and undertook to double it. With the help of Domènec Forns, a professor at the Barcelona Conservatory, he identified the best string, brass and woodwind players in the city, and hired them for two six-week seasons a year.[11] Since sixty-six of the musicians chosen came from the orchestra of the Liceu, Casals scheduled his programmes around the theatre's spring and autumn opera seasons. The remaining twenty-two players emerged after open auditions held at the musical academy Enrique Casals had opened in the Rambla de Cataluna. Most members of the new orchestra were professional players; a few had no orchestral experience. All were recruited on the basis of Casals' assessment of their musical potential. And almost every one was a Catalan. Enrique himself would be leader of the orchestra, with Enrique Ainaud, a friend of Casals' teenage years, as assistant concert-master. Another friend, Bonaventura Dini, was asked to lead the cellos, with his seventeen-year-old nephew within the ranks of the second violins. The only major difficulty was filling places within the brass section, and two of the orchestra's four horn players had to be imported from Paris, at least for the first few seasons. But by the end of 1919 the selection was complete and Casals left for his first post-war American tour, intending to begin rehearsals of his new orchestra when he returned the following spring.

The most immediate problem, however, was money. Casals had expected that his own prestige, together with general enthusiasm for a project of Catalan distinction, would generate substantial financial backing. This did not happen. Apart from his own family, and some close friends, support was limited. The local aristocracy and the wealthiest sections of the Barcelona business community were discouraged by a critical press and the antagonism of the rival musical institutions. In a sense Casals had indeed over-estimated the cultural appetite of the city: this was not, after all, Paris, London or Vienna. The demand needed to be created, it could not be assumed. But Casals named the orchestra decisively after the Catalan form of his name – the Orquestra *Pau* Casals – and established a board of directors to supervise its administration. His friend Joaquim Pena i Costa became the orchestra's secretary, with Felip Capdevila i Donato its treasurer; Capdevila's wife Franchisca, herself a cello teacher, became the organizational backbone of the enterprise. To raise funds, the board began a drive to recruit 'subscribing members', in particular a group of 'protector' supporters – the *patronat* – willing to pay a double fee to help underwrite the orchestra's costs. Casals was a wealthy man and had expected to put some money into his orchestra. But he had not planned to subsidize it completely. As the orchestra became successful, a small annual grant was received from the city government. But in the first eight years of the Orquestra Pau Casals' existence, Casals himself made up the deficit at the end of each season. It amounted to about 500,000 pesetas a year, in total a sum equivalent to almost half a million US dollars.

Casals remained in America throughout the spring of 1920, concluding an arduous tour of forty-one concerts with eight days of recording – between 21 April and 5 May – in Columbia's New York studio.[12] Back in Barcelona he launched immediately into the orchestra's first six-week season of rehearsals and concerts. But on the eve of the first rehearsal at the beginning of June, Casals collapsed from exhaustion and nervous tension. Frustration and disappointment at the city's response to his plans to create an orchestra, together with months of stress involved in its organization, were manifested in an attack of iritis (technically *anterior uveitis*), or inflammation of the irises of both eyes. The treatment of the time, involving repeated injections of milk, almost certainly rendered the inflammation chronic: it undoubtedly led to the pounding headaches from which Casals suffered for many years afterwards. After the attack it was four months before he could resume conducting. In the meantime the players themselves continued to attend, expensively but honourably, at rehearsal times – 2.30 in the afternoon and 9.45 in the evening – for individual practice, musical discussion or, at most, preliminary rehearsals led by Enrique. It was only at the beginning of October, after the summer holidays, that Casals felt strong enough to conduct again. At the first full rehearsal he launched the orchestra into a brisk run-through of Wagner's familiar 'Ride of the Valkyries', from *Die Walküre* – to show them how well they knew the work – followed immediately by a painstaking, bar-by-bar dissection of the work – to show them that they did not.

The orchestra's opening concert took place at Domènech's Palau de la Música Catalana on 13 October. The large but not capacity audience – Casals maintained his opponents had sought to engineer a boycott[13] – heard one of Bach's Orchestral Suites in D, Beethoven's Seventh Symphony, Ravel's 'Mother Goose' Suite and Liszt's tone-poem *Ideals*, all taken from musical scores which Casals had purchased from Hans Richter's widow after the great conductor's death.[14] At the four subsequent concerts of the season the orchestra performed works by Beethoven, Mozart, Mendelssohn, Schubert and Strauss, as well as Emanuel Moór's Improvisations for Orchestra, and two *sardanas* by Juli Garreta, the self-taught Catalan composer whose compositions, along with those of Granados, Albéniz and de Falla, Casals took immense pride in performing.[15] One of the early concerts was presented in conjunction with the Associació de Musica 'Da Camera' de Barcelona, a chamber music organization for which Casals had performed in the past. The Orfeó Gracienc, a choir based in the neighbouring suburb of de Gracia, soon agreed to perform with the orchestra, but the Orfeó Català remained apart. It was a long haul to acceptance by the city Casals imagined he was seeking to honour.

The one advantage of bearing the full burden of responsibility for the orchestra was that Casals could run it as he chose. He could perform the works he enjoyed, promote the composers he favoured, and hire the soloists he appreciated. And he could rehearse his players as thoroughly and as frequently as he wished. Casals demanded high standards in music and discipline. Rehearsals began precisely on time and every member attended: there was no substitution, even for the leading players. And even those not involved in a particular work – such as, quite frequently, the harpist or double bassoonist – would attend all rehearsals, sitting, if necessary, in the front row of the auditorium. For as the musicians of the Orquestra Pau Casals discovered, like those of the orchestras at Prades, Puerto Rico and Marlboro after them, rehearsals, for Casals, were not simply a preparation for public performance. They constituted an opportunity for a collective exploration of great works of music, for the understanding of their 'inner meaning', and the search for the most satisfying means of displaying it. 'We share a great privilege,' Casals told his players, 'the privilege of bringing masterpieces to life. We also share a sacred responsibility . . . the duty of interpreting these masterpieces with utter integrity.'[16]

Before 1920, Casals had seized opportunities to conduct orchestras in several countries, but he was by no means an experienced conductor. It was less common then than now for soloists to make the transition to the podium, and in the age of the legendary conducting maestros of the late nineteenth and early twentieth centuries, it was seen as something of a presumption. For Casals presumption did not come into it. What interested him was the performance of music, and an orchestra, like a cello, was an instrument through which it could be performed. There was no narcissism in Casals' wish to conduct, but there was a confidence that he knew how to do it. For all his statements of enthusiasm for the 'co-operative' nature of orchestral playing, he was no campaigner for a policy of collective musical interpretation. Casals exerted complete artistic control, and his players soon learned it was unwise to press an alternative line. While he was not a conductor who resorted to histrionics, it was always fairly clear, as one of his musicians put it, 'when a thunderstorm is brewing'.[17]

Throughout his life, Casals was more comfortable as a conductor – and conspicuously more successful – when he knew the orchestral musicians individually, lived with them, cared about them, and grew to understand their musical personalities. He was notably less effective in performances with orchestras he had met only two days earlier and had rehearsed with for a brief three hours. And the critics noticed it. In Barcelona, the reviews were almost always very strong. Abroad there was less unanimity. At Casals' formal conducting debut in New York, at Carnegie Hall on 7 April 1922, the *New York Times* critic was won over by a performance which included Beethoven's 'Pastoral' Symphony and Brahms' First Symphony, reporting that 'he led eagerly, with persuasive force, clear upward beat and colorful variety'.[18] Three years later he conducted his first concert in London, playing Brahms' 'Tragic' Overture and Schubert's 'Unfinished' Symphony with the London Symphony Orchestra at the Queen's Hall. The *Times* reviewer decided that 'he is a great conductor because he is a great artist:

> under him the orchestra carves out every phrase as if with the bow on the strings . . . that intense absorption in the task which makes him shut his eyes and turn his head away when he plays the violoncello but crouch and peer earnestly through his spectacles when he conducts, secured his authority.[19]

In the *Sunday Times*, however, the critic, Ernest Newman, felt Casals' technique was as much a hindrance as a help to the players: 'in his anxiety to get them to phrase as he desires he makes them exaggerate the accents and break the back of the rhythm . . . he cannot make an orchestra play with the ease and the flexibility that are the charm of his cello playing'.[20] A year later Casals was back in London. This time Newman responded more enthusiastically to the new conductor, though reporting that '[Casals] is not exactly a model of deportment when he conducts, and to watch him is to have one's auditory impressions somewhat influenced for the worse by his ungainly movements'.[21]

If Casals eventually won over the critics, he did not always succeed with the players. Musicians in his own orchestra learned, after a period of heavy rehearsal, to interpret his unconventional and sometimes unpredictable conducting style. For players in orchestras unfamiliar with him, however, it was more tricky. Bernard Shore was principal violist of the BBC Symphony Orchestra when, during the 1930s, Casals was guest conductor at several notable concerts. He wrote that 'the orchestra often finds it impossible to grasp what he is striving for, and at times wish to heaven he could play it on the cello . . . [it] needs something more than that he himself should be living in the music'.[22] Some players were less sympathetic. Asked about the programme of a forthcoming concert, one Viennese player replied: 'I'm sure I don't know what Casals is going to conduct. *We* are going to play the "Pastoral" Symphony.'[23]

In May 1923 Casals and his orchestra came under the interested scrutiny of the young British conductor, Adrian Boult. Invited to Barcelona to conduct two English works at the orchestra's performance on 26 May – Holst's *Perfect Fool Ballet* and Butterworth's *Folk Song Idyll* – Boult spent three weeks attending Casals' rehearsals and absorbing his technique, and wrote up his experience for *Music and Letters*.[24] What struck him most forcibly was the sheer quantity of rehearsals. For two of the three concerts he attended, there were nine sessions of two and a half hours each. For the third there were eleven, ten hours of which were devoted to a single work, Schubert's C Major Symphony. In theory, Boult reckoned, this should be a route to 'performances of the most uncommon perfection and dullness'. In practice the rehearsals became fascinating lessons, for, as he observed, 'Casals the teacher is no less eminent than Casals the player.'

Boult noticed that Casals would rehearse works in cycles. A full run-through of each new piece would be followed by a painstakingly detailed bar-by-bar dissection of it. Once the process had been completed on one work, Casals would move to the rest of the programme. After a break, the entire cycle would be repeated. Where there was the slightest problem or lack of precision, Casals would stop and rehearse two or three bars with one instrument alone. 'It is interesting to note,' Boult recorded, 'that the Spanish temperament makes it possible for the rest of the orchestra to sit in perfect silence without even a surreptitious puff at a cigarette during an interval of this kind.' Matters of bowing, fingering, intonation, rhythm and tone were discussed and related to the particular work under consideration. Nothing was dependent upon any arbitrary rule: every detail emerged out of the work as a whole:

> Everything was explained, every member of the orchestra was made to feel the passage himself in its inevitable relation to the expression of the moment and the style of the whole work. In this respect Casals was the exact opposite of Nikisch, who exaggerated everything at rehearsal . . . in order that the quicker pace and greater tension of performance should allow these details to drop into their proportionate places.

For Boult it was clear: Casals was a good conductor because he was a good teacher, and a good teacher because he had a mathematical fastidiousness about each individual note – and its relationship to the whole. Membership of an orchestra conducted by Casals amounted to a saturation course in musicianship.

The Orquestra Pau Casals presented, each year, two series of ten concerts, one in the spring and one in the autumn. In the sixteen years of its existence it gave close on 370 performances. Few orchestras can have had so steady and so continuous an association with a single conductor; fewer still can have known none other – apart from guest conductors – than its first. But the sound of this remarkable musical construction is now almost completely lost. Of all its performances, only two, or perhaps three, were recorded and issued on disc. Barcelona was a long way from the centre of the early phonograph industry, and it was only after Fred Gaisberg had recorded Cortot, Thibaud and Casals performing piano trios in London in 1926–8 that it seemed feasible or desirable for HMV (which merged with Columbia to form EMI in 1931) to transport its equipment to Spain. In 1932 the orchestra was recorded in performances of Beethoven's First and Fourth Symphonies, and the overture to the incidental music for *The Ruin of Athens*, the discs being issued in Europe but not in the United States. But the great surviving recording of Casals and his orchestra was made three years earlier, on 10 and 11 June 1929, when Alfred Cortot conducted Casals and Thibaud in Brahms' Double Concerto in A Minor for Violin, Cello and Orchestra (Op. 102).[25] The orchestra's sound in this performance is disappointingly emaciated and reedy, almost certainly the result of primitive techniques of microphone displacement in early ensemble recording. It suffers, too, in conjunction with the ravishing tone of Thibaud's solo violin and Casals' cello. This is the earliest recording we have of Casals in a full-length performance with orchestra. He was already fifty-two years old.

The programmes of the Orquestra Pau Casals very much reflected its conductor's own preferences. But Casals' personal taste was much broader than is often imagined. During the last years of his life Casals was the victim of musical journalists who liked to bait him on the 'touchy' subject of twentieth-century music. Casals enjoyed this verbal sparring and would often adopt a deliberately provocative and extremist position.[26] But he was far from a musical reactionary, locked in the romanticism of his youth. He was not even against experimentation with atonality, when used with great skill to create an impression.[27] What he could not share was any enthusiasm for atonality as an exclusive system; and he was, of course, not alone in that. For Casals, 'music which is not expressive has no reason to exist', and he chose not to perform it. In terms of musical style, he selected what he cared to play from the work of each composer: he did not select – or exclude – a composer in totality. He performed and admired the early work of Schönberg and Stravinsky, but not their later work. It was for him a question of sense and nonsense:

> At moments I can see that these musicians do great things even in their nonsense. But I have not been able to overcome the suspicion that these men and their followers are what they are because they are afraid to be considered old-fashioned.[28]

But the work of innovatory twentieth-century European composers was as well represented within Casals' Barcelona programmes as in the repertoire of any other major contemporary symphony orchestra. The great classical and romantic works formed the backbone of every performance, but the name of one or other working artist of the day was invariably present in the programme. Apart from the best-known Catalan composers, like Garreta, Granados, Albéniz, Millet, Cassadó, Enric Morera and Roberto Gerhard, Casals introduced and regularly conducted works by Béla Bartók, Richard Strauss, Gustav Mahler, Darius Milhaud, Zoltán Kodály, Prokofiev, Webern, Honegger, as well as Schönberg and Stravinsky. Alban Berg did not feature, but then neither, very often, did the composers of Casals' youth, Ravel, Debussy, or indeed Fauré. For Casals distrusted them as men of principle: he never forgave Fauré or Ravel for their earlier casual disregard for the music of Brahms. And, most conspicuously, he never overcame what he saw as his betrayal by Debussy during a celebrated row in Paris just before the First World War. At a benefit concert for the Colonne Orchestra, Casals was due to play the Dvořák Concerto under the conductor Gabriel Pierné. Pierné, a follower of the new French music, uttered carelessly disparaging remarks about the quality of the Concerto, just before the performance, and Casals refused to play under him. Debussy witnessed the incident, but declined to endorse Casals' protest. The performance was abandoned and Casals was sued for breach of contract, eventually paying heavy damages. Music – Casals insisted once again – was a question of moral principle, 'not something to be turned on or off like tap water'.[29] It was a tough, and probably impractical, line in a compromising world, but he stuck to it. And Debussy was never reprieved.

If Casals was proprietorial about what his orchestra played, he was not unduly jealous of his right to direct it: in its seventeen years of existence, almost sixty guest conductors were invited to do so. The choice was an interesting spread of individuals, and included instrumentalists – like Cortot, Arbós, Fritz Busch, Tovey and Ysaÿe – as well as professional conductors such as Monteux, Weingartner, Koussevitsky, Ansermet and Klemperer. Casals particularly enjoyed asking composers to conduct their own work, and Schönberg, Stravinsky, de Falla, Richard Strauss and Vincent d'Indy were among those who did so. Most of the guest conductors were personal friends, or musicians whom, in one way or another, Casals rated highly. None was unknown to him. And none was selected simply on the basis of popular appeal.

The air of private indulgence extended also to Casals' choice of visiting soloists, of whom there were perhaps seven or eight each year.[30] In conjunction with the orchestra's organizing committee, he tended to select Spanish artists, partly of course for reasons of cost. Visitors from abroad were almost always old friends, the violinists Ysaÿe, Kreisler and Thibaud, for example, or the pianists Cortot, Horszowski and Wanda Landowska. Foreign performers wrote to suggest themselves, but were rarely taken up.[31] The cellists that came – bravely – to perform concertos with Casals were invariably pupils or to some extent disciples: Diran Alexanian, Cassadó, Maurice Eisenberg, Pierre Fournier or Gregor Piatigorsky. All performed within the troublesome acoustics of Casals' favourite Palau de la Música Catalana, its glass walls amplifying the street noise outside 'like drum skins'. Josep Pla, Barcelona's great chronicler of the early twentieth century, described its effect on an otherwise 'spellbinding' concert by Casals and Kreisler:

> The first sonata was interrupted again and again: first by the bell
> of a nearby church; then by a slow wagon going down the street
> . . . a wagon so close that it seemed to be moving through the hall;
> then from the next floor one heard the off-key song of a maid-

servant doing the dishes . . . and finally one heard a cock repeatedly crowing. . . . The last part of the concert was shattered by the movement, honking, klaxon-blowing, braking and gear-changing of innumerable cars, showy but very primitive and noisy contraptions, creeping round the Palau and getting ready to take their owners away.[32]

The Orquestra Pau Casals was a highly personal construction. It was not that Casals was vain, but he had a strong sense of his musical prerogative and, since he had the resources, saw no point in repressing it. The orchestra's concerts were by no means a vehicle for the celebration of his gifts, but rather of his good fortune. He performed his own pieces very rarely, in fact only twice. In May 1929 he conducted the first performance of his Sardana for a Double Octet of Cellos – arranged then for thirty-three players – a work which used the national dance of Catalonia to demonstrate the range and versatility of sound that the cello could produce. And in 1935 a group of his songs were sung by the Catalan soprano Concepció Badia. Nor did Casals perform often as a solo cellist, and not at all before 1927. Here it was not primarily a question of modesty, but of commerce. What the Barcelona public most wanted to hear was Casals playing the cello. Until his orchestra was self-supporting he did not give them the opportunity.

Perhaps the most heroically indulgent occasion in the orchestra's life came in 1927, when Eugène Ysaÿe appeared in two concerts to mark the centenary of Beethoven's death. Ysaÿe was in a poor physical state, weakened by rheumatism and diabetes. His last solo concert had been a disaster, and he had withdrawn from all performance other than conducting. Visiting Brussels the previous year, Casals had persuaded him to come out of retirement to perform the Beethoven Violin Concerto in Barcelona. Ysaÿe had not played the Concerto for fourteen years: he agreed, 'as long as a miracle happens'. Weeks later his son Antoine reported Ysaÿe's agonizing attempts to practise and to recover his skill.[33] No one knew if he could succeed: Casals began to fear that all he had engineered was a painful humiliation. On 19 April Ysaÿe conducted Beethoven's 'Eroica' Symphony and the Triple Concerto, with Cortot, Thibaud and Casals as soloists. Four days later he returned to the Palau to attempt the Violin Concerto. Casals was almost as nervous as the trembling Ysaÿe, but coerced from him a performance which included real moments of his former brilliance. The audience erupted in frenzy and, in the dressing-room afterwards, Ysaÿe knelt, took Casals' hand and, in tears, repeated 'Resurrection! Resurrection!'[34]

The gradual but certain success of his orchestra enabled Casals to make plans for the realization of another personal ambition – a regular series of inexpensive concerts for workers. Throughout his life Casals displayed a genuine and uncomplicated sympathy for the experience of being poor. Neither his father nor mother had been, by any definition, working-class, but they had known poverty. Casals' musical talent rapidly brought him wealth and social prestige; from an early age he had access to every level of society, from monarch to labourer, and became, as Alfred Cortot put it, 'a curious mixture of grand seigneur and peasant'.[35] Although Casals enjoyed his money and was unembarrassed by what it made possible, he gave much of it away, but always to endeavours which he himself either invented or was able to control.

Casals knew that his concerts were beyond the reach of working people: the least expensive seat cost almost half what a factory-worker earned in a week. He believed, too, that their bleak lives deserved the comfort of good music. Conditions for the poor in Barcelona were certainly grim. Since February 1919 a sequence of strikes and demonstrations, and the excessive brutality with which workers had been confronted by factory-owners and police, had led to the virtual collapse of civil order in the city, with frequent street assassinations conducted by free-roaming gangs of *pistoleros* of varying allegiance.[36] The relative peace brought by the dictatorship of Primo de Rivera, who seized control of Spain from a divided Cortes and a weak monarchy in September 1923, was soon vitiated by punitive restrictions on Catalonia as a whole.

Casals' example was the visionary Josep Anselmo Clavé, whose mid-nineteenth-century choral societies had inspired a renaissance in the performance of traditional Catalan song. He approached the Ateneu Politecnicum, a workers' night-school and cultural society, with the idea of an annual series of orchestral concerts exclusively for the low-paid and unemployed. A trial concert at the Teatro Olimpico, attended by an enthusiastic audience of 2000 workers and trade unionists, overcame suspicions that the scheme represented either patronizing charity or clever promotion for the orchestra. The Associació Obrera de Concerts (Workingmen's Concert Association), with membership by subscription, was founded in 1926, and held its first concert in May. On six Sundays each year for a decade, Casals took his audience through the full classical and romantic repertoire, with soloists and conductors borrowed from the orchestra's main season, as well as such surprises as an all-Schönberg concert conducted by the composer. The Association grew from an initial 2500 to a staggering 300,000 members, with branches throughout Catalonia, its own amateur orchestra, and a mass-circulation journal, *Fruicions*. It was, Casals claimed, the musical innovation that gave him more pride than any other.

If, during the 1920s, Casals limited his solo appearances within Spain, he stepped them up everywhere else. And he needed to do so in order to meet the costs of his burgeoning domestic establishment. Casals now maintained two sizeable homes – in Barcelona and San Salvador – as well as his orchestra: as many as a hundred musicians and other staff depended on him, if not for their full income, at least for the greater part of it. His popularity in England was now at its height, and he toured there each season between 1921 and 1930, playing principally with the Hallé Orchestra in Manchester, and the London Philharmonic, the London Symphony and the Royal Philharmonic in the capital. He played mainly under Weingartner, Bruno Walter, Sir Thomas Beecham and Malcolm Sargent, but in 1927 encountered a new conductor, John Barbirolli, standing in for Beecham at a London Symphony Orchestra performance in December. Barbirolli, himself a cellist, had first met Casals at a Royal Academy young people's concert in 1911. Now, aged twenty-eight, he found the prospect of conducting the world's greatest cellist, at short notice, in a performance of the Haydn Concerto in D Major highly daunting. During rehearsal the orchestra grew fractious until Casals calmed it – and the young conductor – by telling the players: 'Gentlemen, listen to him. He *knows!*'[37] At the concert the Concerto was performed 'with enthusiasm and cordial noise', *The Times* observing that 'Mr Casals attempted to conduct it by proxy'.[38] The same year a more successful concert had Casals and Kreisler performing the Brahms Double Concerto, Kreisler being so overwhelmed by the beauty of Casals' opening solo that he completely missed his own cue.

Post-war England continued to pay Casals well. He declined individual concerts where the fee was beneath £100, and complete tours if there were too few concerts to rationalize the expenses. According to his London agents, Ibbs and Tillett, Casals in the 1920s was paid what the pianist Solomon received in the 1950s.[39] But his major opportunity for sustained earning, both from concerts and from recordings, was in North America, and his tours there each winter were prolonged, demanding and remunerative. In 1922, for example, Casals opened with a concert in New York on 2 January and closed with one in Peoria, Illinois, on 11 April. In between he had thirty-six bookings ranging from Montreal to New Orleans, earning $1000 for each performance in New York, and $800 outside it.[40] Four years later his New York agent, the Metropolitan Musical Bureau, announced his 1926 tour in a broad-sheet headed 'The World's Greatest Cellist – no cellist plays like him; no one draws like him!' While this was a modest tour in terms of length – for much of which Casals was accompanied by Harold Bauer – it was an ambitious one in terms of hype. Casals' recital on 17 January 1926 at the New York Town Hall on 43rd Street was a sell-out, the audience of 1800 being the highest ever for a music concert in the hall. The takings were $2792, of which, after advertising and commission, Casals received $1826. A detailed itinerary of the tour has survived:[41]

| Dec. 31 | 10.00 am: | rehearsal Boston Symphony |
|---|---|---|
| Jan. 1 | 2.20 pm: | matinée concert |
| 2 | 8.15 pm: | evening concert [total fee: $1000] |
| 6 | 10.00 am: | rehearsal, New York Symphony, Carnegie Hall |
| | 8.15 pm: | Scranton, Pa., Town Hall recital with Edouard Gendron (piano) [$800] |
| 7 | 2.30 pm: | matinée, Carnegie Hall, with NY Symphony |
| 8 | 8.15 pm: | evening performance, Carnegie Hall [$1000] |
| 11 | 8.15 pm: | recital with Harold Bauer, Memorial Hall, Joplin, Mo. [$800] |
| 13 | 8.15 pm: | recital with Paul Kochanski, Women's Club Auditorium, Louisville, Kentucky [$800] |
| 15 | 8.15 pm: | recital with Harold Bauer, New Lyceum Theater, Minneapolis, Minnesota [$700] |
| 17 | 3.00 pm: | recital, New York Town Hall |
| 18 | 11.00 am: | New York Waldorf Astoria (Bagby Musicale) [$800] |
| 21 | 4.30 pm: | Washington, DC, National Theater [$800] |
| 22 | 8.30 pm: | Philadelphia, Witherspoon Hall [$800] |
| 24 | 3.30 pm: | Boston, Symphony Hall [50 per cent of gross] |
| 25 | 7.30 pm: | Athens, Ohio, Men's Gymnasium [$700] |
| 31 | 3.00 pm: | recital with Harold Bauer, Indianapolis, Marat Theater [$800] |
| Feb. 4 | 10.00 am: | rehearsal, Detroit Symphony |
| | 8.30 pm: | evening performance, Detroit Orchestral Hall |
| 5 | 8.30 pm: | second Detroit performance [$1000 total] |
| 7 | 3.30 pm: | recital with Harold Bauer, Studebaker Theater, Chicago [$1300 joint] |

|   |   |   |
|---|---|---|
| 8 | 8.15 pm: | recital with Harold Bauer, City Auditorium, Lincoln, Nebraska [$800] |
| 11 | 8.15 pm: | Winnipeg, Canada: Women's Musical Club [$800] |
| 18 | 10.00 am: | rehearsal, Chicago Symphony |
| 19 | 2.15 pm: | matinée, Orchestra Hall, Chicago |
| 20 | 8.15 pm: | evening performance, Orchestra Hall, Chicago [$1000] |
| 22 | 8.15 pm: | New York Town Hall |
| 25 | 8.30 pm: | recital with Jacques Thibaud, His Majesty's Theater, Montreal, Canada [$900 joint] |

After the Canadian recital, Casals sailed immediately for Europe to begin an eight-concert tour of Austria which, between 12 and 27 March, earned him $9200.[42] In two and a half months he had earned just under $30,000, half the amount required to subsidize his orchestra for the year.

The length and duration of Casals' visits to America had a good deal to do with the state of his relationship with Susan Metcalfe. There is little trace of Casals' wife in his own archive: she is mentioned only very occasionally in letters and documents that survive, and never appears in the family photographs of summers spent at San Salvador. But we know from her own correspondence in other collections, and from programmes of her concert appearances, that she and Casals were together for much of each year until the spring of 1928. Metcalfe was remembered by some of the players as attending all the concerts of the Orquestra Pau Casals, and most of the rehearsals: 'she was a lovely lady, *une grande dame*, a worthy wife of a prince of musicians'.[43] And guests at the Casals' home at 440 Diagonal frequently heard husband and wife performing together contentedly during private evenings.

Casals himself continued to promote his wife's singing career, as he had done in New York during the war. Returning to Barcelona in the late spring of 1919, one of his first appearances was as her accompanist. At a recital on 22 June under the auspices of the Associació de Musica 'Da Camera', held at the Palau, Metcalfe received the star billing, her name decisively above his. She also appeared three times as soloist with the Orquestra Pau Casals, singing arias from Handel's *Acis and Galatea* in October 1923, the soprano part in Mahler's Fourth Symphony in November 1924, and six Beethoven songs during the centenary celebration in April 1927. Concert impresarios occasionally approached Susan Metcalfe as a route to Casals himself: in October 1920, for example, the Dutch Concertdirectie Scheveningen offered the couple 8000 florins to give a series of six concerts together in Holland.[44] Sometimes the joint approach worked: during Casals' visit to London in December 1926, to conduct the London Symphony Orchestra, a Wigmore Hall booking was arranged for Metcalfe. On this occasion it was she who obtained the better reviews, the *Daily Telegraph* critic referring to her *lieder* recital as 'one of the most completely satisfying of the season'.[45]

Few outside an intimate circle knew that the marriage was falling apart. Susan Metcalfe never became reconciled to life in Spain: Enrique Casals noted that the only time she was happy in Barcelona or San Salvador was when her nephew, Louis Metcalfe Kobbé, came on a visit.[46] Towards the end of 1920, after the Casals' first full year in Spain, and at the close of the orchestra's opening season, Metcalfe left to return to New York – alone. The shock of her departure plunged Casals into heavy depression and triggered the return of the illness which had dogged him all year. He felt unable to work or play the cello and, at the last minute, cancelled his planned three-month winter tour to North America, forfeiting income of $50,000 from the forty-three concert schedule.[47] 'My wife left me in the midst of my illness,' he wrote to Harold Bauer, 'on the pretext of not being able to live with my family. What preceded and followed her departure would truly fill a hundred pages, and I cannot think about it without becoming ill.'[48] Bauer and Jacques Thibaud had both been due to join Casals on the tour, and their own schedules were thrown by the sudden change.

Susan Metcalfe returned to Spain the following spring, and the crisis was temporarily resolved. But she began to press for longer periods in the United States, and the idea was raised – but turned down by Casals – that he might return there permanently, or accept a regular six-monthly conducting contract with an American orchestra. In particular Metcalfe used her connection with Elizabeth Sprague Coolidge to try to bind Casals more permanently to American musical life. Elizabeth Sprague Coolidge was one of America's most generous and discerning musical benefactors: Alexander Schneider has described her as doing more for the arts 'than anyone since Jefferson'.[49] Widowed at a young age, she dedicated her life, and half her immense annual income – inherited from her father, the founder of the world's largest wholesale grocery business – to the advancement of chamber music around the world, but particularly in the United States. She founded the Berkshire Festivals – in Pittsfield, Massachusetts – in 1918, inspired and commissioned new work by contemporary composers and, through the Elizabeth Sprague Coolidge Foundation at the Library of Congress in Washington, DC, established a basis for the funding and encouragement of chamber music in perpetuity.

The purpose of Mrs Coolidge's philanthropic intervention was to facilitate 'the composition and performance of music in ways which might otherwise be considered too unique or too expensive to be ordinarily undertaken . . . [not] with a view to extravagance for its own sake . . . but as an occasional possibility of giving precedence to considerations of quality over those of quantity'.[50] This struck a chord, of course, in many musicians. During the early 1920s both Casals and Susan Metcalfe were in regular contact with Mrs Coolidge, and soon she was sponsoring chamber recitals in venues as prestigious as Carnegie Hall, to amounts of up to $5000 a concert.[51]

As well as being very rich and very generous, Mrs Coolidge was also very demanding: 'a sort of Cosima', Tovey termed her. She tried, probably with Metcalfe's encouragement, to engineer Casals' attendance at the Pittsfield Festival, and, failing that, sought to attach him to the musical entourage which accompanied her around the world. Mrs Coolidge, as Alfredo Casella has described, lived for long periods in luxurious hotels where she liked to be surrounded by creative musicians and performing artists:

> The arrival at the hotel of that tall, spectacled lady, followed by a retinue of twenty or thirty persons, most of them armed with musical instruments, was impossibly funny. . . . Her guests were supposed to hold themselves at her disposal all day long and even late at night if she so desired.[52]

It was never likely that Casals would submit to this degree of control, though he and Metcalfe did perform privately for Coolidge and her guests, first in Chicago, and later, in early January 1927, in the Chinese Room of the Mayflower Hotel in Washington. On that occasion Casals played the Bach C Major Suite, Mrs Coolidge writing afterwards to Metcalfe that 'it was the first thing I heard him play, and I have never heard anyone else do it without twinges at the inevitable comparison.'[53]

By the early spring of 1928 the marriage between Casals and Susan Metcalfe appeared finally to be reaching its end, after fourteen years of conflicting expectations and intermittent estrangement. Casals gave the last recital of that season's American tour to a sparse matinée audience at Town Hall, New York, on 26 February, playing – with his accompanist Nicolai Mednikoff – a group of shorter pieces of the kind they had, over the previous two years, been gradually recording for the Victor Company.[54] Two days later they returned to the Victor studio in Camden, New Jersey, for a final session, recording a mazurka of Popper and Casals' own arrangement of Granados' Spanish Dance in E Minor. The next day, 29 February, Casals left to return to Europe. Writing to his brother the week before, he had still not known if he would be travelling 'alone, or with Susie'. But he had taken the precaution of making a will, nominating Enrique as his executor, and lodging the document with his New York bank.[55]

Casals did not set foot in the United States for the next thirty years: in fact the 26 February concert in New York Town Hall had been his last ever public solo recital in America. After fourteen years of regular annual visits, it seemed a sudden and uncharacteristic change. In a sense there was no longer a need for Casals to make deliberate fund-raising tours to North America; the Orquestra Pau Casals was now virtually self-financing, and tours within Europe were sufficiently remunerative to cover his domestic expenses. Nor, indeed, after the 1929 stock-market crash, was the United States an especially ready source of cash. Approaching his mid-fifties, Casals had in any case been performing continuously for three decades. He no longer relished the heavy demands of lengthy, far-flung tours, and decided to cut them out.

While all these explanations are plausible, and doubtless partly accurate, it is a good bet that Casals' abandoning of America had something to do with the collapse of his marriage to Susan Metcalfe. Renewed tours of America in the 1930s would certainly have been feasible, but, as Fred Gaisberg observed, Casals refused them 'for purely domestic reasons'.[56] It may have been that, by avoiding America, Casals was discreetly evading legal constraints instigated by Metcalfe's family. Or he may simply not have wanted to run the risk of encountering her. For although the ending of the marriage was as much to do with the practicalities of their lives and the conflicting demands of their careers as with a breakdown in their affection, it was not an easy severance. After an agreed separation in summer 1928, Casals and Metcalfe met twice more – in Paris and Amsterdam towards the end of 1929 – in an attempt to settle the details of their financial and domestic affairs. These were difficult encounters: Metcalfe refused the divorce Casals requested, and they never saw each other again. When Casals eventually returned to New York, he came with another wife.

The break with Susan Metcalfe proved painful, and both took time to recover. Casals became ill and depressed during the autumn of 1928, and cancelled all concert appearances for four months. 'At the moment rest, long walks and golf are my only preoccupations,' he told his agent.[57] By the following summer, however, his spirits were rising. In a note to Enrique, later that autumn, describing his last encounters with Metcalfe, he mentioned, for the first time with special affection, the name of Franchisca (informally Frasquita) Capdevila.[58] Metcalfe, too, was aware of the name. Later, living in Paris in the early 1930s, she made contact with Casals' friend and pupil, Maurice Eisenberg, to enquire about Casals, his family, and the state of his relationship with 'Madame Capdevila'.[59]

Susan Metcalfe's mother had died, and now, ironically, she no longer felt a need to remain in the United States. She established herself with homes in Paris and in Menton and disappeared from Casals' life for more than twenty years.

Emotional upheaval had a profound effect on Casals. On the one hand it left him incapable of composition; on the other it inspired the most brilliant performances of his career. For most of his life Casals composed regularly and productively. During the twenty-two years he spent with first Guilhermina Suggia and then Susan Metcalfe, however, he wrote only two works – a *cobla*, or dance, entitled *Festivola*, in 1909, and his Sardana in eight parts for Cello Orchestra in 1927. But the very factors that inhibited his creativity seemed to stimulate his gift for musical interpretation and expression. Casals made his greatest recordings at times of private crisis. This is true of the Bach Unaccompanied Suites, the Dvořák Concerto and the Beethoven Cello Sonatas, all recorded during the tumultuous years of the Spanish Civil War and the first few months of Casals' exile. And it is true of his recordings of piano trios with Alfred Cortot and Jacques Thibaud, classics of the early era of electrical recording and achieved between July 1926 and December 1928, as his marriage with Susan Metcalfe gradually but terminally unravelled.

The Trio which Casals had formed with Cortot and Thibaud is probably the most famous in musical history. It was certainly among the longest-lasting – with its opening concert in December 1906 and its last in May 1933 – and the first to achieve international celebrity. There have been other great trios, of course, such as the Busch (with Rudolf Serkin, 1920–50), the Hungarian (1930–50), and the Beaux Arts (with Casals' pupil, Bernard Greenhouse as cellist), which may have travelled more widely and recorded more copiously. And Casals himself played in many other notable combinations, with Horszowski/Alexander Schneider, Végh/Serkin, and Eugene Istomin/Yehudi Menuhin for example, or – most legendary of all – with Paderewski/Kreisler. But no other trio needed to establish the credibility of the ensemble in the same way, and none has lodged itself so firmly in musical memory.

The Cortot–Thibaud–Casals Trio has, however, been surprisingly little studied. There are few serious accounts longer than the sleeve-notes of an average recording, and the players' own memoirs treat it as a vehicle for amusing anecdote rather than musical analysis.[60] For the players themselves it was very much a part-time enterprise; they rehearsed during gaps in their individual solo itineraries and performed when a hall was conveniently available or an impresario willing to pay their minimum rate – usually 4500 francs a concert in the years before

1914. The Trio, known privately as 'Pa-bu-lo', had no formal name: its members did not imagine that it needed one, or that it would survive. They ceased to play, in any case, when one or other was abroad for an extended period, or when personal differences arose amongst them. The Trio was most active in the years between 1906 and 1913, with regular tours in France, Germany, Italy, Belgium, The Netherlands, Switzerland and Spain: 1908 was its record year, with twenty-six concerts. It did not perform at all during the First World War, nor indeed after it – owing to a *refroidissement* in relations between Cortot and Casals – until 1922.[61] In the years that followed, even with Casals based in Barcelona, the Trio managed an annual spring season, adding Britain to its regular touring itinerary in 1925.

An element in the survival of the Trio, described by Ysaÿe as 'God in three persons', was the respect each player had for the others. They were the same age and had achieved a more or less comparable level of public recognition: within France, indeed, Cortot's was the biggest name. Unlike the trio ensembles of Casals' later years, which tended to be led from the bass line, Cortot, Thibaud and Casals somehow fused their temperaments to produce music of great drive and unanimity. In the great recordings engineered by Fred Gaisberg between 1926 and 1928, there is a powerful sense of cohesion and discipline within which the players could display their individual personalities without threatening the overall balance of the music.[62] Casals' *cantabile*, so flawless that it could appear sentimental in solo performances, sounds pure and firm in the Andante of the Schubert B Flat Major Trio. Even Cortot's celebrated technical unreliability and wrong notes – in Beethoven's 'Archduke' Trio, for example – seem not to matter in the context of the intensity and vitality of the collective sound.

The greatest accomplishment of Cortot, Thibaud and Casals was to present as wholly fresh and spontaneous works they had rehearsed strenuously and performed repeatedly. A detailed analysis of ninety-two of their concerts – they gave a total of 158 during the life of the Trio – reveals their repertoire to have been astonishingly small.[63] Out of 150 trios they might have played – Haydn alone wrote forty-five – they performed only thirty-three at all, and of those about thirteen regularly. They played only one Haydn Trio, the G Major (the so-called 'Gypsy Rondo'), and one of Mozart (E Major, K 542), those composers giving the cellist very little of interest to do: performing the Haydn, Casals would in any case double Thibaud's line in the Adagio. A solid core of five trios, precisely those recorded by Gaisberg, were repeated again and again during their twenty-seven years of performance. These were the Haydn, the Schubert in B Flat (Op. 99), Mendelssohn in D Minor

(Op. 49), Schumann in D Minor (Op. 63) and Beethoven in B Flat Major – the 'Archduke' (Op. 97). Of these the Schubert Trio, performed at as many as forty-nine out of ninety-two concerts, became virtually their signature-piece.

The limited repertoire was only partly to do with a lack of rehearsal time: the players knew far more chamber music than they performed. It has to do with the fact that Cortot, Thibaud and Casals played essentially for their own enjoyment and not in order to impress an audience. Time and again they returned to the works they most loved, to explore what more they could find and how differently they could present them. For the artists, each performance, if based on a solid rock of shared understanding, was new. It is almost incidental that its impact on the audience was equally powerful. The performances of the Cortot–Thibaud–Casals Trio have become musical legend: the artists survive in living memory probably as much, or more, for their work as a trio as for their solo careers. Victor Gollancz recalled the Trio's London performances in the late 1920s as the musical highlights of his youth.[64] Many others felt the same.

Cortot, Thibaud and Casals had very different personalities. Contrasts, and sometimes conflicts, between them may have been invigorating during their twenties, but became irksome as they grew older. Gradually they ceased to play together. The Trio gave no concerts in 1929, only two in 1930, eight in 1931, four in 1932 and three in 1933. And then it ended. Casals, perhaps more so than the others, ran out of steam. Busy with his orchestra, his tours and his domestic responsibilities, he outgrew them. 'Mr Gaisberg knows perfectly well that I am not interested in playing in London Trio concerts', he wrote in response to pressure to make further recordings in August 1933, 'and I am surprised at his insistence.'[65] But it was the same Casals who felt most bitterly betrayed when, during the early years of his exile from Franco, Cortot and Thibaud reconstituted the Trio with the cellist Pierre Fournier, and performed in Europe for several seasons. After thirty years of intimate music-making, it felt as though a family had been levered apart.

The war revealed quite how remarkable it was that the Trio had survived so long. As Casals retreated in horror from fascism everywhere, Cortot entered into open collaboration with it. Between 1940 and 1943 he occupied minor, but official, positions within the education and cultural ministry of the Pétain–Laval Government and, invited by Furtwängler, made concert tours to Berlin and five other German cities in June and November 1942. Casals was devastated, and later years were marked by the depressing spectacle of Cortot begging forgiveness at Casals' feet.[66] Cortot's biographer makes an earnest case for the political naïveté of the pianist, the innocuous nature of his official activities, and the strength of his later recantation.[67] But while Cortot succumbed, Casals did not, in immensely more provocative circumstances: it gave him a lifelong moral advantage which he used delicately but also, at times, strategically. Jacques Thibaud, who had himself played publicly in occupied France, but also lost a son in action against Nazi Germany, later repudiated the whole moral nightmare, stating in an interview at the start of an American tour in 1946, that 'I have not been very lucky with my fellows. They have become politicians. Cortot bad. Casals a little mad.'[68]

Thibaud died in an air disaster in September 1953, on his way to entertain French troops in Indo-China, without having made his peace with either of his colleagues. Casals and Cortot had a hugely emotional reconciliation in July 1958, when Cortot made a pilgrimage to Prades. Peace had been signalled over the previous two years when both men had celebrated their eightieth birthdays. In a card to Cortot, Casals wrote that 'we were as brothers, united by the same devotion to music'. Referring to Thibaud as 'le regretté . . . notre cher disparu', Casals saluted the memory of the Trio, 'dans cette phase crépusculaire de nos existences'.[69] At Casals' invitation Cortot joined him for a performance at the Prades Festival, playing Beethoven's Sonata in A Major and the Variations on 'Ein Mädchen øder Weibchen'. Cortot was deeply overwrought and found it difficult to play. After the first movement of the Sonata, Casals put down his cello and crossed to him for a further bout of emotional hugging, reassuring Cortot afterwards that his timing was far surer than that of the 'younger pianists': 'It is as if you had stolen a metronome adjusted by Beethoven himself.'[70]

Apart from the Trio, the greatest joint accomplishment of Cortot and Casals was the Ecole Normale de Musique in Paris. The Ecole was essentially Cortot's creation, prompted by Auguste Mangeot, the proprietor of the influential journal, *Le Monde Musical*, and both Casals and Thibaud were brought in as artistic directors. Mangeot's idea, in 1919, at the end of the war, was to establish a school based on French rather than German musical principles, and one which would train not only composers and virtuosi, as the Paris Conservatoire did, but fully rounded professional musicians. Casals invested $20,000 in the enterprise, and it was set up in a small hotel at 64 rue Jouffroy. The school had sixty part-time professors, including Landowska, Marguerite Long, Marcel Dupré, Stravinsky, Honegger and André Hekking, and a small number of permanent instructors. Diran Alexanian was recruited as resident cello teacher, succeeded in 1929 by Maurice Eisenberg, though Casals returned each summer to give a masterclass in interpretation.

Alexanian, a dour Armenian, was a formidable perfectionist who, though younger than Casals, often assumed a kind of *de facto* seniority. Saul Bellow's *To Jerusalem and Back* quotes Alexander Schneider's recollection that Alexanian was 'just as particular about music as other people are about seasonings. Alexanian said to Pablo Casals after a performance of some of the [Bach] Suites, "You made three bad mistakes. Terrible." Casals did not answer. He knew Alexanian was right.'[71] Casals himself, equally terrifying to his pupils, had rather more sophisticated pedagogic skills. Opening his first Paris masterclass, in 1921, he reassured the student cellists that 'c'est très difficile de faire une note; et trois notes, alors!'[72]

For seventeen years, between his return from America in 1919 and his exile in 1937, Casals spent more time in Catalonia than outside it. It was the only period, in a life of ninety-six years, that he was able to live permanently in his own home. Each summer, and as often as possible during the rest of the year, he returned to San Salvador where, fourteen years older than his brother Luis, and sixteen older than Enrique, he naturally assumed the role of *pater familias* to the growing brood of nephews and nieces.[73] Each morning he would play Bach, usually from *The Well-Tempered Clavier*, on his father's piano, and ride along the beach on his jet-black Andalusian Arab, Florian. There would be walks, perhaps with his elder nieces, Pilar and Enriquetta, and certainly with his dog, a German shepherd called Follet, and rounds of tennis. And throughout the day Casals would practise, read scores and work on his programmes for the next season of concerts.

Casals was now a celebrated Catalan figure and the recipient of awards and honours from his own and neighbouring towns and villages. Catalonia has a great tradition of paying conspicuous homage to its national heroes, and a good deal of it was paid to Casals. In 1927 he was designated *fill predilecte* – a favourite son – of El Vendrell, and a plaque was erected to commemorate his birthplace in the carrer Santa Anna. Casals conducted the Orquestra Pau Casals in the town square, performed on the cello, and gave a formal address as troupes of costumed acrobats skilfully built and rebuilt the traditional *castells* – the human pyramids characteristic of the region. Later a square in the town was renamed Plaça Pau Casals, and the organ his father had played in the Church of Santa Anna was restored with funds provided by Casals himself.

Casals' estate had developed into a substantial holding. Luis managed the property and supervised the farm, which had excellent vineyards providing grapes for the local wine-producers, as well as livestock – cows, ducks, geese and fowl. The villa itself was further remodelled and extended between 1920 and 1929, with a formal Italianate garden laid out to the west, and an impressive terraced walkway on two levels separating the grounds from the sea. Electricity had come to San Salvador in 1923. In 1934 and 1935 the tennis court was removed and a substantial new wing constructed on the eastern side of the main house, looking on to an inner courtyard. It comprised three large interconnected rooms, one a recital hall capable of seating two hundred, another a gallery to display Casals' growing collection of the work of Catalan artists. The decoration of the third room was purchased intact from the Barcelona residence of the Marqués de Moya in Puertaferrisa Street and installed at San Salvador complete with wall and ceiling panels (painted by Vigotà) presenting pastoral and allegorical scenes, ornate crystal chandeliers and a tiled floor. Throughout the house were busts, portraits, drawings and commemorative medals depicting Casals himself, some retained because they were good, others because they could not be thrown away.

Most extraordinary of all was a statue of Apollo, commissioned from the Catalan sculptor and pupil of Rodin, José Clará. Clará was amazed at the anachronistic commission but, convinced by Casals as to the timeless status of Apollo as the god of harmony, music and medicine, the guardian of travellers, and a warrior for peace, created a prize-winning and perhaps prophetic work. His Apollo now stands with its back to the ocean, looking out over the pools and pathways, the pine, cypress and lemon trees, through the heavy metal gates and on to the busy tourist street beyond.

Situated on the beachfront of a modest holiday resort, Casals' villa had become something of an absurdity. It was too small for its pretensions, and its accretion of styles and periods had made it an architectural jumble. But it was the house Casals wanted and in which he was comfortable. Two years after its completion he was forced to leave it and, after 1939, saw his home only once more during his lifetime. It was as if, sensing that he himself could not be there, he had erected a solid and permanent manifestation of his character upon the earth he loved.

Recovering from the depression which followed the ending of his marriage to Susan Metcalfe, Casals embarked upon his heaviest touring programme since 1914. In December 1929 he travelled to Czechoslovakia and Romania for the first time in fifteen years, followed by tours in France, England, Switzerland and Spain. In November 1930 he was in Brussels to perform the Lalo Concerto with Eugène Ysaÿe in what would be Ysaÿe's final concert: he died the following May. The same month Casals had thirteen other major engagements in Europe, and in the first two weeks of December played in Copenhagen, Stockholm, Vienna,

Budapest, Prague and Florence.[74] The hectic schedule continued into 1931, with a dozen concerts in six countries booked for March. Casals was in Geneva on 13 March when word came of the death of his mother, aged seventy-seven, two days earlier in San Salvador. He continued with his tour, lost in a daze. One month later elections throughout Spain resulted in an overwhelming vote in favour of a republic. Alfonso XIII left the country, and the Second Spanish Republic was proclaimed on 15 April. Later that week, in the palace on Montjuïc, overlooking Barcelona, an audience of 7000 heard Casals lead his own orchestra, and the Orfeó Gracienc, in a performance of Beethoven's Ninth Symphony to celebrate the new order. Privately, and politically, the new decade would be strikingly different for Casals.

# 8

## Catalonia and the Spanish Republic, 1931–1939

> Do not commit the crime of letting the Spanish Republic be
> murdered. If you allow Hitler to win in Spain, you will be the
> next victims of his madness. The war will spread to all Europe,
> to the whole world. Come to the aid of our people.
>
> *Pablo Casals, 1938*[1]

Casals had been born two years after the defeat of the First Spanish Republic. He had been waiting all his life for the arrival of the second. From boyhood he had known that a republic was the most equitable and honourable
political option, the inevitable consequence of true democracy, the source
of justice and freedom for the largest number, the enemy of privilege and
the scourge of arrogance and corruption. But more than anything he knew
that republicanism would signal the end to Castilian domination, and
autonomy at last for the Catalan people. 'Yes, for me, the birth of the
Spanish republic represented a culmination of my dearest dreams.'[2]

Casals had not spent the 1920s in a political vacuum: it was simply
that there was not very much he could do. In September 1923 the
Captain-General of Barcelona, Primo de Rivera, had proclaimed himself
Dictator, ruling through a military directorate and with the connivance
of the King. Even a dictatorship seemed preferable to the corruption of
the former parliamentary regime, and in any case it was widely expected
to be a temporary disposition leading to the summoning of a constituent
Cortes. In fact Primo de Rivera survived for almost six and a half years,
in the early part of which, at least, he engineered some real successes,
such as the pacification of Morocco, and the introduction of surprisingly
progressive labour legislation. But de Rivera turned out to be too idle
and unimaginative to build upon his advantages, and gradually alienated
each of the groups – the Church, the army, the middle classes – whose
support, individually or collectively, was essential to keep him in power.
In any case, as Gerald Brenan observed, 'in a country where half the
population sits in cafés and criticises the Government no dictator can
prosper for long.'[3]

For Catalans, Primo de Rivera's dictatorship was distinguished by its almost complete destruction of their aspirations. The Mancomunidad, the modest forum of regional autonomy established in 1913, was dissolved, and the Catalan language forbidden in schools and public places. The flag could not be flown and even the national dance, the *sardana*, was made illegal. Not surprisingly, when national elections were finally held in spring 1931, the Catalan vote was overwhelmingly republican and, on its own, substantially responsible for bringing down both the dictatorship and the monarchy.

For one who was both Catalan separatist and ardent republican, Casals' connections with the royal family remained remarkably intimate. He himself never saw it as a point of difficulty and never allowed it to become an embarrassment. Somewhat innocently, he imagined that his relationship with the Bourbon monarchy had nothing at all to do with politics. Throughout his life Casals displayed an endearing trust in people who were his natural enemies; it had something to do with his unshakeable belief that nobody nice could be bad. In reality Casals' contact with the Spanish royal family grew more distant as his political views became better known. Since Alfonso XIII succeeded to the throne in 1902, Casals had seen relatively little of his childhood friend or of the Queen Mother, María Cristina. At the height of Primo de Rivera's anti-Catalan repression, however, he decided he would attempt to make his feelings known.

The immediate provocation was a particularly inept and ill-timed reference on the part of Alfonso, during a speech in Barcelona, to his early eighteenth-century predecessor, Philip V, a notorious enemy of Catalonia. Casals journeyed to Madrid to alert María Cristina to the strength of the Catalan reaction, but though friendly and welcoming, the Queen Mother deftly evaded the issue, and he returned to Barcelona crushed and miserable. Sometime later, however, the Catalan message was communicated in a different and rather more effective manner. While on a visit to Barcelona for the International Exhibition of 1929, the royal family – in its entirety – indicated a wish to attend a concert of the Orquestra Pau Casals. According to prearranged protocol, the King and his party arrived at the Liceu in mid-programme, to be received by the audience with only modest applause. But when Casals stepped on to the platform to begin his concerto, the Catalan audience erupted in an excessively vigorous and noisy ovation which amounted, quite obviously, to a political demonstration. Casals was not invited to the royal box after the performance, and assumed that his relations with the King were at an end. Some weeks later, however, he was summoned to the Palacio de Oriente in Madrid to perform during the state visit of Victor-

Emmanuel and Queen Elena of Italy. After the performance and in full view of the audience, Alfonso approached Casals and engaged him in extended conversation, concluding with the remark: 'Well Pablo, I want to tell you how happy I was to see how the Catalans love you.'[4] The following day the papers were full of the incident.

Casals did not think of himself as a political animal. He did not much care for politicians, he never joined a political party, and except briefly in the early 1930s was never in a position to exercise a vote. Yet in the sense that politics is, essentially, about humanity's struggle for a decent life, Casals was a politician from the first breath he took, and political activity was the primary focus of his life. The position he most favoured was one of sufficient familiarity with the people in power to be able to act as counsellor, conscience, prompt and irritant as the occasion demanded. In the Second Spanish Republic he was able to be exactly that. At the Catalan, and to an extent the national, level Casals admired and in some instances knew the leaders of the day personally: his artistic status in any case gave him a platform from which to comment on general issues. The new Republican Cortes was an unusually cultured and intelligent chamber, and its leaders included notable scholars: 'I do not believe that there had ever been before any government made up of such a group of savants and humanists.'[5] Among those Casals most respected were two of the Republic's early prime ministers: Manuel Azaña was a novelist and essayist, and Spain's foremost translator of Voltaire, Dr Juan Negrín a university professor and physiologist of world standing.

But Casals' primary allegiance was reserved for the nationalist leaders in Barcelona, and in particular for Colonel Francisco Maciá, who, after a long campaign of resistance to Primo's dictatorship, had become a Catalan hero. Maciá was the recipient of Casals' first ever electoral vote – exercised, in 1931, at the age of fifty-four. Immediately after the announcement of the results of the election, Maciá had proclaimed an independent Catalan republic, even though no overall federal structure yet existed, nor was envisaged. Persuaded by Madrid to change the name of his administration to *Generalitat*, the name given to Catalonia's prototype representative institution of the mid-fourteenth century, a statute granting limited provincial autonomy was approved by the Cortes in September 1932. Invited by the leader of the new Generalitat, Luis Companys, and its minister of culture, Ventura Gassol, Casals accepted the role of president of the Junta de Música, an organizing committee responsible for spreading the benefits of art and education throughout Catalonia.

If Casals had been a 'national glory' in 1895, he was, almost forty years later, a veritable hero of Republican Spain. Honours and privileges showered upon him and declarations of *homenatge* came from all areas of artistic and public life. In November 1933 the Associació de Música da Camera awarded him the title – after 300 concerts of his orchestra – of *Mestre*, and from the President he received the Generalitat's 'medal of the state'. The following year he was made an honorary citizen of Barcelona and an avenue in the centre of the city was named after him: at a celebratory concert in the Palau Nacional he conducted the Sardana arrangement for thirty-two cellos he had written in 1927.[6] In December the following year Casals was similarly honoured in Madrid, and inducted into the Academia de Bellas Artes de San Fernando – the Spanish Academy. The Republican Government offered him the gift of a Stradivarius cello from the royal collection – which, interestingly, he had never been shown during his years of friendship with Alfonso and María Cristina – but he declined.

For the moment the excitement and activity generated by political issues took precedence over Casals' own concert engagements: he had been, he wrote to friends, 'bouleversé' by recent events.[7] The Orquestra seasons continued as usual in Barcelona, but plans for a solo tour to London in autumn 1931 were shelved because of the impossibility of finding suitable dates.[8] Casals did play concerts in Holland, Switzerland and Hungary just before Christmas that year, but until 1934 he spent, for the first time in his career, the largest part of the year at home. The summer and winter breaks were always spent at San Salvador, where Casals used his holidays for detailed work on solo and orchestral scores for the coming season. He enjoyed his house, and entertained a good deal, helped after his mother's death by Frasquita Capdevila. When, thirty-five years earlier, Casals began teaching in Barcelona, Capdevila had been one of his first cello pupils. She had married Felip Capdevila, one of his closest friends and later treasurer of his orchestra. After her husband's early death in 1921, Capdevila continued to help with the administration of the orchestra and teach her own cello pupils at Enrique's Institut Musical Casals.[9] Several years later she moved into one of the three guest cottages Casals had built next to the main house at San Salvador, and gradually became part of the household. After 1928 friends would include greetings to Capdevila in letters addressed to Casals, and in due course began to refer to them as a couple.[10] Señora Capdevila looked after Casals and organized his home throughout the 1930s; in 1939 she chose to leave her home and family and accompany him into exile. The relationship seems to have been based on a combination of charity, dependence and affection – on both sides. For over twenty-five years, until her death in 1955,

Frasquita Capdevila provided Casals with his closest companionship.

Among the most regular guests at San Salvador was the American cellist Maurice Eisenberg and his wife Paula. Eisenberg was born in Königsberg, to Russian–Polish parents who emigrated to the United States when Maurice was a baby. At the age of ten he began to study the violin, but soon took up the cello and within a year had won a scholarship to the Peabody Conservatory in Baltimore. There he was spotted by Leopold Stokowski and, at sixteen, recruited for the Philadelphia Symphony Orchestra, later moving to become first cello in the New York Symphony Orchestra under Walter Damrosch. Having identified technical difficulties in his own performance, Eisenberg travelled to Europe in 1921 in the hope of studying with Casals, whom he had met and heard perform in America during the war. Casals sent Eisenberg to study first with Julius Klengel and Hugo Becker in Germany, and then to his own Ecole Normale in Paris for lessons with Alexanian.[11] During the late 1920s, Eisenberg followed Casals' career with close interest, eventually performing with the Orquestra Pau Casals and achieving his goal of lessons with the Maestro himself.

Eisenberg was quintessentially Casals' ideal pupil. He was highly talented, expertly trained and absolutely loyal. Intellectually and emotionally the two men were a perfect fit, each offering something the other found highly appealing. They became firm friends, indeed their whole families became closely associated, and remained in regular contact until Eisenberg's early death in December 1972. Maurice Eisenberg's career was largely defined by his relationship with Casals: he succeeded Alexanian as professor of cello at the Ecole Normale in 1929 and later, after spending the war and the years after it teaching in the United States, returned to Europe in 1953, at Casals' prompting, to establish the International Cello Centre in London. Eisenberg became artistic director of the Centre, with his pupil Milly Stanfield as administrative secretary.[12] Casals was its honorary president, largely *in absentia*, since he did not revisit Britain until 1963.

Though Eisenberg himself was a highly experienced and distinguished teacher, giving regular masterclasses and concert-lectures in Switzerland and Portugal as well as in Britain and America, the dynamic of his relationship with Casals was always as pupil to teacher, never as cellist to cellist. Even in his fifties Eisenberg would report back to Casals on his concerto performances around the world, seeking his advice and detailed response. Eisenberg was always the supplicant, and Casals the benefactor. In a sense, of course, this was unexceptionable: Casals was always in advance, technically and musically, of every cellist of his generation and of the next. It was Eisenberg's good fortune to have permanent access to his guidance. In a sense, also, Casals needed to be told it, and Eisenberg did so, throughout his career. It was a bargain, and both were the winners.

Although the two had met before on a number of occasions, the relationship between Casals and Maurice Eisenberg took off in 1928, as Casals emerged from his winter of depression. Eisenberg was invited to play the Schumann Concerto with the orchestra in Barcelona, and then, with his wife, went to stay at San Salvador for several weeks of intensive tuition. The lessons began with the Schumann Concerto. Nervously, Eisenberg got ready to play:

> Before I had a chance to begin, [Casals] asked me to sing the first note, a sustained E. I did this. 'Good,' said he. He then requested me to conduct the note as though holding a baton. He asked me whether there were fluctuations of curves in the line of the note when I sang or conducted it. I of course answered in the negative. 'Then why did you use curves in your wrist and bow action when playing it on the cello?'[13]

For Eisenberg, this was a revelation: 'I suddenly realized the uselessness of the complicated methods adopted by my earlier teachers . . . which I had previously accepted without question. . . . By the next lesson my technique had undergone a complete change.'

The great shock, repeatedly, for all who studied with Casals or played under his baton, was that the answer to every musical problem seemed – in his presence – unnervingly simple. 'I will say only elemental things,' he would often tell an orchestra before rehearsal, 'nothing complicated – as everything ought to be. But you must know that the simplest things are the ones that count.' The simplest things are, of course, also the most difficult to achieve, and take years of work. When Casals was in the room, he represented a kind of conduit to perfection. Lessons consisted, for most students, of a series of epiphanies. Having Casals in front of one, pleading 'Exhaltation, we must have exhaltation!' was enough to make any student provide it. The problem was to do it next time, without him. That took massive effort and practice, and that was what Casals wanted to inspire.

So far as aphorisms and apt quotations were concerned, Casals was monumentally fecund, at least when he was speaking anything other than his first language, and probably even then.[14] He always spoke slowly, carefully, sometimes with flashes of startling exclamation, and almost always with a pipe – generally unlit – in his mouth. Fixing the orchestra or individual students with his freakishly bright blue eyes, he could, through timing and effect, transform a fairly routine utterance into a spectacular *pensée*. For Casals' innate command of sound applied not only to music, but also to speech. From him the statement, 'All music is a succession of rainbows', would resonate like a universal truth.

But what most profoundly communicated itself to musicians confronted by Casals was the inescapable authenticity of his emotional response to the music, reflected in the directness of the instructions he would give. Rehearsing on one occasion the Schumann Concerto, and sensing the mental agony the composer experienced when writing it, Casals cried out, 'Pain, pain. . . . All is pain – the poor man!'[15] To a student about to begin the Dvořák Concerto, Casals once exclaimed, 'Announce the hero!' – and the student did. Or he would ask that an orchestra 'play frankly', meaning forthrightly, without sentimentality. Perhaps the most devastating response was given to a student who once asked: 'How do you count here, Maestro?' The answer came back: 'With my soul.'

For a musician, an encounter with Casals was thus a spiritual experience. The intensity of his own honesty demanded – and almost invariably obtained – an equally candid emotional response. After two full summers of lessons, Maurice Eisenberg wrote to acknowledge the nature of Casals' 'inspiration': 'you make me breathe a different atmosphere which reflects itself not only in my playing but in my whole spiritual self. I always feel a better man when I am with you.'[16]

Until 1936 the Eisenbergs spent each summer at San Salvador, and often a week or two at Christmas, staying as Casals' guests in one of his cottages: it was an idyllic combination of holiday and study. Sometimes they were joined by other friends – Milly Stanfield came in 1933 and 1934 – and in 1932 they had brought their new baby son. Pablo Eisenberg, named after Casals – his godfather – later began to study the piano, cello and clarinet; but when the family returned to the United States in 1939, he opted to concentrate on sport. As some compensation to his godfather (known always as *padrinet*), he became, as well as a brilliant student at Princeton and a post-graduate at Oxford, a US youth champion at tennis. Casals watched young Pablo play on two memorable occasions, one of which was a match against a player of world rank. Eisenberg won the first set but lost the match.[17] Casals was openly disgruntled. He had a highly developed sense of competition and enjoyed victory. He liked, in life as in movie westerns, 'to see the good guys win'.

Back in Paris during the rest of the year, Maurice Eisenberg kept Casals in touch with old friends like Alexanian and new ones like Yehudi Menuhin, and acted as messenger in transactions with their mutual agent, Charles Kiesgen.[18] Casals was not used to remaining in one place for long, and missed the regular stimulus of friends and colleagues. The death of Ysaÿe was closely followed by that of Emanuel Moór – in Switzerland – in October 1931, and of Röntgen the following September, a month before a planned trip to conduct Casals' orchestra in Barcelona.[19] But back in Casals' life was Donald Francis Tovey, whose reinvigorated friendship provided energy and activity until Tovey's own death in 1940.

Tovey had been appointed Reid Professor of Music at the University of Edinburgh in 1914, at the age of thirty-eight. Two years later he founded the Reid Symphony Orchestra, early difficulties in the administration of which foreshadowed problems Casals would encounter in Barcelona. Guilhermina Suggia performed with the Reid Orchestra in April 1920 (she and Tovey had repaired their relationship and given a joint recital at Northlands the previous year), and Casals himself travelled to Edinburgh for a concert with Tovey in 1925.[20] But if, as some friends claimed, it took a year to know Casals, it took a good deal longer to repair a deep hurt: it was a further five or six years before the two men were back to their old intimacy. In the interim Tovey had played a concert – Beethoven's Choral Fantasy – with the Orquestra Pau Casals in October 1927, after he and Casals had met in New York in January.[21] Tovey's New York recitals, during which he performed the Goldberg and Diabelli Variations, earned him impressive notices, the *New York Telegram* describing him as 'among the major pianists of the epoch'.[22] Casals began to realize what the hiatus in the friendship had denied him.

Sometime during the first half of 1931, Tovey began to give serious thought to the idea of composing a cello concerto for Casals. He had first considered the possibility of a concerto during the 1920s, but an extended period of illness and recuperation during 1932 and 1933 gave him the leisure to sketch out his thoughts. By spring 1933 he had already scored 250 bars, and described the work to Sophie Weisse as 'the only full-sized cello concerto (in classical form), except the Dvořák, in the world'. The first movement promised to be a 'record-breaker', the longest single section Tovey had ever written, 'and much the juiciest'.[23]

Casals had been pressing Tovey to get on with the concerto ever since first hearing about it during the summer of 1931, and was delighted to hear that work had begun: 'the day your cello concerto reaches me will be stamped in the calendar of my life'.[24] Sections of the score indeed soon began to arrive, and Casals spent a good deal of the summer working through it in detail. In October he wrote to reassure Tovey that he had discovered nothing that was technically impossible; apart from some minor alterations to the bowing, he proposed to play it as written.[25] Letters were exchanged on detailed points of bowing and figuration throughout the winter of 1933–4, and a visit by Tovey to Barcelona in April 1934 – to play his Piano Concerto, and receive honorary membership of the Orquestra Pau Casals – provided an opportunity to explore the cello concerto together. Casals asked Tovey to play it through 'on the dismantled sewing-machine they sent to my hotel for practising'. Spain was primitive as to pianofortes, Tovey explained to Weisse. 'The concert grand was a Bechstein put out to grass after having been played on by Liszt.'[26] But Casals had 'glorious plans' for the Cello Concerto: he wanted to give the first performance with the Reid Orchestra, in Edinburgh, in November. By June the date had been fixed, and Casals wrote that 'the twenty-second of November will be the most important date of my musical life. Joachim must have felt the same joy and honour the day he first performed the Beethoven violin concerto and that on which he first heard the Brahms.'[27]

1934 was a good year for Tovey. In February he learned from the Master of the King's Musick, Sir Edward Elgar, that he was to receive an honour. Did he 'have any objection to titles?' wondered Elgar, in a letter that month.[28] The knighthood was conferred the following January. In May he arranged for Casals to be offered an honorary Mus.Doc. by the University. The degree was conferred *in absentia*, Casals being too busy preparing the Concerto, and too unsettled generally, to come in person.[29] And in the autumn, not only was Tovey's Concerto to receive its first performance by Casals, but Albert Schweitzer, also the recipient of an honorary degree at his instigation, was to come to Edinburgh to deliver the Gifford lectures in theology, and stay with Tovey for their duration. Since the visits of the two great men coincided, Tovey was able to introduce them – their first meeting – and preserve the moment in a classic, if unflattering, photograph of the three men of music in their doctoral robes.

The première of the Tovey Concerto, for which Casals had insisted he receive no fee, took place as scheduled on 22 November, in Edinburgh University's Usher Hall. Plans for a second performance in London on 6 December fell through, and the *Times* music critic lambasted the BBC Symphony Orchestra and the Royal Philharmonic for their failure to take on the work: 'If both decide to ignore a work which is clearly one of considerable power and intimate beauty and which, moreover, is sponsored by the greatest exponent of violoncello playing in the world, they will be very foolish.'[30]

Tovey's Cello Concerto is long, complex and diffuse. Christopher Bunting has described it as 'of symphonic proportions and aspiration:

Brahmsian, Brucknerish and Sibelian gestures being never far below the surface'.[31] In its twenty-five-minute First Movement, dramatic bursts of orchestration cut across extended sonorous cello passages: Constant Lambert said it reminded him of his 'first term at school'. The Concerto as a whole has many moments of great beauty, but makes severe demands on the listener seeking to relate them. *The Scotsman* was obviously right to observe that it could not be fully understood on first hearing, and for some years it was probably only the composer and the soloist who did.[32] Despite a painful infection in his left thumb on the night of the first performance, Casals produced a rich, controlled and powerful tone which gave the work a sense of real authority. The cause of the infection, however, eluded specialists and prevented Casals from playing for two months, until a physician in the Catalan town of Figueras extracted, with his tweezers, a nailbrush bristle.

The Tovey Concerto had its second performance in Barcelona, in April 1935, with the composer conducting. The local journal, *Carnet Musical*, declared that it contained 'fragments of great beauty and luminous inspiration which some would regard as incompatible with the British temperament'.[33] The first London hearings were not until 11 and 12 November that year, when inadequate rehearsing of the orchestra and loose conducting by Tovey himself, produced two dangerously confused performances. The composer's conducting, the *Observer* reported, was 'unhappily an enemy to Casals and his own music'. Ernest Newman, writing in the *Sunday Times*, remained puzzled by Tovey's programme notes which described the finale as becoming, in diminution, 'like the centrifugal drops from the faithful retriever who irrigates his master after rescuing the walking-stick from the pond'. Newman admitted he was 'hopelessly shut out from Professor Tovey's . . . human and meteorological world'.[34]

The Concerto's London reception damaged hopes that it might soon be recorded. In June 1936 Fred Gaisberg proposed the recording of both the Tovey and the Elgar Concertos, and Casals spent the summer working on the Elgar score.[35] He played the concerto with Boult in London in November, but plans to record both it and the Tovey were scrapped at the last minute, leaving Casals irritated and angry at the wasted effort. He continued to work on the Tovey score, however, adding bowings and fingerings for the published edition. He remained confident the Graphophone Company would eventually record the work, and counselled Tovey not to push things.[36] He was right. Almost exactly a year later, on 17 November 1937, with Casals and the BBC Orchestra – safely conducted by Sir Adrian Boult – the Concerto was recorded (on to seventeen glass discs covered with acetate) and simultaneously broadcast across Europe. Fritz Busch heard it on the wireless in Copenhagen, and Suggia in Portugal. She wrote to Tovey that 'it sounded beautiful . . . I am convinced there is only one 'cellist in the world who could have done it'.[37] *The Times*' review grudgingly conceded that 'we begin to think of the concerto as a work we could live with'. Casals taught the Concerto to a student, Peggie Sampson, in summer 1948, but otherwise no one has needed to try. The release of the recording – finally, in 1992 – may change that.[38]

Casals remained wholly convinced of Tovey's brilliance, both as pianist and composer. 'The fact is,' he later recollected, 'I regard Tovey as one of the greatest musicians of all time.'[39] Tovey died barely two and a half years after the recording of his Concerto, in considerable distress and confusion. In his final conscious days he confided to his doctor his intense admiration for Casals: 'you must listen to him in the flesh – there is no player on earth like him, and nobody so musical'.[40]

The extent to which Casals rationed his time and focused his energies on the Tovey Concerto is evident from the fact that two other concertos, written for him at almost exactly the same time, by composers he knew and valued, got nowhere. In 1931 Alexander Glazunov, who had left Russia in 1928 to compete in an absurd competition (sponsored by Columbia Graphophone) to 'finish' Schubert's 'Unfinished' Symphony – and never went back – completed a cello concerto, his 'Concerto–Ballade', and dedicated it to Casals.[41] After some years, and having never performed the work, Casals passed it over to Maurice Eisenberg. Persuaded by Glazunov on the grounds that he was dying, Eisenberg prepared the Concerto in four weeks flat and, in October 1938, gave its first performance with the Pasdeloup Orchestra in Paris, the composer conducting.[42] By the time of the second performance, with the BBC Orchestra the following year, Glazunov was dead.

The case of Arnold Schönberg was more telling. Between October 1931 and May 1932, Schönberg was a guest in the Barcelona home of the Catalan composer Roberto Gerhard. There primarily to improve his health, Schönberg met Casals on several occasions, played tennis with him, and conducted a performance of the Orquestra Pau Casals. By January 1933 Schönberg had completed a Cello Concerto, freely adapted from a keyboard concerto by the eighteenth-century composer G. M. Monn. He wrote to Casals that 'it has turned out a very brilliant piece', adding, probably wisely in view of Casals' opinion of some of his more experimental compositions, that it approximated in style to Haydn, and nowhere goes 'much further than Brahms'.[43] Schönberg invited Casals to give the first performance. Casals' later recollection was that he worked on the Concerto for two years and, on the point of playing it, was charged a copyright fee by Schirmers, its publishers, which he refused to pay.[44] It seems clear, however, that he did perform the work privately. Hearing this, Schönberg wrote again in September 1933, asking Casals to give the premiere in London on 29 November, with the BBC Orchestra.[45] Schönberg had lost his job and badly needed the money. Casals was by then, however, in the midst of his preparation of the Tovey Concerto, and the schedule was impossible. Both Gregor Piatigorsky and Emanuel Feuermann were keen to give the first performance, and indeed Feuermann did so, with the London Philharmonic under Thomas Beecham, in the autumn of 1935. 'In spite of the remarkable performance he gave,' Casals later observed, 'the work had no success at all.'[46]

Casals very rarely commented publicly on other cello virtuosi, unless they had been his students. Indeed, he very often gave the impression of not being aware of the existence of any. He could of course afford not to, though it is probable that his keen competitive instinct kept him well informed about his rivals, or those who saw themselves as such. By the mid-1930s Emanuel Feuermann was enjoying a glittering reputation and travelling the world as Casals had done twenty years before. Exactly one generation younger, he was the player, if any, most likely to steal the crown. He had, above all, a brilliant technique. 'Difficulties do not exist for Mr Feuermann,' wrote Olin Downes in January 1935.[47]

At the age of eleven, Feuermann had heard Casals perform in Vienna. It proved that the cello could indeed support a solo career, and ignited his ambition to attempt one. Feuermann's brother, Sigmund, had been a spectacular prodigy on the violin, playing the Brahms Concerto at the age of ten in the capitals of Europe. After the Casals encounter, however, the more sheltered 'Munio' soon outstripped Sigmund. Feuermann was a pupil of Klengel. He never studied with Casals: indeed there is no evidence that they even met, or spoke. But throughout Feuermann's brief life – he died at thirty-nine – Casals was his idol and his obsession. Feuermann scrutinized Casals' recordings for signs that the master's interpretative shaping was the result of attempts to evade technical demands. He listened, in 1937, with George and Sophie Szell, to the first pressings of Casals' April recording of the Dvořák Concerto, comparing it anxiously with his own of 1930. And, after its release in 1940, he listened repeatedly to the Maestro's full recorded set of the Bach Unaccompanied Suites. Intimidated, and knowing he could not match the performance, he gradually dropped the Suites from his programmes. He wrote to salute Casals on them, and was jubilant when he received a reply from Prades. Some years after Feuermann's death his widow found, among his papers, the draft of an unpublished article on the history of cello performance. She sent a paragraph to Casals:

> Finally, the great personality appeared on the cello horizon, and through him, this one man, the cello was established as the fully-fledged worthy member of the family of solo instruments. This man's name is Casals. Everyone who has heard him knows that a new period for the cello has come.[48]

In Spain the Republic was in crisis. The political system Casals had long hoped for was proving difficult to sustain. In part it was a consequence of the global economic slump, which increased the urgency for widespread social reform while compromising the Government's ability to provide it. And in part it reflected the fact that, split as it was into mutually antagonistic interests, Spain was virtually ungovernable anyway. Each direction it turned, the Government alienated some important section – conservative Castilians for its approval of Catalan self-government, the landowners for its (limited) plans for agrarian reform, and almost everybody for its precipitate attempt to reform the Catholic Church. Strikes, demonstrations, acts of sabotage and armed revolts continued all over Spain, and in January 1933 a major anarchist uprising took hold of Barcelona, and spread to other cities. The Government took surprisingly harsh and immediate action, made itself deeply unpopular, and resigned in September 1933. The new Cortes was dominated by the Right, and the Anarchists declared open war against it. A general strike was declared in June 1934, and another in October. A socialist uprising in Oviedo was brutally put down, and the ensuing mood of revulsion eventually led to another fall of Government. After further elections, in February 1936, Spain was led by a broadly socialist Popular Front.

There are, and will be, many studies of the background to the Spanish Civil War. What Casals saw was a good idea tearing itself apart: 'sometimes one felt the country was a seething volcano'.[49] His own family was touched by the crisis: very few were not. When Luis Companys, president of the Generalitat, declared Catalonia independent on 5 October 1934, Luis Casals somehow became involved in the short-lived battle to defend it, and was imprisoned for ten weeks before being released – to the family's intense relief – just before Christmas.[50] The violence and uncertainty made Casals nervous, dispirited and intermittently ill. Friends noticed he was often tired and unhappy, and commented on it in letters. In April 1936 Maurice Eisenberg spent Easter at San Salvador and found Casals 'very depressed and downcast'.[51] But the spring orchestra programme was about to begin, and Casals returned to Barcelona to conduct what was to be its last season. The concerts concluded on 28 June, but the orchestra had a final engagement to fulfil: it was due to perform Beethoven's Ninth Symphony, again on Montjuïc, this time at the opening of the Barcelona Olympiad, arranged in opposition to the Olympic Games in Berlin. The final rehearsal took place at the Palau de la Música Catalana on the evening of Saturday 18 July. That morning news had come through of a military revolt two days earlier in the Spanish zone in Morocco, and there were rumours of sympathetic uprisings in garrisons throughout Spain. Casals took the orchestra through the first three movements of the Symphony, and as the chorus came on stage for the final Chorale, a messenger came with a note. It was from the Catalan Minister of Culture, Ventura Gassol: a military revolt was expected in the city that evening, and Casals was instructed to discontinue the rehearsal and allow the musicians to return home. Casals asked if the singers and musicians wished to leave at once, or to finish the rehearsal. The decision to continue was unanimous. As the choir sang Schiller's timeless phrases, 'all mankind are sworn brothers where thy gentle wings abide', Casals found tears were obscuring the score. Outside, barricades were being set up in the streets.

In Barcelona and Madrid, the rebellion was crushed. But the military junta and right-wing politicians had, at their disposal, the major part of the armed forces of the country, together with the promise of weapons and aid from Germany and Italy. The Republic could rely upon only an Assault Guard and a poorly equipped air force. But it had behind it the courage and energy of the majority of the people, and civil war became inevitable. For the first few days, Casals watched from San Salvador:

> All war is terrible but civil war is most terrible of all. Then it is neighbour against neighbour, brother against brother, son against father. And that was the nature of the war that was to rack my beloved country for the next two and a half years. They were a nightmare of unrelieved horror.[52]

Between the July insurrection and the beginning of September, some 75,000 Spaniards were killed. Civil law collapsed, and the anarchists terrorized the countryside around Barcelona, taking summary vengeance against suspected enemies of the Republic or Falangist sympathizers. Casals remained in the Villa Casals, which began to appear alarmingly opulent and dangerously exposed. Casals was later told that his name, and that of his brother Luis, frequently came up at the daily meetings of the El Vendrell extermination council, but that someone was always present who knew enough of his history to secure a reprieve.[53] On one occasion an armed anarchist gang did come to the house, looking for one of Casals' neighbours, Señor Renom, a wealthy Barcelona businessman. After a search in the vicinity, the gang located Renom and his wife and brought them to Casals' house, looking for a telephone to send for a cart. Casals instead telephoned the Anarchist mayor of El Vendrell, who backtracked and ordered the gang away.[54] Later, when anarchists arrived to burn the Ermita – the historic local chapel – Casals again intervened to prevent gratuitous destruction.

While the *anarquistas* were in control of the region, Casals felt himself and his property to be relatively safe. But when local communists took over later in the summer, he knew there was a greater risk, and arranged for a quantity of papers and other items to be wrapped and carefully buried; correspondence between himself and the royal family was burned. Indeed, the random nature of what might have been interpreted as incriminating documentation explains why so little of Casals' correspondence survives in Spain.

Casals' instinct, throughout the Civil War, was to remain in Catalonia to protect his family, and when colleagues and powerful friends – such as Ventura Gassol – suggested he continue his international tours as a means of communicating to the world the reality of the Spanish conflict, he suspected they were trying to protect him. After the summer of 1936, and despite intermittent savage bombing from German and Italian planes, Barcelona remained free, until much later in the war, of ground-fighting between Republican and Nationalist forces, and Casals was able to travel and to return without special difficulty. But what he did not know was where he wanted to be, and his itinerary for these years reveals a sense of unfocused desperation. Whenever he was abroad he would insist on being informed of the latest appalling news from Spain. Whenever he was in Catalonia, there was always the possibility he might be shot.

What is most powerfully obvious – yet has not been clearly observed – is that the two and a half years of the Spanish Civil War coincide almost exactly with the most significant period in Casals' career as a recording artist. Between November 1936 and June 1939, he recorded a sizeable proportion of the principal works of the cello repertoire: the full set of Bach Unaccompanied Suites (the only occasion on which he did so), four of the five Beethoven Cello Sonatas, the Dvořák B Minor Cello Concerto and the Boccherini B Flat Major Concerto, as well as Bruch's *Kol Nidrei* and Tovey's Concerto. Among these are the works which many agree to be the greatest of Casals' recording life – the Bach Suites, the Beethoven Sonatas, and the Dvořák Concerto. Casals had spent a good deal of his performing life evading the harassment of recording companies, or requesting fees which the companies could not meet. Now, heading past his sixtieth birthday, he recorded the bulk of the important works in one relatively concentrated burst.

With the merger of HMV and Columbia Graphophone (Europe) in 1931, Fred Gaisberg became head of the artistic policies of the recording conglomerate EMI. It was the vigorous Gaisberg who had contrived the recordings of the Cortot–Thibaud–Casals Trio in 1926–8, and of the Orquestra Pau Casals in 1932. He, if anyone, could persuade Casals back into the recording studio. How he did so, however, is not clear. Within the larger company Gaisberg may have been able to offer a higher fee. And the arrival of Emanuel Feuermann – a Columbia acquisition – on to the EMI label may have given him greater leverage over Casals: the cellists could not, by and large, record the same works.[55] Doubtless there were also circumstantial factors, such as the simultaneous presence in London of Casals and his great friend Mieczyslaw Horszowski, which enabled Gaisberg to bring them together on 26 and 27 November 1936, in the Abbey Road studios of HMV, to record the Beethoven Sonata No. 4 (Op. 102, No. 1). But two days before this, Gaisberg had 'persistently worried' Casals into making his first serious recording of the Bach Unaccompanied Suites (Nos. 2 and 3). Two days after it they proceeded to record the Boccherini B Flat Major Concerto with Sir Landon Ronald and the London Symphony Orchestra. In between, if the archives are to be believed, Casals also recorded Bruch's *Kol Nidrei*, again with Ronald and the LSO, and at Abbey Road.

In April the following year, Casals was due to visit Prague to play the Dvořák Concerto with George Szell and the Czech Philharmonic Orchestra. Gaisberg persuaded them to repeat the work the following day, for a recording. He recalled that:

> Casals flew from Barcelona, arriving more dead than alive. . . .
> The dress rehearsal and concert before packed houses were a huge success. Casals's *élan* and stamina kept him going for the whole of the next day when over twelve unsurpassed (78 rpm) records were made, and then the little man collapsed, every ounce of his strength exhausted . . .[56]

While in Paris in June 1938, Casals was persuaded to record a further two Bach Suites, and he completed the set on 13 June 1939. This was his only recording of the full set, and though it became a classic Casals himself was never completely satisfied with the sound: he told Lev Ginsburg that he would like to hear them 'at least one tone sharper in order to recover the liveliness that was lost during mechanical recording'. A week later he and Horszowski concluded the cycle of Beethoven Cello

Sonatas, recording Nos. 1, 2 and 5. Casals had recorded No. 3 with Otto Schulhof in 1930, and did not think he could improve on it.

The recording of this substantial corpus of important work – which, as we have seen, might also have included the Elgar Concerto – was not an accident, nor simply the result of Gaisberg's perseverance. In a period of acute physical danger and emotional turmoil, Casals *needed* to play. At the same time, his opportunities for performance were becoming fewer. Apart from an occasional concert in Barcelona – in aid of war victims – he could no longer perform in his own country. Nor, since Hitler's assumption of power in January 1933, had Casals given a concert in Germany. Invitations had come from Wilhelm Furtwängler, whom he admired and to whom he replied with care, indicating an understanding of the conductor's position on the division between art and politics, but rejecting it. Fascist Italy, too, was out of the question, and the United States remained off his touring schedule. Casals needed different outlets. He found them partly by accepting engagements in new, and unusual locations, and partly by agreeing to make recordings. 'The only weapons I have ever had are my cello and my conductor's baton.'[57] If he could not use them on the concert platform to the extent he wished, Casals would do so by means of the gramophone.

On 18 September 1936 the Orquestra Pau Casals reassembled at the Liceu for a concert to raise funds for victims of the summer's violence; Casals performed a Haydn concerto. Troubled and restless, he travelled to Paris to be with Maurice and Paula Eisenberg, but was back in Spain in October, to begin his English tour, and series of recordings, in the middle of November. In London for only a few days, he felt an overwhelming urge to return home, but friends counselled him to continue with his concerts.[58] In late December, this time with Señora Capdevila, he again left San Salvador, crossing the Pyrenees into France and, at the suggestion of a friend, Luis Guarro, staying in the small French–Catalan town of Prades, where Guarro and his nine children had taken temporary refuge.[59] 'I am having some rest in the Pyrenees for a while,' he wrote on 23 January to his London agent.[60] Casals and Capdevila stayed at the town's Grand Hotel, travelling twice to nearby Perpignan to consult a doctor, René Puig. Eisenberg wrote inviting them to Paris: Prades was 'much too depressing'.[61] They did indeed travel to Paris after the Prague concert in April, stayed until 13 May, and then returned to Prades. In June Casals was back in Barcelona, where he performed another Liceu benefit concert on 12 July. It was the final concert of the Orquestra Pau Casals. Five days later Casals sailed from Boulogne for an eight-week tour of South America, his first since 1904.

On his return to Europe, Casals began a full autumn tour, with concerts in London (including the Tovey broadcast), Amsterdam, Prague, Vienna, Budapest, Bucharest, Zürich and Paris, before returning to San Salvador for his sixty-first birthday. In February he went to North Africa – his first and only visit – for two weeks of concerts in Rabat, Casablanca, Oran, Algiers and Tunis. He returned exhausted, and recuperated in Prades.[62] Proceeds from most of the concerts during these years went to war charities: Casals was honorary chairman of the US-based Musicians' Committee to Aid Spanish Democracy. But his particular concern was for child victims of the conflict. On 19 October 1938, as Nationalist forces moved closer to Barcelona, he gave a concert in the Liceu on behalf of the Children's Aid Society. It was his final concert in Spain. With musicians from his own orchestra, and others, he played overtures by Gluck and Weber, and two concertos – Dvořák and Haydn. During a rehearsal for the performance there had been a bombing raid, and the players had dived for cover. When it was over, Casals picked up his cello and began a Bach Suite, until the musicians were ready to resume. At the concert itself, which was to be broadcast, Casals delivered a message appealing to the world not to let Hitler win in Spain, for 'you will be the next victims of his madness'.

Casals' autumn tour began in Belgium, and continued through southeastern Europe to Turkey, with a final concert in Athens at the end of November. At the beginning of December he played concerts in Cairo and Alexandria. A tour of Japan had been mooted for early 1939, but on 23 December Franco had launched his final offensive against the Republican army in Catalonia, and Casals decided to return to San Salvador. He found his villa crowded with refugees. The assault on Barcelona began at the end of December, and by 26 January the Nationalists were in control of the city. Two days earlier an honorary doctorate had been conferred on Casals by what was left of the University of Barcelona, the certificate hastily written by hand and presented at a last-minute ceremony. Most of the faculty present left at once to go into exile. Casals followed a few days later.

# PART 4

## *The Exile*

# 9

## War and Exile, 1939–1949

J'irai à Paris, ainsi qu'à Londres et New York, comme partout
ailleurs, quand l'ignominieuse présence de Franco cessera chez
nous. Tant que celle continuera, mon esprit ne peut être avec la
musique.

*Pablo Casals*[1]

One of the most permanent and painful images of the Spanish Civil War
is of the exodus of refugees across the Pyrenean border with France in
the first, cold and desperate weeks of 1939. Barcelona was already choked
with fugitives, many of them children, from other areas of the conflict
in the south and west. When news came that Nationalist forces had
reached the river Llobregat, tens of thousands began the 160-kilometre
trudge north to the frontier. At midnight on 27–28 January, France
finally and reluctantly opened its border, and the first of almost half a
million men, women and children, civilians and disarmed Republican
soldiers made their way in drenching rain and snow as Nationalist planes
bombed the roads. Wrapped in blankets and carrying what they could
of their possessions, they were fed into transit centres and sorted for
relocation into one of about fifteen internment camps. Soldiers were
separated off into sections of beach marked out with barbed wire at
Argelès, St-Cyprien and Barcarès, and guarded by Senegalese troops.
Some burrowed holes in the wet sand to give themselves a modicum of
protection from the weather.

On leaving Barcelona, Casals had gone straight to Prades. Within days
of the border being opened he visited several of the refugee camps and
was appalled by the conditions: there was no sanitation or medicine, very
little shelter and almost no food. 'There are no words to describe the
horror of what is going on here,' he wrote to a friend on 5 February.[2]
Casals knew at once that he had to help. He gathered friends, like Juan
Alavedra – the Catalan poet – also now in exile in Prades, and set up a
*de facto* relief operation. His bedroom at the Grand Hôtel became the

headquarters, and he and his team began sending out appeals for help to individuals and organizations throughout Europe and the United States. As gifts of food, clothing and money began to arrive, Casals rented both truck and driver and set out to distribute supplies to the inmates of the camps. For the next ten years Casals' primary energies would be directed towards alleviating the suffering of his fellow-exiles. Music had to take second place. 'If I've done one thing in my life well,' he said, several years afterwards, 'that is it.'[3]

Ibbs and Tillett had organized a concert in the Royal Albert Hall on 28 March in aid of Spanish children. Casals travelled to London as news broke of Franco's final assault on Barcelona, and as he returned to the Piccadilly Hotel after the final rehearsal, friends tried to divert his attention from newsstands announcing its fall. At the concert, with Albert Coates and the London Symphony Orchestra, Casals played three entire concertos – by Elgar, Dvořák and Haydn – to a highly emotional audience. Four days later, on 1 April, Franco made the terse declaration that 'the war is finished', and Casals knew there was now no possibility of a return to San Salvador. His public opposition to the Falange had recently led to a brutal taunt during a radio broadcast by the Nationalists' chief propagandist, General Gonzalo Quiepo de Lano: when Casals was caught, he jeered, both arms would be cut off at the elbow. A year later it was reported that the Falange had imposed on Casals a 1 million peseta fine.[4]

Casals went instead to Paris, to stay with the Eisenbergs. There, in their large seventh-floor apartment overlooking the Place de la Porte de Champerret, he spent the next fifteen days in the deepest black depression of his life, curtains closed, speaking to no one, and wholly inconsolable. Encouraged by Alavedra, to whom Maurice Eisenberg had appealed for help, and tended by Frasquita Capdevila, Casals recovered sufficiently to travel first to Cannes for a concert booking, and from there, in the middle of April, back to Prades.[5] Back in the Grand Hôtel, Casals threw himself into the continuing effort to distribute food and clothing to the refugees who, like himself, knew they were now permanently in exile.

On 1 September Germany invaded Poland and the war began. It was what Casals had dreaded. Poland fell in a month, and as the Nazi army headed towards France, Prades seemed daily less secure as a refuge. But Casals continued to accept invitations to perform. On 12 November he played the Lalo and Saint-Saëns concertos with the Lamoureux Orchestra in Paris, marking the fortieth anniversary of his solo debut in the city, and in February the following year he was in Amsterdam and The Hague for a series of concerts with the Concertgebouw. Then, in the spring and early summer, Belgium, Holland and Luxembourg fell, and Hitler's armies entered Paris on 13 June. Nine days later France itself surrendered.

For months friends had been encouraging Casals to move to England or the United States, and it would in practice not have been difficult to do. Concert agents in America pestered him to return for a tour, with promises of enormous fees: he received at least one blank cheque. But so long as half a million of his compatriots were effectively imprisoned in camps between Perpignan and the Spanish border, Casals could see no justification for leaving. Nor, at such a time and surrounded by such misery, could he think about music. But at the end of June the decision was taken for him. Casals was instructed by the head of the Préfecture in Prades that he must leave France. If Franco joined the war, Nationalist forces would cross immediately into France, and Casals, with Alavedra and many others, would almost certainly face execution. Enquiries revealed that a French passenger ship, the *Champlain*, was heading for Bordeaux and was due to sail in a few days for South America. Tickets and travel documents were hurriedly arranged and, for the enormous sum of 250,000 francs, two taxis were found to take Casals, Capdevila, the Alavedras and their two young children, together with Enrique's elder daughter, Pilar, who was with them, on the difficult, 400-kilometre journey to the Atlantic port. Before they left they destroyed any papers which, if found by fascists of any description, might incriminate them or their correspondents.

The journey – first east to Perpignan, then north and west through Narbonne and Toulouse – took two days, and when they reached Bordeaux they found the city in turmoil and under threat of bombing. Casals and Alavedra headed for the municipal offices to obtain the required embarkation documents. In the confused and crowded building Casals fainted. Alavedra located a French official he knew, and the two men managed to lift Casals to a couch. Pushing through the crowds to secure the papers, Alavedra reportedly encountered Alfred Cortot, himself in Bordeaux in an attempt to board a vessel, the *Massilia*, for Morocco.[6] Alavedra appealed to Cortot for aid in attending to Casals, but the Frenchman, according to several sources, excused himself saying, simply, 'Give him my regards and tell him that I wish him well.'[7] Cortot's family later denied that the pianist had known Casals was in the city.[8]

Casals was sixty-three years old. The course of the remainder of his life might have been radically altered that night, had the *Champlain* not struck a mine dropped by German aircraft and sunk off La Pallice, 30 kilometres outside Bordeaux. The two families were exhausted, hungry

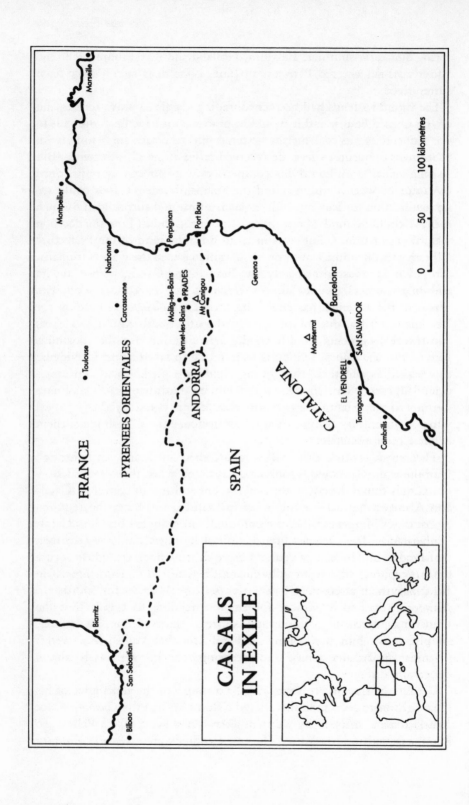

CASALS
IN EXILE

and distraught, but had no option but to recover their taxis and return to Prades along roads clogged with troops and refugees. The first night they slept in the cars. At midnight on the second they reached Prades. The Grand Hôtel was locked and dark, and the proprietor, when roused, refused to give them rooms. Casals, a known enemy of the Nazis, was a bad risk, he claimed: he would put everyone in jeopardy when the Germans arrived in the town. Fortunately not everyone in Prades was so craven. Opposite the hotel, across the street, was Le Café Grand. Awakened by the commotion, Pierrette Hostelrich, the wife of the proprietor, offered them makeshift accommodation for the night. Several days later Casals and Alavedra found a small house for rent on the Route Nationale. Madame Hostelrich provided furniture and household effects, for they had nothing, and the two families had a home.[9]

Prades, with its population of around 4600, was then, and is still, the leading market town of the area known as Conflent, part of the *département* of the Pyrénées Orientales. Apart from its eastern edge, the town is encircled by the mountains of the Pyrenees, and stands in the immensely fertile and well-irrigated valley of the river Têt. Forty kilometres to the east is Perpignan, capital of the Roussillon; to the west, across the Pyrenees and through the principality of Andorra, is Puigcerda and the border with Spain. The mountains that surround Prades are the source of thermal springs which, since the Romans, have attracted visitors seeking *bains de délices* and their legendary health-giving properties. The Church of St Pierre, in the centre of the town, incorporates in its seventeenth-century structure, walls from an earlier Roman settlement on the site.

Casals came to Prades not for its vines and fresh produce, but for its proximity to Spain. Roussillon lies in French Catalonia, and despite three centuries of linguistic and cultural intimidation by France, retains a split inheritance. The Catalan language is still commonly heard in the streets of Prades, and indeed pronunciation of the town's name (as also Perpignan/Perpinyà) signals an individual's allegiance. The town is not itself distinguished or beautiful, and there is a perpetual sense of light but lingering dust, as if God had forgotten to vacuum. But it can be colourful. In winter it is grey and bitterly cold, but in summer its buildings, constructed of the pink stone and terracotta slate of the area, stand out against the lush green of the surrounding valley. Prades is best appreciated at a distance.

Route Nationale 116 runs straight through the town, but changes its name three times on the way; it is the Route de Marquixanes on the east, the Route de Ria on the west and, now, Avenue du Général de Gaulle in the centre of the town. After almost a year in their first and temporary home, Casals and his household moved further down the road to a pretty, double-storey cottage let to them by Madame André Four. The Villa Colette, which faces the gardens of the Hôtel de Ville, became their home for the next nine years. The Alavedra family occupied the ground-floor rooms. On the second level, approached by an external staircase, Casals and Señora Capdevila each had a bedroom, and at the back there was a small additional room which Casals used as a study, and eventually for teaching. From his window at the front of the house he had a clear view of Mount Canigou, at almost 3000 metres the highest peak of this northerly extension of the Pyrenees. Canigou, celebrated in the verse of the nineteenth-century Catalan poet, Jacint Verdaguer, retained a powerful mythological significance: on its slopes stood the Abbey of Saint-Martin, founded in the eleventh century by the legendary Count Guifred. For Casals the mountain became a symbol of Catalan freedom: as he walked each morning with his now elderly dog, Follett, he would lift his hat in emotional greeting.

In Villa Colette the two families lived as one: they shared meal-times, and Casals was contentedly involved in the daily lives of the Alavedra children, checking schoolwork and going to honours evenings.[10] There were many callers, often Catalans – fellow-exiles, journalists or former Republican officials – and politics was high on the agenda. Luis Companys, the Catalan president, had led the Generalitat into exile, until he was arrested by the Gestapo, returned to Spain and immediately executed. A campaign was launched to persuade Casals to take over as president, but he declined; Josep Irla was appointed to lead the Generalitat-in-Exile after 1940, followed in 1954 by the former republican minister, Josep Tarradellas.

Casals continued to work for the refugees, many of whom were now becoming permanent inhabitants of the camps, if not conscripted into the French army or forced to work in organized labour battalions. He was deluged with individual appeals, many of which he would earlier have met from his own resources. But after June 1940 Casals' Paris bank accounts were frozen, and at the same time it became more difficult for donations and supplies from Allied countries to get through. For two years his only performances had been for the benefit of refugee charities, organized by the Red Cross or the French Legion in neighbouring cities of unoccupied France – Montauban, Montpellier, Toulouse, Grenoble, Béziers and Bordeaux, for example. But in the spring of 1941 it became necessary to raise money for his own sustenance as well as for refugee assistance, and Casals arranged a number of professional concert engagements in Switzerland, beginning with a performance in Zurich Town Hall, attended by 1800, on 13 May. During an autumn tour later that year – seven weeks of concerts between July and September – he earned over $8000.[11]

In November 1942, Germany took control of unoccupied France, and life for Casals became immediately more difficult: 'From the moment Hitler had come to power in Germany, I had refused to play . . . but now the Nazis had come to me. We were virtual prisoners of the Germans.'[12] The administration of Prades was now in the hands of the Gestapo and the Vichy militia, and the Villa Colette came under continuous surveillance. Soon agents visited the house, examined Casals' papers and warned him against any kind of political activity.[13] The scrutiny alone had an impact on his standing in the town. People who had formerly been friendly began to turn away: some became openly hostile. Casals was too famous to be inconspicuous, and his sympathies too established to be denied. He became the victim of every rumour – that he was in secret touch with the Resistance organizations, or the Maquis, or indeed that he was working for the Communists. The Communist taint proved difficult to shake off, and lingered for many years: even in 1956 Casals was concerned about inviting the Soviet violinist, David Oistrakh, to the Prades Festival, in case it should be taken as 'confirmation' that he himself was a fellow-traveller.[14] Oistrakh was invited anyway.

As well as an atmosphere of suspicion, the Gestapo brought favouritism and graft. Food was short, but Nazi rationing made it scarcer still. Casals, Capdevila and the Alavedras existed on turnips, beans and green vegetables: milk and meat were rare luxuries, and there was no possibility of sugar or coffee. The winter was severe, and coal – indeed even firewood – was hard to find. For the first time Casals felt signs of rheumatism in his shoulder, and it began to affect his playing. 'At times I felt old and isolated from the world.'[15]

From the earliest days of the German occupation, Casals lived in expectation of arrest, or worse. One day he thought the moment had come. An official car drew up outside the villa and three German officers approached the door. They were young, smooth, elegant and exaggeratedly polite. Once inside Casals' tiny room they clarified the purpose of their visit: they sought Casals' consent to travel for a performance in Berlin. When he declined they persisted, seeking explanations, baiting him to make a false move. They asked to see his cello: he removed it from its case but used his rheumatism to evade the pressure to play. After a taut two hours, during which Casals had not invited the Germans to sit, they left, taking photographs of the house as proof of their visit. On another occasion Casals was warned that his name was on a list of local figures to be apprehended and dealt with. After a Maquis attack on the Gestapo headquarters in Prades, during which two Germans were killed, Casals prepared himself for swift and brutal reprisals. Miraculously, he again escaped.

Casals' decision to remain in France under Nazi occupation was entirely his own. Friends continued to encourage him to abandon Europe, as he had during the First World War. They undertook to procure visas, to arrange his passage, to guarantee him engagements and teaching opportunities in the United States. But Casals was now in his mid-sixties. He had commitments in Spain, and among the refugees, and if he could not be with his brothers and family, he would at least not make it impossible for them to be with him. Since 1936 his whole world had been at war, and he could not simply wipe it from his mind and resume his musical career as if nothing had happened. 'Everything is more important than music', he explained, 'when it is a question of human pain.'

During the period of Nazi occupation, Casals had not given a single public performance. In December 1944, following the Allied landing in Normandy and the withdrawal of Nazi forces from France, he resumed local concerts in aid of the victims of war. On the day before Christmas, the *New York Times* printed a letter revealing to its readers that Casals was not in fact in 'a Franco concentration camp', but 'living in seclusion in the south of France'.[16] It triggered a deluge of invitations from American orchestras and impresarios. A similar inundation had already arrived from Paris, where fifty-six separate organizations had offered to stage the Maestro's first post-war appearance. He decided to ignore them all and to appear in England instead.

During four embattled years in Prades, Casals' principal source of information about the rest of the world had been through the Foreign Service broadcasts of the BBC. Often he had listened under a blanket to hide the sound from outside ears. It was Britain, so it seemed to him, that had defeated Hitler and saved Europe. Now, he felt, Britain held the key to the future of a free Spain. Indeed – more than that – he considered Britain carried a real obligation. For it had been the British Government's policy of non-intervention that had prompted France to withhold aid from the Spanish Republic in 1936, and justified the United States' subsequent decision on neutrality. Churchill had undertaken to eliminate fascism wherever it existed. Now he would surely attend to it in Spain. On 3 May Casals wrote confidently to his former pupil, Germaine Grottiendieck, in Belgium:

The villainous Franco does not seem to want to go. He has betrayed the monarchy, the Republic, his friends and collaborators . . . but happily I know the English. At the point at which they give him the signal to leave, he will go. I expect to be returning to Spain after my concerts in Switzerland at the end of August.[17]

Unhappily, Casals did *not* know the English. Nor did he seem to have appreciated that what a coalition Prime Minister may have said – and the BBC may have reported – during a war was not necessarily what would happen after it. The whole question of the restitution of democracy to Spain shows Casals at his most innocent and gullible. If the British had been capable of swallowing the sham of non-intervention in 1936, while arms for Franco's Nationalists were flooding in from Hitler and Mussolini, they were not likely, after an exhausting war, to embark upon another military initiative in Europe – particularly one from which they now had little to gain. For Churchill and the Conservative Party, neutrality had never been less than an acquiescence in Franco's campaign, tempered by moral revulsion for the violence of his methods. Even the British Labour movement, the source of most of the financial and humanitarian aid to Spanish republicanism, is known now to have been far more equivocal in its attitude to the Civil War than the rhetoric of its leaders suggested at the time: fears of Communism, and resistance to the Republic's persecution of the Catholic Church weakened the overall socialist commitment to the aspirations of a 'free' Spain.[18] For the British, the end of the Civil War had meant the end of 'the Spanish problem'. There was never a chance that the country would seek to dislodge Franco. The only question was how long it would take Casals to find it out.

Casals made two prolonged visits to Britain in 1945. When he arrived for the first, at the end of June, there was in practical terms no real government to deal with: a general election had been declared for 5 July, and the country was at the hustings. But for Casals the visit began in a glow. British Airways refused to accept payment for his ticket, and customs officials declined to interfere with his baggage. His first concert – indeed his first performance with an orchestra since 1939 – took place at the Royal Albert Hall on 27 June when he played the Schumann and Elgar Concertos with the BBC Symphony Orchestra under Sir Adrian Boult. It was a capacity audience and, in addition, a huge crowd had gathered outside the Hall. Germany had surrendered twenty days earlier, Casals was a humanitarian hero, and almost 12,000 people had come to cheer him: after the performance the police had to carve a path to his car. Waiting at the stage door had been his old friend, the Spanish cellist Augustín Rubio, whom Casals had first met at the Café Tost in Barcelona almost seventy years before. 'Remember,' Rubio said, 'that night I told Albéniz the time will come when this little one will make a big stir!'[19]

Immediately after the Albert Hall performance, Casals was taken to Broadcasting House where the concert, recorded that evening, was to be re-broadcast to Catalonia on the Foreign Service. He played his arrangement of *El Cant dels Ocells* (The Song of the Birds), the traditional Catalan melody with which, since he resumed performing the previous November, he had concluded all his concerts. Clenching his jaw to control his emotion, he spoke a few words in Catalan about the song, concluding with the hope 'for a tomorrow of peace, when Catalonia will again be Catalonia'.[20]

Casals had requested Gerald Moore as accompanist for several recitals during the tour, though they had not met before. Moore had established a reputation as one of Europe's finest accompanists and, between the wars, had performed with Guilhermina Suggia, Gaspar Cassadó and, in 1936, with Susan Metcalfe, among many others. The invitation to accompany Casals staggered and terrified Moore: 'After six years of existing in a blackout came this blinding light; I was to play for the world's greatest living musician. It was the biggest assignment I had ever had.'[21] At their first rehearsal they began with the Second Movement of Beethoven's Cello Sonata in D Major (Op. 102, No. 2): Moore had practised the sonata 'with devilish care' for weeks:

> [Casals] sang on his cello and I crouched over my keyboard with every nerve alert and my very soul in my finger-tips. Thus we played away together without exchanging a word. Then, when we had covered two dozen measures, Casals abruptly stopped playing, laid his cello gently on its side and, looking very straight at me, said, 'I am very happy'.[22]

By the time Casals returned to Britain in the second week of October, atom bombs had fallen on Hiroshima and Nagasaki, Japan had surrendered, and the war was over. A Labour Government was in power at Westminster, the talk was of a welfare state and post-war restructuring, and newspaper coverage of Spain seemed sickeningly conciliatory towards the Franco regime. Casals was astonished. The central plinth of his life, the assumption on which everything had been predicated for the last six years, seemed not even to be on the political agenda.

> Was it conceivable, I asked myself, that the Spanish people . . . were to be doomed to continue living under fascist rule? And the hundreds of thousands of refugees who had believed an Allied victory would mean the return of democracy to Spain . . . were they to be condemned to permanent exile?'[23]

The answer, plainly, was yes.

The first concert of the tour was scheduled for 17 October, in London. It was to be followed by four further orchestral performances around the country, six recitals, and a number of private appearances, concluding on 8 November. But first Casals had a commitment to record both the Elgar and Haydn D Major Concertos for Gaisberg's successor, Walter Legge of EMI. The recording of the Elgar, on 14 October, took seven hard hours in the Abbey Road Studios, the second movement needing several reruns. At intense moments of performance Casals would commonly emit quite audible moans and grunts, often anticipating the first notes of the bar he was about to play. On this occasion, the story goes, the emissions were particularly conspicuous. 'Maestro,' protested the engineer, 'we're picking up all your grunts.' 'In that case,' Casals replied, 'you can charge double for the record.' The following morning, again with Boult and the BBC Symphony, Casals recorded the first two movements of the Haydn. But the orchestra was booked elsewhere for the afternoon, and there was no opportunity to record the third.[24] The Concerto has never been released.

The Elgar recording was a repeat of Casals' June performance at the Albert Hall. It was the fourth time he had played the Concerto in London, and the third with Sir Adrian Boult. At the first, in November 1936, the critics had, almost to a man, disliked it. It was, according to the *Daily Telegraph*, 'a reading unstable from beginning to end'; Casals had failed, said the *Musical Times*, 'for the first and probably the only time in his long career'. Thoughtfully, *The Times* explained what had gone wrong: 'Experience goes to show that players who are not Elgar's fellow countrymen find considerable difficulty in catching his particular tone of voice.' Casals had not established, the reviewer considered, 'a basic rhythm for each movement', and by the final coda, 'in which the threads should be gathered together, the concerto was in pieces past the possibility of restoration'.

But in the columns of the *Radio Times*, however, there was a different report. The critic Ralph Hill called the performance 'finer than any I had ever heard before'.[25] Moreover, he ridiculed the view that the Concerto contained some secret national code that foreign artists could not crack. If that were so, he argued, then surely it applied to the music of other countries too? 'Why then is Toscanini viewed as a great interpreter of Debussy, or Thomas Beecham of Sibelius and Wagner?'

Casals' personal files are thick with review clippings, frequently identified and dated in his own hand. If he rarely spoke of them, it seems fairly certain that he read them. Coming to London in the spring of 1945, he knew the critics would be poised to attack, and he tried out bits of the Concerto on several English friends in advance of the performance. This time he seemed to have got it. He played, according to *The Times*, 'rhapsodically, extracting the last drop of autumn sweetness . . . the way that Elgar's melodic line demands'. Indeed Elgar, according to another paper, would now gladly have entrusted the work – despite its 'English-ness' – to Casals, for the cellist 'reached to an Elgarian mood of wistful-ness that few artists now understand'. Adrian Boult was asked to explain the difference between Casals' pre-war and post-war interpretations. 'None,' he replied.[26]

There is a certain irony in the fact that, just at the point Casals came to satisfy the English critics, the English ceased to satisfy him. By the end of the first week of the tour, the realization that Britain intended to do nothing about Franco had destroyed his will to continue. On the way to Reading for a recital with Gerald Moore he announced to his shocked companions that this would be his final visit to the country. Plans for a further tour the following spring were abruptly cancelled, and dis-cussions with HMV about a recording of the Brandenburg Concertos were immediately scrapped. Casals was somehow persuaded to fulfil the scheduled concerts of the current tour, but he refused to participate in any peripheral jollifications. He declined a luncheon arranged in his honour by the Worshipful Company of Musicians on 30 October, and turned down the offer of honorary degrees by both Oxford and Cam-bridge Universities. Myra Hess, by then a national heroine by virtue of the wartime concerts she had arranged at the National Gallery, accom-panied Casals at his final recital, and used her contacts to secure meetings for him at first the House of Commons, and then Buckingham Palace. Casals spent an hour with Sir Alan Lascelles, private secretary to George VI, but refused to meet with the Labour Cabinet Minister, Sir Stafford Cripps: '[He] would speak about politics, and I about morals. We would not understand each other.'[27] For it was what he saw as the socialist betrayal that most disgusted him: 'This is politics without feeling and without honour – a worker's party that bases its electoral appeal on the cry "Down with Franco" and then, having won, bolsters the very same dictator.'[28]

At what would be his last ever solo concert in England, Casals played the Dvořák and Elgar Concertos with the Liverpool Philharmonic and Malcolm Sargent. As he left for France he asked his secretary, Milly Stanfield, to send a cheque for £1000 – almost the entire proceeds of the tour – to the RAF Benevolent Fund.[29] The day after his departure, by some miscalculation, Buckingham Palace sent a car to the Piccadilly Hotel to invite him to speak with the King and Queen.

France was as much a disappointment to Casals as London had been, perhaps more so. Popular acclamation at his first post-war Paris appearance was predictably immense. The Grande Salle Pleyel was packed; no one could remember a comparable demonstration of mass affection. Casals again played the Elgar Concerto, but here there was no preciousness about 'English wistfulness', nor any caution over adjectives. The performance, *Le Soir* observed, was 'réinventant, rajeunissant, réparant, consolant, équilibrant, compensant, animant, [et] ennoblissant'.[30] Casals himself, however, could share none of the lofty sensations: the applause, the honours and the awards came to feel somehow nauseating and shameful when a quarter of a million Spanish Republican refugees remained interned along the Pyrenean border in what had become little more than forced labour camps. During the early spring of 1946 he gave a number of further benefit concerts, and made a single tour to Switzerland. But by December – and his seventieth birthday – he had resolved not to perform in any country that acknowledged Franco's legitimacy. Soon afterwards he decided not to perform at all.

It is unlikely that Casals ever seriously believed that – on its own – his boycott could reverse the inactivity of the West. But he did know that, as a public symbol of opposition to Franco, the honours bestowed on him, by organizations, individuals and indeed governments, served principally to displace their own guilt at their failure to act. He would not give them that comfort. Personally, moreover, he did not have a choice. So long as thousands of his compatriots were denied their fundamental freedom, Casals could take no pleasure in the rewards and gestures of admiration that were so readily offered. He knew that – unlike his own brothers, for example, who had families to support – he was in a position to afford his own conscience. For the rest of his life his actions were defined primarily by his determination not to betray 'the forgotten people'.

Casals' initial expectation of a co-ordinated post-war confrontation with Franco had been unrealistic, but not entirely fanciful. Britain, the United States and France all made declarations of support for some imagined internal upheaval which might oust the dictator and lead to the return of electoral democracy in Spain. In December 1946 the General Assembly of the newly established United Nations voted to exclude the country from its activities and, as member nations, sever diplomatic connections with the Falangist regime. Even some individuals had a significant personal impact on the character of resistance to Spanish fascism. But despite universal admiration for his humanitarian example, Casals himself would never be in the first rank of external threats to Franco. However inappropriately, his standing was compromised both by the rumours of Communism that dogged defeated Republicans across the globe, and by the unedifying rivalry and infighting that seemed a corollary of the exile condition. The historian and writer Salvador de Madariaga, roughly Casals' contemporary and a fellow intellectual, had in contrast left Spain at the beginning of the Civil War. By avoiding association with any particular faction of the Opposition, Madariaga now had access to the highest levels of the British Foreign Office and the US State Department.[31] He too grew rapidly dispirited by the absence of any real British commitment to remove Franco. But he, at least, had the satisfaction of being heard.

Within Spain, too, Madariaga, as a right-winger and political activist, represented a more substantial threat. But for Franco no liberal intellectual was ever more than a minor irritant: 'exiled pieces of Spanish grit', was Jan Morris's sobering description.[32] While constantly attacking his liberal critics, Franco deftly harnessed their opposition to domestic advantage. Rather than mentioning exiles by name, he assaulted them collectively and obliquely – referring bitterly to unspecified subversives, Communists, intellectuals, royalists, and Freemasons – and constructing an overall sense of vicious foreign conspiracy. The historian Paul Preston, in fifteen years of intensive research on Franco, found only two occasions on which 'the Caudillo' had any public connection with Casals' name.[33] Both were in the 1950s, the first in February 1956 when Casals, through the US State Department, applied for the renewal of his Spanish passport. The response, which almost certainly came direct from Franco, was that when the cellist himself made the application, it would be granted. The second, in June 1958, involved a visit to New York by Don Juan, the Bourbon Pretender and son of Alfonso XIII, and a request by him to see Casals. The Spanish Ambassador was detailed to persuade Don Juan that Franco would disapprove of any meeting, in his words, with 'el separatista'. Indeed it was Casals' identification with both Catalan separatism and the exiled royal family that provided the Falange with its most powerful ammunition against him.[34]

For Spanish artists and intellectuals in general, exile was a double-edged sword. At worst – like Lorca – they were killed. Those who survived faced a choice of endorsing Franco or being forgotten inside Spain.[35] If they returned to the country, like Joan Miró for example, they were turned into propaganda trophies, and had to stomach a lifetime of censorship. If they remained in exile they gradually lost touch with their roots, and sometimes their inspiration. The Nationalist victory deprived Spain of an entire generation of writers, musicians and artists, and the country declined, as a result, into a cultural wasteland. Franco himself was astoundingly uncultured. He had no appreciation of literature or classical music – the *zarzuela* being the upper level of his musical taste – and could dismiss their exponents without any sense of loss. Within Spain Casals had always been the property of a cultured elite: Bach was not a mass preoccupation. After a decade of exile he, like many others, had been largely forgotten, except by a Catalan few. Spain was deprived of a quality musical culture for almost forty years.

Casals' decision to silence his cello in response to the world's neglect of human rights in Spain was 'the greatest sacrifice of my life'.[36] It was therefore hardly surprising that he should react with fury and disgust to those of his colleagues, and especially his friends, who had not only capitulated to fascist entreaties to perform, but who now, after the war, continued with their careers as if there was no shame in the world. What Casals sought was a sense of repentance. What those involved could not comprehend was why they needed to repent to him. It caused enormous pain on all sides. Casals had seen Jacques Thibaud in London in November 1945, but they had not been able to agree: 'He only made excuses,' Casals told friends, 'he did not say he had been wrong.'[37] Wilhelm Furtwängler, in exile in Switzerland, came in 1945 to seek Casals' support in the enquiry into his wartime record. Casals could do little, nor would he have sought to contribute to an exoneration. But the mood of the encounter itself brought an element of peace to the relationship. Pressed later to perform the Brahms Double Concerto with Yehudi Menuhin under Furtwängler, Casals told Menuhin he was willing in theory, since Furtwängler was 'a clean man'. But in practice it was impossible: 'I am considered the leader of the anti-fascists . . . and they would not understand.'[38]

While Casals' greatest fury was reserved for Cortot, and a little less for Pierre Fournier, his manifest brutality was exercised upon Gaspar Cassadó. For a Spaniard to remain 'apolitical' over the Spanish Civil War was bad enough. For him then to perform in Nazi Germany, and live in Fascist Italy, was beyond forgiveness. In what the critic Stephen Walsh has termed Casals' indulgence of 'Jesuitical reasoning without Jesuitical intent', he publicly supported the New York boycott of Cassadó when the cellist attempted to play there in 1949.[39] Menuhin himself identified the primary impulse as coming not from Casals himself but from 'a coterie of my New York colleagues who more or less ran the first few festivals at Prades, making wonderful music with Casals but also using his prestige for their own purposes, including punishment campaigns against suspect musicians'.[40] He intervened on Cassadó's behalf and found Casals as swiftly merciful as he could be suddenly ruthless.

Returned to Prades in enforced if not contented retirement, Casals found he now had the time and inclination for activities which for years had been impossible. He began to compose again, and soon he resumed some teaching, but for the next ten years the major part of his energy was devoted to refugee aid. A sizeable proportion of the original Republican exodus had returned to Spain. Of those who remained – 160,000 by the early 1950s – many had been absorbed into the local economy. But there remained a substantial number, including the old, the sick and the impoverished, who were incapable of caring for themselves. Casals became involved in the welfare of some 600 families, and his correspondence was crowded with the detail of their lives. 'Casals is my friend,' wrote a Montauban factory worker, 'he knows my entire life . . . my denture, my stomach and my sadness.'[41] Casals was associated with the Paris-based refugee charity, Chaînes du Bonheur International, and consulted by them on the disbursement of substantial sums to children's organizations within and outside Spain.[42] In January 1953 he became joint chairman of Spanish Refugee Aid Inc., a New York-based charity organization which solicited funds within the United States on behalf of families in exile in France. Casals wrote personally to every substantial donor, and kept a precise record of where and for what purpose the money – over 100,000 francs each month – was spent.

Cultural aid, too, became a priority. As Franco began the harshest persecution of the Catalan language in history – it was prohibited in schools, the press and literature in 1939 – the annual Jocs Florals de la Llengua Catalana went into exile. The Jocs Florals (Floral Games), founded in the fourteenth century and revived in 1859, consisted of an annual cultural competition celebrating the Catalan language and its literature: it was in effect the 'spinal column', as one critic put it, of the Catalan Renaissance. After the Civil War the Games were held in Latin America, Cuba, France and, in 1947, in London. Casals was prominently involved in Catalan cultural activities abroad, and a special edition of the *Adam International Review*, produced that year to give Catalan writers an outlet in English and French, was dedicated jointly to him and to his fellow-exile Pompeu Fabre, the philologist and scholar, who died in Prades two years later.[43]

When the Jocs Florals were celebrated in Perpignan in 1943, Juan Alavedra won a prize for a poem, written for a child, on the subject of the Nativity. Casals, one of whose earliest memories had been the sight of the crib on Christmas morning as he came, a five-year-old chorister, to sing mass at the Church of Santa Anna in El Vendrell, immediately began work on setting the poem to music. After two years the piece had grown into a full-length oratorio, *El Pessebre* (The Manger), which, when finally completed in Puerto Rico in 1960, more than ten years later, became the pivot of the campaign for peace which dominated the final years of Casals' life.

For a man brought up to reject the trappings of organized religion, it is remarkable that the bulk of his compositions, certainly those that survive, were written for the Church. One of the profound spiritual influences of Casals' life was the monastery of Montserrat, a community of eighty-four Benedictine monks, 60 kilometres north-west of Barcelona and both physically and emotionally sunk into the heart of the rock of Catalonia. For eight centuries the monastery has been a place of pilgrimage – to the Black Virgin of Montserrat, a twelfth-century wooden image of the Madonna – and of music: its choir school, the Escolanía, is thought to be the oldest in Europe. For Casals the combination of Montserrat's fantastic setting, its Catalan heritage, its musical traditions and the simplicity of its monastic order was irresistible. He discovered, when first teaching in Barcelona after 1896, that the monastery contained some of the finest scholarly and artistic minds of Spain, and between 1920 and 1936 he was drawn back to it and became close to many of the monks. All his choral works were dedicated to Montserrat, and first performed in the Abbey. Scored for male chorus and organ, the best-known pieces, *O vos Omnes* (1933), *Nigra Sum* (1942) and *Tota Pulchra* (also 1942) reveal Casals' deep familiarity with the structure of Gregorian chant and medieval polyphony. Before his reinterment in Spain in November 1979, Casals' remains lay in the Sacristy at Montserrat as the choir of the Escolanía honoured him with his own cantatas.[44]

Late in 1946, the first pupil to be taught by Casals in exile arrived in Prades. Since the end of the war there had been many enquiries, but he had turned them away or referred them to other teachers. The American cellist Bernard Greenhouse had studied with Felix Salmond at the Juilliard School, and subsequently at the terrifying hands of both Feuermann and Alexanian. But Casals had always been his idol: at the age of ten, in Newark, New Jersey, he had practised with the window wide open in case Casals should walk by and hear him.[45] Despite a recommendation from Alexanian, Casals turned down Greenhouse's first enquiry. But the thirty-year-old cellist travelled to Paris, enrolled at the American School at Fontainebleau, and sent a postcard to Prades. Casals relented and offered to hear him, provided Greenhouse would donate $100 to Spanish refugee charities.

For Greenhouse it was a leap in the dark. He spoke no French, barely knew where Prades was, and had little idea what he would do if Casals turned him down again. He took the train to Perpignan, and on to Prades, where the proprietor of the Grand Hôtel, seeing his cello, refused him a room: the last cellist to stay there – Casals – had disturbed the other guests. He took a tiny room in a private house and, two days later, presented himself at the Villa Colette for his audition. Casals, who was in his pyjamas, invited Greenhouse to warm up while he changed, and disappeared. After playing for twenty minutes, with his back to the door, the young man turned around and saw Casals listening at the keyhole. He was still in his pyjamas: he had not wanted Greenhouse to be nervous. They talked for an hour about Greenhouse's background and motivation, and finally Casals agreed to take him as a pupil. The cost would be $20 a lesson. The Grand Hôtel, into which Greenhouse eventually inveigled himself, charged a dollar a night including meals.

Of all Casals' pupils, Greenhouse struggled hardest for the privilege of studying with him: it was he who broke down Casals' resistance to the idea of teaching at all, of taking time from his focus on refugee aid. In return Greenhouse received the most intense and thorough tuition: he studied for a year, having two or three lessons a week, each of about three hours. The first hour was spent playing, and the second in discussion of musical technique. The third hour Casals devoted to reminiscences about his life, as he did later with José Maria Corredor and Albert Kahn. The difference was that Greenhouse, alas, did not write them down.

Subsequent students did not receive such indulgence: for them it was solid work, and solid music. Zara Nelsova came at the end of 1947, and spent seven weeks in Prades. Greenhouse would practise all day, but as he returned from dinner each night he would hear Nelsova still working in her room at the hotel. During the lessons, Casals would sit with his cello, facing his pupils, frequently playing with them, or rehearsing a piece bar by bar. He had a 'molecular subtlety', Christopher Bunting remembered, and was 'unbelievably analytical, obsessively analytical'. Bunting arrived in 1952, and for ten months studied nothing but the Dvořák Concerto and the Bach Suite in D Major. Casals would sit across the room, pipe in his mouth, saying 'again . . . again . . . again', and finally, 'exactly'.[46] Bunting would emerge from the lessons drained and exhausted, and return to his room to practise relentlessly. It was however far from a sadistic method of teaching, Bunting recalled, though it would not be acceptable today. It represented an intensive joint search for the right interpretation, though in the end there would be only one interpretation. 'If you did not want to accept this, you did not learn with Casals.' Some students could not accept it, and left sooner than they had expected to. After three months, in 1955, the Israeli cellist Uzi Wiesel found himself 'playing like [Casals] – imitating the smallest gradation of colour, intonation, speed, glissandi, phrasing . . . I was becoming a lesser replica . . . and I felt artistically strangled, so I had to leave before it was too late'.[47]

Students responded to the approach in different ways, of course. In general it is probably true that Casals did not take as pupils the most inspired, self-confident solo virtuosi – or at least his pupils did not become that. Those, commonly, stayed away. But students who made it through the Casals experience of intense disciplinary control found they could, afterwards, apply the approach to almost any work. In Bernard Greenhouse's case, Casals spent several weeks on a single Bach Suite, the D Minor. Finally they sat down and played it together, with identical fingerings, bowings and phrasings: 'It was as if that room had stereophonic sound – two cellos producing at once.'[48] When they had finished, Casals asked Greenhouse to sit and listen. He played the Suite again, changing every bowing, every fingering, every phrase and every emphasis. The sound was heavenly. Casals put down his cello. 'Now you've learned how to improvise in Bach.'[49]

Some pupils came for help with interpretation, and others to concentrate on technique. Pamela Hind O'Malley arrived for an audition in December 1949 and had her first lesson two days later. At it she played the Prelude from the Bach Suite in C, and pieces by Mendelssohn and Rossini. Casals announced that both her right and left hands were weak, but that he would teach her if she had 'patience and interest'.[50] O'Malley remained until the end of January, and returned the following winter for a further sequence of lessons. In the interim she published an account of her experience in the magazine of the Royal College of Music.[51]

Amaryllis Fleming came to Prades in the summer of 1950 with a very tricky pedigree. The daughter of Augustus John – the painter of Guilhermina Suggia – she had indeed studied with Suggia in Porto, as well as with Cassadó and Pierre Fournier, both of whom Casals had, of course, condemned for their connections with fascism. Fleming asked to study the Schumann Concerto, on which she had previously worked with Fournier. Casals proceeded to alter – perhaps deliberately – every bowing and fingering Fleming had learned from Fournier, and it was two years before she could approach the Concerto with a clear mind.[52]

What all Casals' students came to recognize was that there was no law of the cello he would not break if he thought the music required it. The paramountcy of the sound over the methods used to achieve it was for many a complete artistic liberation. There are numerous accounts of the specifics of Casals' technical instruction for string performance.[53] From them several common features emerge. The first is the issue of intonation. Casals was fanatical about intonation: 'You hear when a note is false the same way you feel when you do something wrong in life.' But it did not mean that he was bound by any pre-ordained mathematical formula. For Casals, notes were not independent entities of fixed position, but variable stages in a developing organic line. Semitones, in particular, were bound in a relationship of 'gravitational attraction' to the tonics to which they led. Casals' pupils absorbed a theory of 'expressive intonation', whereby semitones could be sharpened, or flattened, in relation to their place within the directional pull of the music. The technique impressed even pianists: Daniel Barenboim declared it had made him very conscious of the 'geographical position of the notes'.[54]

Similarly, Casals introduced techniques of an almost sacrilegious nature in other areas. Because of his obsession with clarity and articulation, he recommended a percussive technique with the fingers of the left hand to set the string in vibration. The fingers were to be 'thrown' like sprung hammers on to the strings, and relaxed immediately. He encouraged his students to rehearse pieces without the use of the bow. In terms of fingering, Casals eliminated formal shifts, encouraging a lizard movement, with jerks down, to produce a sound which was clean, clear and compelling. The player should use the stronger fingers wherever possible: 'The cello is so difficult to play that we must make use of every natural facility. . . . We never gain anything by trying to do things against nature.'[55] Nor in terms of bowing was Casals frightened of dropping the bow upon the string. Preparing to play the opening theme of the Dvořák Concerto, Casals' bow would 'hover for a moment high in the air – like an eagle watching its prey – before slashing upon the string with stunning impact'.[56]

Many pupils came to Casals with what they imagined to be an accomplished and elegant vibrato, and were surprised to have it totally reconstructed. 'Vibrato', he argued, 'is a means of expressing sensitivity, but it is not a proof of it': again, it needed to be harnessed to the requirements of the music. Bernard Greenhouse thought he was in Prades to learn about interpretation, but Casals announced that there was 'a slight vulgarity' to his playing: 'You do not use the vibrato to make music.'[57] He asked him to begin practising without a vibrato, then gradually reintroduced it in different forms: an arm vibrato for the lower strings, an elbow vibrato for the middle strings, and a finger vibrato for the higher register. 'This ability to vary the speed and the width of the vibrato changed my whole approach to phrasing,' Greenhouse later admitted. 'It was like a whole new spectrum.'[58]

Only a small proportion of the cellists who applied to Casals were accepted. Most were referred to other teachers, a few were invited to make the long journey to Prades for an audition. It was a risk. In 1949 a young player travelled from New Zealand. After a brief hearing, Casals declined to take him, and he returned home.[59] Those who succeeded had to make distinct sacrifices for the privilege. Living in Prades was one of them. Conditions were often primitive, and the winters were particularly bleak. Christopher Bunting and his wife lived in a garret in rue de la

République, with cold running water and a butane gas stove for heat. Bernard Greenhouse practised with an electric toaster under his chair, to provide at least a modicum of warmth. Amaryllis Fleming could not afford the price of meals at the Grand Hôtel and was ejected from her room: the brothers Pepito and Ramon, relatives of Casals' sister-in-law Teresina, found her a cheap room with a Catalan family, and with cockroaches.

By 1950 there was always a handful of students in the town, though they rarely associated. Their primary bond was with Casals, and he clearly preferred it that way: he was consistently well informed about occurrences in the town. If Bunting went dancing at the Casino, one of Prades' few places of entertainment, he would be told next day that it had affected his playing. One summer's day Amaryllis Fleming bathed naked, and alone, in the river Têt. At her next lesson Casals observed that she should be careful of her health. And if his pupils stayed up too late at a party, or became too friendly with the young people of the town, Casals would angrily accuse them of neglecting their work. For Casals, life was not a recreation. Music was a serious business. For most of his students it was the greatest musical experience of their career.

# 10

## Resurrection: The Bach Festival, 1949–1950

C'est vous, Sasha, qui a pris pitié de mon silence.
*Casals to Alexander Schneider*, 1950[1]

In December 1949 Casals turned seventy-three. He had been in exile for a dozen years and had long since abandoned any realistic expectation of an early return to Spain. His friend and biographer, Lillian Littlehales, visiting Prades in 1948, referred to him simply as 'in retirement'.[2] By now Casals was a legendary figure, politically as well as musically: his unequivocal condemnation of the failure of the Western alliance to take action against Franco after 1945, and his refusal to perform in any country whose government recognized the Spanish dictatorship, had made him much more than simply a great artist. In the words of one critic, he had become 'a symbol of the living endeavour of art to change the physical condition of life'.[3] But international honour and respect seemed slight reward for shouldering the burden of moral principles which the rest of the free world appeared to have shelved. And popular acclaim did not bring private contentment. Casals had forfeited his home, his music, his family and most of his friends, without prospect of recovery. Political exile had turned into artistic incarceration.

In the twelve years after leaving Spain, Casals had had few opportunities to perform. Since 1946 he had given no major concert, except for occasional recitals in neighbouring towns and villages in aid of Catalan refugees. His life was a routine of teaching, practice and composition, appealing in a way for a man of his age, but much less than he was used to. After ten years of what began as a 'temporary' billet in the tiny Villa Colette, he had at least now moved to larger and moderately more imposing quarters in the gardener's gatehouse cottage of the Château Valroc, a substantial family mansion, adjoining the Hôtel de Ville on the Route Nationale. Juan Alavedra and his family, who had accompanied Casals into exile, had returned to Spain earlier in 1949, along with other Catalans for whom the excitement of exile, such as there was, had been replaced by the inexorability of it. Señora Capdevila was continually unwell and often depressed. Casals, as powerfully loyal to her as she had long been to him, refused all invitations which required his absence from Prades and from her side. The result was a highly circumscribed life for the world's most celebrated musician, and there was no prospect that it would change. Despite his energy, and despite himself, he was becoming an old man.

The year 1950, however, was to bring one of the most rejuvenating musical experiences of Casals' life, and a radically new mood. The catalyst was Alexander (Sasha) Schneider. Schneider, a brilliant Lithuanian violinist, had been concert-master of the Frankfurt Symphony at seventeen, before becoming, in 1933, second violin with the Budapest String Quartet. In the United States after 1947 and a member of the Albeneri Trio, he had taken the decision to set aside chamber playing in order to work in detail on Bach's Unaccompanied Violin Suites. A chance meeting with Bernard Greenhouse, just back from France, led to his interrupting a tour of Europe to travel to Prades early in June to visit Casals: Schneider came bearing an introduction from his teacher – and Casals' friend from Paris days – Diran Alexanian. The encounter was immediately successful. Schneider described the three days he spent with Casals as the best of his life.[4] Schneider was forty-one, ebullient, impetuous and an exceptionally gifted musician. As a Jew from Vilna he too was in exile. Although Sasha and his brother Mischa had escaped Nazi Europe, his mother, sister and elder brother Grisha had been taken to the concentration camps. Only in 1947, in Paris, did Schneider see Grisha and his family again – for the first time in seventeen years. At the same time he learned that his mother and sister had died in Auschwitz. It transformed his view of the world. And he wrote to Casals that 'since I have seen the tragedy of Europe there is nothing left in my mind of any sort, nor is there left any kind of personal egotism about my own ambition'.[5] Casals' reaction to post-war Europe had been to retreat in horror and disgust. Schneider's was to throw himself with passion and vigour into music-making. He was exactly what Casals needed.

Schneider returned to Prades the following summer, living in the Grand Hôtel and working each day on the Bach Suites. That autumn he performed them in public in the United States for the first time before returning again to Prades in the summer of 1949. By then Schneider, who had a taste for the good things in life, musical and otherwise, began to chafe at the restrictions and deprivations Casals had imposed upon himself. Already he had taken steps to relieve the austerity. In July 1948, as a kind of early birthday gift, Casals had received a set of the complete Bach *Gesellschaft*, forty-six volumes of the photo-offset edition issued by

Edwards Publishers in Ann Arbor, Michigan. Hearing of the gift in advance, Casals recommended it be labelled 'cadeau – hommage' to avoid customs duties; to receive the *Gesellschaft* was, he told his friend Rafael Moragas, 'one of the purest joys of my life'.[6] The gift was co-ordinated by Schneider, but readily paid for by 10-dollar donations from musicians, friends and admirers of Casals in the United States, starved of his playing for twenty years.[7] Among the donors were Alexanian, Adolf and Fritz Busch, Paul Hindemith, Artur Schnabel, Bruno Walter, Arturo Toscanini, Arthur Rubinstein, Rudolf Serkin, Igor Stravinsky and Serge Koussevitzky.[8] When he learned of the gift some months later, Eugène Ormandy was incensed at not having been approached to contribute.[9] Next from Paris came a Pleyel grand piano, chosen on Schneider's behalf by the pianist Yvonne Lefebure, and paid for – $800 on the black market – by a friend, Cameron Baird of Buffalo, to replace the out-of-tune upright which was all Casals had.[10] Casals welcomed the new instrument, but kept the old one all the same.

In the summer of 1949 Schneider's treat was to bring to Prades outstanding musicians with whom Casals might play chamber music. There was Schneider's Frankfurt violin teacher, Adolf Rebner, a viola player, Milton Thomas – who was there for lessons at $50 a time – and two of Casals' former pupils, Madeline Foley and Zara Nelsova. Their return to London at the end of July left 'a big emptiness', partly filled by the arrival of Alexanian and Bernard Greenhouse, and the singer Doda Conrad.

A rare joy though the opportunity for chamber music was to Casals, it was only a taste of the plans Schneider was developing. From their first meeting, Schneider had raised the possibility of a series of North American concerts. To him it seemed an appalling waste that a talent such as that of Casals should remain unused in a dusty French town, and he engineered huge financial inducements. It was endearing but hopeless. The longer Casals remained silent, the greater his market value, of course, particularly within America. But the longer his sacrifice, the firmer too his commitment to his principles. Invitations to play, conduct and record in all the major capitals were politely refused, or ignored. The greatest temptation was the approaching bicentenary of the death of Bach, and the many invitations to participate in events being organized to mark it. For Casals these were close to irresistible. But he did resist, and Schneider soon realized it was useless to try further. An alternative idea came from Mieczyslaw Horszowski, who knew Casals better than anyone, and was communicated to Schneider over dinner in October 1948. If Casals would not be brought to America, America would be brought to him. Schneider wrote suggesting 'a Bach Festival next summer, in June or July, in Prades or Perpignan, under your direction'.[11]

The new plan was to select a group of leading orchestral players from Europe and America and bring them to Prades for a series of chamber concerts which Casals would conduct. Among the concerts would be some solo recitals, during which Casals would play the six Bach Cello Suites. In theory it seemed an absurd plan: Prades was inaccessible and unsuitable; it had no adequate hotels, no auditorium, and no obvious audience. Casals said no, just as, at the same time, he refused many other invitations: to a major Bach celebration at the US Library of Congress, to a concert at Bach's own Thomas Kirche in Leipzig, and to perform with Schweitzer in Strasbourg.[12] These were not insignificant invitations, and his refusal was no light matter. To an extent it was a matter of confidence. As well as not having performed since 1945, Casals had heard precious little live music during those years. A new generation of cellists was performing in the concert-halls of the world. He did not know them. He no longer knew how he compared, whether he still had his touch: 'Bit by bit I lay aside any idea of returning to an active musical life.'[13] The realization after 1945 that fascism in Spain would not be eliminated as it had been in Germany and Italy led Casals to the decision not merely to withhold his talent, but to withdraw from performance permanently. To the world he announced that what had begun as a boycott of the countries that recognized Franco's Spain had turned into a more general disappointment with what he saw as the complicity of the West in a profound moral wrong:

> It is because I think it is immoral that people have forgotten that the German war cost about thirty million lives . . . every nation has forgotten and receives – as if nothing has happened – all the people that took the side of the Germans. . . . I do not want to mix up in this kind of a world.[14]

In the quiet of exile, Casals saw no alternative but to retire from music. For more than half a century he had performed, taught, travelled and recorded. Now, for reasons he saw as overwhelmingly conclusive, his performing life was over. But it was not quite that easy. Within every great musician is a permanent tension between the urge to perform and the fear of performance. After crushing his left hand on Mount Tamalpais in 1902, Casals had felt a strange, momentary elation as if a curse had been lifted: 'dedication to one's art', he later observed, 'does involve a sort of enslavement'.[15] Alexander Schneider's achievement was to recover Casals' need to make music in the face of his determination to withhold it, and to convince him that a festival in the place of his exile would not diminish his protest, but reinforce it. By summer 1949 Casals had sanctioned the idea of a Bach Festival, and the course of his life had irretrievably altered. Although between 1950 and his death in 1973 Casals' commitment to freedom and his opposition to totalitarianism remained uncompromised on his own or any other terms, he had been liberated to use his most powerful weapon – his musical gift. The silence was over. Schneider set energetically to work to arrange a festival for June 1950.

Planning a festival in one country, to take place in another, 5000 miles away, was bound to be complicated. In New York Schneider established an 'executive committee', made up of musicians – Horszowski and Leopold Mannes – and wealthy figures prominent in the arts – Elizabeth Sprague Coolidge, Cameron Baird, Rosalie J. Leventritt and Carlton Sprague Smith. A further committee was set up in Perpignan, under Casals' close friend and private doctor, René Puig, to co-ordinate the European arrangements, with sub-offices in Paris and London, where Casals' English secretary, Milly Stanfield, ran a fund-raising operation nominally headed by John Barbirolli and Adrian Boult. The crucial decisions on programming and the choice of artists were effectively taken by Schneider in consultation with Casals. Throughout the winter of 1949–50 letters and cables went backwards and forwards between Prades and Schneider's home in Beekman Place, New York. What was not in short supply was goodwill: in January Schneider reported that he was pursued by musicians willing to upset their contractual bookings to come to Prades and join the Festival orchestra.[16] In March 1950 he flew to Zurich and travelled on by train to Prades to check final details with Casals.

The main anxiety was money. The phenomenon of Casals, after years of silence, playing the full set of Bach Unaccompanied Suites and conducting the Brandenburg Concertos was clearly superb box-office. The problem was that he was doing it in an inaccessible French town no American had heard of. An application to the Fulbright Foundation was turned down. Schneider's next idea was that the entire Festival should be recorded, the royalties subsidizing festivals in subsequent years, and providing Casals with funds to support his work for Catalan refugees. The first choice of recording company was His Master's Voice, with whom, in Europe, Casals had recorded for some time. But HMV's royalties were paid in England, and Casals' British interests had, since the German invasion of France, been frozen in his London account at the Midland Bank in the Strand. Friends in England had appealed to the British Foreign Office for the release of assets now described, in a phrase highly uncongenial to Casals, as 'enemy property'.[17] But pending an appeal to the Office des Charges in Paris, under the Custodian of Enemy

Property legislation, an exclusive two-year deal was made with Columbia Records in New York, who would pay unencumbered in US dollars.

Columbia agreed to advance $25,000 – payable after the Festival on delivery of the recording-tapes – to cover administrative overheads. The thirty-five invited musicians would come essentially for nothing, receiving expenses and $300 apiece. The initial expectation was that Casals himself would receive $30,000 in the first two years of the Festival, subsequently revised to $50,000.[18] Since Casals had been capable of earning twice this amount in a single tour of the United States twenty years earlier, the sums in question seemed fairly modest. In the context of post-war France, however, and given that he had not earned anything for five years, it was certainly useful money. But even this was unachievable: early forecasts of both the costs of the Festival, and the revenue accruing from it, proved seriously unrealistic.

Towards the end of April the musicians chosen for the proposed chamber orchestra began to arrive in Prades. Twenty came from the United States, including John Wummer, first flute of the New York Philharmonic–Symphony, Marcel Tabuteau, first oboe of the Philadelphia Orchestra, and Daniel Saidenberg, a cellist and conductor of the Connecticut Symphony Orchestra. Rehearsals began on 5 May in the dining-room of the Collège Moderne des Jeunes Filles. At the start of the first rehearsal Casals said, simply and emotionally, 'Thank you for coming. I love you. And now let's begin.' The Festival Orchestra was manifestly an oddity: an aggregate of some colossally gifted individuals, chosen from around the world, alongside 'a few who would be barely passable in a first-rank American ensemble'.[19] They had not played together before; some had not played in an orchestral ensemble for years. But it was a highly select group, there being at least three realistic candidates for every place in the orchestra among those who had put themselves forward. By and large they were young, confident performers some of whom, twenty years on, would be among the first rank of international soloists. And there was a sense in which they had been picked 'to continue the tradition'. Casals chose Schneider as his concert-master, with his own brother Enrique as leader of the second violins. Paul Tortelier was first cellist, with some of Casals' best pupils alongside him. The most obvious absentee, and perhaps the player most missed, was Maurice Eisenberg. Eisenberg had been in Prades to see Casals earlier in the spring, but in May had had to return to the United States for the high-school graduation of his son – and Casals' godson – Pablo.

The rehearsals began with the First Brandenburg Concerto. Tortelier, who had had no contact with Casals since 1945, later remembered the emotional power he extracted from the slow movement, and particularly the poignant D minor dialogue between violin and oboe. 'Performing that movement with Casals was unutterably moving. It was, I think, the most beautiful moment of my musical life.'[20]

What the members of the Festival Orchestra experienced, between the first rehearsal and the close of the Festival on 19 June was, in effect, a gigantic Bach masterclass by his supreme interpreter. There were two rehearsals each day, at 9.30 in the morning and then at 5.00 in the afternoon, with the concert beginning at about 9.00 p.m. For visitors to Prades, a special attraction was the opportunity to attend a rehearsal – a privilege guarded and granted by Schneider himself – to see and hear how Casals worked, how he built up a reading of a musical work, phrase by phrase. For the players, too, the rehearsals were the inspiring highlight. As they wrote to Casals in a collective letter after the Festival:

> When we first played together, people from different nations, languages, beliefs, religions, personalities and styles of playing . . . we had much spirit but little ensemble. Patiently, you explained a phrase. We listened, and played what we understood you to mean, if not what you meant. As the weeks went by, each gave up a little of his individuality, a little of his ego . . . blended his style to the ensemble. The results were obvious.[21]

The first concert of the Bach Commemorative Festival took place on 2 June in the Church of St Pierre, the only venue in Prades suitable for an orchestral concert. The performance, scheduled for 9 p.m., did not begin until 10, when the Bishop of Perpignan began a lengthy speech of welcome and praise for the whole idea of the Festival. As he spoke, Casals warmed up in the sacristy, then entered the church, carrying his cello and wearing an expression, in the words of Cyrus Durgin, music critic of the *Boston Globe*, 'blended of impassivity, bewilderment and preoccupation'.[22] Since this was a church, there was no applause: the audience simply rose in silent greeting. A chair had been set on a raised platform in front of the heavily ornate gold and pastel blue altar. Casals sat, twitched the chair about, ran his fingers briefly over the fingerboard to test the strings, and began the Prelude of Bach's First Cello Suite in G Major. The tension of the moment was palpable. The church was packed with reporters, critics, visiting dignitaries and professional musicians from around the world. And it was heavily wired for sound recording, even though, at Casals' insistence, the equipment was not switched on until after the opening Suite. Only a handful of close friends had heard Casals play in recent years, and no one knew what nerves or the emotion of the occasion would do to his performance. For a decade

Casals had maintained that 'his cello was his only weapon'. The world waited to discover whether the weapon still had force, and whether the Festival itself was to be more than an orgy of sentimental nostalgia. Even the members of the Festival Orchestra were on the edge of their seats: for the entire month of rehearsals, none had heard Casals put bow to strings. But it required only a few bars to reveal that nothing had faded; Casals played simply, smoothly and precisely. For the audience it may have been ten years since they had heard that sound. For Casals it was one more performance of a Suite he had played virtually every day for the past sixty years. The French correspondent of *The Strad* magazine called it 'strong, ethereal, gruff, elusive', while Cyrus Durgin described it simply as 'the supremely fine music-making of the greatest cellist in the world'.[23] When Casals had finished the Suite, he bowed and walked slowly from the chancel, as the audience again rose to its feet. Quite plainly, he, rather than Bach, was now the centrepoint of the Festival.

The first concert continued with Casals conducting the orchestra in the Second and Third Brandenburg Concertos and the D Minor Piano Concerto, with Yvonne Lefebure as soloist.[24] In a formal sense, the Festival consisted of twelve such concerts, half of them chamber recitals and half orchestral concerts. More accurately, though, Prades was, for six weeks, the centre of a musical experience. There were musicians everywhere, practising where they could. Even among those not performing, there was a good deal of impromptu music-making: for visitors the random presence, in a town of no musical pretensions, of soloists like Rudolf Serkin, Clara Haskil, Joseph Szigeti, Isaac Stern and Mieczyslaw Horszowski, made for an exciting atmosphere. There was a shortage of rooms to practise in, and a shortage of pianos: Serkin found himself rehearsing on an ancient, abused instrument discovered in the neighbouring spa village of Vernet-les-Bains, much to the pleasure of a visiting Englishwoman lodging next door.[25] Musically the Festival was something of a shock. Though Casals had made recordings and played notable concerts in the mid-1940s, he had not made an international tour for a generation; apart from a few isolated trips to Switzerland, no one had heard him since 1945. He had become almost a mythological figure: was the memory accurate? The Bach Festival answered the question. But for younger musicians who had grown up unfamiliar with his approach, it was a surprise to encounter, suddenly and unexpectedly, a musical style so at odds with the purist orthodoxy now widely followed and represented most conspicuously in the style of Toscanini. For some the contrast was merely a curiosity. For others it was a revelation, as the pianist Eugene Istomin later recalled:

The predominant performing style of our times, which most of my contemporaries naturally acquired, is a kind of electric, antiseptic style. We got very good at it, and at the drop of a hat could go into a hall and give a perfect, brilliant, and meaningless performance. Casals, by his example and his nature, reminded us of something we had forgotten, or hadn't dared contemplate: the importance in music of color and variety, of feeling, warmth, involvement . . . of ultimate human values and meaning.[26]

The Bach Festival was a landmark in Casals' history as a recording artist. Before 1950 a choice but small proportion of his performances had been recorded. Thereafter virtually everything of importance was cut on disc, if not issued on it, and from 1957 a good deal also was filmed. In return for its initial $25,000 advance on royalties in 1950, Columbia secured the right to record every moment of the Bach Festival except Casals' own solo performance – up to ninety sides, or thirty hours of music. Five months later, on 13 November, it issued its treasure, from which it expected to make between $500,000 and $700,000.[27] On ten discs it included the six Brandenburg Concertos, the Sonatas for Viola da Gamba and Harpsichord (Nos. 1, 2 and 3), the Orchestral Suites (Nos. 1 and 2), the Italian Concerto, the Concerto for Violin and Oboe in C Minor, the Concerto for Two Violins in D Minor, the Violin Concertos in A Minor and D Minor, the Clavier Concerto in F Minor, the Triple Concerto, a trio sonata for violin, flute and continuo, the Sonata for Flute and Harpsichord in B Minor, the English Suite No. 5 in E Minor, as well as several 'filler' piano solos played by Serkin, Istomin and Lefebure.[28] Also recorded in June 1950 and issued later as part of a series of 'meditational music' were the Bach Largo, Casals' 1943 composition of a Catalan *sardana* (*Sant Marti del Canigou: Sardana del l'Exili*) and Enrique's orchestration of *El Cant dels Ocells*. A similar volume of music was recorded at the 1951, 1952 and 1953 Festivals, providing Columbia with a vast reservoir from which to draw for new releases, reissues and premium offers for many years. It was a remarkably effective investment.

It is of course an unkind legacy for an instrumentalist that two-thirds of the work by which he is remembered should date from his seventy-fourth year and beyond. Casals was close to forty by the time he made even his earliest acoustic recordings: at the same age, Emanuel Feuermann, the cellist most often ranked with him this century, was already dead. Casals was sixty before he recorded the full set of Bach Unaccompanied Suites, or any of the major cello concertos. From these later solo performances, together with the great chamber recordings of the 1920s and early 1930s, the listener can only imagine the quality and sound which Casals would have produced at the peak of his solo career. But the real sound of the young Casals at full strength is lost, and we shall never know what he made of those staples of his early repertoire – the Lalo or Saint-Saëns Concertos, for example – which he failed to record at any time. The omission is to be regretted, but no more. Casals himself set little store by recorded performance: the sound was never as he remembered it. In an age in which a recorded rather than a live perform-ance represents the most frequent musical experience, it is worth recog-nizing that, very often, recording is a betrayal of the actual. For a major element in performance is, of course, the moment. And if the techniques of recording can contrive perfection – or the sins of perfection – they rarely capture the emotional moment, and the performance is perma-nently diminished. So it was with Casals, whose presence was a critical part of his performance. Charisma, commitment, the total involvement of soul and sound, was the experience of Casals in performance, an actuality that did not always survive the transfer to disc.

This is nowhere more effectively demonstrated than in the recordings of the first four Prades Festivals. Those present at the performances themselves, touched by the poignancy of the moment and the spirituality of the location, heard music of the finest quality: new life was breathed into familiar pieces, and Casals' philosophy of music 'permeated the work of every artist'.[29] When Columbia issued the recordings, generally fifteen months after each Festival, the discs were again perceived and reviewed within the emotional context of the original performances. Even when Columbia later reissued a selection of Prades recordings in a five-disc anthology commemorating 'The Musician of the Century', reviewers wrote of their 'vibrancy' and 'sense of occasion'. But upon the second reissue, a memorial tribute released the year after Casals' death, a reviewer commented that, 'in a way that is hard to describe', Casals seemed 'a remote presence' in the collection.[30] The performances began to be evaluated as disembodied musical specimens, and, as a result, they suffered. Compared with more recent recordings, including some of Casals' own, they were described as 'waywardly Romantic' and 'un-characteristically lack-lustre', with Casals himself accused of 'irascible sobriety'. It may be true, in retrospect, that in 1950 Casals was past his prime as a cellist but before his best as a conductor. But forty years on, musicians who played at the first Prades Festivals acknowledge without embarrassment defects and deficiencies in some of the early perform-ances. For what mattered was not simply the sound, but what Casals had to teach, to impart and to reveal about the role of music and the place of the musician in the world.

If Prades had been a shock for Casals when he arrived a dozen years earlier, the Festival was a very real surprise to the citizens of Prades who until now had not fully absorbed the international stature of the Catalan refugee living amongst them. Suddenly the town was full of foreigners, some with rooms in the Grand Hôtel, sharing its single bathroom, others lodging where they could with families in the town or in neighbouring villages, or staying in larger centres as distant as Perpignan, and crowding the bars and cafés by day. Beyond those billed to perform, there were musicians of world rank, political leaders, American philanthropists and minor royalty: President Auriol, Baron de Rothschild, the Comtesse de Polignac, Mrs Rosalie Leventritt, and – incognito – Juan Negrín, the President of the Spanish Republic in exile. The first concert was well attended by the American and European visitors, but it was not a sell-out: a third of Prades turned out to stand in the town square and survey the cars and the clothes, but they did not join in.[31] By the second concert, at which Casals and Paul Baumgartner played the three Bach Sonatas for Viola da Gamba and Harpsichord, the realization had dawned that something unprecedented and special was going on, and there was not a spare seat.[32] In the church the prayer-kneelers were removed and the pews placed more closely together: the side-chapels were pressed into use to accommodate the overflow. At a squeeze 1200 people could get in. Sometimes even the pulpit was occupied.[33] Outside, the citizens enthusiastically joined in the Festival spirit. Coloured lamps and Catalan flags were hung in the square, and biographies and posters of Casals were suddenly everywhere.[34] The bakery displayed an iced cake the shape and size of a cello. In the Route Nationale, the Grand Hôtel restaurant was heavily booked, and people crowded into the Grand Café opposite for coffee and aperitifs. Up the street the cinema, the Folies Pradennes, was showing Bette Davis and Glenn Ford in *La Voleuse*. Everyone, from the photographer, Alexandre Fruitet, to Madame Dolores Gouzy, who ran the local shoe-shop, felt the excitement. Even the local prostitute, in the rue Voltaire, reported a good deal more activity than usual.[35]

After the music the Festival was perhaps pre-eminently a press event. Self-sacrifice always makes good copy, and Casals' exile had been widely covered. Now his decision to break his silence, together with his prominent anti-Franco position, turned it into an irresistible story, particularly for the American public. The choice of a modest church in the Pyrenees, rather than any of the great concert halls of the world, for this dramatic event added to its power. As the world's press converged on Prades, Franco was reported to have denounced the Festival as 'Moscow's diabolical machinations against Spain' and attempted to inhibit travel across the Pyrenees border. Whether or not it was true, Franco's opposition

*Prades: Casals performing with Mieczyslaw Horszowski in the Church of St Pierre during the 1955 Festival. Queen Elisabeth of the Belgians is seated in the front row (right).*

*Casals and Marta Montañez, with Schweitzer, at Gunsbach, 1955.*

*Casals and Marta disembarking from the* Flandre *upon arrival in Puerto Rico, December 1956.*

*Casals, in 1957, showing Marta 20 Villa Molitor, his home in Paris between 1906 and 1913.*

*Casals performing at the United Nations,*
*New York, 1958.*

*Casals conducting, September 1961.*

*Concert at the White House, November 1961, with John F. Kennedy, Luis Muñoz Marín and Jacqueline Kennedy.*

*With Rudolf Serkin and Marta at the Marlboro Festival.*

*Casals and Marta at home in Isla Verde, Puerto Rico, with Mieczyslaw Horszowski and Alexander Schneider, 1966.*

*Casals with Marta, November 1972, photographed by Fritz Henle.*

*Casals with Schneider in Israel, September 1973, two months before his death.*

*A monument to Casals in his home town of
El Vendrell, by Josep Viladomat.*

was widely assumed, and a number of Catalan loyalists simply set out and walked the 250 kilometres from Barcelona to Prades. At the close of the final concert a young couple dressed in Catalan costume presented Casals with a bouquet in the Catalan national colours. Casals passed it to his brother Enrique, who silently placed it upon the altar. Although the Festival was explicitly a musical rather than a political event, it inevitably became, in subsequent years, a kind of emblem of Catalan cultural regeneration.[36]

As an exercise in public relations the Festival was a triumph. The first major press feature had been a *Life* magazine cover story, published in May 1950 under the heading 'Pablo Casals: at last he is preparing to play in public again'. It was based on an extended interview with Casals by Lael Wertenbaker, with photographs by Gjon Mili.[37] The article's prominence was wildly out of proportion to Casals' popular stature, but it triggered international media interest. The *New Yorker* ran a 'Letter from Prades' in June, and during the Festival itself the American photographer Margaret Bourke-White, then living with Alexander Schneider, photographed rehearsals and performances, again under commission from *Life*. Prades was full of photographers, reporters, music critics and sound engineers: the 1950 Bach Festival remains one of the most copiously documented musical events in history. After each concert critics cabled reviews to papers round the globe. Music-lovers everywhere knew exactly what Casals had played and how he had played it: confirmation came with the Columbia recordings when they were issued several months later. The massive attention catapulted Casals to international media stardom, especially in the United States where he had not been heard since 1928. Schneider, back in New York after the Festival, reported affectionately that Casals' popular esteem had risen to 93 per cent: 'if there would be the slightest chance for you to run for President of the United States you would certainly win with a landslide'.[38]

Considered rationally, a festival featuring the world's most famous instrumentalist and an orchestra comprising an unlikely but overwhelming collection of talent in a remote French town in the middle of a hot summer was a nonsense. But for everyone there, players and tourists, the unreality helped make it an unforgettable experience. None felt it more than Casals. The Festival had given him seven weeks of intense and exhilarating music-making: after it, and returned to the vacuum of exile, he felt restless and disturbed. 'Cher Alexander', he wrote to Schneider, using French and still addressing him rather formally as 'vous', 'you have achieved the miracle of unlocking powers which I believed were beyond me.'[39] He was, after all, not dead, and there was more to life than the Prades routine of semi-forgotten retirement: morning walks, practising, teaching and hours of correspondence. Signs soon came of revived curiosity about the world outside and a willingness to be part of it – the acceptance of an honorary doctorate from the Philadelphia Academy of Music, and a Polish award. Schneider took the opportunity to float the idea of a visit to America, to play for President Truman at a concert commemorating the 150th anniversary of the birth of Washington: 'if you wish you can have Rudi Serkin play with you, even God Himself'.[40]

But until September 1951, Casals did not leave Prades. The reason was simple. Señora Capdevila – 'Tití' as she was affectionately known – was increasingly ill with Parkinson's disease, and became severely nervous at the mere idea of Casals' absence. Casals' letters at this time were preoccupied with news of Tití's fluctuating condition and the doctors' prescription of 'a long period of absolute rest'.[41] It became Casals' primary anxiety for the next three years.

One of the clearest benefits of the Festival had been Casals' reintroduction to youthful musicians: not pupils – for that was a different kind of relationship – but profoundly gifted fellow-players. Schneider was just forty-one, and Tortelier thirty-six. Younger still were Isaac Stern, who turned thirty in July 1950, and the Spanish–American harpsichordist, Fernando Valenti, who was twenty-three. But the favourite was the American pianist Eugene Istomin, just twenty-four at the time of the Festival, and to be the most powerful new friendship of this period of Casals' life.

Istomin, though young, had a considerable musical past. The child of Russian parents, both professional musicians, he had been born in New York. Spotted by Casals' old Russian colleague, Alexander Siloti, he was taught, from the age of twelve, by Serkin and Horszowski at the Curtis Institute in Philadelphia. Spectacular wins of the Philadelphia Youth Contest and the Leventritt Award in 1943 brought him, aged seventeen, a broadcast performance of the Brahms Second Piano Concerto with the New York Philharmonic, and immediate fame; at nineteen he made his first recording, of Bach's D Minor Concerto. Deeply impressed by his performances, Schneider recruited Istomin to Prades to play a Bach trio, with Stern and John Wummer the flautist. As it happened, he also filled in for Serkin as pianist in the Brandenburg Concerto No. 5 in D, since Serkin, having recorded the work elsewhere, and being of monogamous disposition, declined to record it for Columbia. Istomin, like several of the young talents in Prades, was not shy about his abilities, and wrote asking for an advance meeting with Casals in April.[42] A single encounter, at 'El Cant dels Ocells', the name Casals had given his gatekeeper's cottage, transformed cockiness into pellucid devotion. The two men played four hands on one piano – a canon of Schumann in an arrangement by Debussy – and some Bach.[43] Then Casals picked up his cello and played the D Minor Suite, the reflection of light from his spectacles giving the appearance of a halo. For Istomin it was an epiphany: he was overcome and captivated. Casals, who was not unaware of his effect on young musicians, sensed this to be the beginning of a relationship of unusual intensity and permanence. Neither man knew quite how special it would become.

After the 1950 Festival ended, and the musicians separated to resume their individual careers, Eugene Istomin remained behind. He was acutely aware of Casals' fragility and his need for stimulus, and could not bear to abandon him in this musically deprived state: 'he's been living down here without anyone even to play the piano for him, and you just can't let things like that happen'.[44] Part of what Istomin felt resulted of course from a young man's hero-worship. Two weeks after the final concert, and from just a few doors away, he wrote appealing for more of Casals' time which he sensed was squandered generously but unworthily on things of little importance: 'if I really mean something to you, as you do to me, then open the door (the inner one) to the Cathedral and let me in'.[45] In Prades until October, Istomin saw the friendship deepen. Musically the two men had enormous respect for each other. Some said Istomin was fortunate to be a pianist, that Casals' most profound musical relationships could not be with artists of his own instrument.[46] On a personal level, the age gap was such as to make it all great fun, bringing the bond of grandfather to grandson within which Istomin could behave outrageously, yet do no wrong. Soon he was addressing Casals as 'dear old boy!', and secretly practising hard on some tricky piece before springing it on Casals as a challenge.

The relationship invigorated them both, even if it briefly delayed Istomin's resumption of a brilliantly promising career. In the longer term the impact on Istomin's musicianship was, as Howard Taubman of the *New York Times* observed, 'astonishing'.[47] Istomin himself perceived it immediately:

> That first Casals Festival in 1950 had such a profound influence on my musical thought and personal development. [I] returned many times again in later years to be near the man who personified so many of my ideals. . . . Curiously enough, although his influence was very broad, it was never direct . . . taste, depths of feeling, love – big words, big things – and none of them can be learned or rehearsed. They can, however, be drawn out and encouraged by revelation.[48]

What Istomin, in return, provided was a continuity of trust and honesty. He became one of a highly select number of friends who, during Casals' lifetime, had the courage – and the permission – to tell the great Maestro what they really thought.

As one musical friendship began, another connection ended. In thirty-eight years, since their break in 1912, Casals and Guilhermina Suggia had met on only a handful of occasions, and then briefly and by accident. But on 10 May 1950 Suggia wrote from her home in Porto, seeking help in securing tickets and accommodation for a short visit to the Festival. Apologizing for the interruption, Suggia explained that she had been seriously ill: 'Cher ami . . . I write to you with emotion and in the hope that you will not refuse me . . . but I should not wish to die before hearing you, cher maître, and seeing you again.'[49] Aware that a taboo was being broken, Suggia suggested that Casals' secretary might respond, if he did not care to do so himself: 'Remember me always as your devoted admirer – do you forget the little eleven-year-old who came to take lessons with you at Espinho? Au revoir – j'espère.' There is no indication of a reply. And Suggia did not travel to Prades. At the beginning of July she was back in London to see her doctors and undergo an emergency operation. On 1 August she died, in Porto, aged sixty-two.[50]

# 11

## *The Prades Festival, 1951–1955*

Casals' mastery is colossal. It seems that the first blossoming of the creative talent of the great artist is still continuing. I think it is the only instance in the entire history of our art. Perfect intonation, free movement of the hand along the fingerboard, the greatest refinement and polish of any bowings – that is a real miracle. I have never before seen anything like it.

*David Oistrakh*[1]

Intonation is a question of conscience.

*Pablo Casals*

The institution of an annual 'festival in exile' at Prades was the greatest gift Casals could imagine. But in music as in the rest of life nothing comes entirely free, and the Festival that bore his name became, at times, a serious burden.

Difficulties first emerged during the winter of 1950, as forward plans were made for the 1951 Festival. The problem was not lack of interest, but excess of it: too many wanted to be on the Festival letterhead, and as Schneider pointed out, 'the fewer people we have mixed up in the Festival, the easier and more successful it will be'.[2] The main questions were who should play what, and where? Casals wanted the same players, the same orchestra, the same focus on Bach: he wanted to re-create the spirit and atmosphere of the first Festival.[3] Others knew it could never be the same. For one thing, the Bishop denied a second use of the Church of St Pierre: the opening Festival of 1950, as a celebration of the Bach bicentenary, had been, he argued, a special case.[4] An argument developed over an alternative location, Schneider writing from New York to register a preference for the tenth-century Abbey of St Michel de Cuixà, 2 miles outside Prades, where an unscheduled daytime concert – the central nave of the Abbey had no roof – had been held with great success towards the close of the 1950 programme. René and Geneviève Puig, who ran the Festival office in Prades, pushed strongly for Perpignan, where they lived. Casals intervened, opting for Perpignan on the assurance of improved acoustics, a factor which concerned him after hearing the tapes of the 1950 concerts.[5] But these were minor difficulties, common to any festival. Then, as later, Casals was – as the Catalans put it – *molt senyoral*, or 'very gentlemanly': he delivered his opinion clearly and straightforwardly, but ceded to the advice of his colleagues, provided there was a consensus. In any case, as he told Schneider, 'Je ne peux avoir aucune préférence quand il s'agit de la musique des dieux.'[6]

There was, however, one area of particular sensitivity, where things could easily go wrong. And they did. In Casals' mind, the Bach Festival was a Catalan event, celebrated, for political reasons, in French Catalonia rather than within Spain itself. For the French, however, Prades was a French town and its Festival very definitely a French festival. In reality, of course, the Bach Festival was almost exclusively an American musical event – financed, recorded and very largely performed by Americans – transplanted to France. The affluence and confidence of the American contingent, in the context of post-war recession, provoked resentment among some of the European players. And what the Americans in turn regarded as a certain sloppiness in the performance standards of some of the European contingent became a point of tension. The atmosphere was very difficult at times. Several of the European players chose to avoid it the following year by accepting engagements which clashed with the dates of the Festival. In an attempt to defuse tension, the Festival Committee hired the singer Doda Conrad to handle relations with the French government in 1951. Conrad's negotiations with the Ministry of Information led to a contribution of 1 million francs from RadioDiffusion Française in return for broadcasting rights to some of the concerts. But the agreement was rescinded by Festival officials at the very last minute on the grounds that the sum offered was insufficient. Conrad erupted in anger and disappointment. Any contribution from France was highly praiseworthy, he argued, since the Festival was not notably useful to French tourism, offered little opportunity for French artists and none at all for French music. The money France offered from its diminished post-war budget was greater than it paid for rights to any other festival. That France was poor, he stressed in his report to the Committee, 'should indeed not deny a nation the privilege of making available to the greatest number of its citizens, through one of its public services, music presented on its soil at a festival facilitated by its taxpayers' support'.[7]

Despite the problems, the second Festival, now called the Casals Festival, took place in Perpignan in July 1951. The concerts were performed in the courtyard of the Palace of the Kings of Majorca, a spectacular location with the Pyrenees on one side of the medieval ramparts and the

Mediterranean Sea on the other. The atmosphere was less intimate, and Casals less accessible, travelling back and forward to Prades each afternoon between the rehearsal and the performance to the comfort of his own bed and the security of Capdevila's cooking.[8] The highlight of the Festival in the view of many who attended was Myra Hess's playing of the Mozart E Flat Piano Concerto (K.271). Milly Stanfield observed that, following Hess's performance at the Festival, British artists were treated with a marked increase in respect.[9]

Although the Prades Festivals were a constant preoccupation during the early 1950s, they were by no means all Casals thought about. His involvement in the welfare of the Catalan refugees was an almost daily affair: he now knew hundreds of exiles and their growing families, and corresponded closely with parents about the schooling and progress of their children, whom he often knew individually and by name. There was also the relentless correspondence with friends and strangers all over the world. Quite apart from the regular letters from close friends – Eisenberg, von Tobel, Grottiendieck, and the family in Spain – Casals' archives contain many thousands of notes, cards and telegrams from admirers, students, opportunists and (sometimes) critics, each one fastidiously preserved, annotated and answered by hand. His handwriting, large and expansive earlier in his life, had now become tiny and cramped, reflecting not only the shortage of paper but also the diminution of his hopes. The burden of Casals' correspondence was noticed by one of his visitors, José María Corredor, a young Catalan living in Perpignan, who regularly came with friends to see Casals on Sunday afternoons. Corredor, himself a poet and linguist who had studied at the universities of Barcelona and Madrid, offered to help and, for several years in the early 1950s, came once or twice a week to receive instructions on answering a proportion of the incoming mail. The instructions naturally prompted further questions about Casals' life and opinions, and gradually Corredor began to take notes of the responses and assemble them under headings. With Casals' approval he published his record of the dialogue in both Catalan (*Converses amb Casals*) and French (*Conversations avec Casals*) in 1955, and it was issued two years later, in an English translation by André Mangeot, as *Conversations with Casals*.[10] The book, a sort of 'testimony from exile', was an enormous success. It has been translated into eleven languages and used as a core source for almost every subsequent account of Casals' life. Written during some of Casals' lowest and most static years, its effect has been to project a false sense of *gravitas* and finality over the life as a whole. Rarely was Casals as calm, measured, philosophic – or humourless – as he emerges from these conversations.

Casals composed little during the early 1950s, a reflection perhaps of his mood. But he did continue to teach: there were always three or four students at the Grand Hôtel, or lodged in rooms about the town. Pamela Hind O'Malley, the student of Ivor James, had first arrived in the winter of 1949/50, and returned for a second series of lessons in December 1950, studying four of the Bach Suites.[11] Christopher Bunting had reached Prades in the autumn of 1952, and stayed ten months, overlapping with Vera Canning and several other young English cellists.[12] The lessons stopped when Bunting's scholarship ran out, but he stayed on to attend the 1953 Festival, and some of Istomin's parties. In common with all Casals' pupils he found the lessons intense and exacting, not simply a musical but a spiritual experience: Casals remained the centre of Bunting's musical world for the rest of his life.

Equable and avuncular though Casals appeared and was portrayed by the world's press, those close to him were aware of a sudden and sometimes alarming capacity for passionate outbursts. For a man who had travelled the world and been fêted by it, Prades was a small stage, and sometimes felt that way. In a community of barely 4000 inhabitants, minor things were magnified into major ones, and everyone knew each other's business, or thought they did. Casals could not always remain detached from rumour, particularly since, as a sort of king, he was consistently surrounded by court intrigue. In addition he had that quality, evident in some genuinely inspirational men, of making everyone want to be, and many feel they are, his favourite. Casals sought and gave attention continuously, and people competed for his approval, a rivalry he did not always discourage. Access to the great man was difficult: many felt they did not get enough of his time, and that others got too much. Visitors to Prades noted that although Casals affected exhaustion at the stream of callers, he took no steps to curtail it:

> A notably large number of women and girls from all over the world went in and out – nieces, aunts, students and gate-crashing Festival fans. Some kept house for him, others . . . spent the whole year as disciples in Prades. The master rewarded even the slightest help with an embrace and kisses on both cheeks.[13]

Demands on Casals' energy and resources were made by his brothers, when in Prades, and by their children, by musicians and pupils anxious for his endorsement, and by fellow-Catalans seeking his leadership and charity. Each group resented the importuning of the others, and felt them over-indulged. Certainly it made the organization of the Festivals themselves more complicated and inefficient, with different parties lobbying for conflicting interests and priorities. Occasionally, too, there was local irritation at the disruption caused to life in Prades by the fact of Casals' presence. His landlord, Admiral Troy, complained more than once at finding the path to his château blocked by a large limousine. When told that the car belonged to Queen Elisabeth of the Belgians the Admiral exclaimed that this was his home, and here he was king. Then he put the rent up.[14]

Even in the 1950s Casals suffered fits of black depression. He was vulnerable to migraine and sometimes took to his bed for a couple of days in a mood of desperate gloom. The cause may have been something quite elementary, like indigestion, but Casals was determinedly pre-Freudian when it came to exploring his psyche. He appeared never to analyse his indisposition, but simply to respond to it. On occasions, too, he exhibited outbursts of powerful sexual jealousy, suspecting friends and pupils of quite unlikely misdemeanours, or of too close an association with one or other of his nieces. When Istomin took Enrique's pretty daughter Marionna Casals to the cinema, it turned into a local scandal. One young male pupil even recalled being accused of paying excessive attention to Madame Capdevila. Casals became intensely distraught, and while it is far from clear whether his primary concern was Capdevila's dignity, or indignation that attention was being displaced from himself, his rage and hurt were, either way, wildly out of proportion. These outbursts were invariably brief, however, and after several days of awkwardness, the issue would be forgotten. Casals never held a grudge for long: he too easily saw the good in people.

Given the imbroglio of the French subsidy, the 1951 Casals Festival was again almost exclusively underwritten by Columbia Records, which allocated a $25,000 advance to the 'Prades Musical Society' against future recording royalties.[15] Having paid the piper for two years – albeit with a good return – Columbia now sought to call the tune more specifically, and the Festival administration began to crumble in response. Essentially there was a wide gap in expectations. What Casals sought from the Festivals was an opportunity, such as he was not getting elsewhere, to direct a medium-sized chamber orchestra in a programme of orchestral works and concertos, predominantly by Bach. But what Columbia wanted to record was not Casals conducting, but Casals himself performing the core repertoire of classical chamber music. For it was not the case that anything bearing Casals' name would be an automatic commercial success. Chamber music was cheaper to programme, easier to record in the less than ideal conditions of the remote Pyrenees, and much more saleable in the market-place. Both Casals' view and that of Columbia were altogether understandable, but they were at odds. It amounted to a clear clash between artistic and commercial priorities.

Casals came to realize that the Festivals, established in his honour and for his enjoyment, were not to be wholly at his discretion.

The debate over the nature of the Prades Festival was not settled for three years, until 1954, and generated strong feeling, tension and some bitterness; Schneider, as the executive director of the Festival, found himself at the centre of the argument. As plans for a broader Bach, Mozart and Beethoven programme for 1951 came together, Casals pressed to change them back to Bach. Schneider urged him to leave things as they were. Columbia's priorities were Beethoven sonatas and trios, and since Columbia was underwriting the Festival, he explained, 'I think we should try to be as considerate to them as they are to us.'[16] Later that year, in discussing plans for 1952, Casals again pushed hard for a small chamber orchestra, with which he offered to play, amongst other works, the Schumann Cello Concerto. Schneider knew it would not work and could not be afforded: the recording of full orchestral works in Prades required artists of a higher calibre who would need to be paid extra to remain for recordings after the close of the Festival, and full rehearsals which would consume Casals' time and energy.[17] When Casals persisted, Schneider consulted with Istomin and, at the end of January 1952, cabled an ultimatum that if the orchestra idea went ahead, he would not continue as concert-master.[18] Casals knew there was no possibility of replacing Schneider, controlling costs and retaining Columbia's backing – and he gave in. From then on the choice of music owed a good deal to box-office appeal, and the selection of soloists equally to considerations of talent and their connection with the Columbia label. All Columbia's artists contributed, led by their star pianist, Serkin, chosen in preference to Yvonne Lefebure who was not known in the United States. There were no artists from the EMI stable.[19] The same short-list of soloists appeared repeatedly at the first few Festivals: Jennie Tourel and Genevieve Warner as singers; Serkin, Horszowski, Istomin, Myra Hess and Leopold Mannes as pianists; Stern and Schneider, violinists; Milton Katims and Milton Thomas, violists; Casals and Tortelier, cellists; Torello, double bass; Wummer, flute and Tabuteau, oboe.[20] Although Casals thanked Schneider for having created 'this magnificent family',[21] the truth was that the family bond owed most to the artists' drawing-power on recordings produced by Columbia. 'The Prades Festival', Virgil Thomson wrote, 'is a recording deal.'[22]

The day-to-day organization of the Festival programmes involved Schneider in choreographing works and artists 'like jugglers at a circus'. For professional impresarios this would not have been a surprise, but for Schneider it was exasperating. In 1952, for example, he discovered that Isaac Stern would come if he could play trios with Casals and Myra

Hess. Hess wanted to play with Szigeti or Schneider but not, at first, with Stern. Serkin spoke of missing the Festival, but was thought likely to accept if invited personally by Casals. In this atmosphere of abundant egos, Schneider appealed to Casals to make amendments only in the programmes of Mannes or Horszowski, who were flexible, but not of any of the others.[23]

The argument over the future of the Festival extended into a polariz-ation of the Prades regulars, with Madeline Foley and Leopold Mannes supporting Casals' position, and Eugene Istomin taking Schneider's view of the Columbia association. In March, Foley circulated a suggestion that the players might stay on after the close of the Festival to play orchestral music. The idea was dropped, however, when several of the European instrumentalists, including Tortelier, replied that they could not afford continued unpaid absence from their schedules.[24] After the Festival, Foley articulated the players' dissent, saying that the whole situation needed 'more energy and fight':

It is my opinion that Columbia has made a pretty slick deal with Casals all along, and they have had more from him than any com-pany has had from any artist, for less money and less time expended in making records. It is now our turn to dictate terms. I think we should let Columbia know that we are going to have a Festival, with orchestra, whether they give us a nickel or not.[25]

It was all too much for Schneider whose concentration, in any case, was distracted by the new passion of his life, the actress Geraldine Page. He resigned on 2 September 1952, accusing Casals of playing a game of 'politics and compromise'.[26] Casals was 'paralyzed' with shock, and could not respond for a month. When he did, he said there was nothing he had said or done which he could regret.[27] Responsibility for the day-to-day administration of the festivals devolved to Dr Russell B. King-man, a wealthy New Jersey businessman, President of the American Lawn Tennis Association, and a member of the Festival Committee since 1950. Kingman was an enthusiastic amateur cellist, and the owner of Emanuel Feuermann's Stradivarius instrument, among other notable cellos.[28] Schneider's early preparation ensured the success of the 1953 Festival, held between 14 June and 7 July and for the second year in Schneider's favourite location, the Abbey of St Michel de Cuixà. Ironi-cally it proved possible, before the start of the Festival, to conjure up a small orchestra and for Columbia to record Casals playing the Schumann A Minor Concerto, Eugene Ormandy, who happened to be on holiday in the South of France, being brought in to conduct. It was the first time Casals had performed a full concerto in public since 1945 and, excepting a performance – which he later disavowed – of the Dvořák Concerto in Puerto Rico in 1960, the last occasion on which he was to record one.

Without Schneider's confident presence at the Festival, however, there was tension between individual players and Columbia officials, and the atmosphere soured. This time Leopold Mannes joined Istomin in deploring Columbia's treatment by some of the musicians, writing to Casals that he was 'saddened by what took place'.[29] The Committee dissolved itself and Casals was asked to appoint a new one. Schneider was approached but, a year on, was found to be 'completely hostile'.[30] He performed once more at Prades, in 1966, but otherwise was lost to the Festival he created. And it changed things permanently. During its first four years the Prades Festival had the character of a medieval centre of musical learning, with artists attending out of simple devotion, with a real sense of privilege and no expectation of reward. With professional management it turned gradually into an institution, like so many other music festivals around the world.

From the beginning the problem was money, and Casals' own attitude to it. Dr Kingman swiftly identified dangers in the Festival's hitherto relaxed system of financial management. He warned Foley that, while the 1952 subsidy, from various sources, had been $45,000, the following year's Festival had secured only Columbia's now standard $25,000 advance, and ran a serious risk of insolvency.[31] As it had been organized, the Festival was an expensive indulgence. It could not run the risk of a deficit, which would damage the 'attraction power' of the Festival and hit the confidence of the performers. Worse still, as the Festival Committee was currently constituted, a deficit would theoretically be Casals' own responsibility.[32] Casals had taken little from the early Festivals, but he had taken what there was. He was far from mercenary, and frequently highly generous. But his nature was essentially frugal, and he was embarrassed by and inhibited from discussion of financial matters. Casals had agreed to the Festivals, he had not invented them. Not unreasonably, he came to regard them as a kind of personal benefit, and for some years failed to perceive the considerable financial sacrifice other artists were making to attend, or the amount of time those involved in organization were having to devote to the Festivals. The issue was simply not mentioned, and it contributed to Schneider's disaffection, and to that of Istomin too for a short while. In particular it punctured Casals' relationship with Madeline Foley who, for years, had given her wholehearted energy to the organization of the Festivals, without any financial recompense. Following pressure from Kingman, an agreement was reached in June 1954 to re-route some of the Festival surplus to its executive officers and principal artists, 'as a gesture'.[33] Once the principle had been established, most of the artists waived their share in Casals' favour. Foley, however, did not, and accepted her $430 entitlement. This was viewed as a signal transgression, and it took more than a year before the resulting awkwardness and hurt could be overcome.[34] Visiting the Festival for the first and only time in 1955, the young German lieder singer Dietrich Fischer-Dieskau found Foley distressed and embittered by 'the Prades cult'. He himself identified 'the very specifically miserly intent of keeping from the participating artists even the slightest remuneration'.[35]

The overall difficulty, however, remained securing a surplus at all. In January 1954 the New York arm of the Festival Committee was reconstituted as the Prades Musical Society Inc., with Russell Kingman as President and three subordinate committees dealing with finance, music and orchestral matters respectively. John M. Barnes was appointed salaried executive secretary, based in Prades – the first time the Festival had been run from France. Despite the organizational improvements, the finances looked so bleak at the start of the year that any Festival in 1954 seemed at risk. Serious fund-raising secured a deal with RadioDiffusion Française and some private donors. But the programme needed to be cut, and Istomin was chosen to break the news to Casals, in terms that he would understand. He explained that until 1953 the Festival had attracted artists of the highest calibre, but that 'with the desertion of Sasha Schneider most of these artists were lost to us'. 1954 looked thin: no Stern, Szigeti or Schneider. Nor was there input from Columbia Records which, after four successive Festivals, had decided against recording that year. The solution was a severely truncated Festival, restricted to Beethoven's chamber music. So it went ahead, between 7 and 23 June, with only six artists (Casals, Istomin, Horszowski, Serkin and the violinists Szymon Goldberg and Joseph Fuchs) and the Trio Pasquier playing eight concerts.[36] As an emergency measure it worked. The Festival remained solvent and, with a surplus of almost 2 million francs, was able to proceed to a significantly more expansive programme in 1955.[37]

But by then Casals had other preoccupations. Towards the end of 1954, Tití's condition had deteriorated rapidly. For several years, bulletins on Señora Capdevila's illness had been a regular feature of Casals' letters to his friends: 'Tití continue avec les hauts et bas.'[38] In 1954 an invitation from Queen Elisabeth of the Belgians, who had attended that year's Festival, to visit Liège, had to be cancelled because Tití was not well enough to travel. In October they did go to Switzerland, but it was not a comfortable trip: Tití wanted to return home, declaring, 'I don't want to die here'. Back in Prades she was happier: as Casals wrote to his old friend Germaine Grottendieck, 'she is reunited with her home, her routines and her doctors'.[39] By November all Capdevila's family had arrived in Prades: 'l'irréparable' could come at any time.[40] It came on 18 January, and Casals lost 'la compagne de ma vie'. Casals and Capdevila had been close friends for thirty years, and since the late 1920s had lived side by side. She had accompanied him into exile, relinquishing her life, home and friends, and had made Prades bearable. She was a strong woman, of independent means, and a positive force. It was she who had first welcomed the idea of the Festival, partly of course as a way of keeping Casals content in Prades. And it was she who had kept house and rationed the demands on Casals' strength. Capdevila was in a sense a kind of surrogate mother, and made no demands for a life of her own: it was the kind of relationship that Casals found most congenial. As she lay close to death, the priest was summoned and Casals and Capdevila were married.

It was an act of deep loyalty and affection. But it could not be more than that. Though Casals had not seen Susan Metcalfe for twenty-seven years, she had not been agreeable to a divorce and legally she was still his wife. That marriage had been by civil ceremony. Marrying Tití was a form of religious experience, and it lasted for a few brief hours. The niceties of legal distinction would not have concerned Casals, who had learned from his mother to honour moral principle above formal legalities. Two days later, Casals' gratitude to Capdevila was demonstrated even more powerfully by his decision to accompany her body back to Spain for burial. For the first time in fifteen years, and having secured special dispensation to re-enter the country, he travelled to Barcelona and on to San Salvador, to be welcomed by his brother Luis, then living in and looking after Casals' villa. Capdevila was buried in the small cemetery just outside Vendrell, beside Doña Pilar. She had asked that Casals play *El Cant dels Ocells* at the grave, but he was too distressed, and Luis' wife, Teresina, played a recording on a portable phonograph. Though Frasquita Capdevila came from a notable Barcelona family, and left her effects, including land, an apartment in Barcelona and a Guarnerius cello, principally to her nephews and nieces,[41] Casals very much wanted to remember her as part of his own. He wrote to Schneider that 'the only thought that consoles me is having, with my own hands and my own arms, placed Tití's body next to that of my mother'.[42]

After the burial, Casals remained in San Salvador for almost a week, walking through the house and its gardens, revisiting old friends, becoming better acquainted with his nieces and their husbands. Returning home was a poignant experience, but Casals felt more wistful than disturbed by it. Though he had not seen his home for seventeen years, he had never been wholly out of touch. In recent years especially, visits from his brothers, their wives and children, and trips to San Salvador by Schneider and Istomin, for example, had brought him in contact with the regular problems of leaks, repairs and alterations. Perhaps what he now felt most profoundly was loneliness. The sharpest pain of exile was gone: he had been away too long for that and in any case could not imagine a simple resumption of his life in Spain. Nor, without Tití, did he have any strong desire to return and continue his life in Prades. It was an unsettling and, in a way, dangerous few months, and his friends sensed it. Seeing a *New York Times* report that Casals had 'broken his exile', Eugene Istomin telephoned him in Prades, advising him to delay any serious decisions about his future, such as moving from Prades. He should regard this, Istomin wrote, as a period of 'spiritual convalescence'.[43]

Capdevila's death left Casals, as he wrote to Grottendieck, 'in a state of emptiness and confusion that excludes me from reality. Every feeling has changed, for me and in me.'[44] Indeed, all had changed. Casals returned to Prades in one sense serene, but rootless. He spent a couple of weeks away from the town with his niece Enriquetta and her husband, and visited friends in Monaco. Sasha Schneider was back in touch, and came to see Casals at the beginning of June, bringing with him Geraldine Page, whom he had married the previous month. Then it was time for the Festival, and Casals was again busy with his meetings, teaching and correspondence.

The 1955 Festival, the sixth consecutive Casals Festival, was a decidedly more relaxed event than its predecessors. This was partly because it was once again held in Prades, in the Church of St Pierre, and partly because, now the Festival was being professionally managed, its finances were less critically close to the edge. There was no orchestra, but an especially distinguished group of soloists and chamber performers, Horszowski and Istomin being joined this time by the violinsts Yehudi Menuhin and Sándor Végh. Columbia was once again absent, though most of the performances were recorded by RadioDiffusion Française which, since 1953, had held broadcasting rights to the Festivals. But since the majority of the artists were under contract to Columbia, many of the performances were not free for release on rival labels. Some appeared through pirated copies of radio broadcasts, but most were not made commercially available on disc until 1982.[45] Some have never appeared, and it represents a serious loss, for among the performances were many powerful, unrepeatable moments: Casals playing Brahms Trios with Menuhin and Istomin, and Dietrich Fischer-Dieskau, accompanied by Gerald Moore, singing Schubert's *Die Winterreise* song-cycle. For the Fischer-Dieskau recital Casals sat in the first row, next to Queen Elisabeth of the Belgians, and whispered a clearly audible 'Lovely!' at the end of each song.[46]

The Festival of 1955 was particularly intimate, Casals inviting personal friends to hear chamber rehearsals in his own villa. For some this indicated a breakdown in the 'strong organization of the disciplinary managers of former years'.[47] Rather more plausibly, it stemmed from Casals' own altered state of mind. For alongside his grief, he appeared to feel a sense of liberation, both from the daily routines and patterns of his life but also from the restricted horizons of the long years of exile. What began to alarm his closest friends was that it appeared also to signal a loosening of his political resolve. Quite suddenly Casals began to speak of the prospect of travel, the possibility of going somewhere new. And the country on his mind was Puerto Rico, the Caribbean dependency of the United States, the home of the Defilló family, forebears on his mother's side, and the birthplace of Doña Pilar herself. The worry was not so much that Puerto Rico was a part of the United States and a visit would seem to knock the central argument of Casals' exile. It was more the indication that Casals planned to begin his journey in Barcelona. Istomin wrote urging against this: everyone sympathized with the return to San Salvador for Capdevila's burial, but a second trip to Spain would have serious consequences. Many Americans, Istomin reminded him, had supported Casals' moral stand and 'greatly deranged themselves in order to help you adjust to your exile'. Another visit to Spain would change the whole position:

> You can explain only so much away. No one would hold it against you if you definitely returned to live in San Salvador. It is the most understandable thing. However you cannot go in and out of Spain and be an exile from Spain at the same time.[48]

The interest in Puerto Rico was not, however, accidental. It was prompted by Casals' newest and possibly most gifted pupil of the moment, Marta Montañez. Marta, known then by the affectionate diminutive Martita, had first encountered Casals in 1951 when her uncle, Rafael Montañez, had accompanied her on a visit from their home in Puerto Rico to the Perpignan Festival. Casals took a kindly interest in the little party from Puerto Rico, welcomed them to El Cant dels Ocells and listened to Martita play. She was not yet fifteen years old, and though she had an obvious talent for the cello, the impracticality of a young teenager living and studying so far from home prompted Casals to recommend that she return to New York and continue her general education. After elementary school in Santurce in Puerto Rico, Martita had transferred in 1950 to the Marymount College in Manhattan. In New York she was studying the cello with a former pupil of Casals, Lieff Rosanoff, at the Mannes College of Music.

Casals was often disproportionately receptive to young people, both those with a genuine gift and those with assertive temperaments – or parents. But there was something else at work on his occasion, which Casals sensed but did not yet understand. 'This is no stranger who comes to visit me', he later remembered thinking.[49] In part he was simply deeply affected by greetings brought from his mother's Defilló relatives in Puerto Rico. He was conscious, too, that Martita reminded him of Doña Pilar, her bearing, her colouring, her origins. The resemblance has often been observed, and linked with the intriguing coincidence that Martita's mother was born in the same house (21 calle Méndez Vigo, in Mayagüez) as Casals' mother, and on the same day of the year.[50] But at a deeper level, what Casals may have perceived in Martita was that combination of personal strength and moral confidence that he had found in no other woman in his life beyond his mother. Doña Pilar had broken every convention of her time in respect of gender, background and class in order to achieve what she held to be most important. Marta Montañez would show a comparable decisiveness.

For the moment Casals simply enjoyed the company of his Puerto Rican visitors. He introduced them to the Festival Orchestra at rehearsal, and shared with the players the gift of cigars they had brought, each one in a cellophane wrapper bearing Casals' picture.[51] Casals did not see Martita again until November 1954 when, having graduated with top honours from both Marymount and the Mannes School, and won a $1000 cello competition in San Juan, she returned to Prades with her mother, Angélica Montañez y Martínez, to begin intensive study with the master. After a month, Señora Montañez returned to Puerto Rico, and Martita remained, boarding locally and cycling to her lessons with Casals. She became friendly with Enriquetta, Casals' niece, and often joined the little family at El Cant dels Ocells in the evenings. In the months that followed Tití's death and Casals' return from San Salvador, Martita found herself increasingly at Casals' side, helping with the correspondence, driving him on visits to refugee settlements, sharing the burden of guests and callers, or simply accompanying him on his walks.[52] He gave her a photograph of himself, inscribed 'Tio Pablo' ['Uncle Pablo'], and in press photographs of the two together she was frequently identified as his niece, or adopted daughter; often he called her, not Martita, but simply *nena*, or child. Very soon it became clear to Casals that he could not manage without her, and moreover that he did not want to be separated from her.

The appeal Martita held for Casals was hardly difficult to decipher. He was alone, and her generous and uncomplicated temperament filled a painful void. At almost eighteen, Martita had grown into a strikingly beautiful woman. Fifty years before, Casals had been drawn to another talented and striking pupil, also eighteen years old, olive-skinned and dark-featured. But there the analogy ends. Martita was unusually composed, competent and self-sufficient. She made Casals' life easier, she infused it with energy. Guilhermina Suggia had drained it, becoming more rival than lover. Martita, unlike Suggia – or, of course, Susan Metcalfe – was a native Spanish speaker, and there was no obstacle to communication. She also spoke French and English, and very swiftly picked up Catalan. Musically she was both naturally talented and well trained, without which there would have been no access to Casals' inner world. And Martita had a tremendous capacity for fun. Fellow-pupils at the time noticed how, in her company, Casals was rejuvenated, how she, like Istomin, could take affectionate liberties (she did a spectacular Donald Duck impersonation) without Casals feeling his dignity threatened.[53] But Casals was never short of a 'palace guard' of admiring women, and there were many willing candidates for the role of nurse, companion or secretary. The particular strength of the bond between Casals and Martita had something very much to do with the difference in age between them: the seventy-eight-year-old Maestro and the dazzling eighteen-year-old were comfortable with each other precisely because there was nothing conventional about the relationship: there was no risk of equality between them and therefore no possibility of a threat.

Once the Festival had ended, it was time for Casals to go to Zermatt for the annual chamber music Summer Academy of Music organized by his friend and pupil, Rudolf von Tobel. He had attended the school in 1952 and 1954, and enjoyed the intimacy of these 'master classes in the mountains'. But he did not want to go alone, and asked Martita to accompany him. After Zermatt they continued on to visit Albert Schweitzer in Gunsbach and then Charlie Chaplin at his home in Vevey. The trip turned into a kind of royal procession, with visits to Wagner's house in Lucerne and, rather surprisingly, a small recital at Beethoven's birthplace in Bonn. Finally, fulfilling an invitation that Tití's illness had ruled out the previous year, Casals and Martita went to Belgium as guests of Queen Elisabeth in Laeken.

It was natural that Martita, a young student far from home, should after a year away want to return to see her family in Puerto Rico: respite from the discomforts of life in Prades was in any case very welcome. By now it had become inevitable that Casals should not wish to be alone. So at the beginning of December 1955, Casals and Martita sailed from Le Havre on the *Flandre*, Casals' first transatlantic journey for twenty-five years. The visit would last six weeks, and change the whole focus of his life.

PART 5

*The Superstar*

# 12

## Epiphany: The Discovery of Puerto Rico, 1955–1959

The first music I remember was a lullaby. The first words that
I understood from my mother were 'Puerto Rico'. It is a dream
I have had all my life.

Pablo Casals, 1956[1]

When the *Flandre* docked in the bay of San Juan at 8.05 a.m. on 11
December, over 200 residents were waiting to greet it. Up the gang-
plank to welcome Casals came the wife of Puerto Rico's Governor, Doña
Inés Muñoz Marín, the formidable Mayor of San Juan, Felisa Rincón de
Gautier, the Chancellor of the University of Puerto Rico, Jaime Benítez,
and two Defilló cousins, Pilar de Acevedo and Concepción de González.[2]
Lining the harbour, cheering, smiling and wearing their Sunday best
were many more Defilló relatives, whom the emotional and somewhat
overwhelmed Maestro greeted and kissed, one after the other. 'La tierra
de mi madre', he repeated, 'the land of my mother'. The San Juan daily,
*El Mundo*, had anticipated the scene in a cartoon printed the previous
day which depicted Casals arriving to a large crowd of locals, each
waving a placard announcing the bearer as a 'Defilló'.[3] Casals' mother
had been one of eight children and the descendants of that large family
all seemed to be here. After the tearful welcome, and an introduction to
Martita's parents, Aquiles Montañez Rivera and Doña Angélica, Casals
and Martita were driven with a police escort through old San Juan to the
Plaza Colón for an informal ceremony and brief performance by a
student chorus, before being taken to the apartment officially placed at
their disposal in the Condado area, 3 miles along the coast from the
centre of the capital.

Clearly this represented rather more than a spontaneous welcome for
a returning son of Puerto Rico. Indeed, it had been carefully planned.
Casals had often thought of making a visit to the island his mother had
left at the age of seventeen, and had frequently been invited, but the

nearest he had been was the neighbouring island of Cuba. Now, at seventy-nine, encouraged by Martita and her family, and with little left in Prades to hold him, it seemed an appropriate moment. Since 1950 Rafael Montañez had been exploring Casals' Puerto Rican origins and, with his encouragement, tracing Defilló relatives and attempting to locate the house in Mayagüez in which Doña Pilar had been born.[4] From early in 1955 Governor Luis Muñoz Marín had taken a personal interest in the investigation, and began to promote a strong welcome for Casals. On the eve of the arrival, both the Governor and the State Legislature issued proclamations declaring Casals to be an honoured guest. A car and chauffeur were placed at his disposal throughout the visit and every procedure made effortless. Encouraged by the Governor's wife, Jack Delano, a young Russian composer–producer now resident on the island, began to record a television documentary account of the visit, broadcast in 1956 as *Pablo Casals En Puerto Rico*, and a journalist started taking notes for a book devoted exclusively to the thirteen-week visit, *Pablo Casals: Pelegrino en America*.[5] By the time Casals left on 23 March 1956 to return to France, he had given a commitment to return to the island and sensed that his connection with Puerto Rico would be permanent.

Casals and Puerto Rico were indeed a near-perfect match. The Bach Festivals had highlighted what he was missing in terms of making music and seeing musical friends, and after Capdevila's death Prades seemed diminished and depressing. Since a return to Spain remained impossible, Puerto Rico appeared the next best opportunity: it was the closest Casals could get to Catalonia without setting foot in Franco's Spain. The climate in San Juan was similar to that in San Salvador, if warmer in winter and wetter in summer: the humidity was sufficient, it was popularly said, for envelopes to seal themselves. The vegetation, terrain and in particular the beaches reminded Casals powerfully of his home: 'much of the time I felt I was in Spain'.[6] Although the native language was Spanish, and the customs hispanic, the island's life had a perceptible American influence which Casals, after almost thirty years away from North America, found appealing too. Puerto Rico was also the closest Casals could get to the United States without, in his view, flouting his moral commitment. And here, after the relatively solitary and deprived existence in Prades, he found himself with a large, exuberant, warm and ready-made family.

For Puerto Rico, the arrival of a world-famous cultural figure, especially one with genuine local connections, was precisely what it needed. After 450 years of external domination, first by Spain and then by the United States, this 3 million-strong Caribbean community had embarked on a deliberate programme to establish its independent economic and cultural identity. Since its conquest by Spain in 1493, Puerto Rico's strategic location ensured that it would not be left alone by nations seeking military and geo-political advantage in the West Indies. During the Spanish–American war of 1898 Puerto Rico had been annexed by the United States and administered since then as a 'non-incorporated territory' – in effect a colonial possession – with an American-nominated governor reporting to the US War Department and, after 1934, to the Department of the Interior.[7] In 1900 the Foraker Act of the US Congress had defined the nature of Puerto Rican civil government, and created the post of a Puerto Rican resident commissioner in Washington, with speaking but not voting rights in Congress. For forty years adjustments in the island's political status depended largely on the relationship between the Governor in San Juan and the responsible under-secretary in Washington, and on their joint effectiveness in persuading Congress to relax its hold over the island.

Other than its strategic importance, Puerto Rico was seen by the United States largely as a source of ready labour and cheap sugar. Heavy American investment subverted small-scale coffee plantations and reduced the *haciendas*, the traditional form of peasant landholding, to little more than units for the production of bulk sugar and tobacco for the US mainland. After Puerto Ricans were granted American citizenship in 1917, through the Jones Act, the mass emigration of displaced agricultural workers began, providing a virtually limitless supply of impoverished labour for poorly paid and menial jobs across the United States.

The Americanization of Puerto Rico had a devastating effect on its national culture, as well as on its economy: English was declared the official language and hispanic traditions marginalized. But just as it had been wrecked by American money, indigenous culture was rescued by economic decline. The recession of the 1930s and the weakness of the sugar and tobacco industries permitted a populist upsurge led by Luis Muñoz Marín. A scholar and a poet, Muñoz Marín proved a highly charismatic leader of the majority Partido Popular Democrático (or 'Populares' Party) within the Puerto Rican Senate after 1940. Under a newly designated constitution after 1952, the Popular democratic administration sought the cultural regeneration of the island through its transformation to an industrial economy. The industrialization programme, known as 'Operation Bootstrap', aimed to divert US capital into manufacturing. By 1956 the island's Economic Development Administration, or 'Fomento', had achieved substantial success.[8] 'Operation Bootstrap', in the words of *Life* magazine, quadrupled the island's income and

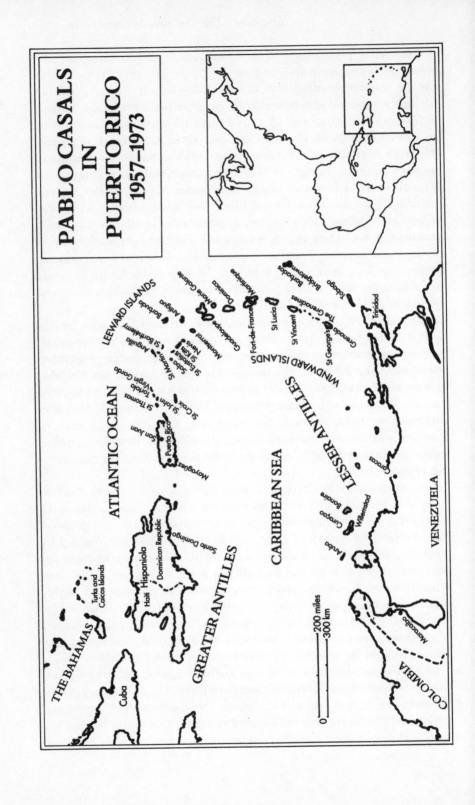

# PABLO CASALS
## IN
## PUERTO RICO
### 1957–1973

THE BAHAMAS

Turks and Caicos Islands

Cuba

Haiti  Hispaniola

Dominican Republic

Santo Domingo

GREATER ANTILLES

ATLANTIC OCEAN

San Juan

Mayagüez  Puerto Rico

St Thomas

St John  Tortola  Virgin Gorda

St Croix

Anguilla  St Barthélemy

St Martin

Saba  St Eustatius  St Kitts

Nevis

Montserrat

Barbuda  Antigua

LEEWARD ISLANDS

Guadeloupe

Marie Galante

Dominica

Martinique

Fort-de-France

St Lucia

St Vincent

The Grenadines

Grenada

St George's

Barbados

Bridgetown

Tobago

Trinidad

WINDWARD ISLANDS

CARIBBEAN SEA

LESSER ANTILLES

Aruba  Curaçao  Bonaire

Willemstad

Caracas

Maracaibo

VENEZUELA

COLOMBIA

200 miles

300 km

0

transformed it 'from a pesthole to a shiny exhibit of democracy and free enterprise in action'.[9]

If the remarkable Muñoz Marín was the driving force for change on the island, he was powerfully aided in Washington by Abe Fortas, a brilliant young lawyer who, as head of the Division of Territories within the Department of the Interior, was responsible for the formulation of US policy towards Puerto Rico. With Muñoz Marín, whom Fortas termed 'a spectacularly great figure', and Rex Tugwell, US-nominated Governor between 1941 and 1948, Abe Fortas sought a 'New Deal' for the island, the first success of which was the achievement of an element of democratic choice and the establishment of an elective governorship, to which Muñoz Marín succeeded, in 1948.[10] Even in private legal practice during the 1950s, Fortas maintained an unwavering concern for Puerto Rico's interests: according to his biographer, 'it became the one cause to which he was unconditionally committed', his attitude being 'proprietory, protective, and loving'.[11] The top Washington practice of Arnold, Fortas and Porter was retained by Puerto Rico on a modest annual retainer of $10,000, and Fortas' contacts with powerful members of Congress eased the passage of legislation favourable to the island. In particular it was Fortas' links with the future Democratic majority-leader in the Senate, Lyndon Johnson, that helped the passage of Public Law 600, legislation which, in 1950, empowered Puerto Rico to draft its own constitution. Although Fortas never succeeded in dismantling the US conviction of a unilateral right to govern Puerto Rico – indeed, paradoxically, everything he did bound the countries more tightly together – his aggressive defence of the island's interests did permit Muñoz Marín unprecedented autonomy in day-to-day administration.

Between his arrival in Puerto Rico in 1955 and his death in 1973, Casals' life was to be fundamentally influenced by the advice and guidance of Abe Fortas, though neither yet knew to what extent. Indeed, the beguiling combination of sharp wits and smooth operation that eventually saw Fortas almost to the head of the US Supreme Court largely defined the character of Casals' final years. The caesura between the hidden years in Prades, when Casals was guided by his own pained conscience, and the glittering years of celebrity in Puerto Rico, when he was guided with supreme dexterity to within a hair's-breadth of his own moral frontier, could not have been more dramatic.

It was Abe Fortas who articulated the idea that the cultural regeneration of Puerto Rico should be subsidized by government along with its industrialization. 'Operation Serenity' was invented to accompany Operation Bootstrap, and to expose the Puerto Rican people to 'the best culture that the world offers'.[12] The intention was to foster a sense of national identity, which Puerto Rico conspicuously lacked, through the promotion of its artistic heritage, and in 1955 an Institute of Puerto Rican Culture was founded to co-ordinate that endeavour.[13] In literature and painting the result was a burst of creative work with a nationalist and popularist content, strongly influenced, interestingly, by a group of distinguished artists and intellectuals who had come to the island in the early 1940s as exiles from Franco's Spain.[14] In terms of music, Operation Serenity began with, amounted to, and wholly resulted from the connection with Casals. Fortas, a fine amateur violinist and chamber music player, alerted Muñoz Marín to the enormous advantages of Casals' presence on the island. He helped persuade Casals to support a festival in San Juan along the lines of that in Prades, and subsequently to lend his prestige and expertise to the foundation of a Puerto Rican conservatory of music and a symphony orchestra. Fortas became a trusted friend of both Casals and Martita and acted as Casals' personal lawyer for the rest of the Maestro's life.[15]

In terms of Puerto Rico's cultural self-discovery, Casals' arrival was clearly providential. In that context, what began as a private visit to the land of his mother's birth turned into an organized and highly publicized encounter with the whole island, and indeed with a wider area of the Caribbean. A considerable effort was made to ensure that he liked what he saw. The afternoon after their arrival, Casals and Martita were received at La Fortaleza, the Governor's sixteenth-century 'fortress' palace from which, in 1595, Sir Francis Drake had been pummelled into defeat. A sequence of fiestas and ceremonies of welcome followed, and on 17 December Casals crossed the island to visit the house in Mayagüez in which his mother had been born a little over a century before. Accompanied by Martita and Doña Inés Muñoz Marín, Casals moved quietly through the house, number 21 calle Mendez Vigo, before playing *El Cant dels Ocells* on a balcony overlooking the street in which a crowd had gathered. To Casals' profound emotion, Doña Inés then unveiled a commemorative plaque identifying the house as the birthplace of Pilar Defilló i Amiguet: Casals' connection with the island was confirmed.[16]

Casals' seventy-ninth birthday on 29 December was marked by serenades sung by the University of Puerto Rico chorus, and celebrated with a large iced cake which, because it was decorated in the shape of a cello, Casals pretended to refuse to cut. Mieczyslaw Horszowski had travelled from the United States for the occasion, and the party was joined by Russell Kingman and Lieff Rosanoff. A substantial reception was given at La Fortaleza by Muñoz Marín on 19 January, at which 400 guests heard Casals perform a vigorous arrangement of a Handel Sonata with Martita and the pianist Jesús María Sanromá, Puerto Rico's best-known musician and a former pupil of Alfred Cortot. It was the first opportunity Martita had had to display the results of her year of study in Prades, and after the joint performance by teacher and pupil she played alone a suite of pieces by Couperin. The following day *El Mundo* noted that Puerto Rico now had 'a violoncellist who will make her mark in the world of art'.[17]

On 23 January 1956 Casals left San Juan via Miami for a visit to Mexico where, for seven exhilarating days, he was fêted with honours, tributes and receptions. Mexico had consistently withheld recognition from Franco's regime and, from the earliest days of the Civil War, had offered a home to Spanish exiles and Catalan patriots – a good number of whom Casals was able to meet. On 29 January he was honoured at a banquet held by the Spanish Republican Center and attended by over 900 Spanish exiles, including officials of the former Republican government whom Casals had known during the early 1930s. The following day Casals returned to Puerto Rico, stopping for a few hours in Havana, Cuba, for further celebrations. It was like a royal tour, for the giving and receiving of flowers and affection, and Casals felt honoured and moved, if a little staggered at the extent of his celebrity status. Above all he felt fatigued, for a visit intended to provide a change of view, some relaxation and perhaps some opportunity for composition, had turned into a relentless public procession, everywhere followed by Jack Delano's camera.

By late February Casals was certain that he wished to return to Puerto Rico after the Prades Festival in the summer, perhaps even to make a permanent home there. He wanted to help a people in need, and if Catalonia was out of reach, he would give his energy to the land of his mother's birth. Musically the island had little to offer him, apart from a clean slate and the promise of funds to create his own cultural environment. And that indeed was what most suited him. It was years since Casals had attended a public musical performance in which he had not himself participated. And not since 1920 had he sought the stimulus of a richly artistic metropolitan life. First in Barcelona and then in Prades, Casals had constructed his own musical world, according to his own musical priorities. All he needed was a basic organizational structure, resources to import talented performers, and the support of his friends. These Puerto Rico could guarantee, in unprecedentedly generous proportion, and Casals turned automatically to Alexander Schneider to put it all together. 'I am in love with this country', he wrote on 24 February, '. . . and am so sad to leave it. I feel so much that I am at home here that I have had a wonderful idea. What would you say of a Prades Festival in Puerto Rico in April 1957?'[18]

Even before the letter could reach him, Schneider had been tracked down in Florida, where he had been booked by the Daytona Beach Symphony Society for two performances with the Florida Symphony Orchestra, and summoned to Puerto Rico by Governor Muñoz. Never one to miss an event, Schneider caught a plane from Jacksonville immediately after the second performance on 2 March. He was met at San Juan airport by Casals and a representative of the Governor, and spent his first night on the island in the guest suite at La Fortaleza.[19] A further visit and several meetings later the plans were fixed. Casals would be musical director of the Festival Casals Inc., with Schneider as his assistant. A board of directors was appointed, which included Abe Fortas, and the organization established under the aegis of Fomento, with an initial budget of $75,000.

With the first San Juan Festival firmly scheduled for April 1957, and Schneider engaged to arrange it, Casals left Puerto Rico on 23 March. Having discovered that all available passenger ships bound for Le Havre were scheduled to put in first at a Spanish port, he decided to travel by plane. It was Casals' first transatlantic flight and he and Martita travelled via Pan-American Airways to Paris, then by smaller aircraft to Perpignan. The following two months were spent in preparations for the seventh Prades Festival, an especially rich celebration of chamber music at which Casals played Schumann trios in combination with both Menuhin/Istomin and Végh/Serkin, and Schumann's Adagio and Allegro in A Flat Major with Clifford Curzon. After it he travelled once again to Zermatt for a further series of masterclasses and then, as in the previous year, to visit Queen Elisabeth in Belgium. The high-point of the autumn was a concert of homage in the Grand Amphitheatre of the Sorbonne, in Paris, on 10 October, held to celebrate both the fifty-seventh anniversary of his Paris debut and his approaching eightieth birthday. Appropriately, Casals conducted the Lamoureux Orchestra, and a group of eleven cellists – which included Gaspar Cassadó and Rudolf von Tobel – in Fauré's *Elégie* for cello and orchestra, and in a section from his own oratorio, *El Pessebre*. The climax of the evening was the performance, by an ensemble of 102 cellists, of a version of Casals' own Sardana for Cello Orchestra.[20] The eightieth birthday itself, on 29 December, was celebrated in Puerto Rico, to which Casals had returned with Martita at the end of November, this time accompanied by his brother Enrique, his sister-in-law Maria, and a quantity of books, papers and personal possessions. Governor Muñoz gave a dinner of honour at La Fortaleza, followed by a reception and concert in the gardens. Hundreds of greetings cards, letters and telegrams arrived from friends and well-wishers all over the world; most were acknowledged, and all noted and carefully stored. After his eightieth, each of Casals' birthdays prompted considerable celebration and activity, with parties in his honour, presentations and special concerts. Coming of course as it did between Christmas and the end of the year, the birthday enhanced but prolonged the festive period and, increasingly, left Casals exhausted at the beginning of each new year.

In almost every respect the Casals Festival in Puerto Rico was a direct beneficiary of the painful administrative lessons learned in Prades. Artistic decisions – the choice of performers and programme – were taken by Casals and Schneider alone, and implemented through the Festival's New York office. There Schneider, with two secretaries and an 'orchestra contractor', operated out of the premises of the Puerto Rico Division of Tourism on Fifth Avenue. This time Schneider held out resolutely against committees, patrons and other extraneous involvement: the Festival, he maintained, was a Puerto Rican affair and 'not of any social American importance'.[21] Administratively that was true enough, for the business arrangements of the Festival, being part of the island's strategy for economic regeneration, were impressively handled by Pridco, the Puerto Rico Industrial Development Company, and its vice-president for Finance, Gaspar Roca. Pridco had lawyers, business managers and financial experts. And above all it had cash. Casals was to be paid $24,000 for his role as musical director, and the orchestral musicians, who would need to be members of the Musicians' Union, would receive at least the minimum union rate of $150 a week. In terms of those able to attend the Festival concerts, however, the Puerto Rican advantage was heavily, and deliberately, circumscribed. Fearing that the full complement of 2300 seats for each performance would be swiftly bought up by Puerto Ricans, only 1000 were released for local sale, the remainder being held back for tourists and visitors, largely from the United States.

During the winter of 1956–7, Casals and Schneider finalized the Festival details. The basic core of soloists and orchestral players were those who had become regulars at Prades – Serkin, Horszowski, Istomin, Stern, Katims and Szigeti among them. But since union rules debarred the hiring of orchestral musicians from Europe, their place in the orchestra was filled by instrumentalists from North America, such as bass player Julius Levine, flautist Julius Baker, clarinetist David Oppenheim, bassoonist Elias Carmen and horn player John R. Barrows, as well as Schneider's own Budapest String Quartet. Unavoidably but conspicuously, there were few eligible Puerto Ricans other than Jesús María Sanromá, the young soprano Olga Iglesias, one or two members of the very musical Figueroa family, and Marta Montañez herself. Casals agreed to open the Festival with a performance of the Bach C Major Suite, now something of a tradition. But in general he was concerned not to over-extend himself, to avoid the risk of becoming ill and letting people down. Schneider thought him 'as strong as a bull', but Casals knew how draining he had found the October performances in Paris.[22] 'If I couldn't finish the Festival it would be a disaster; you would probably have to return the money . . .' When an infected finger had prevented him from playing a concert at Prades, he remembered, 'more than a hundred people returned their tickets'.[23]

Casals' fears proved cruelly prescient: on the day of the first rehearsal for the first Puerto Rico Festival, he suffered a serious heart attack. It was 16 April 1957, and the orchestra had assembled in the University Theatre on the campus of the University of Puerto Rico in Rio Piedras, six days in advance of the first advertised concert of the Festival. There was an audience of several hundred in the auditorium and Casals, with the minimum of preliminaries, took the orchestra through Mozart's A Major Symphony (No. 29), in order that they might 'get to know each other'. The theatre was warm and the air-conditioning, on Casals' instructions, had been turned off; by the time they broke for an intermission, his shirt was soaked with perspiration. Casals was enormously pleased with the sound the orchestra was producing, and he began a run-through of Schubert's Symphony No. 8 in B Minor (the 'Unfinished'). Twenty bars into the Allegro moderato first movement he made a point about an accent, beating his chest emphatically and shouting 'Voom! Voom!' to mark the beat in typical fashion. He completed the movement and began the second.[24] Some minutes later, and quite suddenly, he put down his baton, murmured a general apology to the orchestra and staggered from the podium. Clearly in acute pain and his faced drained of colour, he was helped backstage into a dressing-room. Within half an hour four doctors had arrived, including Casals' own physician, Dr Jose Passalacqua. A heart specialist, Dr Ramón Suarez, followed at the request of Inés Muñoz Marín, and after three hours of intense pain in the lower chest and left side, an electrocardiogram confirmed that Casals had suffered a coronary thrombosis. He had remained conscious throughout the attack. He loathed hospitals and insisted on returning home to the calle Bucaré apartment, where a hospital bed and oxygen equipment were rapidly installed.

It was a crisis for Casals, of course, for the fledgling Festival and for Puerto Rico itself. The possibility that Casals might die had to be considered, and to insure itself against the adverse publicity that would inevitably follow the Maestro's death in San Juan, Governor Muñoz called in a leading US cardiologist, Paul Dudley White. Examining the patient almost three days after the attack, White revealed that Casals' attack had been a major one, in medical terms an acute anterior myocardial infarction – a blood–clot in one of the heart muscle walls.[25] The prognosis was cautiously positive, but by no means certain. At the very least, Casals would be in bed for a month.

On the evening of the heart attack, Schneider and the Festival administrators gathered for a crisis-meeting that lasted six hours. The Festival was a sell-out and San Juan's hotels were solidly booked for the following three weeks. The decision was made to continue the Festival, in honour of Casals, even, at worst, in memoriam. A press announcement was made and the following morning the *New York Times* headlined its story 'Casals Stricken; to Miss Festival'.[26] Schneider, already scheduled to conduct many of the rehearsals and some of the performances, was asked to take over as musical director, in addition to his role as leader of the orchestra. After a sleepless night he came up with a radical solution for the survival of the Festival: there would be no conductor.[27] Schneider would lead from the concert-master's chair while Casals' high stool on the podium remained empty throughout the Festival. It seemed to work: perhaps the near-tragedy compelled it to. The full programme of concerts continued as planned, the soloists gave powerful performances, the audiences did not stay away, and the festival showed a profit of almost $3000.

Casals' absence from a Festival constructed by, around and for him was an emergency which might be overcome once; but everyone knew that what was crucial was Casals' recovery in time for the second Festival in April 1958. Several things ensured it, the main one being Casals' own astonishing physical resilience. Nursed by Marta, by Maria Casals and, each evening for five weeks, by a young Puerto Rican doctor, Heber Amaury Rosa Silva, he made extraordinary progress. Ten days after the attack he was sitting up; two weeks later he was free of the intravenous tube and eating normally. A month later he was walking half a mile each day at a respectable pace. What he missed most was music, and after two months of deprivation he was back playing the piano for about three hours each day. At first the cello was too arduous a prospect, and Casals wondered if he would have to learn to play all over again, if the fingers of his left hand would ever recover their dexterity. Marta noticed that his core preoccupation was the fear that he was becoming 'a stranger with the cello'.[28] But gradually he became stronger: by July he was practising for an hour and a half each day, his intonation apparently unimpaired and his bowing arm firm. Casals made his own acknowledgements:

> . . . as I once more found the music of my cello, I marvelled more than ever before at that other instrument which made it possible

for me to play again. Man has made many machines, complex and cunning, but which of them indeed rivals the working of the heart?[29]

Whatever the cause of Casals' thrombosis – and a full medical examination in Mexico the previous year had described his constitution as that of a man of thirty-five – one reason for his survival was clear: he still had a great deal of living to do. He had now established himself in a fresh and stimulating environment, with new friends, a new way of life and an ambitious and challenging range of opportunities for music. And he wanted to get married. In Puerto Rico as in Prades, Marta Montañez was constantly at his side, coping with the practical requirements of an eighty-year-old man in constant demand on two continents. Single-handedly she had made him want to live again, and shown him not only that it was possible, but that it could be fun. For two years now they had scarcely been separated: since the heart attack she had nursed him assiduously. There was now no possibility that he could manage alone, even if he cared to try. If they were to marry, this seemed the ideal time, and on 3 August the ceremony took place in Casals' own apartment in the calle Bucaré.

Casals and Marta had themselves already privately discussed the possibility of marriage, and the closeness of the relationship had inevitably provoked considerable gossip. Earlier in 1957 Marta had declined to join the Festival orchestra, arguing that she needed to devote her full energies to Casals. In advance of that decision she had sought the advice of Doña Inés, since 'naturally my parents will not be happy'.[30] Aquiles and Doña Angélica Montañez had been, understandably, startled and distressed. They had dispatched their daughter on a scholarship to study with the greatest cellist in the world; what two years before had seemed a magnificent opportunity now appeared to be leading to her abandoning the instrument. More than this, there was even talk of marriage. However much they may have admired Casals personally, or been in awe of him, the idea that their twenty-one-year-old daughter should not only give up her career but, as they put it, sacrifice 'her life' to the Maestro came as an extraordinary shock.[31] Despite Doña Inés' intervention, they opposed it and Marta, being under-age, could not be married from her own home. None of her family attended the wedding nor saw the couple off on their honeymoon the following day. Even Marta's uncle, Rafael, was absent, issuing a statement, printed in the *Morning Post*, that 'the Montañez family is very honoured to have such a distinguished "in-law", but the difference in age makes it difficult for us to accept the marriage'. It was two years before Marta's father was in any sense reconciled:

only her grandmother came sooner to an understanding of what had happened.[32]

It is less surprising that Casals should have proposed than that Marta should have accepted. Thirty years later it remained difficult for her to explain: 'something propelled me that I still don't understand'. She knew that she had become essential to Casals, and it seemed a natural course. 'I was very clear I wanted to contribute to his life, and that is what I did.'[33] Her decision very probably gave Casals another seventeen years of alert and active life. And whatever the private options she herself relinquished in terms of family and children, the marriage to Casals provided Marta Montañez with privileged access to a genius, the responsibility for his memory, and an experience few can share or imagine.

Before he could marry Marta, however, Casals needed a divorce from Susan Metcalfe. Casals and Metcalfe had been married for forty-three years, but had not met for thirty. After their separation she had lived in Paris, and her last known recital had been in 1951 at the Ecole Normale de Musique.[34] Sometime in the early 1950s Susan Metcalfe Casals had been found in France in a distressed and confused state, and Casals had been contacted. He arranged for her to be cared for in a hospice run by a sister of Capdevila, and subsequently to return to her family in New Jersey. In 1957, not knowing if she was alive, Casals began proceedings for divorce. The decree, issued in Mexico on 17 May, listed the grounds for the ending of the marriage as Susan Metcalfe's desertion of the matrimonial home, radical incompatibility, and the prolonged thirty-year separation.[35] With some alarm it was discovered, only days before the wedding ceremony on 3 August, that the Metcalfe divorce decree had not been formally witnessed. Jack Delano was summoned to the San Juan office of Casals' lawyer, and the formalities were expedited. Thanking Delano warmly, Casals offered to return the favour when necessary.[36]

A marriage between a man of eighty and a young woman of twenty-one was bound to provoke shock, incredulity, rumour and a certain degree of ridicule. None realized it more clearly than Casals and Marta themselves. Casals, disarmingly candid, referred to it later in his memoirs:

> I was aware at the time that some people noted a certain discrepancy
> in our ages – a bridegroom of course is not usually thirty years
> older than his father-in-law. But Martita and I were not too con-
> cerned about what others thought; it was, after all, we who were
> getting married – not they.[37]

It was easier, none the less, to marry quietly and quickly, with the minimum of attention, and slip away to give the world time to absorb the news. The civil ceremony in Casals' apartment was witnessed only by Dr José Passalacqua and the music critic, Alfredo Matilla. A religious ceremony followed in the Capilla de la Piedad in the nearby suburb of Isla Verde, performed by a family acquaintance and attended by a few close friends. The next day, 4 August, the couple left for Europe on board the liner *Antilles*, and on 5 August Superior Court Judge Martin Almodovar disclosed the marriage to the press.[38] In San Salvador, Luis and Teresina Casals heard the news via a radio broadcast. Not even Sasha Schneider was warned: a postcard from Casals written the day before the wedding failed to mention it. It took Schneider a while to respond: 'I meant to write for a long time,' he said in a letter sent to Prades on 5 September, 'to wish you all the happiness in the world.'[39]

The newly married couple arrived back in Prades to a certain amount of unavoidable consternation, the reception being, as Casals described it, 'in part good and in the other bad'.[40] Some old friends kept their distance, though many registered open delight. What was most inopportune was the request of Admiral Troy, the owner of El Cant dels Ocells, that Casals vacate it for the Troys' own use. With Casals not yet back to full strength, it was not the right time. It proved difficult to find an alternative house and the staff at the Mairie were conspicuously unhelpful. Casals was stressed and emotional, though Meicio Horszowski arrived with impeccable timing to cheer him with the prospect of some Beethoven cello sonatas. Eventually the proprietor of the Hôtel Grand Thermal in the neighbouring spa village of Molitg-les-Bains offered Casals and Marta a small apartment adjoining the hotel. Furniture, music and papers were packed and transported the 5 miles to Molitg, which became Casals' headquarters for the period of the Festival during the next nine years. Whether or not the removal from Prades had anything to do with feelings in the town following the marriage, it certainly made it easier for Casals when the time came in 1966 to sever permanently his connection with the Festival. The marriage of Casals and Marta was ultimately no one else's business, though it became everyone else's fascination. None that knew them or saw them together during the final years of Casals' life could doubt, however, that they married for love.

The heart attack had knocked a hole in the heavy schedule of engagements for 1957. For the first time Casals had missed the Prades Festival, which took place without him in July. Plans for five concerts with Horszowski in the Beethovenhaus in Bonn were postponed until the following year, and the first Concours International Pablo Casals, a cello competition in Paris held in honour of his eightieth birthday, had to be postponed from June until October: Casals attended, but did not join the panel of judges, which included Barbirolli, Eisenberg, Cassadó, Fournier and Rostropovich.[41] Casals also missed his now annual visit to Queen Elisabeth in Belgium, but at the end of August he and Marta did go to the Zermatt Summer Academy, although he did not teach and did not play. For Zermatt was one of his private pleasures, where he went to enjoy the clean air, the tranquillity, the spectacular mountain scenery and the companionship of the most gifted young cellists in Europe. Generally, at Zermatt, Casals would take small classes of cellists through sections of the classical chamber literature – quartets, trios or sonatas – and give a number of private and relatively informal concerts with Horszowski, Sándor Végh, or whichever other friends were there. This was the music-making Casals preferred, small groups of motivated artists, living and playing together for several weeks without public pressure. He had not taught in this way since his classes at the Ecole Normale in Paris in the early 1920s, and would not find another such opportunity until invited by Rudolf Serkin to the Marlboro Festivals during the 1960s.

Occasionally Zermatt threw up an astonishing talent: in 1960 a 'brilliantly talented teenager from England' stood out among the younger players and was chosen as soloist in the Saint-Saëns A Minor Concerto at the students' concert on the evening before Casals' departure.[42] The teenager was Jacqueline du Pré, fifteen years old and, by a neat irony, sponsored in Zermatt by the Suggia Gift, the scholarship willed by Guilhermina Suggia and funded through the sale of her Stradivarius instrument. Du Pré won the Suggia award for seven successive years, and it provided her with the means to an independent career which Suggia herself had so conspicuously lacked at the same age. Casals was immediately struck by du Pré's power and energy, and surprised when she revealed that she was English: 'With such temperament? Impossible.'[43] But du Pré was young, headstrong and, in her own phrase, 'bolshie'. She did not acknowledge authority automatically, and could not stomach the overt manifestations of the Casals cult – the deference, the circle of admiring women, the apparent dogmatism. As a result she failed to explore what Casals may have had to offer her, and resisted anything that appeared to rival the advice of her own teacher, William Pleeth. The following year, however, persuaded by Horszowski and by Pleeth himself, she wrote to ask for private lessons during the autumn of 1962.[44] The lessons never materialized, and du Pré studied instead with Tortelier at the Dartington Summer School. She did, however, with her husband, Daniel Barenboim, later attend and perform at the Casals Festival in San Juan.

After early autumn in Europe, Casals and Marta returned to Puerto Rico for the winter. Their first home together was not in the busy Santurce area of San Juan, but about 8 miles outside the centre of the city at Isla Verde. A light, modern house was built by the ocean, to which they moved at the beginning of 1958. There Casals rested, practised and made preparations for the second San Juan Festival, due to open in April. From 1957, and for the last sixteen years of his life, the pattern of Casals' year was dominated by the Festivals he headed and the musical retreats he liked to attend. With the Puerto Rico Festival in the spring, Prades in the early summer, the Zermatt Summer Academy in August and, after 1960, the Marlboro Festival in July, eight or ten weeks of the year were routinely blocked out in his calendar. Planning and programming for Prades and Puerto Rico consumed weeks besides: in effect, the two festivals that bore his name involved a year-round effort. And in practice they provided him with a very substantial degree of musical patronage. With Schneider, Casals selected the orchestral players for Puerto Rico, determined the programme and picked the soloists. With Enrique, who after 1956 had taken over the day-to-day administration in France, he did the same for Prades. In Zermatt and Marlboro he rapidly became the central attraction, with young players making a kind of pilgrimage to be with him. Along with several cello competitions established in his name and under his adjudication, masterclasses around the world, the pupils he accepted or declined to teach privately, and the talented individuals placed in his line of scrutiny wherever he turned, his power to promote and to endorse musical careers was strikingly evident.

Inevitably, too, Casals had strong views and clear favourites. In 1959, for example, he favoured the pianists Rubinstein, Arrau, Hess and Kempff for Puerto Rico, but not the 1954 Leventritt winner, Van Cliburn ('not for us or for the quality we want to maintain') or Glenn Gould who, he observed to Schneider, 'has not aroused enthusiasm'.[45] Leonard Bernstein, however, who had been introduced to Casals at Schneider's fiftieth birthday party in New York in 1958, was invited both to conduct and to play a piano concerto. Sometimes the guests had equally strong opinions. Invited to Puerto Rico in 1965, Arthur Rubinstein agreed to two concerts provided Casals did not conduct. Sometimes they were simply hurt. Paul Tortelier, stung by his omission from the jury of the Pablo Casals competition in Acapulco in 1959, wrote a long analysis of their relationship since 1945. Then, after hearing Tortelier for the first time, Casals' only criticism had been 'that you have conquered me'. Fourteen years on, Tortelier asked if it had been at Prades that he had 'annoyed' Casals, by his independent spirit, his 'syndicaliste' politics, or his primordial Gallic passion.[46]

For young players, catching Casals' attention could make their career. The twenty-six-year-old American, Leslie Parnas, won the first prize of 350,000 francs in the 1957 Paris Concours International, and was catapulted to a successful solo career. In Israel in 1961 and wherever he travelled, a procession of extravagantly gifted string-players was presented to Casals. His interest was pricked by some more than others. Parents sometimes employed a more direct approach. In November 1961 Casals received a note from H. T. Ma, informing him that his six-year-old son, Yo Yo, 'thinks of you almost every day'.[47] In 1966 Mrs Won Sook Chung brought her children, Kyung-Wha and Myung-Wha, to play for the Maestro in San Juan. Others were simply unlucky. Young students, like Thomas Igloi, continued to request individual lessons, but, with Casals in his late eighties, the masterclass seemed a more effective use of his time than private teaching.

Of all Casals' musical interests, those in Puerto Rico were the most important, at least in the eyes of the Puerto Ricans. As the subsidiary of an industrial development programme, the Casals Festival was unusually privileged for a cultural event. It received subsidies, tax advantages and other benefits common to all Fomento projects, and administrative decisions were made swiftly and flexibly under existing legislation by the head of Pridco, Theodore Moscoso. But there was a catch. As part of a wider programme for the economic, social and cultural regeneration of the island, the central purpose of the Festival, and later of the Symphony Orchestra and Music Conservatory, was not simply to honour Casals, but to foster and promote indigenous creativity. Soon there was pressure, from government and the Federation of Labour Musicians' Union, to include more Puerto Rican music on the Festival programme, and to recruit local musicians for the orchestra. Casals was by no means unaware of the pressures, or the extent to which he was seen as a means to an end. He recommended the Puerto Rican Jesús María Sanromá as Director of the Conservatory for its first three or four years, since that would go down well.[48] The post in fact went to the Argentinian conductor–composer, Juan José Castro.

When faced with an idea he did not care for, Casals deployed a strategic gift for missing the point which invariably resolved the matter in his favour. Invited to use the Puerto Rico University Chorus, or to select a particular local violinist, Casals responded that he did not mind where musicians came from, so long as they were able to maintain the quality of the Festival. Pressed to establish a yearly benefit to raise $50–60,000 for Puerto Rican cultural interests, he regretted that commitments elsewhere precluded acceptance. Where, however, there was a straightforward clash between the island's interest and his own, he was immovable. Offered an honorary doctorate by the University of Puerto Rico early in 1956, Casals discovered that a fellow recipient was to be the Supreme Court Justice of Spain, José Castán Tobenas, visiting the island as part of a convocation of international jurists. Casals declined the degree, accepting one instead at the Inter-American Polytechnic University soon afterwards.[49]

At the 1958 San Juan Festival Casals performed Beethoven sonatas and Brahms sextets in several chamber recitals but, on doctors' orders, still did not conduct; not until the third Festival, in April 1959, did he play a full part in the programme. That the Festival began without its founder was, in a sense, a liberation, both for it and for him. Whereas Prades was pivoted on his presence, and risked collapse if he did not attend, Puerto Rico was forcibly weaned from a similarly intense cult of personality, and became more flexible and more varied as a result. Casals did not need to attend every concert and, as he grew older, he did not care to: the programme continued and the audiences attended, even if Casals was at home watching the proceedings on television. On one occasion a ticket-holder complained that her seat had been taken by a stranger. About to effect an ejection, the usher was disconcerted to discover that the usurper was the Maestro himself, who had come to the concert unexpectedly.[50]

After the seventeen-day Festival, Casals and Marta returned to Prades, and settled into the Molitg-les-Bains apartment. Molitg, then as now, was a popular but fairly exclusive *station thermale de la beauté*, and the large, pink and imposing Hôtel Grand Thermal catered to comfortably-off city-dwellers seeking health with their holiday. The hotel was equipped with sun-terraces, gymnasiums and 'thermal cabins' in which guests soaked in marble baths or endured plankton mud treatment while looking out, through one-way panoramic windows, at the eucalyptus and palm forests beneath them. Bathing in the hotel's lake, fed by a 35°C spring, was said to benefit the skin, allergies in general and most respiratory and rheumatic conditions. The only disadvantage was the pervading odour of sulphur. Casals' accommodation was in an annexe to the main hotel building, a sort of pavilion with a clock-tower and later a working carillon which the hotel proprietor constructed in his honour.[51] The apartment had a fine view over the winding road from Prades, and it is said that Casals, with the carillon keyboard in his room, sounded the Belgian national anthem when he saw in the distance the approach of Queen Elisabeth's limousine.[52]

There is no evidence that Casals, in nine summers spent at Molitg, took any interest in the treatments available, or that he was at all faddish about his health. By late 1958 he already seemed fully recovered from the thrombosis of the previous year, and the attention of Marta to routine details of everyday existence which Casals found uninteresting left him healthier and more energetic, as well as better-dressed, than for years. The surgical removal of a birth-mark on the left of his forehead certainly left him rather more photogenic. Casals' longevity, together with his remarkable physical robustness, did prompt bizarre interest. There were rumours that he had received injections of sheep's placenta while in Switzerland. And, because of his 'extreme youthfulness', he was in 1964 included in a survey undertaken by Dr Manfred Clynes, director of the Bio-Cybernetics Laboratory at the Rockland State Hospital, New York, to 'shed some light on the problem of what constitutes essential elements of retaining youthful characteristics in spite of biologic age-ing'.[53] So far as he thought about it at all, Casals attributed his longevity to work and continued activity: 'to stop, to retire even for a short time', he said, 'is to begin to die'.[54] He began his memoirs on the same theme, declaring that he was then ninety-three: 'That is not young, of course. In fact, it is older than ninety. But age is a relative matter. If you continue to work and to absorb the beauty in the world about you, you find that age does not necessarily mean getting old.'[55]

Sasha Schneider, of course, did not allow Casals to become overly pompous about age. In Prades in 1966 he arranged for a hoax letter from the Georgian Caucasian Orchestra, inviting Casals to be guest conductor. The invitation – based on an article about longevity in the Soviet Cau-casus, published in the *Illustrated London News* – declared that although members of the orchestra were required to be over 100 years old, an exception would be made, 'despite your youthfulness', in view of Casals' talent. Casals fell for it. 'Isn't this wonderful!' he told Marta. 'Let's go.'[56]

After Marta Montañez, Alexander Schneider was the most critical agency in Casals' life at this time. For the last twenty-five years of the Maestro's life, Schneider was wholly devoted to him, and totally loyal. Even the 'feet-of-clay' period, the break at Prades between 1953 and 1955, was very probably more a consequence of the shifting of Schneider's emotional centre of gravity – during his relationship with Geraldine Page – than any personal difference between the two men. And Casals knew this. When the marriage with Page was over, Schneider plunged back into Casals' life without a moment's recrimination on either side. Casals' relationship with Schneider was different from almost any other. Schneider was honest, open and fearless, with none of the obsequiousness displayed by – and perhaps required from – most other of Casals' pupils and disciples. And while many of the very greatest musicians of the time kept their distance from Casals, fearing perhaps being burned or blinded by too close a proximity to the sun, Schneider not only sought him out but accepted the potentially fraught role of his musical deputy or *doppelgänger*. Schneider's great energy and enthusiasm for people and experiences have led his career down unusual paths, and his outspoken candour has brought others to a sudden halt. But his activities – generally on several fronts simultaneously – and immense artistic generosity have invariably resulted in the improvement and promotion of the careers of his friends and colleagues rather than of his own professional interests. Casals was one of his greatest beneficiaries. Schneider was concerned with every aspect of the Maestro's comfort and well-being. He badgered the Puerto Rican authorities to provide Casals with improved and more convenient accommodation. He discovered the best source of good food and fresh vegetables in San Juan, and encouraged Casals to take advantage of it.[57] He travelled where Casals travelled, smoothing his way, and was constantly to hand at every critical performance or public occasion. He interposed himself between Casals and his critics and was everywhere willing to shoulder the burden and deal with the blame. After Casals' death the cellist Pierre Fournier wrote to Schneider that he had earned the gratitude of every musician for having 'unified the whole musical world around Casals'.[58]

Schneider's memoirs reveal, however, that his limitless musical respect and personal devotion were mixed with a healthy realism about what he saw as Casals' flaws and inconsistencies. For Schneider, the issue of moral principle was wholly clear-cut and straightforward. His own mother and sisters had died in Auschwitz: there was no question that he could ever play in Germany or Austria again. So while he fully comprehended Casals' refusal to perform in countries that recognized Franco, he could not understand what he took to be the cumulative modification of Casals' moral position. For Schneider, amending an absolute position meant destroying it. Once Casals had set foot in Spain, once he had performed in Germany, and once he had settled in a country which was unarguably part of the United States, Schneider failed to see any purpose in continued compunction. He observed that: 'Somehow, even Casals always found a reason for excusing his actions. These excuses were nonsense in my opinion. It is unfortunate that most great artists . . . can be great compromisers, particularly when they want or need something for their personal beliefs.'[59]

The issue in September 1958 was Casals' visit to Germany to give two private recitals at the place of Beethoven's birth in Bonn. It was only his second visit to Germany since the 1930s – his first, also to the Beethovenhaus, had been on 23 September 1955 – and once again Schneider, otherwise irrepressible at every one of Casals' great international occasions, was absent. Instead, Sándor Végh joined Casals and Mieczyslaw Horszowski in Trios Nos. 3 in C Minor (Op. 1, No. 3) and 5 in D Major (Op. 70, No. 1) which were recorded by Philips in the dismal acoustics of the Beethovenhaus. For some, remembering Casals' hostility to the plans of Furtwängler and Cassadó to perform in the United States after the Second World War, it was hard to swallow. But for Casals it was a deeply emotional act of homage to the memory of Beethoven, an act which transcended simple politics. Horszowski later recalled the performance as the most moving in his career with Casals.[60]

Casals had responded indulgently to Schneider's surprise about the move to Puerto Rico: 'I cannot blame you for not understanding my moral position. You must know and be sure of my friendship and love.'[61] The truth was, however, that Casals continuously redefined his personal convictions, carefully and cautiously as most people do, within the context of practical reality. The purest manifestation of his embargo had been compromised the moment he played at the first Prades Festival in 1950; and technically his conducting of two of his own works during a visit to Zurich following the Perpignan Festival in September 1951, in Paris in 1957 and in Puerto Rico during 1958 were further 'infringements' of his own code. Long before 1957 Casals had recognized that while his stand had impressed many individuals, it had not changed the policies of governments. Moreover, he knew that Franco was not likely to bow to the protests of a handful of exiled intellectuals, nor that many within Spain were aware of his continuing embargo in any case. But he knew that his age, distinction and fame made him a symbol for the thousands of Catalans around the world whose exile was now, like his, a permanent condition. Their hopes remained his primary concern and one he would not betray. But continued self-sacrifice and personal deprivation were no longer a precondition of making his point. Paradoxically, Casals' humanitarian credentials were now so well established that whenever he performed in a major world centre the effect was to reinforce the power of his statement rather than to breach it. He had, in a sense, done his time. People knew what he stood for. Now he could take his message into their back-yards.

Schneider was right to see the move to Puerto Rico as a critical point. He himself was pleased to see Casals 'getting out of Prades', but advised that it was important 'to explain to the world why you are going to have a Festival in Puerto Rico'.[62] Because Casals had not deliberately planned the move, but rather acquiesced in it, his immediate rationalization – that Puerto Rico was distinct from the United States by virtue of having no direct representation in Washington – was unconvincing. But his real and more plausible response, over the next five years, was to broaden the scope of his political position to take advantage both of his proximity to the United States and the status he now clearly shared, with Schweitzer and Einstein, as a global humanitarian icon. It remained important to him to draw a distinction between playing and conducting, a narrow distinction, one writer observed, 'but if it satisfies his conscience, it can scarcely be questioned by others'.[63] But increasingly Casals' focus shifted from a single-minded opposition to European fascism, to encompass the nuclear threat and the campaign for world peace.

War had played a prominent part in the first seventy years of Casals' life: peace would be the dominant preoccupation of his final years. In his early twenties he had seen the personal consequences of Spain's final, desperate and fruitless struggle to retain the colonies of Cuba, Puerto Rico and the Philippines. He had bought military exemption for his brother Luis, but with that option closed, Enrique had to be dispatched to Argentina in 1912 to escape compulsory mobilization to fight Spain's savage war with Morocco. In Paris in 1914, Casals' life and career were totally disrupted by the First World War. Twenty years later, civil war in Spain, followed by the Second World War, led to permanent exile for him and for hundreds of thousands of fellow Catalans, and to the abandonment by the international community of principles he considered fundamental to civilized life. If war could be beneficial, he had not seen it. He knew that if he had a platform, he should use it to celebrate peace and warn of the madness of war.

Casals had first met Albert Schweitzer in Edinburgh in 1934, and then again in Zurich, seventeen years later. Between those meetings, and afterwards, the Hermit of Lambaréné and the Hermit of Prades had maintained a respectful correspondence, first about Bach, a shared passion, and then about politics. Their exchanges, inevitably, rarely extended beyond universals and abstractions, but at their September 1951 encounter the dialogue fastened on the obligations of the artist in a troubled world. Schweitzer's decision was to 'create', Casals' to protest. But by the mid-1950s the reality of the Cold War, atomic testing and rearmament impelled each to do both. During April 1958 Casals was strongly affected by three radio appeals broadcast by Schweitzer under the title 'Peace or Atomic War?' That summer the two men issued a joint statement to the Soviet and US governments, calling for an end to nuclear testing and a cessation of the arms race. Soon afterwards Casals accepted an invitation to perform at the General Assembly of the United Nations, during the annual United Nations Day concert held to mark the anniversary of the organization's foundation.

The invitation, from the United Nations Secretary-General Dag Hammarskjöld, had come in February, when an emissary had spent three days with Casals in Puerto Rico, seeking his acceptance. But the UN was located within the United States, where Casals had undertaken not to perform; Spain, moreover, was a member-state. He at first refused but subsequently, persuaded that the land on which the United Nations headquarters stood, by the East River in Manhattan, was extra-territorial and politically neutral, Casals recognized that the invitation was an important opportunity. The concert took place on 24 October, the programme beginning with Charles Munch conducting the Boston Symphony Orchestra in Arthur Honneger's Fifth Symphony. After an address by Hammarskjöld, Casals and Horszowski played Bach's Sonata No. 2 in D Major, followed by *El Cant des Ocells*. In additional segments of the concert in Paris and Geneva, there were performances by Yehudi Menuhin, David Oistrakh and Ravi Shankar, while Ernest Ansermet conducted the 'Ode to Joy' from the final movement of Beethoven's Ninth Symphony.

Casals had planned to preface his performance with a substantial message of peace, but since only delegates or political representatives were permitted to speak in the hall of the General Assembly, his statement was included in the printed programme. In it he indicated why he was there:

> . . . it is not because anything has changed in my moral attitude or in the restrictions that I have imposed upon myself and my career as an artist all these years, but because today all else becomes secondary in comparison to the great and perhaps mortal danger threatening all humanity.[64]

Casals called for an end to nuclear experiments and appealed to governments – and to all men 'not living in unconsciousness' – to seek the dignity of peace rather than the 'inhumanity and uselessness of war'. He recommended music as a universal language and source of communication among men.

The United Nations Day concert was the most widely broadcast musical event in history. It was carried via the new technology of a transatlantic cable to radio networks in seventy-five countries and on all five continents, and transmitted on television by CBS. The event attracted enormous press coverage around the world, and the image of Casals as a campaigner for peace was projected into millions of homes. Prades and the publicity resulting from it had presented Casals as a figure of conscience, primarily to Europe and North America. The United Nations appearance transformed him, virtually instantaneously, into a globally recognizable symbol of peace and, in the uncomfortable but accurate phrase, a 'geriatric superstar'.

The visit to the United Nations meant of course a visit to New York. Casals had not been to the city for thirty years, and the volume of press attention was overwhelming. The six days he and Marta spent in New York brought home to them both the exhilaration of celebrity status, and the price to be paid for it. A deluge of requests followed the announcement of the visit, demands for interviews, invitations to dinners, requests to conduct and play, pleas to visit and address Spanish refugee communities: 'I am refusing almost everything,' Casals wrote to Schneider, 'because if I were to accept I would have to stay there a year!'[65] In New York, they gained some privacy by accepting Eugene Istomin's offer of his apartment, but the pressure continued – telephone messages, letters, cards, telegrams, requests for autographs and photographs, demands to comment on one or other issue of the day and widespread solicitations for his money and his time. For the remainder of his life, this would be the norm: the burden of fame. Every step he took generated newspaper comment, every remark was scrutinized. For an artist with a fairly conspicuous ego, the attention and admiration were welcome in principle. But for a man who retained his almost Victorian reticence about matters he considered personal and private, the indiscriminate curiosity of the outside world was a painful imposition. Protected by Marta, Casals limited his engagements. On 21 October he attended Schneider's fiftieth birthday party at the Golden Horn restaurant, and there met Leonard Bernstein for the first time. There was also an emotional encounter – but for the last time – with his old friend Fritz Kreisler, whom he had not seen since 1936 when together they had played the Brahms Double Concerto in London. The day after the UN concert Casals visited students at the Manhattan School of Music, and heard Istomin play Schumann's Piano Concerto at Carnegie Hall.[66] He then returned to Puerto Rico to begin to answer the 5000 letters and telegrams that had arrived in response to the American visit.

# 13

## Music and the Fight for Peace, 1960–1973

Perhaps I shall never see Catalonia again. For years I believed
that freedom would come again to my beloved land before I
died. Now I am unsure.

*Pablo Casals*[1]

In 1958 Casals was nominated for the Nobel Prize for Peace. He did not
win: it went instead to a monk of the Dominican order in Belgium,
Georges Pire, in recognition of his work for political refugees. It is not now
clear how far Casals' candidature went within the mysterious processes
of the Nobel apparatus. But it was almost certainly scuppered by the
overtly partisan nature of the nominating committee, the Agrupación
Catalana 'Montserrat', an organization of Catalans living predominantly in Peru and Chile, who pushed for the Prize as recognition of the
Catalan nation as a whole, rather than as an explicit acknowledgement
of Casals as an individual. But the fact of the nomination, and the attention it received from individuals such as Schweitzer, Eisenhower and
Queen Elisabeth of the Belgians, confirmed Casals' global credibility as,
in the committee's words, 'une lumière irremplaçable dans la lutte de
notre humanité'.[2]

The aura of saintliness that settled over Casals in the last dozen years
of his life separated him to an extent from his past. A number of life-long
friends sensed that he was no longer accessible to them, or at least not
under the same conditions. In reality this was probably inevitable. For a
start, he was living in a completely different environment, on an island
in the Caribbean Sea. For friends in North America, Puerto Rico was no
more inaccessible than Prades had been for Casals' European colleagues,
indeed probably less so. But it felt a long way from London, or Paris,
or indeed from San Salvador: in his last years Casals saw far less of his
immediate family, his brothers and their children, than he had during
the first eighty years of his life. And he may not have minded. The
conditions of his life were so vastly more comfortable, and the opportu-

nities for making music so rich and interesting, that the fact that he had been effectively 'annexed' by his friends in North and Latin America could not have worried him unduly. The pity, for him, was that it had not happened sooner.

Some felt disconcerted, too, that in his old age Casals appeared rather to 'believe in his own sainthood',[3] a view apparently corroborated by the publication in 1970 of *Joys and Sorrows*, the volume of reminiscences compiled by Albert E. Kahn. As well as material of great charm and fascination, the book included passages which appeared embarrassingly self-regarding: 'the sad fact is that one can discuss one's own humility only so long without arousing suspicion in one's listeners'.[4] This did not seem to damage the book, however, which sold 20,000 copies in its first year and was translated into many languages. But it did ascribe to Casals a degree of vanity and self-righteousness which is wholly absent in his letters and which, according to those who met him, was conspicuously absent in the man. Casals did indeed have a very strong sense of himself; he knew he was important, but it did not manifest itself in terms of conceit or narcissism. As Lael Wertenbaker observed in 1950:

> Casals has egotism and pride, but it is detached egotism, almost impersonal, essentially humble. He holds his gift in his hand as a gift from God, and admires it without false modesty. His great pride is feeling he has proper respect for the gift . . . and has fulfilled his duty. . . . Personally he is gentle, benign, modest, friendly and utterly unaffected.[5]

The pressures of celebrity did, however, require some restraint. As the 'first cultural citizen of the world' and a kind of moral head of state, Casals was pestered and cajoled from all sides, and his own instinct was to say yes to everything. It could not go on. In December 1960 he entered his eighty-fifth year. No one knew how many years he had left: the 1957 heart attack signalled a continuing coronary vulnerability. Casals had things to do and needed to focus his energy. Yehudi Menuhin has said that 'there is no more successful old age I can think of than that of Casals'.[6] It was entirely due to the care and protection of Marta that this was so. After performing the Boccherini B Flat Major Concerto in December 1959, with Casals conducting, in the Puerto Rican cities of San Juan and Ponce, Marta abandoned her own highly promising solo career to devote all her energies to 'the Maestro'. Casals frequently maintained that Marta had been his best pupil. But she knew she could not both have a professional career and attend to his needs. By now in any case it had been fairly well established that Casals preferred his closest companions not to be professional musicians. Marta made her choice.

The single event that most effectively projected Casals on to the world stage was his performance for President John F. Kennedy at the White House in November 1961. Casals had of course played for monarchs and leaders throughout his life, and had indeed played at the White House itself, fifty-seven years earlier. But the performance in Washington on 13 November 1961 was of a different order. Kennedy was a highly visible President, and this was the most publicized of all White House concerts, probably of any concert in America.[7] It was broadcast by NBC and ABC, recorded by Columbia, and attracted massive press interest from around the world. It was also Casals' first deliberate public performance on American soil since the start of his boycott in 1946. And it very nearly did not happen at all.

Casals was in Israel when a letter from the White House arrived in September. The origin of the invitation is unknown: one account suggests that the idea was suggested to Jacqueline Kennedy by Greta Garbo.[8] It is more likely to have come from Abe Fortas, by then established as Casals' personal lawyer as well as legal adviser to Kennedy's Vice-President, Lyndon Johnson, and a well-known Washington figure. In principle Casals was very keen to accept. Since his re-emergence into active life five years earlier, he had looked for a political figure in whom he might place his trust and hopes for the world. He found it in John Kennedy. Kennedy's predecessor as President, General Eisenhower, had gone to Madrid in 1959, declaring it had been his 'life's ambition' to visit Spain and 'meet the Spanish people'. What he really wanted was Franco's continued agreement to the location of US military bases in the country. After Kennedy's election in 1960, Casals had twice written to the White House, pushing for a reversal of the Spanish policy of the previous administration. But the idea of a public visit to the White House was more significant and, as he explained to Fortas, 'extremely delicate . . . every move I make must be carefully considered and traced in my line of ideals and actions'.[9] Casals would go to Washington to 'convey publicly my confidence in Kennedy as leader of the West', provided the invitation was a personal one from the President and provided Casals could play 'privately' for Kennedy and his friends. In particular there should be no press conference or any reference to the Spanish question:

For example, I would certainly be asked: have you abandoned your position in regard to Spain? I would have to answer 'No'. If I were asked: do you now agree with the US policy towards Spain? my answer would be 'No'. If I were asked: Why does Franco still hold power after so many years? I would have to answer: 'It is due, mainly, to the United States' aid and support.' As you see, this would be very dangerous and disagreeable.[10]

At that point it all went wrong. A memorandum from Fortas to the President's adviser, Pierre Salinger, had summarized Casals' conditions, but had been overlooked.[11] The announcement of the concert to the press declared that the State Dinner – which Casals had declined since he made it a rule not to eat before a performance – was now to be in honour of President Muñoz Marín and the Commonwealth of Puerto Rico, and would be followed by the performance by Casals. The implication was that Casals was lifting his performing embargo as a mark of respect for Muñoz Marín, and the press – particularly in Puerto Rico – took it as such. Casals was shocked by the sudden change of emphasis and threatened to pull out of the event: it took every ounce of Fortas' celebrated persuasive skill to convince him otherwise. In four letters and a telegram to Puerto Rico, Fortas appealed against a reaction which could 'strike a blow at the presidency and at the cause to which you are devoted'. Kennedy, he explained, 'sometimes acts on the advice of subordinates and without careful consideration'. The invitation to Muñoz Marín was an afterthought, and the essential focus of the evening still that 'Pablo Casals is to honour President Kennedy as a leader in the fight for peace'.[12]

Whether or not Fortas was believed, his appeal worked. Kennedy's invitation, and Casals' carefully worded letter of acceptance, were published as a hurried press release on 24 October. But it had been a painful awakening: the US Government, like the British Government in 1945, clearly did not take Casals' moral position as seriously as he took it himself:

> I realized when the idea of my going to Washington began that I
> would have to accept the risks of misunderstanding and disapproval
> . . . for many years I have maintained my stand against all kinds
> of criticisms, condemnations and even calumnies, and they have
> never bothered me because I had my convictions. But what would
> bother would be that those who have confidence in me would think
> that I had betrayed them.[13]

If the White House concert involved a compromise for Casals, it proved to be a highly effective political manoeuvre for Kennedy. 'A nation reveals itself', he had said, 'not only by the men it produces but also by the men it honors.'[14] Honouring Muñoz Marín was not only a means of endorsing the economic miracle in Puerto Rico as a model for modernization in Latin America in general, but of signalling gratitude to

the estimated 300,000 Puerto Rican voters in New York who had cru-
cially assisted Kennedy's wafer-thin presidential victory over Richard
Nixon in 1960.[15] Entertaining Pablo Casals did Kennedy no harm, either,
with the peace lobby, and nourished his administration's reputation as
one friendly to the arts. Indeed the Casals concert was followed by
evenings in honour of Stravinsky, André Malraux, Isaac Stern and Ernest
Hemingway, and created, in the words of Thornton Wilder, 'a whole
new world of surprised self-respect'.[16]

The concert itself was a substantial success. The day before the performance, Casals, who was to be accompanied by Mieczyslaw Horszowski and Alexander Schneider, rehearsed for three hours in the Diplomatic
Reception Room. The White House piano, an ornate 9-foot Steinway,
reminded Casals of a Cadillac convertible Marta had recently purchased.[17] The following evening, 200 of America's most prominent
musicians assembled in the mirrored and heavily draped East Room
before the President, with Inés Muñoz Marín on his arm, led in the dinner
guests. Among the audience were the conductors Leopold Stokowski,
Eugene Ormandy and Leonard Bernstein, composers such as Aaron
Copland, Samuel Barber, Elliott Carter, Roger Sessions and Virgil
Thomson, critics, diplomats, patrons of the arts and members of Washington society. The programme, which lasted just over an hour, began
vigorously, with Mendelssohn's Trio in D Minor (Op. 49) catching
the audience's attention with its showy runs for the pianist. Casals and
Horszowski then played a suite of concert pieces by Couperin, followed
by a heavily romantic interpretation of Schumann's Adagio and Allegro
in A Flat Major for cello and piano. The musicians were nervous, and
gave a relatively scrappy performance. And remarkably – for the apex
of American musical culture at its most conspicuous outing – applause
broke out after each movement. But Casals' performance of *El Cant dels
Ocells*, the concluding piece of the evening, was probably the most
moving version he ever recorded – slow, dense and heavy with emotion,
his grunts turning to sobs as he reached the final bars.

What the President himself made of the performance is not clear:
Jacqueline Kennedy was reported as saying that 'the only music he really
appreciates is "Hail to the Chief"'.[18] What mattered to Casals was that
he had had an opportunity, earlier in the day, for a forty-five-minute
private talk with John Kennedy, and that at the informal supper following the concert they were able to speak again. Casals was deeply affected
by Kennedy's serious concern and attention, and sensed that the President's personality had begun to bring 'a new idealism to the life of the
US and of the world'. After several minutes Kennedy excused himself
to attend to other business – somewhat surprising Schneider and

Horszowski by asking them, as he left, if they were from Puerto Rico[19] – and Mrs Kennedy accompanied Casals and Marta to their car.

In terms of the sensitivity behind its organization, the concert had been a nightmare. Fortas confessed to Isaac Stern that he would never again get involved in a similar event, even 'if Jesus Christ were available for a Jew's Harp concert'.[20] In terms of public response, however, the reaction was overwhelmingly favourable. At a highly public level, Casals had performed for – and been seen physically to embrace – the leader of a country which actively recognized Franco. But the hundreds of letters that followed came not from disappointed Spaniards who felt their suffering and exile had been betrayed, but from disappointed music lovers all over the world who were reminded of what they were missing. Once again, by breaking his vow, Casals had reinforced his message. Fortas had earlier observed that 'the crisis of this moment in history demands something in addition to the symbol that has done such wonderful service in the past: it is marvellous . . . that [Casals] has had the flexibility, courage and dedication to see the need and take the risks of a different kind of action to serve his great cause'.[21] Casals himself did not see it quite that way. Despite performances in many countries of the world throughout the next decade, he was convinced that his essential renunciation remained intact. For although he taught, conducted and performed frequently at festivals and private occasions, Casals did not once take his cello in his hand, walk out on to a concert platform in front of an audience that had paid to attend, and play a Bach Suite. For a man who had travelled more widely and performed more ferociously than almost any musician in history, that was a major statement of self-denial. And for everyone else it was a major loss.

Barely a month after the White House Concert, the US Secretary of State, Dean Rusk, publicly praised Spain as an ally of the West in the world's defence against Communist aggression.[22] Casals was appalled and wrote to Kennedy deploring the statement.[23] Over the ensuing months he continued to correspond with the President on questions of humanitarian concern, gently cautioned by Abe Fortas as to likelihood of a practical response:

> I believe that people like Bertrand Russell, Erich Fromm and above all Maestro Casals can have a tremendous effect in appealing to the conscience of the world, but I feel that it is almost always a mistake for them to make suggestions that are . . . specific.[24]

The news of Kennedy's assassination in November 1963 came as a severe blow: it left Casals physically ill and deeply depressed, and for much of the winter he was unable to leave Puerto Rico. Kennedy's death meant the loss of the single individual Casals had contrived to make his ideological hero. And he had not been wrong to do so.

Casals had spent a good deal of his life doing what he felt he *had* to do. Friends now thought it was important he should be encouraged to do what he *wanted* to do. His primary political obsession in the final years of his life became not Spain, but the issue of peace, and in particular the liberation of the world from the threat of nuclear war. Casals had joined a number of disarmament organizations, including the Committee for a Sane Nuclear Policy, but felt the need to do something more direct and persuasive. In 1960 he conceived the idea of using his oratorio *El Pessebre* in a kind of 'crusade' for world peace. When the oratorio was first composed in Prades between 1944 and 1946, the intention had been that the first performance should honour the end of the World War and the restoration of democracy to Spain. Following his United Nations performance in 1958, Casals began to think it might be harnessed as a plea for world peace rather than a celebration of it. Alavedra was asked to write a concluding section emphasizing the theme of peace and con-fraternity, and Casals orchestrated this final Adoration in six sections, culminating in a triumphant Hosanna and Gloria for soprano, chorus and orchestra. Then he set out to perform the work wherever he was invited.

*El Pessebre* dominated Casals' last performing years and became his cen-tral artistic preoccupation. His obsession with communicating a global message of peace through a full-scale work of his own composition was an expression of massive self-confidence on the one hand, and of desperate sadness about the fate of mankind on the other. Friends sought to dissuade him, not only because they were concerned about the critical reaction, but because of the physical strain. But Casals was determined: 'it seemed to me that the very fact that I might not have much longer on this earth was all the more reason for acting while I could'.[25]

The first complete performance of *El Pessebre* took place in Acapulco on 17 December 1960, in the amphitheatre of the Old Fortress of San Diego, overlooking the ocean. Mexico was chosen for the premiere in recognition of its open acceptance of Spanish exiles during and after the Civil War. But the peace crusade itself was launched with a performance of the oratorio in the San Francisco Memorial Opera House on 19 April 1962, Casals' first commercial concert on the US mainland for thirty-four years. Prior to the concert there had been some evidence of alarm among anti-fascist Spanish organizations that Casals was finally about to break his vow, but the emotional reaction of the 3000-strong audience over-came any sense that the conductor was undermining his own moral conviction. Casals conducted from a swivel-chair. But at moments of particular excitement he rose, sang out loud and stamped his feet, communicating, as Alexander Fried of the *San Francisco Examiner* wrote the following day, 'the sheer power of his living will'.

Over the next ten years the oratorio received fifty-one performances around the world, thirty-three of them conducted by Casals himself.[26] Several performances were conducted in Barcelona by his brother Enrique, who was also responsible for a revival of the work in Spain after Casals' death. To an extent this level of performance represented serious over-exposure, since the quality of the work did not of itself warrant repeated hearings – as the reviews were not slow to point out. *El Pessebre* is essentially a work of nineteenth-century romanticism, and even if the imagery is a little stretched – a chorus of shepherds, angels and fishermen adoring the Christ Child, articulate livestock, and a communal *sardana* danced around the manger – the music is not a surprise. Harold Schonberg observed after a Carnegie Hall performance in June 1962, that 'nobody expected anything but what actually did occur'.[27] One orchestral musician declared the score was difficult to play since 'it always reminds me of something else I have already played'.[28] The British critic Felix Aprahamian, after the October 1963 performance at the Royal Festival Hall in London, wrote in the *Observer* that 'from the opening *sardana* . . . to the final chorus of peace and goodwill, all is blamelessly diatonic without even a hint of modality to lend the score some regional Iberian charm'.

*El Pessebre* was clearly an indulgence, both on Casals' part and on the part of those who agreed to present it. The recorded version, made in Puerto Rico in 1972, reveals a polished and lyrical work with a broad range of styles, and resonances of Bach, Wagner, Dvořák and, it has to be said, movie soundtrack.[29] Indulgence does not sit well with genius: the effect of the oratorio – as Casals' only public manifestation during the last years of his life – was to suggest that he was losing his musical edge. The evidence of his performance elsewhere, however – at festivals and summer schools where he could present the great works of the traditional repertoire – revealed that he had in fact lost nothing of the sort. The point about *El Pessebre* was that it represented one man's passionate message of peace. For those who witnessed a live performance, conducted by the composer when close to or already in his nineties, it was an overpoweringly emotional experience. On every occasion the reception was overwhelming, clamorous and tearful. At Budapest in 1964 the audience could not be persuaded to leave the auditorium until the lights were totally extinguished. In Caracas in 1972 the ovation for conductor and soloists continued long after the orchestra had boarded a bus for the airport.

International curiosity about Casals ensured that there was never a shortage of applications to host performances of the oratorio, despite the size of the undertaking and Casals' own specific requirements. A standard rubric was dispatched to every interested promotor indicating the size and standard of the required orchestra and choir (200 voices), the number of rehearsals and the minimum rest-time required between perform-ances. The text of the full oratorio, in the language of the host country, was required to be printed within the programme, together with a mes-sage of peace written by Casals himself. A fee of $2500 was to be paid to a Foundation, established in 1962 to avoid awkwardness over the sharing between Casals and Alavedra of proceeds from the peace crusade.[30]

An invitation to stage *El Pessebre* in Moscow in 1962 came from Casals' friend Lev Ginsburg of the Moscow Conservatory. Despite Casals' own enthusiasm, the plan foundered on both practical and political details; Abe Fortas had discouraged the visit, in any case, on the grounds that Casals 'is a great and powerful symbol of opposition to dictatorship . . . I expect the Russians will distort his appearance . . . as an endorsement of their form of government.'[31] But the 1964 performance in Budapest, when Casals was reunited with Zoltán Kodály for the first time in thirty years, did take the oratorio behind the Iron Curtain.

The visit to perform *El Pessebre* in London in October 1963 was Casals' first visit to England since 1945, and the final one of his life. He had brought his cello and, in his suite at the Westbury Hotel, gave an impromptu recital to his local agent, Wilfred Stiff of Ibbs and Tillett. It was in effect his final solo performance in the country, sixty-four years after the recital for Queen Victoria at Osborne.[32] While in London Casals met Pierre Monteux, then eighty-eight, and Adrian Boult, who reported the Royal Festival Hall performance as a 'wonderful triumph'.[33] At this stage of Casals' life, and after two decades of exile, his tours often involved emotional encounters, nostalgic reminiscence, or – more poig-nantly – the discovery that old acquaintances had died. Casals' distress at the death of friends was so acute that Marta, when necessary, chose a careful moment to break bad news, such as the death of Bruno Walter in 1962. As well as a peace crusade, this was inevitably a tour of farewell.

Two performances of the oratorio were of special significance. In October 1963 Casals conducted the Festival Casals Orchestra and the Cleveland Orchestra Chorus in the General Assembly of the United Nations, his second performance in the building, at the invitation of the Secretary-General, U Thant. It was the most widely disseminated performance of the work, being broadcast throughout Europe, the Middle East, Latin America and Africa, and shown on educational television within the US. Three years later, and just before Casals' ninetieth birthday, a performance at Prades, in the Abbey of St Michel de Cuixà, commemorated the 1000th anniversary of the Catalan Assembly of Tologes, an early medieval administrative structure established, appropriately, in an attempt to regulate feudal anarchy.

Performances of *El Pessebre* – generally between four and seven a year – punctuated Casals' calendar but did not dictate it. The rhythm of his life in the early 1960s was dominated, as before, by the festivals to which he was committed – San Juan, Prades, Marlboro, and the Zermatt Summer Academy. When private opportunities for chamber playing are added to these regular engagements, it is clear that, in his last years, Casals had access to as much live music as he had ever had, and indeed since he was no longer repeating a limited collection of concertos night after night, probably to a greater overall range of work. At the San Juan Festivals in Puerto Rico, he would both conduct and perform, though his cello appearances gradually diminished: he played no solo concertos at all during the 1960s. In 1959 he had played the Brahms Double Concerto with Isaac Stern, and in 1961 performed the Beethoven Triple Concerto with Stern and Rudolf Serkin. In 1967 Casals conducted a performance of the Schumann Cello Concerto, with Gregor Piatigorsky as soloist, but the final occasion on which he himself played was in 1969, when the programme included a Brahms piano quartet, performed with Yehudi Menuhin. That year Jacqueline du Pré visited the Festival, but her performance – of the Elgar Concerto – was conducted not by Casals but by her husband, Daniel Barenboim. Two years later Pierre Fournier attended, playing the Haydn D Major and a Saint-Saëns concerto. Again, and not unexpectedly, Casals did not conduct.

The bulk of Casals' conducting took place at the Marlboro Festivals in Vermont and that was where, year by year, he found most happiness. The Marlboro Music School and Festival had been founded in 1951 by Adolf Busch who, with his brother Hermann on cello, had formed the celebrated Busch Quartet in Europe during the 1930s. Casals had known Adolf Busch since 1910, and his son-in-law Rudolf Serkin since the 1920s. All three had met in Edinburgh in the autumn of 1934, when Casals had come to collect his honorary doctorate, and the Busch Quartet to perform for several of Tovey's Reid Concerts. Adolf Busch died in 1952, but Serkin took over as artistic director and, in 1958, prompted by Alexander Schneider, wrote to suggest that Casals might visit the Festival: 'you can do whatever you want in Marlboro, little, much, conducting . . . playing chamber music . . . lecturing or just being there listening'.[34] Casals came in 1960, and on 10 July conducted

Mozart's Symphony No. 29 at his first concert. Schneider's hunch was right, Marlboro was exactly what Casals enjoyed: a group of between seventy and a hundred enthusiastic professional musicians, a cross-section of ages, instruments and abilities, living and playing together for up to eight weeks in lush and peaceful rural surroundings, with no pressures other than those they placed on themselves. The road-sign at the entrance to the College read: 'Caution – Musicians at Play'. Busch had dreamed of a 'non-competitive summer of chamber music', and that is what Casals discovered it to be.[35] He returned every year, except for 1961, until two months before his death.

At first Casals and Marta came for two weeks early each July. They would stay in an attractive timber farmhouse, and acquaintances from New York, Puerto Rico, Europe and elsewhere knew they would always find the Maestro in an especially relaxed mood. At Marlboro, Casals could conduct what he chose – generally the core symphonic repertoire of Beethoven, Mozart and Schubert, with some Bach, Mendelssohn, Handel and Brahms – and give masterclasses, and he would be paid. The musicians would rehearse as much as they cared to, often late into the night, and perform publicly for family, friends, neighbouring Vermont residents and each other, at weekends. In due course Casals' rehearsals themselves became *de facto* masterclasses: aspiring conductors would attend to study the workings of his technique and the construction of his interpretation. In 1963 David Blum, the twenty-six-year-old director of the Esterhazy Orchestra in New York, visited Marlboro to observe Casals' rehearsals and performances. Later, based on this and similar experiences at Prades, Zermatt and San Juan, he wrote an outstanding account of Casals' conducting and teaching, *Casals and the Art of Interpretation*.[36]

Casals became Marlboro's most famous, and certainly most venerable, regular performer. He tended, more by default than by intention, to dominate the Festival during the weeks he was there. It was hard to maintain the pretence of a community of equals when Casals was around, and a few of the students may have resented the accoutrements of his aura which invariably manifested themselves when his car drove into view: the visitors, admirers and photographers. Inevitably, too, within an annual gathering of intense, committed and brilliant young musicians, there were some who responded critically to his liberties of style, particularly in relation to the interpretation of Bach. This was not the first time Casals had encountered purist criticism, or indeed purist pedantry, and in so far as he noticed it at all, he knew how to handle it: he kept on playing. Years earlier, during a rehearsal, Wanda Landowska had carped, 'You play Bach your way; I'll play him his way.' Casals had spent all his life studying Bach, and knew every note the composer had written. He could engage on every level of musicological debate except the most mathematical. But he would have had nothing to say to the kind of post-modernist empiricism exhibited in a recent scholarly dissection of his performance of the Saraband from the D Minor Bach Suite, which begins: 'Insofar as sentimentality is untrue, it represents a failure of the artist's critical judgment.'[37]

The accusation of indulgence in Casals' reading of Bach often stems from the apparent leisure and fullness of his interpretations. Revealingly, when the BBC compared performances by a number of cellists of the Prelude to the G Major Suite, Casals' 'relaxed' reading was found to be nearly the quickest.[38] Casals himself of course never insisted there was a single valid interpretation of anything, but simply knew what was right for him at a particular moment. Reacting to a musician's complaint, during a rehearsal of the Fifth Brandenburg Concerto, that Bach had not written the work 'that way', he retorted: 'I will take the responsibility if Bach should complain about it.'[39]

Most young participants at Marlboro, however, simply grabbed the opportunity to work under Casals. In 1973 the unlikely figure of Glenn Gould visited the Festival to record a programme for Canadian Broadcasting entitled 'Casals: A Portrait for Radio'. It featured young members of the Festival Orchestra speaking in astonishment of Casals' obsessive concentration: forty minutes, for example, on the first four bars of a work. At ninety-six Casals was driving himself to exhaustion doing what he had done all his life: searching for the most perfect musical expression. Those who could not be there had the opportunity, through a remarkable series of filmed masterclasses given at the Music Extension Division of the University of California, Berkeley, in 1960, to study with Casals through television. Nathan Kroll's films, now available on video-cassette, provide over four hours of intensive teaching of the Boccherini, Haydn, Dvořák and Saint-Saëns Concertos, the Bach Suites and a Brahms sonata.[40]

The attraction of Marlboro eventually displaced Prades from Casals' annual schedule. It was San Juan that had first appropriated the atmosphere of the early Prades Festivals. Enrique Casals had inherited responsibility for the administration of the Prades programmes in 1956, after his brother began to devote more time to Puerto Rico. He began immediately to redress what he had seen as the traditionally excessive American involvement at Prades, and the Festivals became gradually more European in their focus. By 1959 almost all the principal artists were from Europe – Menuhin, Kempff, Christian Ferras, Alberto Lysy, Sándor

Végh and Victoria de los Angeles, for example. Casals remained pre-eminent, performing in each of the twelve concerts that year. Rudolf Serkin continued to appear regularly, and in 1965 his eighteen-year-old son, Peter, accompanied the eighty-eight-year-old Casals in a Bach sonata. By the mid-1960s, too, Prades had shifted its schedule to occupy the final week of July and the first week of August, which meant that Casals had to leave Marlboro in mid-July and travel immediately to Europe. There he would play in the majority of concerts and receive an endless stream of visitors from Catalonia. At the age of ninety it became too much. 'The Prades Festival will not take place,' wrote Marta to a friend in April 1967. 'He will do Marlboro.'[41]

Casals' final visit to Prades, in 1966, had coincided with the extended celebrations of his ninetieth birthday. He played in seven out of the twelve concerts, and many of his closest musical colleagues had come: Horszowski, Kempff, Végh, Serkin, Oistrakh, Katchen, von Tobel and, for the first time since 1953, Alexander Schneider. On the first morning two Spanish buses arrived outside Casals' apartment at Molitg-les-Bains, and a crowd of string players from the Barcelona Symphony Orchestra got out. They serenaded Casals with Mozart's *Eine Kleine Nachtmusik*, reboarded the buses and left.[42] At the first concert, in the Church of St Pierre, Serkin, Schneider and Casals played Beethoven's Piano Trio in E Flat. 'When a musician is almost ninety', Julius Katchen remarked to a journalist, 'one may legitimately worry about how he is going to play.'[43] After the final notes of the Trio had been played, the journalist turned to David Oistrakh. 'Never in the history of stringed instruments', Oistrakh observed, 'has there been such a musician!'

After twenty-seven years the Prades Festival had become welded to the economy of the town, and it had to continue, even without Casals himself. Casals gave permission for the continued use of his name, provided the artistic level of the concerts was maintained. The Casals Festival at Prades has now existed without Casals as long as it did with him. For some years a handful of Casals' close colleagues continued to attend. Each year a concert of homage to Casals was performed, and until his death Paul Tortelier was a frequent guest. Tortelier's daughter, and Casals' godchild, Maria de la Pau, who was baptized during the founding Festival in 1950, and first performed there in 1970, herself provides a continuity with the past. But the music no longer brings kings and presidents to the streets of Prades: the atmosphere has irrevocably gone.

The Marlboro Festival came to provide everything that Casals wanted and that Prades and San Juan had lost: a sense of community, a range of instrumentalists chosen by quality rather than by nationality, unlimited time for rehearsal and a complete absence of commercial pressure. Each year he began to spend more time in Vermont. In 1967 his last concert took place on 30 July. The following year he stayed until 18 August. From the point of view of the world of music, however, there was one seminal drawback: almost nobody heard the music. There were those who realized time was short, and that everything had to be recorded. Rudolf Serkin became aware of this first, in 1963, as he heard Casals rehearsing Beethoven's Symphony No. 8 and Mendelssohn's 'Italian' Symphony. He contacted Columbia in great excitement, asking the company to come to record the performances. Columbia had several versions of the works in their catalogue, however, and declined. Serkin pushed harder: Marlboro would underwrite the cost of the recordings – he wanted to hire a production team. As Thomas Frost, executive producer of Columbia Masterworks, later recalled: 'I arrived in Marlboro that summer somewhat sceptical – and left with some of the most glorious tapes! Columbia promptly bought them, and a record was soon issued.'[44]

Columbia returned to Marlboro each year, recording not only the concerts, but also some of Casals' rehearsals. Some of the recordings they released at once, others appeared for the first time only in 1991, to mark Marlboro's fortieth anniversary.[45] Other tapes presumably still await release. But Casals provided superb value. In 1969, when he was ninety-two, he recorded five Beethoven symphonies, four of them within a period of ten days. Casals was important to the Columbia label, and the company rewarded him. In 1966 Frost put his way a recording of two Bach Chorales ('Sheep May Safely Graze' and 'Jesu Joy of Man's Desiring'), part of the annual Goodyear Tire Company Christmas Recording, for which the fee was $20,000. Casals earmarked it for charity.[46] In a contract signed in January 1969 for recordings of Mozart's Symphony No. 40 and Schubert's 'Unfinished', Casals received a royalty advance of over $18,000.

The organizers of the Puerto Rico Festival had made recording arrangements from the outset. But Columbia, which had agreed to record the initial Festival in 1957, suffered a loss after Casals' heart attack and resulting absence from the schedule, and pulled out of subsequent years. Thereafter recording was handled by three different agencies: the local radio network, WIPR, run by Jack Delano, the Voice of America, which took recordings for national broadcasts, and a wealthy local physician, Dr Franchesci, who possessed his own recording equipment and from whom Columbia subsequently acquired several concerts retrospectively.[47] Each operator experimented with microphone and recording techniques within the context of the acoustics of the performance hall, but until the first stereophonic recordings in 1971, the quality was variable. In 1960 a commercial recording company, Everest Enterprises, undertook a recording of Casals' performance at the Festival of the Dvořák Concerto, but subsequently released it without seeking Casals' approval of a test pressing. Abe Fortas sued the company on Casals' behalf, and a settlement of $12,500 was agreed in 1961.[48]

In Abe Fortas, Casals had one of America's finest – and most expensive – legal minds permanently at his disposal, and at no cost. From the early 1960s Fortas took care of all Casals' contractual dealings with impresarios, festival and masterclass organizers, recording companies and broadcasting authorities – and Casals' income rose substantially as a result. But Fortas did much more. He counselled Casals on personal and political matters, made connections and introductions for him in Washington, New York and Puerto Rico, organized the repair of his Gofriller cello (which suffered in the San Juan humidity) whenever necessary, and, in the final years, provided solid, wise and warm support for Marta. In 1965 Fortas was appointed to the US Supreme Court, but retained two private clients: Pablo Casals and the President, Lyndon Johnson. He noted that Casals was 'obviously . . . not impressed by the fact that I am no longer in law practice', and decided not to disturb him by proposing a change.[49]

Fortas was a friend, and occasional quartet partner, of both Isaac Stern and Alexander Schneider, and with them helped introduce Casals to a shared fascination with the State of Israel. In 1960 Stern had invited Schneider to help organize Israel's first music festival. Schneider in turn involved Casals, and the America–Israel Cultural Foundation agreed to sponsor and host the Third International Casals Cello Competition at the same time as the Festival. At a preliminary fund-raising concert, held on 11 October 1960 at the New York home of David Rockefeller, Casals performed Schubert's Quintet in C Major and Mendelssohn's Trio in D Minor with Horszowski, Schneider and the Budapest String Quartet. One of the 100 guests, each of whom had paid $500 to attend, was Golda Meir, Israel's representative at the United Nations. Casals had taught Mrs Meir's son, Menahem, and, just before Casals' United Nations performance in 1958, the diplomat, later to be Israel's Prime Minister, wrote him a note: 'I am Mrs Golda Meir. You will know me better if I tell you I am Menahem's mother . . . tomorrow will be one of the greatest experiences of my life.'[50] It was largely Golda Meir's personal warmth and humility that attracted Casals and secured a commitment to Israel which lasted until his death.

Casals travelled to Israel for the festival and the cello competition in September 1961. In Jerusalem he joined the Budapest Quartet in playing Schumann and Schubert quintets, and Rudolf Serkin for Beethoven's Sonata in D Major. In Tel-Aviv he conducted the Israeli Philharmonic

Orchestra in a programme of Mozart and Beethoven. And with Schneider, the Budapest Quartet and the Istomin–Stern–Rose Trio, he performed a final, impromptu concert – the first in possibly 1500 years – at the Roman amphitheatre in the Plain of Sharon, near Caesarea, on which restoration was then beginning. From among the many highly talented young Israeli instrumentalists paraded for Casals' inspection during the visit, he singled out one in particular: the encounter transformed the life of the young Pinchas Zukerman.[51]

Casals' enthusiasm for travel – and the habit of it – persisted until his final months. During the 1960s, in addition to Israel and his regular trips to Europe, he made his first visits to the Far East and Japan (in 1961) and to El Salvador and Central America (in 1967). He went twice to Venezuela, once to perform *El Pessebre* in Caracas and once to play chamber concerts with Schneider and Horszowski, several times to neighbouring Caribbean islands, and repeatedly to Mexico. At ninety-five he thought he might make his first visit to Jamaica. 'Well, let's go to the moon!' responded Schneider.[52]

After 1966, Casals and Marta spent longer each year at home in Puerto Rico. Their long, low house at Isla Verde, built on a single level, was cool and spacious, but hardly grand. Everywhere there were testaments to Casals' career – gifts, mementos, pictures and souvenirs. In the living-room was a grand piano, covered by an embroidered Spanish cloth, and through the picture-window, Casals had a clear and uninterrupted view of the ocean. Each morning he would begin, as always, with Bach on the piano, then practise on the cello, read scores, and prepare for forth-coming concerts. After his siesta and more study, or perhaps some composition, guests would begin to call. As H. L. Kirk, a regular guest at the time, observed, Casals had great energy and an appetite for stimulus. He received 'the great, the humble, the interested, the curious, friends who came with friends, friends-of-friends-of-friends, and Catalans in droves'.[53] Inevitably, and less enjoyably, Casals became a fixture on the Puerto Rico celebrity circuit. Visiting dignitaries, diplomats, professors, Latin-American heads of state, humanitarian figures like Martin Luther King, Jr, and show-business personalities – of whose identity Casals often remained wholly innocent – were wheeled to Isla Verde. Extreme old age metamorphoses into a miracle – for all but the old themselves – and Casals became a victim of a pilgrimage of journalists, asking the same bland questions, and writing genuflecting articles in glossy magazines. 'A Serenade to Ninety Years of Greatness' was published in *Life* in November 1966.[54] There were many others. The living myth was created, as Casals looked on and controlled it. Probably it amused him. Sometimes it depressed him. Occasionally he would erupt. Asked for the umpteenth time for the 'secret' of his longevity, Casals rounded on his questioner: 'I *live*! Very few people live.'

What Casals most enjoyed were leisurely walks by the sea – the image of the famous cellist, on the beach with his umbrella, became an affectionate cliché – and private times with Marta and close friends, surrounded by their succession of Great Danes (Pachyderm, Viola or Prince) or the stray cat, 'Piqui', adopted at Marlboro. Late in the 1970s, Casals and Marta built a small weekend retreat on high land near the village of Ceiba, 40 miles from San Juan. From 'El Pessebre', as the house was christened, the view was of fields of sugar-cane, the shoreline and the ocean beyond. There the closest friends of Casals' old age, like Rosa and Luis Cueto Coll, would come to play dominoes, which Casals and Rosa in particular played expertly and fast. Years earlier, in Prades, playing Ludo with his pupils, Casals would announce, 'J'ai gagné!', even when he had not.[55] Now he won anyway, and the friends awarded each other the 'Honorary Degree of Doctor of Dominoes'.

The house at Isla Verde had been built on a narrow stretch of land between the highway and the sea, and was at first relatively quiet and private. Gradually it had been surrounded by hotels and blocks of condominiums, as the pressure of tourism pushed the developers eastwards beyond the Laguna del Condado. Security became a problem, and noise from the now busy freeway, the buzz of marine helicopters, and the jets on the runway at San Juan International Airport, 6000 metres upwind, became a torment. Marta Casals located and extended a substantial house further inland, at Rio Piedras, adding a music salon capable of accommodating 200 guests, a facility Casals had not enjoyed since leaving San Salvador over thirty years before. They moved there in 1971. Late the same year the offer came of a lavish modern home at Guadalajara, the gift of a wealthy Mexican. Casals, Marta and their friends spent several periods of a month or more in the Mexican house, and indeed considered the possibility of permanent relocation when delays in the creation of a Fundació Pau Casals in Spain – and complications in relation to his will – threatened to leave Casals' estate vulnerable to punitive inheritance taxation within Puerto Rico itself. Casals had been grafted on to Puerto Rico. He could be grafted off. But in the end there was no time.

It had sometimes seemed that Casals would go on for ever. It was not that he was relentlessly healthy; indeed, illness – or, rather, anxiety about it – had always been part of his nature. He had suffered intermittent angina since the heart attack in 1957, and diverticulitis gave him frequent intestinal pain. X-rays taken in 1971 revealed signs of arthritis in Casals' hands and feet, but nothing that would threaten his playing. What he did have was a tremendous will to live. There was always another project to anticipate, another trip, another festival, another goal: Marta kept him looking ahead. Between his ninetieth and ninety-fourth birthdays, Casals performed at least fifty works as cellist or conductor.[56] Subsequently, until his death, two months short of his ninety-seventh birthday, he conducted around a further thirty-six performances, in addition to rehearsals, private chamber sessions, masterclasses and his own practising.

After his ninetieth birthday, Casals always travelled with portable oxygen equipment. Only once did he need it – in El Salvador, in 1967, when, during a performance of El Pessebre, the sound produced by an orchestra of local firemen, bolstered by a few string players from the Costa Rica Symphony, was so distressing that he suddenly clutched his chest and staggered off the podium. Schneider took over and returned at the end of the performance to find Casals sitting happily, 'drinking beer, smoking his pipe and smiling'.[57] Much more valuable as travelling companions were Rosa and Luis Cueto Coll, who began to join Casals and Marta for their major trips. On meeting Luis in 1955 Casals had been immediately drawn to him: two of his uncles had fought against the fascists in Spain, been captured and shot. His father, Augusto, had been head of the anti-Franco organization in Puerto Rico.[58] Other new and increasingly close friends were Sylvia Fuhrman, Special Representative of the Secretary-General for the United Nations International School, and her husband Murray, a radiologist. Sylvia Fuhrman had met Casals at his 1957 and 1963 UN performances, but the family friendship developed after a Carnegie Hall benefit, in April 1970, in aid of the UN International School, at which Casals conducted 100 cellos in a performance of his own Sardana. The evening raised more than $150,000, with Harold Schonberg in the New York Times describing the Sardana as 'a sweet piece that is more sophisticated than it sounds'.[59]

Perhaps the first signs of real frailty were noticed during Casals' third UN performance, on 24 October 1971, when he was close to ninety-five. He had been invited by U Thant to compose a hymn to peace for performance on United Nations Day. The preamble to the UN Charter had been suggested as a text, but after Casals had found the technical vocabulary difficult to score, W. H. Auden was approached to prepare a variant. Though initially reluctant, he delivered a forty-three-line ode within three days of the commission, and Casals spent the summer transforming it into a 'Hymn for the United Nations'.

At the performance itself Casals conducted his own Festival Casals Orchestra, brought in to replace the Mexican National Symphony which its country could not, in the end, afford to send.[60] At a rehearsal the previous day at the New School, Casals had not been entirely happy with the Manhattan School of Music Choir: 'Perching forward in a chair, his strong, stubby arms propped against the lectern, Pablo Casals alternately spoke, grumphed and sang.'[61] He sent for the Puerto Rican soprano, Olga Iglesias, who arrived on the 7 a.m. flight, and positioned both her and Marta strategically near the microphones. After the first performance of the Hymn, U Thant presented Casals with the UN Peace Medal. There was more music – including Horszowski, Serkin and Istomin playing a Bach triple-keyboard concerto – and then Casals called for his cello. Speaking quietly to the rapt and motionless audience, he said he had not played in public for forty years, but 'I *have* to play today.' Clasping his cello and about to begin, he raised his right arm and introduced *El Cant dels Ocells*, his voice full of emotion: 'The birds in the sky, in the space . . . singing peace, peace . . . peace . . . and the music is the music that Bach and Beethoven and all the great would have loved and admired. And it is the soul of my country, Catalonia.'

At the San Juan Festival in 1972, Casals conducted rehearsals for Beethoven's 'Pastoral' Symphony, but he was affected by the air-conditioning in the auditorium and Schneider took over for the performance. *El Pessebre* was recorded over four or five days, Schneider again doing the bulk of the directing, Casals taking over for the final Gloria. At Marlboro that summer he took part in four concerts, conducting symphonies by Beethoven, Mozart and Haydn, as well as Mendelssohn's 'Hebrides' Overture. The student orchestra was particularly strong that summer, with the young cellist Yo-Yo Ma attending his first Marlboro, and the violinist Miriam Fried her third. Between the two festivals, Casals had taken *El Pessebre* to Venezuela, and at the end of the arduous season he reported to Schneider that he felt well, even though he had endured five days of hospital tests: 'It is the same thing – the diverticulitis – which gives so much pain, and also arthritis in my hips and spinal chord. The rest, they say, is fine . . .'[62]

Friends thought Casals appeared subdued at San Juan in 1973, but it turned out to be nothing more than a problem of wax in one ear. He repeated his Marlboro programme of Beethoven's First Symphony and the 'Hebrides' Overture, and added a performance of his 'Hymn to the United Nations'. He was cheered in March by a visit from his old Catalan friend, the medical scientist Josep Trueta, who came from Oxford and prescribed a new drug to ease the pain in Casals' legs. The following month he was able to make a fifteen-day trip to Mexico, playing on 23 and 24 April what would be his final concerts with Mieczyslaw Horszowski. At Marlboro he had another heavy programme, conducting Beethoven's First, Second and Fourth Symphonies, and Haydn's Symphony No. 96 in D Major. Before leaving the Festival he heard works by two of his old friends: Tovey's Trio in D Minor (performed by Horszowski, James Buswell and Randall Cook), and Schönberg's early Chamber Symphony (Op. 9). He left Marlboro on 3 August and drove with Marta to New York to celebrate their sixteenth wedding anniversary at the home of Sylvia and Murray Fuhrman. Late at night, after a five-hour drive, dinner, and a cake with anniversary candles, Casals was tearful, but very happy. He took up his Gofriller and played for an hour.

After his first visit, Casals did not return to Israel until August 1970, for a performance of *El Pessebre* in the amphitheatre at Caesarea. He was back in September 1973 to help celebrate the country's twenty-fifth anniversary, and though he took advantage of a wheelchair in the sweltering heat, he came ferociously to life conducting the Festival Youth Orchestra in Mozart's Symphony No. 33: '*Con amore . . . con amore*,' he urged, 'otherwise it means nothing.'[63] Towards the end of the visit, Casals and Marta had to make an exhausting two-hour journey from Jerusalem to Herzliyya under the midday sun. Casals felt it more than anyone, 'but after 50 minutes in the cool and two aspirins, he started with a filmed interview which lasted three hours'.[64] Before leaving Israel, Casals had a deeply moving meeting with Golda Meir, then Prime Minister. He played for her – one of his last performances for anyone – embraced her and quietly informed her, looking over at the Gofriller, 'My cello is my oldest friend . . . oh yes . . . my cello is my companion. I love him and he loves me. And he sounds well to make me happy.' Mrs Meir could say nothing; she hugged Casals, tears rolling down her cheeks.

Pablo Casals was playing dominoes in the Santurce home of Luis and Rosa Cueto Coll when his final heart attack occurred on 30 September. He hated hospitals and insisted on remaining in the Cueto Colls' second-floor bedroom for ten days until he was strong enough to return home to Rio Piedras. Then phlegm began to accumulate on the lungs, and he became noticeably weaker: the doctors persuaded Marta that he should be moved to the Auxilio Mutuo Hospital in San Juan. When the stretcher arrived Casals was angry at having to lie down: he said his back hurt, and asked to ride in front with the driver. Then it was a fast and bumpy trip, with Casals complaining to Marta, 'The driver's a maniac . . . he'll kill us all.'[65]

For ten restless days, Casals lay wired to a respirator and other monitoring equipment. Marta refused to leave his bedside, and an SOS was sent to the Fuhrmans, then attending a radiology congress in Madrid.

On 16 October a telegram reached Enrique Casals in Barcelona: he came immediately to Puerto Rico. Arriving at the hospital he found the waiting-room filled with Defilló relatives, with Luis and Inés Muñoz Marín and other close friends. The local radio station was issuing regular bulletins on the Maestro's condition. Casals was still conscious – the Yom Kippur War had begun and he dictated a letter of support to Golda Meir – but in his agitation kept trying to pull out the tubes and drips. Then he suffered another serious embolism and drifted into unconsciousness. Schneider and Istomin brought headphones and played some Bach. It seemed to make him more tranquil. The machines were switched off, but Casals' ox-like constitution kept him alive for two more days.

# Epilogue

*Sia'm la mort una major naixença.* (Let death be a greater birth.)
*Joan Maragall*

Spain is my country. Let Franco give up his.
*Pablo Casals*

Death is more final for some than for others. Pablo Casals, by his own wish, could not have permanent rest until Spain was free, Catalonia independent and he had returned to the land of his birth. Moments after his death, at 2 p.m. on Monday, 22 October 1973, Marta Casals and Sylvia Fuhrman left the Auxilio Mutuo Hospital by a rear door, to avoid the press, and went to select a sufficiently substantial casket in bronze and lead, which would enable the Maestro's remains to be transported to Spain at the appropriate time.

On the evening of Casals' death, the casket was taken to his Rio Piedras home, and friends came to fill the house with music. Eugene Istomin, Alexander Schneider and the cellist Leslie Parnas played movements from some of Casals' treasured trios, and Marta herself, with Olga Iglesias, sang a setting by Casals of a Catalan prayer. The following morning, thousands of Puerto Ricans filed past the body as Casals lay in state in the grand rotunda of the Capitol in Puerta de Tierra, the seat of the island's legislature.[1] The Puerto Rico Symphony Orchestra played the Second Movement (the Funeral March), of Beethoven's 'Eroica' Symphony, and with Olga Iglesias and the chorus of the Conservatory of Music, presented two sections from *El Pessebre* (the 'Tears of the Infant Jesus' and the final 'Gloria'). Schneider then led a chamber ensemble in the slow movement of Mozart's Clarinet Quintet, and other pieces chosen by Casals.

As the casket, draped in the Catalan and Puerto Rican flags, was transported to the Church of Nuestra Señora de la Piedad in Isla Verde, many hundreds lined the streets. Luis Cardinal Aponte Martínez said a requiem mass, and the sound of Casals' own cello, in a recording of *El Cant dels Ocells*, resonated through the small church. The Puerto Rico Memorial Cemetery was crowded with local residents waiting to honour the man who had made his home on their island, and some of Casals' closest friends had to watch from a distance as the casket was lowered into the ground.

In the June before his death, Casals was to have performed with the Festival Casals Orchestra at a free, open-air concert in Central Park, New York. The concert was cancelled because of rain, but the Mayor, John Lindsay, declared Casals an honorary citizen of New York, posing the question, 'not, is he worthy of us . . . but are we worthy of him?' New York now acknowledged his death at a memorial concert on 8 November at St Paul's Chapel, Columbia University, during which Catalan religious music, including some of Casals' own, was performed. The following month, at five minutes after midnight on Christmas morning, Alexander Schneider led the sixty young musicians of his annual Christmas String Seminar in a Carnegie Hall performance of the Third Brandenburg Concerto, played standing in honour of what would have been Casals' ninety-seventh birthday. On the birthday itself, 29 December, Schneider, with Horszowski and Olga Iglesias, performed a programme in San Juan devoted entirely to Casals' own compositions.

All over the world people acknowledged their sense of loss in obituaries, memorial concerts and letters of condolence to Casals' family in Spain and to Marta – now, in the words of Eugene Ormandy, 'a very young widow of a very great man'.[2] Marlboro seemed very different the following summer, and the first two formal concerts were dedicated to Casals 'with infinite love and gratitude'. Schneider, Horszowski and Serkin led the Festival Orchestra in works of Bach, Brahms, Beethoven, Haydn and Mozart, and Olga Iglesias sang a selection of Casals' songs ranging from *Cançó Catalana* No. 1, composed in 1895, to *Cuando Vuela a Nacer*, written in 1971.

In each of the places in which Casals had lived, steps were taken to establish a permanent memorial. In San Salvador the Fundació Pau Casals, despite financial problems arising from the complexities of Casals' will, and Enrique's own sense of grievance in relation to his brother's possessions in Puerto Rico, opened Casals' house as a standing museum and archive. Four acres of land were sold to provide funds for other activities undertaken by the Fundació, such as sponsorship of concerts and the endowment of scholarships for gifted Catalan cellists. In 1980–1 a striking and stylish auditorium (l'Auditori Pau Casals), designed by Jordi Bonet i Armengol, was constructed on land adjoining the San Salvador villa, under the joint auspices of the Fundació and the

Associació Musical Pau Casals del Vendrell, and with financial support from the State Bank of Catalonia.

In San Juan the Museo Pablo Casals was established in June 1977 by the Corporación de las Artes Escenico Musicales. It houses a permanent photographic exhibition and videotaped recordings from the Festival Casals. In essence, however, Casals' most enduring monument in Puerto Rico is the entire cultural life of the island, since virtually none had existed before he arrived in 1955.[3] In Prades, too, a Musée Pablo Casals was opened in August 1982 to commemorate the Maestro's association with the Festival, and is administered by the Festival Pablo Casals de Prades. In Japan, where Casals has long been particularly revered, and where his recordings have always sold in considerable quantities, a concert auditorium in Tokyo has been named in his memory.[4] No other performing artist in the twentieth century has been so widely and permanently commemorated.

Casals had undertaken, had he lived, to celebrate his 100th birthday in Jerusalem. In fact the Pau Casals Centenary, in December 1976, was celebrated all over the world. In Catalonia in particular there were concerts, festivals, inaugurations, dedications and conferences. Mstislav Rostropovich performed three Bach Suites in the Villa Casals and in the presence of Queen Sophia of Spain in July 1976, and a programme of concerts followed in December, with Stern, Schneider, Istomin and Leonard Rose performing in Barcelona with the State City Orchestra. In March 1977 a bronze bust of Casals was dedicated by Kurt Waldheim, Secretary-General of the United Nations. Sculpted from life by Robert Berks, the powerful work is on permanent loan to the United Nations, and is exhibited in the Visitors' Lobby of the General Assembly building in New York.

Upon Casals' death, Marta Casals became Director of the Festival Casals, and President of both the Puerto Rico Symphony Orchestra and the Puerto Rico Conservatory of Music. She resigned from the Festival Board of Directors in December 1977 and, in 1980, was appointed Artistic Director of the Kennedy Center for the Performing Arts in Washington, DC. To initial surprise but widespread pleasure, Marta Casals married Eugene Istomin in February 1975. Close friends doubted Casals himself could have choreographed events better. Marta declared that 'we will work to bring to life and light the things that Maestro Casals left to us – the museums, the festivals. That will be a very important part of our lives.'[5]

General Francisco Franco died on 20 November 1975, but it was not until November 1979 that Casals' body was returned to Spain. Casals had vowed to remain in exile until Spain reverted to full democracy and

Catalonia became an autonomous self-governing territory. It took four years for those conditions to be fulfilled. A general election had been held in June 1977, and Josep Tarradellas, President of the Generalitat-in-exile, was persuaded to return to Spain to take over a 'provisional' autonomous administration. Tarradellas arrived on Spanish soil and declared 'Ja soc aqui' ('I made it!').[6] But this was still not sufficient. On the advice of Tarradellas, and of the Spanish Prime Minister, Adolfo Suárez, Marta withheld her permission until after a further general election in March 1979, and a referendum in October that year which endorsed a statute granting Catalan home rule. Then, immediately, she made arrangements for Casals' return. The casket was removed from Isla Verde cemetery and sealed by the Spanish consul. A farewell ceremony was held at San Juan Cathedral on 8 November and, with several friends, Marta accompanied the casket on its journey to Spain. The following day Casals' body lay in state at the Palace of the Generalitat in Barcelona. On 10 November a memorial Eucharist was held in the Basilica of the Abbey of Montserrat, and the same afternoon Casals' remains joined those of other members of his family in the small, neat cemetery on the outskirts of El Vendrell. Among the messages received in honour of the reburial was one from Rostropovich:

> This is one of the most stirring moments of my life, when the body of the greatest artist of the twentieth century finally finds peace in that land which he so loved and which brought him so much suffering during his lifetime . . . this humane and symbolic act is especially close to my heart as I perhaps better than others know so well what it means to be deprived of one's country.[7]

In terms of popular perception and mass awareness, Catalonia's twentieth-century triumph came in 1992, with the staging in Barcelona of the Olympic Games. For Casals it was twenty years too late. But he was not forgotten. As the Catalan flag flew again on Montjuïc, the television cameras of the world focused on the restored Bourbon monarch, King Juan Carlos, the grandson of Alfonso XIII, as he stood to hear an orchestra of cellos perform *El Cant dels Ocells*. For Casals it would have brought pride and intense emotion. But at the same time the appalling bloodshed and brutality of the last decade of the century would have made him despair of the human condition.

For Casals was simultaneously blessed and cursed by his accentuated sensibility and unrivalled moral obstinacy. What he sought was a perfect world, and it would always fail him. He could have had permanent wealth, ease and adulation, but this would have required compromise. He would not compromise his principles; indeed, he did not even question them. Casals never lost his belief in the power of good. If he had, he might also have lost the inspiration of his music, for the two were inextricable – his moral conscience and the power of his bow. Without the pain, there would not have been the music. In the final analysis he showed that music could be a force for good. Do good men make better music? Casals persuades us that the answer must be yes.

# Notes

CHAPTER 1: THE QUIET BIRTH OF A GENIUS, 1876–1890

1. Since Carlos Casals did not register the birth for two days – beyond the permitted limit – it was formally registered, by municipal judge M. Pablo Serra Virgili, as being on 30 December, and that is the date that appears on Casals' birth certificate. See certificate details, Casals archives, San Salvador (hereafter PCSS).
2. Enric Casals, *Pau Casals: dades biogràfiques inèdites, cartes intimes i records viscuts*, Barcelona, Editorial Pòrtic, 1979, p. 21.
3. From a genealogy of the Casals family, prepared by Señorita Mercèdes Guarro, December 1971, PCSS.
4. 'Apèndix Important', in Enric Casals, *Pau Casals*, pp. 304–7.
5. See J. Ma. Corredor, *Conversations with Casals* (English edition), London, Hutchinson, 1956, Albert E. Kahn (ed.), *Joys and Sorrows: Pablo Casals*, which carries the by-line 'His own story as told to Albert E. Kahn', New York, Simon and Schuster, and London, Macdonald, 1970, reissued London, Eel Pie Publishing, 1981, and Pablo Casals, 'The Story of My Youth', first published in *The Gramophone*, December 1932, and reprinted in *Ovation*, October 1983. The accounts of Casals' youth in Lillian Littlehales, *Pablo Casals*, New York, W. W. Norton, 1929 and 1948; reissued Westport, Conn., Greenwood, 1970, and Bernard Tapper, *Cellist in Exile: A Portrait of Pablo Casals*, New York, McGraw-Hill, 1962, also owe much to interviews with Casals himself. H. L. Kirk, for his *Pablo Casals: A Biography*, New York, Doubleday, and London, Hutchinson, 1974, harnessed the basic information from these accounts, but pursued them in greater detail with Casals himself.
6. Kahn, *Joys and Sorrows*, p. 20.
7. The gourd has survived and is on display at the Casa Museu Casals in San Salvador. Casals liked to recall that among the pieces he played on it was Schubert's *Serenade* but, even in the hands of a genius, this seems fanciful.
8. Kahn, *Joys and Sorrows*, p. 35.
9. Ibid., pp. 35–6.
10. Kirk, *Pablo Casals*, p. 39.
11. Robert Hughes, *Barcelona*, London, HarperCollins, 1992, pp. 362–73.
12. Kahn, *Joys and Sorrows*, p. 38.

13. Ibid., p. 40.
14. David Blum, *Casals and the Art of Interpretation*, Berkeley, University of California Press, 1977, p. 110.
15. Kahn, *Joys and Sorrows*, p. 41.
16. Josep Pla, quoted in Hughes, *Barcelona*, p. 388.
17. Kahn, *Joys and Sorrows*, p. 46.
18. Corredor, *Conversations*, p. 109.
19. See *La Opinión*, Tarragona, 27 August 1889, and *Ilustración Musical*, Barcelona, December 1890, both kept by Pilar Casals in a scrapbook of early press clippings.
20. Reviews in *La Renaixenta* and the *Diario de Barcelona*, see Kirk, *Pablo Casals*, p. 61.
21. Kahn, *Joys and Sorrows*, pp. 45–6.

CHAPTER 2: PATRONAGE AND DISCOVERY, 1890–1899

1. Casals to Louis Biancolli, in an interview in *McCall's*, May 1966, quoted in H. L. Kirk, *Pablo Casals: A Biography*, London, Hutchinson, 1974, p. 67.
2. Pujal's victory over Casals was publicly criticized in *La Vanguardia* of 26 May 1893. See Kirk, *Pablo Casals*, pp. 70 and 630.
3. Albert E. Kahn (ed.), *Joys and Sorrows: Pablo Casals*, London, Eel Pie Publishing, London, 1981, pp. 50–1.
4. J. Ma. Corredor, *Conversations with Casals*, London, Hutchinson, 1956, p. 28.
5. Ibid.
6. Kirk, *Pablo Casals*, p. 77.
7. H. L. Kirk in a BBC television interview, New York, February 1991.
8. The most prominent painting to hang on Casals' walls was a Watteau – owned, however, by his wife, Susan Metcalfe.
9. Corredor, *Conversations*, p. 31.
10. Kahn, *Joys and Sorrows*, p. 64.
11. Reviews from *El Pensiamento* of 24 September, and *El Alcance* of 25 September 1894, are quoted in Kirk, *Pablo Casals*, p. 87.
12. In addition to Casals and Francés, the Quartet comprised Peraite on second violin and Rafael Gálvez on viola. The pianist José Güervós joined the group for piano quintets. See material on Casals' early life in PCSS.
13. Lists of Casals' compositions are provided in Kirk, *Pablo Casals*, pp. 559–7, and Enric Casals, *Pau Casals: dades biogràfiques inèdites, cartes íntimes i records viscuts*, Barcelona, Editorial Pòrtic, 1979, pp. 326–8. Dating of his work is problematic: these two lists do not wholly tally.
14. The correspondence about the dispute, which involved Casals' apparent

acceptance of some paid engagements without seeking Monasterio's permission in advance, appears in *Academia*, the Bulletin of the Real Academia de Bellas Artes de San Fernando, Madrid, triennium 1955–7, pp. 133–5, and is given in an English translation in Kirk, *Pablo Casals*, pp. 90–1.

15. Corredor, *Conversations*, p. 35.
16. Margaret Campbell, *The Great Cellists*, London, Gollancz, 1988, p. 78.
17. Pablo Casals, 'The Story of My Youth', *Ovation*, October 1983, pp. 12 and 47.
18. Corredor, *Conversations*, p. 37.
19. Kahn, *Joys and Sorrows*, p. 75.
20. Ibid., p. 76.
21. The other members of the Crickboom Quartet were the violinist José Rocabruna and the viola player, Rafael Gálvez, a former member, with Casals, of the Quartet Society in Madrid.
22. Robert Hughes, *Barcelona*, London, HarperCollins, 1992, p. 389.
23. *El Noticiero*, 2 March 1895.
24. Enric Casals, *Pau Casals*, pp. 284–5.
25. Corredor, *Conversations*, p. 40.
26. Enric Casals, *Pau Casals*, p. 285.
27. Hughes, *Barcelona*, p. 415. Robert Hughes' powerful account of the fortunes of Catalonia, especially pp. 415–24, is the source of these paragraphs.
28. Pablo Casals, 'The Story of My Youth', p. 47.

CHAPTER 3: TOURING THE WORLD, 1899–1906
1. Pilar Casals i Defilló, Casals' mother, to a niece, May 1899, quoted in H. L. Kirk, *Pablo Casals: A Biography*, London, Hutchinson, 1974, p. 114.
2. Gertrude Stein, *Paris, France*, New York, Scribner, 1940, quoted in Norma Evenson, *Paris: A Century of Change, 1878–1978*, New Haven and London, Yale University Press, 1979, p. 1.
3. Charles Rearick, *Pleasures of the Belle Epoque: Entertainment and Festivity in Turn-of-the-Century France*, New Haven and London, Yale University Press, 1985, p. xi.
4. Arthur Rubinstein, *My Young Years*, London, Jonathan Cape, 1973, pp. 138–9.
5. See Casals' travel log and diary, PCSS.
6. Kirk, *Pablo Casals*, pp. 117–19. The Queen's private secretary was Sir Harry Ponsonby.
7. Albert E. Kahn (ed.), *Joys and Sorrows: Pablo Casals*, London, Eel Pie Publishing, 1981, p. 88.
8. Ibid.

9. Margaret Deneke, *Ernest Walker*, London, Oxford University Press, 1949, p. 58, quoted in Kirk, *Pablo Casals*, p. 120.
10. From the Journal of Queen Victoria RI, 2 August 1899, The Royal Archives, Windsor.
11. Kahn, *Joys and Sorrows*, p. 92; Kirk, *Pablo Casals*, p. 122. Casals' own account of the Lamoureux encounter is corroborated by Chevillard's own son-in-law, Charles Kiesgen, a pupil of Casals and later his professional manager.
12. Unfortunately there is no known recording of Casals playing the Lalo Concerto, nor indeed the Saint-Saëns Concerto, substantial gaps in the totality of Casals on record.
13. Joseph Salmon in 1931, recalled by Milly Stanfield, 13 January 1992.
14. Margaret Campbell, *The Great Cellists*, London, Gollancz, 1988, pp. 91–2.
15. Elizabeth Cowling, *The Cello*, London, Batsford, 1975, p. 136.
16. These four notebooks are preserved in the PCSS.
17. Kirk, *Pablo Casals*, p. 133.
18. Kahn, *Joys and Sorrows*, p. 94.
19. Ibid., pp. 98–9.
20. J. Ma. Corredor, *Conversations with Casals* (English edition), London, Hutchinson, 1956, pp. 46–7.
21. Rearick, *Pleasures of the Belle Epoque*, p. 130.
22. Bauer later described his first American tour as 'one of the least impressive visits ever made to the United States by an artist who had acquired some status in Europe'. Harold C. Schonberg, *The Great Pianists*, New York, Simon and Schuster, 1963; London, Gollancz, 1981, p. 378.
23. Quoted by Kirk, *Pablo Casals*, p. 308.
24. Ibid., p. 316.
25. Kahn, *Joys and Sorrows*, p. 102.
26. Ibid., p. 101.
27. Kirk, *Pablo Casals*, p. 162.
28. Corredor, *Conversations*, p. 51.
29. Kahn, *Joys and Sorrows*, pp. 110–11.
30. See José Ortiz, 'Inauguracion de una pista', *Stadium*, 18 September 1915, p. 211.
31. See 'Concurso de Espluga de Francoli', *Stadium*, 14 August 1915, p. 522.
32. See the work of Dr Ramon Balius i Juli, a member of the Medical Committee of the Royal Spanish Athletics Federation, 'Un esportista dit Pau Casals', *Apunts d'educació física i medicina esportiva*, XX, 1983, pp. 205–12. And also M. B. Stanfield, 'Following Through', *The Strad*, July 1950, pp. 98–100.
33. Bauer, *His Book*, New York, W. W. Norton, 1958, quoted in Schonberg, *Great Pianists*, pp. 378–9.
34. Bauer observed that they played even the relatively uncommon Grieg

Sonata in A Minor (Op. 36), about one hundred times all over Europe. See Cowling, *The Cello*, p. 141.

35. Kirk, *Pablo Casals*, p. 171.
36. Elise K. Kirk, *Music at the White House: A History of the American Spirit*, Urbana, University of Illinois Press, 1986, p. 180.
37. The rent appeared to remain constant until the end of Casals' tenancy, in July 1913. The receipts, together with a complete sequence of his gas bills, survive in his papers, PCSS.
38. Other star singers, like Felix Mayol, could earn up to 2000 francs an evening at the leading Parisian music-halls. See Rearick, *Pleasures of the Belle Epoque*, p. 70.
39. Casals papers, PCSS.
40. Campbell, *The Great Cellists*, p. 317. During the early years of his career, Yo-Yo Ma also played a Matteus Gofriller instrument, formerly owned by Pierre Fournier.
41. Kahn, *Joys and Sorrows*, p. 108.
42. Corredor, *Conversations*, p. 77, and Montserrat Albet, 'Pau Casals: A Lifetime of Music', trans. by Jacqueline Hall, in *Pau Casals and His Museum*, Fundació Pau Casals, Sant Salvador–El Vendrell, 1986, p. 19.
43. See the excellent sleeve-note, by Jean Loubier, to the 1991 EMI reissue on compact disc of the Cortot–Thibaud–Casals recordings of 1926–9 (CHS 7 64057 2).
44. Corredor, *Conversations*, p. 44.
45. Robert Hartford, *Bayreuth: The Early Years*, London, Gollancz, 1981, pp. 187–8.
46. See Cortot to Casals, 28 April 1913, PCSS.
47. These recordings, digitally remastered from the original London recordings of 1926 and 1928 respectively, are available on compact disc. See 'Compact Discography', pp. 304–20.
48. This itinerary is taken from Casals' travel log for 1899–1913, PCSS.

CHAPTER 4: PARIS, 1906–1910

1. Quoted in C. Bunting and D. C. Pratt, *Cello Technique: 'from one note to the next'*, Cambridge, Cambridge University Press, 1987.
2. Suggia has one brief and not wholly reliable biography, in Portuguese – Mário Cláudio, *Guilhermina*, Porto, 1986 – from which some material in this section has been taken, checked against other sources.
3. The Canadian cellist Zara Nelsova has acknowledged her debt to Suggia, both musically and in terms of fashion. From an interview with the BBC, New York, February 1991.
4. The invitation to appear had come from the Director of the Gewandhaus, Dr Lampekischer. Cláudio, *Guilhermina*, p. 31.
5. The performance took place at the Curtis Concert Club, apparently on 21 January 1905. See van der Straeten, *History of the Violoncello, the Viol*

*de Gamba, their Precursors and Collateral Instruments*, London, William Reeves, 1914, p. 599.

6. Margaret Campbell, *The Great Cellists*, Gollancz, 1988, p. 118.

7. The reference is to the performance of Emanuel Moór's Double Cello Concerto, composed for Casals and Suggia. J. Ma. Corredor, *Conversations with Casals* (English edition), London, 1956, p. 96.

8. Correspondence between Casals and both H. L. Kirk and Joan Alavedra, PCSS. A proportion of the royalties accruing to Kirk's biography, published by Doubleday in 1974, were allocated to Casals in the contract for the book. And see the review of Kirk by Stephen Walsh, *The Listener*, 24 April 1975.

9. Casals to Julius Röntgen, 8 December 1913, Röntgen Papers, The Hague, quoted in H. L. Kirk, *Pablo Casals: A Biography*, London, Hutchinson, p. 292.

10. Casals' papers were apparently rifled by the French police during the war. See Albert E. Kahn, *Joys and Sorrows: Pablo Casals*, London, Eel Pie Publishing, 1981, pp. 150–1.

11. Cláudio, *Guilhermina*, p. 43.

12. A copy of the programme is in the Haags Gemeentemuseum, The Hague.

13. Cláudio, *Guilhermina*, p. 37.

14. Leslie Sheppard, 'Ysaÿe and Kreisler – A Great Friendship', *The Strad*, 1059, July 1978, pp. 221–7.

15. Casals, quoted in Kahn, *Joys and Sorrows*, p. 143.

16. As an agent, Kiesgen wrote to Casals almost every week between January 1913 and October 1937. The correspondence – formal, straightforward and respectful – survives in the PCSS. In 1957 Kiesgen wrote to Casals, offering to represent his new wife, Marta, in her career. See PCSS, Box 8 (a).

17. See S. S. Dale, 'Gaspar Cassadó', *The Strad*, October 1977, pp. 507–9, reprinted in the *Violoncello Society Newsletter*, February 1978. For a survey of Cassadó's career, see Ginsburg, *History of the Violoncello*, New Jersey, Paganiniana Publications, 1983, pp. 233–40.

18. See Adam Ulam, *Russia's Failed Revolutions: From the Decembrists to the Dissidents*, London, Weidenfeld and Nicolson, 1981, p. 200.

19. 5 November by the Julian Calendar. All dates in this section are calculated on the Western calendar.

20. A. A. Borisiak's recollections, in the possession of Lev Ginsburg, and quoted in his *History of the Violoncello*, pp. 165–6, and in H. L. Kirk, *Pablo Casals: A Biography*, London, Hutchinson, 1974, p. 225.

21. Albert E. Kahn (ed.) *Joys and Sorrows: Pablo Casals*, London, Eel Pie Publishing, 1981, p. 121, and Corredor, *Conversations*, p. 55.

22. Alexander Koptyayev, 'Concert by Siloti and Casals', *Sankt Peterburgskiye Vedomosti* [The St Petersburg Record], 24 November 1905.

23. Kirk, *Pablo Casals*, p. 234.

24. Ulam, *Russia's Failed Revolutions*, p. 204.
25. Kahn, *Joys and Sorrows*, p. 120.
26. In 1910, for example, Casals played in Vienna at the beginning of January, travelling to Budapest on the 7th, Moscow on the 14th, and St Petersburg on the 19th. He played a concert in Sweden on the 21st, returning to St Petersburg the following day, and then on to an engagement in Warsaw on the 28th. On 2 February he was back in France, playing a concert in Nice. See Casals' engagement log, PCSS.
27. The concert gained powerful reviews, including one by Alexander Ossovsky: 'On the stage appeared a tiny, skinny little man carrying an instrument almost as big as himself. . . . He walks carefully, as if afraid of spilling the pent-up emotions . . . the first stroke of the bow – and a nervous tremor resounds in the depth of thousands of hearts. The eyes of the virtuoso are closed. The world of reality disappears for him . . . how otherwise would it be possible for a mechanical instrument to sing with such a profound passion, to reveal such important secrets, to be so angry and caressing? [The soloist] would lovingly bend his head toward the instrument as if listening to its whisper. . . . Then at once he would proudly turn his head – all the time without opening his eyes – as if he commanded a crowd of spirits, and these would rush to all the corners of the concert-hall to dispatch the orders of their ruler.' A. N. Ossovsky in the Moscow *Slovo*, 22 November, 1906, quoted in Ginsburg, *History of the Violoncello*, pp. 166–7, and Kirk, *Pablo Casals*, p. 227.
28. Kahn, *Joys and Sorrows*, p. 121.
29. Kirk, *Pablo Casals*, p. 235.
30. Kahn, *Joys and Sorrows*, p. 122.
31. The date of the Vienna debut is given in Kirk and in Albet as November 1910. Casals' own log indicates that he was in Vienna during the first week of January 1910, travelling to Budapest on the 7th. During November he was in Darmstadt (8th), Prague (12th), Bremen (15th), Frankfurt (19th) and Hamburg (28th).
32. Kahn, *Joys and Sorrows*, p. 125.
33. Arthur Rubinstein, *My Young Years*, London, Jonathan Cape, 1973, p. 375.
34. See Seymour W. Itzkoff, *Emanuel Feuermann – Virtuoso: A Biography*, Alabama, University of Alabama Press, 1979, pp. 43–4.
35. Marguerite Caponsacchi was twenty-one years old in 1905, having graduated from the Paris Conservatoire in 1903 as top cello student of the year.
36. Corredor, *Conversations*, p. 92.
37. Kahn, *Joys and Sorrows*, p. 139.
38. Ibid., p. 141.
39. Casals, quoted in Corredor, *Conversations*, p. 93.
40. Dedication of 12 December 1905 to Moór's Second Concerto for Violon-

cello and Orchestra (Op. 64), reproduced in Kahn, *Joys and Sorrows*, p. 141.

41. Max Pirani, *Emanuel Moór*, London, P. R. Macmillan, 1959, pp. 54–5.
42. Louise Llewellyn in *Musical America*, 7 March 1908.
43. Pirani, *Moór*, p. 60. As well as the Double Concerto on 7 February, Casals featured Moór's Triple Concerto at his second Salle Gaveau concert on 28 February (during which he also conducted Suggia playing the Dvořák Concerto), and Moór's Sixth Symphony at the 16 March performance.
44. Pirani, *Emanuel Moór*, p. 60.
45. Ibid., p. 62.
46. For a full account of the history of Moór's double-piano invention, see Pirani, *Moór*, chapters XI–XIX.
47. See Alfredo Casella, *Music In My Time*, Norman, Oklahoma, University of Oklahoma Press, 1955, p. 83.
48. Cláudio, *Guilhermina*, p. 41.
49. Ibid., p. 39.
50. From Julius Röntgen, *Brieven van Julius Röntgen*, Amsterdam, 1934, quoted in Kirk, *Pablo Casals*, pp. 201–2.
51. See Elizabeth Cowling, *The Cello*, London, Batsford, 1975, p. 36.
52. Casals purchased the Bergonzi–Gofriller cello on 15 May with a deposit of 10,000 francs. He paid the remaining 8000 francs in two instalments, on 9 June and 28 October. See receipt from Caressa and Français, 15 May 1908, PCSS.
53. Casals sold the Tononi in 1920. The same instrument was most recently sold by Christie's of London on 26 April 1991 for £143,000.
54. Enric Casals, *Pau Casals: dades biogràfiques inèdites, cartes intimes i records viscuts*, Barcelona, Editorial Pòrtic, 1979, p. 119. Casals passed the replica on to his gifted niece, Enric's daughter Pilar.
55. Casals to the Paris dealer, Vatelot-Hekking, 26 March 1921, PCSS.

## CHAPTER 5: THE ENGLISH CONNECTION, 1910–1914

1. Eisenberg to Casals, 16 February 1932, PCSS.
2. Edward Speyer, *My Life and Friends*, London, Cobden-Sanderson, 1937, p. 86.
3. Speyer, *My Life*, pp. 197–8.
4. Ibid., p. 198, recycled in H. L. Kirk, *Pablo Casals: A Biography*, London, Hutchinson, 1974, p. 263, and misquoted in Albert E. Kahn (ed.), *Joys and Sorrows: Pablo Casals*, London, Eel Pie Publishing, 1981, p. 174.
5. Mary Grierson, *Donald Francis Tovey: A Biography Based on Letters*, London, Oxford University Press, 1952, p. 96.
6. Andrew Porter, *Music of Three Seasons, 1974–7*, London, Chatto and Windus, 1979, pp. 70–1.
7. Grierson, *Tovey*, p. 98.

8. See the account of Sophie Weisse by Tovey's student friend at Balliol, Sir Denys Bray, in a letter to Hubert J. Foss, Tovey's projected biographer, 31 December 1945, Tovey Papers, Edinburgh.

9. The links between Bergson's philosophy and Tovey's musical analysis are discussed by William R. Pasfield in a chapter entitled 'Henri Bergson – Time, Creativity and Spontaneity' in his unpublished manuscript, *Music and Philosophy*.

10. Quoted in Kirk, *Pablo Casals*, p. 270.

11. Casals' travel log for 1910 reveals that he was in Vienna in early January, moving on to Budapest on 7 January. His itinerary for the rest of the year (dates indicate arrival in a city) was: 14–15 January Moscow, 19 St Petersburg, 21 Sweden, 22 St Petersburg, 28 Warsaw; 2 February Nice, 12 Brussels, 16 Amsterdam, 17 Kiel, 23 Amsterdam, 28 St Gall; 1 March Freiburg, 7 Brussels, 8 Paris, 11 Frankfurt, 15 Geneva; 5 April Paris and Nice, 17 Marseille, 21 Dijon, 29 Strasbourg; throughout May in Paris; 2 June London, 7–9 Northlands, 25 Scheveningen; summer in Spain; 20 October London, 21 Northlands, 23 Oxford, 26 Liverpool; 8 November Darmstadt, 12 Prague, 15 Bremen, 19 Frankfurt, 28 Hamburg; 5 December Paris.

12. Sir Henry Wood, *My Life of Music*, p. 321.

13. Grierson, *Tovey*, pp. 145–6.

14. J. Ma. Corredor, *Conversations with Casals* (English edition), London, Hutchinson, 1956, p. 59.

15. Arthur Rubinstein, *My Young Years*, London, Jonathan Cape, 1973, p. 410.

16. Ibid., p. 404.

17. Muriel Draper, *Music at Midnight*, New York, Harper, 1929.

18. Rubinstein, *My Young Years*, pp. 391, 425–6.

19. Suggia to Weisse, 24 September 1911, Tovey Papers, Edinburgh, and Grierson, *Tovey*, p. 152.

20. Tovey, writing from Vienna, to Robert Trevelyan (n.d.), early February 1912, Tovey Papers, Edinburgh.

21. The St Petersburg concert, on 3 February (21 January by the Julian calendar), was conducted by Albert Coates; the Moscow performance, on 6 February (24 January) was conducted by Siloti. See Lev Ginsburg, *Ysaÿe*, New Jersey, Paganiniana Publications, 1980, and Casals' own log for 1912, PCSS.

22. Tovey to Weisse (n.d.), February 1911, Tovey Papers, Edinburgh.

23. See a letter (n.d.) from Enrique Fernández Arbós (Spanish violinist, pupil of Jesús de Monasterio in Madrid and Joachim in Berlin and, since 1894, professor of violin and viola at the Royal College of Music, London) to Casals, PCSS, and Montserrat Albet, 'Pau Casals: A Lifetime of Music,' trans. by Jacqueline Hall, in *Pau Casals and his Museum*, Fundació Pau Casals, Sant Salvador–El Vendrell, 1986, p. 20.

24. The figures come from accounts in Casals' own hand, PCSS. His fees

were $1050 for two concerts in Liverpool, $700 for each of two in London, $600 for a single performance in Belfast, $525 in Oxford and $525 at Northlands, Englefield Green.

25. Again from Casals' own handwritten accounts at San Salvador, his monthly earnings for the 1910–11 season were: October (England) $4100; November (Germany) $5886; December (France) $3100; January (Austria and Russia) $11,107; February (France and Holland) $5574; March (Germany and Switzerland) $6902; April (France) $4330; May (England and France) $4900, making a total of $45,899.

26. Interview, Milly Stanfield, 15 December 1991.

27. Correspondence from Horszowski to Colin Spector, 31 July 1989.

28. Tovey to Weisse (n.d.), September 1912, Tovey Papers, Edinburgh.

29. Tovey to Weisse (n.d.), September 1912, Tovey Papers, Edinburgh, and quoted in Grierson, *Tovey*, p. 161.

30. Tovey to Weisse (n.d.), September 1912, Tovey Papers, Edinburgh.

31. See four postcards from Tovey to Robert Trevelyan, September 1912, Trevelyan Papers, Cambridge.

32. Casals to Weisse, 16 September 1912, Tovey Papers, Edinburgh.

33. Kirk, *Pablo Casals*, p. 467.

34. Tovey's bitter confusion and anxiety about what he referred to as his 'adventures in Spain' are evident in his letters to Elizabeth Trevelyan of 20 October and 6 December 1912, and 13 October 1913, Trevelyan Papers, Cambridge.

35. Grierson, *Tovey*, pp. 161–2.

36. Casals to Trevelyan, 28 November 1912, Trevelyan Papers, Cambridge.

37. Mário Cláudio, *Guilhermina*, Porto, 1986, p. 45.

38. Milly Stanfield in an obituary of Guilhermina Suggia, *The Strad*, September 1950, p. 154.

39. From Guilhermina Suggia, 'The Violoncello', *Music and Letters*, vol. I, no. 2, April 1920, pp. 104–10. The article was accompanied by four photographs, two of Suggia herself, one of her Montagnana instrument, and one of Casals. See also Suggia's 'Violoncello Playing', *Music and Letters*, vol. II, no. 2, April 1921, pp. 130–4, which is very much an account of Casals' principles of performance, especially his 'expressive vibrato' technique. The third article, 'A Violoncello Lesson: Casal's *Obiter Dicta*', *Music and Letters*, vol. II, no. 4, October 1921, pp. 359–63, is attributed to the editor of *Music and Letters*, Arthur Henry Fox Strangeways, but is in fact an account of Casals' public cello classes in Paris during the summer of 1921, 'supplied by Madame Suggia'.

40. See Cláudio, *Guilhermina*, pp. 71–2, and interview, Amaryllis Fleming, 24 January 1992.

41. Kirk, *Pablo Casals*, p. 362. Also in the audience at the Albert Hall concert was the publisher Victor Gollancz. See Victor Gollancz, *Journey Towards Music: A Memoir*, London, Gollancz, 1964, p. 211.

42. From Charles Reid, *Malcolm Sargent*, London, Hamish Hamilton, 1968, pp. 112–13.
43. See correspondence from Horszowski to Casals, 6 July, 12 November, 23 December 1912, 19 May and 29 July 1913, PCSS.
44. Casals to Röntgen, 8 December 1913, quoted in Kirk, *Pablo Casals*, p. 292.
45. Interview, Bernard Greenhouse, 17 April 1992.
46. Casals to Moór, 9 October 1920, in Max Pirani, *Emanuel Moór*, London, P. R. Macmillan, 1959, p. 99.
47. Grierson, *Tovey*, pp. 208–10.
48. See the inventory of Casals' possessions, prepared on 4 November 1914 by M. J. Mansell Ltd, PCSS.
49. Casals' 1937 recording of Tovey's Cello Concerto in C Major (Op. 40) was released on compact disc in 1992 (Symposium 1115). See Andrew Malone, 'Legend lives again in mouldy oldies', *Scotland on Sunday*, 19 April 1992.
50. Corredor, *Conversations*, p. 108.
51. See Cortot to Casals, from the Grand Hôtel, Nancy, 28 April 1913, PCSS.
52. Casals to Granados, 25 December 1913, PCSS.
53. Lev Ginsburg, *History of the Violoncello*, New Jersey, Paganiniana Publications, 1983, p. 170.

CHAPTER 6: AN AMERICAN REFUGE, 1914–1918

1. From a review of Casals' March 1915 performance at the Boston Symphony Concerts by the music critic of the *Boston Post*, see H. L. Kirk, *Pablo Casals: A Biography*, London, Hutchinson, 1974, p. 306.
2. Ibid., pp. 293–4; Montserrat Albet, 'Pau Casals: A Lifetime of Music', in *Pau Casals and his Museum*, Fundació Pau Casals, Sant Salvador–El Vendrell, 1986, p. 22.
3. Lillian Littlehales, *Pablo Casals*, New York, W. W. Norton, 1929 and 1948; repr. Westport, Conn., Greenwood, 1970. See pp. 52–3.
4. Albert E. Kahn (ed.), *Joys and Sorrows: Pablo Casals*, London, Eel Pie Publishing, 1981, p. 142.
5. Juan Alavedra, *Pau Casals*, Barcelona, Plaza y Janes, 1963, p. 271.
6. Casals to Julius Röntgen, 10 July 1914, quoted in Kirk, *Pablo Casals*, p. 299.
7. Casals to Röntgen, 19 November 1914, quoted in ibid., p. 301.
8. Kahn, *Joys and Sorrows*, p. 146.
9. Ibid., p. 147.
10. Quoted in Kirk, *Pablo Casals*, pp. 305–6.
11. Oliver Read and Walter L. Welch, *From Tin Foil to Stereo: Evolution of the Phonograph*, Indianapolis, Howard W. Sams, 1976, p. 216.
12. See Fred Gaisberg's fascinating volume of memoirs, *The Music Goes*

*Round* (also issued as *Music on Record*), New York, Macmillan, 1942.

13. Columbia Graphophone Co. became Columbia Phonograph Co. Inc. in 1924. It was bought by CBS in 1938. CBS was itself purchased by Sony in the late 1980s, so that the bulk of Casals' Columbia recordings now come under the Sony Classical label. Rights in a number of historic recordings have been sub-licensed to various smaller recording labels.

14. Read and Welch, *Tin Foil to Stereo*, p. 209.

15. See Casals' artist contract card, Columbia Masterworks Archives, p. 1.

16. Kirk, *Pablo Casals*, p. 313.

17. Albet, 'Pau Casals', p. 23.

18. Kahn, *Joys and Sorrows*, p. 149.

19. Quoted in Kirk, *Pablo Casals*, p. 295.

20. Richard Aldrich in the *New York Times*, January 1916, quoted in Kirk, *Pablo Casals*, p. 647.

21. See the correspondence between Susan Metcalfe Casals and Elizabeth Sprague Coolidge, from April 1917 until 1927, in the Coolidge Papers, the Library of Congress, Washington, DC.

22. Tovey to Sophie Weisse (n.d.), *c.* September 1912, Tovey Papers, Edinburgh.

23. Enric Casals, *Pau Casals: dades biogràfiques inèdites, cartes intimes i records viscuts*, Barcelona, Editorial Pòrtic, 1979, p. 285.

24. Kahn, *Joys and Sorrows*, p. 147.

25. For the two Madrid performances, on 23 and 26 November 1917, he earned 4500 pesetas.

CHAPTER 7: BARCELONA, 1919–1931

1. Casals to Julius Röntgen, quoted in J. Ma. Corredor, *Conversations with Casals*, London, Hutchinson, 1956, p. 72.

2. Albert E. Kahn (ed.), *Joys and Sorrows: Pablo Casals*, London, Eel Pie Publishing, 1981, p. 150.

3. Corredor, *Conversations*, pp. 61–2.

4. At the New York Bohemian Club concert, Casals and Rachmaninov played Rachmaninov's Cello Sonata. See S. A. Satina, *Memoirs of S. V. Rachmaninoff*, vol. I, Moscow, 1974, quoted in Lev Ginsburg, *History of the Violoncello*, New Jersey, Paganiniana Publications, 1983, p. 170.

5. Manuel Vázquez Montalbán, *Barcelonas*, London, Verso, 1992, p. 80.

6. For a fascinating discussion of Catalan *modernisme*, see Robert Hughes, *Barcelona*, London, HarperCollins, 1992, pp. 391–463.

7. Hughes, *Barcelona*, p. 408. The Casa Terrades was at Diagonal 416–420. The Casals family lived at Diagonal 440.

8. Ibid., p. 458.

9. Kahn, *Joys and Sorrows*, p. 151.

10. Ibid., p. 152.

11. Enric Casals, *Pau Casals: dades biogràfiques inèdites, cartes intimes i records viscuts*, Barcelona, Editorial Pòrtic, 1979, pp. 78–9.

12. The itinerary is given in a letter from Casals to his brother Enrique, 9 January 1920, quoted in Enric Casals, *Pau Casals*, pp. 147–8.

13. See Corredor, *Conversations*, p. 72.

14. I am grateful to Richter's latest biographer, Chris Fifield, for identifying the extent to which the choice of music at the first rehearsals and concerts of the Orquestra Pau Casals was determined by orchestral scores in Richter's collection. Among other works performed in the first series of concerts during the autumn of 1920 were Beethoven's *Coriolan* Overture and the 'Eroica' Symphony, Mozart's Symphony No. 40 in G Minor, the Overture to Weber's *Der Freischütz*, Schubert's 'Unfinished' Symphony No. 8 in B Minor, Strauss's *Ein Heldenleben*, Fauré's *Masques et Bergamasques*, and Debussy's *Rondes de Printemps*.

15. See Kahn, *Joys and Sorrows*, pp. 160–1.

16. Ibid., p. 157.

17. H. L. Kirk, *Pablo Casals: A Biography*, London, Hutchinson, 1974, p. 336.

18. The *New York Times*, 8 April 1922.

19. *The Times*, 8 December 1925.

20. The *Sunday Times*, 8 December 1925.

21. The *Sunday Times*, 12 December 1926.

22. Bernard Shore, *The Orchestra Speaks*, London, Longmans, Green and Co., 1938, pp. 66–7.

23. Carl Flesch, *Memoirs*, London, Rockliff, 1957, p. 118.

24. Adrian C. Boult, 'Casals as Conductor', *Music and Letters*, 4, 1923, pp. 149–52.

25. The Cortot–Thibaud–Casals performance of the Brahms Double Concerto is available on compact disc in two collections: Pearl GEMM CD 9363 ('Pablo Casals Plays Brahms'), and EMI's three-disc set, CHS 7 64057 2 (see Compact Discography, pp. 304–20). Following the Barcelona recording, Gaisberg and HMV travelled to Paris to record Cortot and Thibaud playing Beethoven's Kreutzer Sonata on 27–28 June 1929. The June concert in Barcelona was the only occasion on which Cortot, Thibaud and Casals played together during 1929.

26. See, for example, Jay S. Harrison, 'Pablo Casals Talks About Modern Music', the *New York Herald Tribune*, 4 October 1953.

27. See Corredor, *Conversations*, p. 172.

28. Harrison, 'Pablo Casals . . .', art. cit.

29. Corredor, *Conversations*, p. 136.

30. A full list of the guest conductors and visiting soloists during the sixteen-year life of the Orquestra Pau Casals is given in Juan Alavedra, *Pau Casals*, 4th edn., Barcelona, Plaza y Janes, 1963, pp. 294–5.

31. The American pianist Elie Robert Schmitz, for example, offered to perform in Barcelona during 1930–1. See Schmitz to Casals, 19 February

and 10 June 1930, and Casals' response of 12 April 1930, Pro Musica Society Papers, Yale Music Library.

32. Josep Pla, quoted in Hughes, *Barcelona*, p. 463.

33. Lev Ginsburg, *Ysaÿe*, New Jersey, Paganiniana Publications, 1983, pp. 221–7. In addition to Ysaÿe's performances, the Beethoven centenary included a performance of the G Major Piano Concerto by Mieczyslaw Horszowski.

34. Alavedra, *Pau Casals*, pp. 301–2.

35. Bernard Gavoty, *Alfred Cortot*, Paris, Editions Buchet/Chastel, 1977, p. 103.

36. Gerald Brenan, *The Spanish Labyrinth*, Cambridge, Cambridge University Press, 1950, pp. 65–76.

37. Kirk, *Pablo Casals*, p. 363.

38. Charles Reid, *John Barbirolli*, New York, Taplinger, 1971, pp. 92–3. In 1969, at nearly seventy, Barbirolli came as guest conductor to Casals' Puerto Rico Festival in San Juan.

39. The observation comes from Wilfred Stiff, former managing director of Ibbs and Tillett. And see Casals' correspondence with the agency, Ibbs and Tillett archives.

40. See Casals' itinerary, prepared by the Metropolitan Musical Bureau, New York, PCSS, Box 2 (v).

41. PCSS, Box 2 (ii).

42. See agent's contract, Charles Kiesgen and E. C. Delaet, of Paris, PCSS.

43. A recollection by Willem Valkenier, a member of the Orquestra Pau Casals, quoted in Kirk, *Pablo Casals*, pp. 648–9.

44. Administrator, Concertdirectie Scheveningen, to Susan Metcalfe Casals, 1 October 1920, PCSS.

45. The *Daily Telegraph*, 3 December 1926. The review noted that 'Time deals lightly with this fine artist, whose voice is rich and sweet as ever'.

46. Enric Casals, *Pau Casals*, p. 285.

47. See newsletter of the Metropolitan Musical Bureau, New York. The tour schedule had included five dates in Cuba, paying $2000 a concert.

48. Casals to Bauer, 20 February 1921, US Library of Congress.

49. Alexander Schneider, *Sasha: A Musician's Life*, New York, 1988, p. 86.

50. Quoted in the *Report of the Librarian of Congress*, 1925.

51. See the Elizabeth Sprague Coolidge Foundation Collection in the music division of the Library of Congress. The correspondence with Casals includes a cheque for $5000, dated 3 February 1921, to sponsor a concert during the 1921 season. Since Casals cancelled his 1921 tour, the subvention was probably not used.

52. Alfredo Casella, *Music in My Time*, Norman, Oklahoma, University of Oklahoma Press, 1955, p. 162.

53. Coolidge to Metcalfe, 9 January 1927, Coolidge Papers, Library of Congress.

54. The Casals/Mednikoff recordings are available on compact disc as 'Casals: the Victor recordings (1926–28)', Biddulph LAB 017.
55. Casals to Enric Casals, 23 February 1928, reproduced in Enric Casals, *Pau Casals*, pp. 148–9.
56. Fred Gaisberg, *The Music Goes Round*, New York, Macmillan, 1942, p. 214. Casals considered the possibility of an American tour in the winter of 1931–2, but did not pursue it. See Casals to Tillett, 28 December 1931, Ibbs and Tillett Archives.
57. Casals to Tillett, 13 January 1929, Ibbs and Tillett archives.
58. See Casals to Enrique, from Berlin, 22 November 1929, reproduced in Enric Casals, *Pau Casals*, p. 150.
59. See Eisenberg to Casals, 20 March 1933, PCSS.
60. See Kahn, *Joys and Sorrows*, or Corredor, *Conversations*, on Casals, Gavoty, *Alfred Cortot*, which similarly incorporates direct testimony from the pianist, and Jacques Thibaud, *Un violon parle: souvenirs recueillis par Jean-Jacques Dorian*, Paris, Editions du Blé, 1947.
61. See Cortot to Casals, 15 June 1920, PCSS.
62. The performances of the Trio are available in a three-CD set, from EMI (7 64057 2).
63. See the excellent sleeve-note by Jean Loubier accompanying the Cortot–Thibaud–Casals Trio CD issue from EMI. I make grateful acknowledgement to Loubier's research.
64. Victor Gollancz, *Journey Towards Music: A Memoir*, London, Gollancz, 1964, p. 214.
65. Casals to Tillett, 19 August 1933, Ibbs and Tillett archives.
66. See Renée Cortot to Casals, 24 May 1947, *et seq.*, Casals Papers, Washington, DC (hereafter PCW).
67. Gavoty, *Alfred Cortot*, pp. 159–64.
68. See Irving Kolodin, 'The Big World of Don Pablo', *SR*, 31, December 1966, pp. 43–7.
69. Casals to Cortot, September 1957, PCW.
70. Gavoty, *Alfred Cortot*, p. 192. This final Cortot–Casals performance was recorded by Radio Diffusion Française, but has never been released.
71. Saul Bellow, *To Jerusalem and Back*, London, Alison Press, 1976, p. 6.
72. The 1921 masterclass was recorded verbatim by an unidentified cellist, and interpreted by Guilhermina Suggia for *Music and Letters*, vol. II, no. 4, October 1921, in 'A Violoncello Lesson: Casals's *Obiter Dicta*'.
73. Enrique had four children, Pilar, Enriquetta, Luis and Carlos, while Luis had three, Mariona, Pilar and Pau.
74. The schedule is taken from Casals' engagement diary, 1930–1, PCSS, Box 2 (iii). His income from fees, for the two months of November and December 1930, was $16,300.

CHAPTER 8: CATALONIA AND THE SPANISH REPUBLIC, 1931–1939

1. Casals, speaking during the broadcast of his final Barcelona concert on 19 October 1938, quoted in J. Alvarez del Vayo, 'Pablo Casals – Freedom's Artist', *The Nation*, 17 June 1950.
2. Albert E. Kahn (ed.), *Joys and Sorrows: Pablo Casals*, London, Eel Pie Publishing, 1981, p. 209.
3. Gerald Brenan, *The Spanish Labyrinth*, Cambridge, Cambridge University Press, 1950, p. 84.
4. J. Ma. Corredor, *Conversations with Casals*, London, Hutchinson, 1956, p. 79.
5. Kahn, *Joys and Sorrows*, p. 209.
6. See PCSS, Box 3 (i).
7. Casals and Tovey, 26 August 1931, Tovey Papers, Edinburgh.
8. Casals to Ibbs and Tillett, 4 September 1931, Ibbs and Tillett archives.
9. See Enric Casals, *Pau Casals: dades biogràfiques inèdites, cartes intimes i records viscuts*, Barcelona, Editorial Pòrtic, 1979, p. 286.
10. Interview, Macià Alavedra, 25 April 1990. In most accounts of Casals' life, Frasquita Capdevila has been depicted, if at all, as his housekeeper, an interpretation sharply criticized in the account of Casals' own brother. See Enric Casals, *Pau Casals*, pp. 306–7.
11. For information on Eisenberg's career, see Margaret Campbell, *The Great Cellists*, London, Gollancz, 1988, pp. 150–1; Lev Ginsburg, *History of the Violoncello*, New Jersey, Paganiniana Publications, 1983, pp. 258–63; and Ishaq Araz, 'Always Back to Bach: A Glimpse into the career of Maurice Eisenberg, cellist', *American String Teacher*, Spring 1968.
12. Milly Stanfield had studied at the London Violoncello School, run by Herbert Walenn, where in 1925 she had been prize-winner at the annual students' concert. Sara Nelson (Zara Nelsova) was a prize-winner in 1933. See Campbell, *The Great Cellists*, p. 237, and PCSS, Box 3 (5).
13. From Maurice Eisenberg, 'Casals at Eighty: A Tribute', *Violins and Violinists*, January–February, 1957, pp. 4–6.
14. The cellist Julian Lloyd Webber has published a remarkable anthology of Casals' quotations, or anecdotes about him, as *Song of the Birds: Sayings, Stories and Impressions of Pablo Casals*, London, Robson Books, 1985. There are, of course, many more.
15. This, and other examples of Casals in rehearsal, are taken from David Blum's classic study, *Casals and the Art of Interpretation*, Berkeley, University of California Press, 1977.
16. Eisenberg to Casals, 15 January 1933, PCSS.
17. Interview, Pablo Eisenberg, 6 December 1991.
18. See correspondence between Eisenberg and Casals, 1930–9, in PCSS. Eisenberg performed and toured with Yehudi and Hephzibah Menuhin, and recorded with them for HMV. Yehudi Menuhin became godfather to the Eisenbergs' second child, a daughter, Maruta.
19. See H. L. Kirk, *Pablo Casals: A Biography*, London, Hutchinson, 1974,

pp. 389–91 for an account of the final correspondence between Casals and Röntgen.

20. See Suggia to Sophie Weisse, 11 April 1920, Tovey Papers, Edinburgh, and Mary Grierson, *Donald Francis Tovey: A Biography Based on Letters*, London, Oxford University Press, 1952, p. 202.

21. See Susan Metcalfe Casals to Mrs Tovey, commenting on the success of the Barcelona performance, 21 October 1927, Tovey Papers, Edinburgh. Tovey had visited the United States during the summers of 1924–6, performing first at The School of the Arts in Santa Barbara, California, and later at Elizabeth Sprague Coolidge's Festival in Pittsfield.

22. Grierson, *Tovey*, p. 234.

23. Tovey to Weisse, n.d. (spring 1933), Tovey Papers, Edinburgh, quoted in sleeve-note by Jeremy Upton for Symposium Records' CD issue of the concerto (SYMP 1115, 1992), and Tovey to Grierson, n.d., quoted in Grierson, *Tovey*, p. 276.

24. See Casals to Tovey, 26 August 1931 and 12 May 1933, Tovey Papers, Edinburgh.

25. Casals to Tovey, 8 October 1933, ibid.

26. Tovey to Weisse, 25 April 1934, ibid. At the concert on 11 April, Tovey played the piano part of the Fifth Brandenburg Concerto as well as his own. He described Casals' conducting as 'very interesting', adding that 'I cannot trace any technique in it; the beats seem all over the place and in syncopated passages he is quite likely to mark the syncopation instead of the beats'.

27. Casals to Tovey, 12 June 1934, ibid.

28. Elgar to Tovey, 10 February 1934, ibid.

29. Casals to Tovey 28 May 1934, ibid.

30. *The Times*, 24 November 1934.

31. Christopher Bunting, in an introduction to the CD recording.

32. *The Scotsman*, 23 November 1934.

33. *Carnet Musical*, 5 April 1935.

34. Both the *Observer* and the *Sunday Times* published their notices on 17 November 1935.

35. Casals to Ibbs and Tillett, 27 June and 4 August 1936, Ibbs and Tillett archives.

36. Casals to Tovey, 24 November 1936, Tovey Papers, Edinburgh.

37. Grierson, *Tovey*, p. 313.

38. The recording, which Tovey himself was asked to underwrite to the extent of £300 or the sale of 100 copies, was never released as planned, on 78s, but appeared, in 1992, on CD from Symposium Records (SYMP 1115).

39. Kahn, *Joys and Sorrows*, p. 215.

40. Account of a visit to Sir Donald Tovey, unidentified source, late 1939. PCSS, Box 10 (i).

41. Ginsburg, *History of the Violoncello*, p. 171.

42. Samuel and Sada Applebaum, 'Pablo Casals', in *The Way They Played*, New Jersey, Paganiniana Publications, 1972, p. 297.
43. Schönberg to Casals, 20 February 1933, in Erwin Stein (ed.), *Arnold Schoenberg Letters*, London, Faber and Faber, 1964, pp. 171–2.
44. Corredor, *Conversations*, p. 170.
45. Schönberg to Casals, 22 September 1933, Stein, *Letters*, pp. 182–3.
46. Corredor, *Conversations*, p. 170.
47. See Seymour W. Itzkoff, *Emanuel Feuermann, Virtuoso: A Biography*, Alabama, University of Alabama Press, 1979, pp. 155–7.
48. Included in a letter from Eva Feuermann to Casals, 26 May 1950, PCW. The paragraph is similar, but not identical, to one in an article he published in *Musical America*, 25 February 1940, entitled 'Feuermann inveighs against mechanical methods'.
49. Kahn, *Joys and Sorrows*, p. 218.
50. See Casals to Tovey, 27 December 1934, Tovey Papers, Edinburgh.
51. Eisenberg to Casals, 23 April 1936, PCSS.
52. Kahn, *Joys and Sorrows*, p. 220.
53. Kirk, *Pablo Casals*, pp. 401–2.
54. Corredor, *Conversations*, pp. 213–14.
55. This point about same-label competition is made by Charles Haynes in his sleeve-note to the Pearl CD 'Pablo Casals Plays Brahms' (GEMM CD 9363). He observes that Casals never recorded the Haydn D Major Concerto nor the Brahms E Minor Sonata, both of which Feuermann had already recorded for Columbia. But Gaisberg did record Casals playing the Dvořák Concerto, in 1937, even though Feuermann had recorded the same work in 1930.
56. Gaisberg, *The Music Goes Round*, New York, Macmillan, 1942, p. 212.
57. Kahn, *Joys and Sorrows*, p. 224.
58. See Eisenberg to Casals, 26 November 1936, PCSS.
59. Interview, Sta. Mercèdes Guarro i Tapis, 21 September 1991. In *Conversations with Casals* (p. 214), Casals suggests his first visit to Prades came as late as 1939. Following inaccuracies in obituaries after his death in 1973, *Le Monde* ran an article entitled 'Quand Pablo Casals est-il arrivé à Prades' (9 November 1973), which quoted locals as having seen him there as early as late 1936.
60. Casals to Ibbs and Tillett, 23 January 1937, Ibbs and Tillett archives.
61. Eisenberg to Casals, 2 February 1937, PCSS.
62. See Casals to Tovey, 3 March 1938, Tovey Papers, Edinburgh.

CHAPTER 9: WAR AND EXILE, 1939–1949

1. Casals to Victor Alba, author of *Insomnie Espagnole*, Paris, 1946/7, PCSS, Box 7 (4).
2. Casals to Germaine Grottiendieck, 5 February 1939, PCP (Prades).

3. Casals in conversation with Isaac Stern in a CBS TV documentary, 'Casals at Eighty-eight', 1958.
4. The fine was imposed on 5 September 1940, and listed in the compendium *Crimes Against Catalonia*: reference courtesy Professor Paul Preston.
5. Juan Alavedra, *Pau Casals*, Barcelona, Aldos, 1962, p. 318.
6. Bernard Gavoty, *Alfred Cortot*, Paris, Editions Buchet/Chastel, 1977, pp. 156–7.
7. See Alavedra's own account of the episode, in his *Pau Casals*, p. 336, and Albert E. Kahn (ed.), *Joys and Sorrows: Pablo Casals*, London, Eel Pie Publishing, 1981, p. 237.
8. On publication of the French edition of *Joys and Sorrows*, Cortot's son Jean instituted libel proceedings against Casals for the insinuation. Casals' lawyer, Abe Fortas, sought the advice of Coudert Frères in Paris on the case, which was not pursued.
9. Fifty years later, Pierrette Hostelrich and her daughter Nanou still run their café, now part of the Hotel Hostelrich. Opposite, the Grand Hôtel is derelict.
10. Interview, Macià Alavedra, 25 April 1990.
11. H. L. Kirk, *Pablo Casals: A Biography*, London, Hutchinson, 1974, p. 416. Casals' accompanist in this period was very often Reine Gianoli.
12. Kahn, *Joys and Sorrows*, p. 241.
13. J. Ma. Corredor, *Conversations with Casals*, London, Hutchinson, 1956, p. 216.
14. See Casals to Schneider, 12 April 1956, ASLC (Schneider Papers).
15. Kahn, *Joys and Sorrows*, p. 239.
16. *New York Times*, 24 December 1944. The letter was printed anonymously, but may have been sent by Maurice Eisenberg on Casals' instructions.
17. Casals to Germaine Grottiendieck, 3 May 1945, PCP.
18. See, for example, the argument advanced by Tom Buchanan in *The Spanish Civil War and the British Labour Movement*, Cambridge, Cambridge University Press, 1991.
19. Kahn, *Joys and Sorrows*, p. 253.
20. Corredor, *Conversations*, p. 222.
21. Gerald Moore, *Am I Too Loud?: Memoirs of an Accompanist*, London, Hamish Hamilton, 1962, p. 144.
22. Ibid., p. 145.
23. Kahn, *Joys and Sorrows*, p. 256.
24. Milly Stanfield, 'Looking Back'.
25. *Radio Times*, 15 January 1937.
26. When the 1945 recording was issued the scholar–critic of *The Gramophone*, Edward Sackville-West, still had problems with it: 'Many of us look back upon Casals' playing of the concerto in the Albert Hall, just after the end of the war, as among the great musical experiences of our lives . . . [but] the great cellist's idiosyncrasies take us too far away from

the composer's intention. The long, winding, pastoral theme in the first movement is pulled clean out of shape by a very slow, intensely rubato delivery. It never flows at all . . . over the whole there hangs a heavy cloak of sentimentality.' Fifty years on, performances of the Elgar in the 1970s and 1980s by du Pré and others have put the issue of sentimentality into some sort of context. Casals now looks rather dry and brisk.

27. Corredor, *Conversations*, p. 224.
28. Casals to Grottiendieck, 23 April 1946, PCP.
29. Noted by Milly Stanfield in *The Strad*, 1 January 1947.
30. Jean Weiner in *Le Soir*, 24 November 1945.
31. See Paul Preston, *Salvador de Madariaga and the Quest for Liberty in Spain*, Oxford, Clarendon Press, 1987, p. 22.
32. Jan Morris, *Spain*, London, Faber and Faber, 1964 and 1979, p. 47.
33. I am very grateful to Professor Preston for the information on which this paragraph is based.
34. After 1938 Casals had corresponded with Alfonso XIII in exile, primarily in connection with help for child victims of the Civil War. After Alfonso's death in 1941, Casals met his twenty-eight-year-old son, Don Juan, in Switzerland. Later, in Athens in 1966, Casals met the Pretender's own son, Juan Carlos, later Franco's nomination to the restored Spanish throne. See Kirk, *Pablo Casals*, p. 437, and Kahn, *Joys and Sorrows*, p. 66.
35. See John Hooper, *The Spaniards: A Portrait of the New Spain*, London, Viking, 1986, pp. 144–6.
36. From the profile by Lael Wertenbaker in *Life*, 15 May 1950.
37. Milly Stanfield, *Looking Back*.
38. See David Dubal, *Conversations with Menuhin: A Celebration on his Seventy-fifth Birthday*, London, Gollancz, 1991, pp. 65–6.
39. Casals authorized Diran Alexanian to publish a letter of his about Cassadó in the *New York Times*, 6 March 1949. And see Stephen Walsh's review of Kirk, *Pablo Casals*, in *The Listener*, 24 April 1975.
40. Yehudi Menuhin, *Unfinished Journey*, London, Macdonald and Jane's, 1977, p. 231.
41. Quoted in a leaflet printed by Spanish Refugee Aid, New York, 1953.
42. See, for example, Casals to Roger Nordman, secretary-general of Chaînes du Bonheur, 11 January 1954, on the issue of a 2-million-franc donation for refugee children, PCW, 4 (c).
43. *Adam International Review*, XV, no. 174, PCSS 7 (i).
44. A collection of Casals' sacred music is available, sung by the choir of the Escolanía at Montserrat, on compact disc (SCHWANN 313062, 1991).
45. Interview, Bernard Greenhouse, 17 April 1992.
46. Interview, Christopher Bunting, 10 October 1991.
47. 'Releasing the Inner Fire', a profile of Uzi Wiesel by Margaret Campbell, *The Strad*, June 1992.

48. Interview with Bernard Greenhouse in Nicholas Delbanco, *The Beaux Arts Trio*, London, Gollancz, 1985, p. 51.
49. Ibid.
50. Interview, Pamela Hind O'Malley, 8 November 1991.
51. Pamela Hind, 'Casals as Teacher', *The Royal College of Music Magazine*, vol. 46, 1950, pp. 96–100.
52. Interview, Amaryllis Fleming, 24 January 1992.
53. See, *inter alia*, David Blum, *Casals and the Art of Interpretation*, Berkeley, University of California Press, 1977, especially chapter 5 ('Insights for String Players'); David Cherniavsky, 'Casals' Approach to Teaching the Cello', *Etude*, June 1952; Pamela Hind O'Malley, 'Casals and Intonation', *The Strad*, October 1983; Milly Stanfield, 'Lessons by Example', *The Strad*, September 1950, and *The Intermediate Cellist*, London, 1973; Guilhermina Suggia, 'Violoncello Playing', *Music and Letters*, vol. II, no. 2, April 1921.
54. Daniel Barenboim, *A Life in Music*, London, Weidenfeld and Nicolson, 1991.
55. Blum, *Casals and the Art of Interpretation*, pp. 131–2.
56. Ibid., p. 110.
57. Delbanco, *The Beaux Arts Trio*, p. 51.
58. Ibid., p. 52.
59. Interview, Pamela Hind O'Malley, 8 November 1991.

CHAPTER 10: RESURRECTION: THE BACH FESTIVAL, 1949–1950

1. Alexander Schneider, *Sasha: A Musician's Life*, New York, 1988, p. 127.
2. Lillian Littlehales' short biography, *Pablo Casals*, had been first published by W. W. Norton in New York in 1929. A second, updated, edition was issued in 1948.
3. Stephen Walsh, review of H. L. Kirk, *Pablo Casals: A Biography*, in *The Listener*, 24 April 1975.
4. Schneider to Casals, 16 June 1947, PCW.
5. Schneider to Casals, 26 November 1947, PCW.
6. Casals to Schneider, 4 June 1948, Alexander Schneider Papers, Library of Congress, Washington DC (hereafter ASLC); Casals to Rafael Moragas, 2 April 1948, Biblioteca Nacional de Catalunya, Barcelona, MS 3148.
7. Schneider, *Sasha*, p. 110.
8. Casals letter of thanks to Schneider, 31 July 1948, PCW, File 8d.
9. Ormandy to Misha Schneider, 3 October 1950, PCW, File 8d.
10. See Schneider to Cameron Baird, 10 January 1949, PCW.
11. Schneider to Casals, 11 November 1948, PCW.
12. Undated *c.* May 1950 draft article by Lael Wertenbaker, PCSS, Box 8 (iv). The invitation to the Library of Congress concert came personally from Elizabeth Sprague Coolidge, 7 October 1949, PCW, File 8d.

13. Casals to Schneider, 15 October 1948, ASLC.
14. Wertenbaker interview notes, ibid.
15. Albert E. Kahn, *Joys and Sorrows: Pablo Casals*, London, Eel Pie Publishing, 1981, p. 105.
16. Schneider to Casals, 30 January 1950, PCSS.
17. See Josep Trueta to Foreign Office, 19 August 1949, and Board of Trade reply, 31 August 1949, PCSS.
18. Schneider to Casals, 14 February 1950 and 7 September 1950, PCSS.
19. Howard Taubman in the *New York Times*, 29 July 1951.
20. Paul Tortelier and David Blum, *Tortelier: A Self-Portrait*, London, Heinemann, 1984, p. 103.
21. PCW, file 4e, and quoted in Kirk, *Pablo Casals*, p. 454.
22. Cyrus Durgin, 'Frustrating Silence at Great Casals Concert', *Boston Globe*, 3 June 1950.
23. Durgin, ibid., and Christina Thoresby, 'Bach Festival in Prades', in the 'Music in France' column of *The Strad*, July 1950, p. 106.
24. At the opening concert the Brandenburg Concertos were recorded. Casals' performance of the G Major Suite was not.
25. Interview, Milly Stanfield, 15 December 1991.
26. Istomin, quoted in Bernard Tapper, 'A Cellist in Exile', the *New Yorker*, 24 February 1962.
27. Schneider to Casals, 7 September 1950, PCSS.
28. The inventory of works recorded is taken from Casals' Columbia Masterworks artist contract card, pp. 8–14.
29. Howard Taubman in the *New York Times*, 29 July 1951.
30. Harris Goldsmith, 'Pablo Casals (1876–1973)', *High Fidelity Magazine*, July 1974, pp. 77–8.
31. Hélène Jeanbrau, interview at Prades, 3 June 1991.
32. The recording of this performance is available on CD, Columbia Masterworks Portrait (MPK 46445).
33. Cyrus Durdin, 'Streets Where Casals Played Marble-Paved', *Boston Globe*, 4 June 1950.
34. Prominent among the available biographies were Lillian Littlehales' 1929 study (see note 2 above) and Arthur Conte's poetic *La Légende de Pablo Casals*, printed in Perpignan (Editions Proa, 1950) with photographs by Gjon Mili.
35. Interview, Alexander Schneider, 3 June 1991.
36. J. Alvarez del Vayo, 'Pablo Casals – Freedom's Artist', *The Nation*, New York, 17 June 1950.
37. Wertenbaker's piece appeared in *Life*, 15 May 1950. The full notes of her interview with Casals are in PCSS, Box 8 (iv).
38. Schneider to Casals, 25 July 1950, PCSS.
39. Casals to Schneider, 20 July 1950, ASLC. Casals and Schneider corresponded in both French and English, at different times. Quotations from letters written in French I have translated myself.

40. Schneider to Casals, 7 September 1950, PCSS.
41. See Casals to Germaine Grottendieck, 10 October 1952, Casals Papers, Prades (hereafter PCP).
42. Schneider introduced Istomin to Casals in a letter of 30 March 1950, PCSS.
43. This account comes substantially from Eugene Istomin, interview, New York, 2 October 1990.
44. Istomin, quoted in Paul Moor, 'Casals at Prades', *Theatre Arts*, October 1950.
45. Istomin to Casals, 5 July 1950, PCSS, Box 19.
46. Interview with Christopher Bunting, 10 October 1991.
47. The *New York Times*, 29 July 1951, following the Perpignan Festival.
48. Istomin, 'The Virtuoso and Chamber Music', *Music and Artists*, February/March 1968.
49. Suggia to Casals, 10 May 1950, PCSS.
50. News of Suggia's death came in a card from Madame Maria Adelaide Diego de Freitas Gonzalves, 1 August 1950, PCSS.

CHAPTER 11: THE PRADES FESTIVAL, 1951–1955

1. David Oistrakh, 'At a Festival at Prades', *Sovetskaya Muzyka*, no. 11, 1961, pp. 135–6, quoted in Lev Ginsburg, *History of the Violoncello*, New Jersey, Paganiniana Publications, 1983, p. 172.
2. Schneider to Casals, 26 January 1951, PCSS. One musician for whom a place could not be found in the orchestra was Casals' former pupil, the cellist Zara Nelsova.
3. Istomin, for Casals, to Schneider, 21 October 1950, ASLC.
4. Casals to Thea Dispeker, 17 December 1952, ASLC.
5. See Schneider to Casals, 13 December 1950, and 31 March 1951, PCSS. Hélène Jeanbrau, the Festival secretary in Prades and a friend of Schneider, resigned after the 1951 Festival.
6. Casals to Schneider, 22 December 1950, ASLC.
7. Doda Conrad to Thea Dispeker, executive secretary of the Casals Festival, 29 September 1951, PCW, File 12e.
8. The combination of nerves and unfamiliar cooking was known to make Casals ill. See Conrad to Dispeker, 17 May 1951, PCW, File 12e.
9. From notes of a talk by Milly Stanfield to the International Cello Centre, London, 15 December 1953, PCW, File 12e.
10. The Catalan edition, *Converses amb Casals*, was reissued in an updated edition in 1967 by Editorial Selecta of Barcelona. The French edition, originally published by Albin Michel in 1955, was reissued with new annotations, by Pluriel/Hachette in 1982. In 1967 J. Ma. Corredor published an abridged and illustrated edition, as *Casals: biografía ilustrada* (Ediciones Destino, Barcelona). The English translation, *Conversations*

*with Casals*, was published in New York by Dutton and in London by Hutchinson in 1956.

11. Interview, Pamela Hind O'Malley, 8 November 1991.

12. Interview, Christopher Bunting, 10 October 1991.

13. Dietrich Fischer-Dieskau, *Echoes of a Lifetime*, London, Macmillan, 1989, p. 332.

14. Interview, Enriquetta Touron, Prades, 30 April 1990.

15. See Casals' Columbia Masterworks artist contract card, 2 January 1951, p. 28. Casals' royalty rose from 7.5 per cent of 90 per cent in 1950 to 10 per cent of 90 per cent in 1951.

16. Schneider to Casals, 26 January 1951, PCSS.

17. Schneider to Casals, 14 December 1951, PCSS.

18. Schneider's cable to Casals, 17 January 1952, and Casals' response, 31 January 1952, PCSS.

19. Interview, Eugene Istomin, 9 December 1991.

20. Schneider to Casals, 2 February 1952, PCSS.

21. Casals to Schneider, 27 March 1952, ASLC.

22. Virgil Thomson, 'Casals and the Matterhorn', *New York Herald Tribune*, September 195?.

23. See Schneider to Casals, 21 February 1952, PCSS.

24. Foley circular letter of 10 March, and Tortelier's reply, 23 March 1952, PCSS, Box 12 (iv).

25. Foley to Mannes, 23 August 1952, PCSS, Box 11.

26. Alexander Schneider, *Sasha: A Musician's Life*, New York, 1988, p. 136.

27. Casals to Schneider, 26 October 1953, ASLC.

28. Seymour W. Itzkoff, *Emanuel Feuermann, Virtuoso: A Biography*, Alabama, University of Alabama Press, 1979, p. 213.

29. Leopold Mannes to Casals, 23 September 1953, PCSS, Box 13 (iii).

30. Istomin to Casals, 23 October 1953, PCSS.

31. Kingman to Foley, 16 February 1952, PCSS, Box 12 (iv).

32. Kingman to John Barnes, 8 December 1953, PCSS, Box 13 (iii).

33. The agreement, dated 17 June 1954, was signed by Istomin, Foley, Horszowski and Kingman, and approved by Casals, PCW.

34. From correspondence between Verne Foley (Madeline's father) and Casals, January–February 1956, PCW, File 8a.

35. Fischer-Dieskau, *Echoes of a Lifetime*, p. 333. In fact, Fischer-Dieskau, along with David Lloyd and Eugene Istomin, was offered reimbursement of travelling expenses and a fee of 3500 francs per day. All renounced their entitlement in favour of the Festival or of Casals himself. See PCSS, Box 13 (iv).

36. Istomin to Casals, 14 February 1954, PCSS, Box 19.

37. The forecast balance was 1,837,083 francs, and the artists received 175,000 francs each. See John Barnes' Festival Financial Report, 15 June 1954, PCW, File 12e.

38. Casals to Germaine Grottendieck, 27 February 1954, PCP. Grotten-

dieck, a Belgian cellist, had studied at Liège Conservatoire with Jacques Gaillard, then with Diran Alexanian in Paris. She gave her debut concert in 1926. During the 1920s she had occasional lessons from Casals.

39. Casals to Grottendieck, 12 October 1954, PCP.
40. Casals to Grottendieck, 15 November 1954, PCP.
41. Franchisca Capdevila's will, dated 10 October 1950, in Prades, left to Casals a cameo necklace, and a selection of items from her flat in Barcelona. The principal beneficiary was her nephew, Frederico Vidal Canadell. PCW, File 8a.
42. Casals, in response to Schneider's letter of condolence, 8 March 1955, ASLC.
43. Istomin to Casals, 27 January 1955, PCSS, Box 19.
44. Casals to Grottendieck, 1 March 1955, PCP.
45. The archive of the Festival Pablo Casals de Prades apparently holds recordings of sixty concerts for the years after 1953. A selection of Prades Festival performances, ranging from 1953 to 1959 but principally taken from 1955 and 1956, were issued by Educational Media Associates of America, Inc., in 1982. They were reissued in a two-volume, eight-compact disc set in 1991 by a successor organization, Music and Arts Programs of America, Inc. Other performances from 1955–6 have been issued in Italy under the 'i protagonisti' and AS Disc labels (1989), and in France by Lyrinx – within a series entitled 'Collection Festival de Prades: Les Années Casals'. Perhaps because of the length of time these recordings have remained unavailable, the printed notes accompanying the CDs contain unfortunate errors and inaccuracies in respect of artists' names, the dates of performance and the works performed. See 'Compact Discography', pp. 304–20.
46. Fischer-Dieskau, *Echoes of a Lifetime*, p. 334.
47. Milly Stanfield in *The Strad*, 721, 1955.
48. Istomin to Casals, 16 March 1955, PCSS, Box 19.
49. Albert E. Kahn (ed.), *Joys and Sorrows: Pablo Casals*, London, Eel Pie Publishing, 1981, p. 268.
50. H. L. Kirk, *Pablo Casals: A Biography*, London, Hutchinson, 1974, p. 483. Dona Angélica Montañez kindly provided her recollection of the discovery of the coincidence in a conversation on 17 April 1992.
51. Schneider, *Sasha*, p. 171.
52. Kahn, *Joys and Sorrows*, p. 270. The French press began to print photographs of Casals and Martita, describing her as an 'adopted daughter', or a niece.
53. Interview, Christopher Bunting, 10 October 1991.

CHAPTER 12: EPIPHANY: THE DISCOVERY OF PUERTO RICO, 1955–1959

1. From Casals' speech accepting an honorary doctorate at the Inter-American University, San German, Puerto Rico, 6 March 1956, taken

from 'Pablo Casals En Puerto Rico', a film for television by Jack Delano, 1956.

2. *El Imparcial*, 12 December 1955.

3. *El Mundo*, 10 December 1955.

4. See correspondence between Rafael Montañez and Casals, 6 June 1950, PCW, File 8a.

5. José Garcia Borrás, *Pablo Casals: Pelegrino en America: Tres Semanas con il Maestro*, Tallerers Gráficos Victoria, Bolívar, Mexico, 1957. The Puerto Rico Department of Education also produced an account of the visit, *Pablo Casals en Puerto Rico, 1955–56*, San Juan, 1957.

6. Albert E. Kahn (ed.), *Joys and Sorrows: Pablo Casals*, London, Eel Pie Publishing, 1981, p. 271.

7. This survey of the political and historical genesis of Puerto Rico is based substantially on Raymond Carr, *Puerto Rico: A Colonial Experiment*, New York and London, 1984, and *Puerto Rico: Five Hundred Years of Change and Continuity*, published by the Institute for Puerto Rican Affairs, Washington, DC, 1991. See especially, in the latter, Maria de los Angeles Castro Arroyo, 'A Profile of Puerto Rican History', pp. 2–11.

8. Marcia Rivera, 'Puerto Rico: A Mirror with Many Images', in *Puerto Rico: Five Hundred Years of Change and Continuity*, pp. 65–72.

9. Quoted in Laura Kalman, *Abe Fortas: A Biography*, New Haven and London, Yale University Press, 1990, p. 170.

10. Ibid., pp. 86–7.

11. Ibid., p. 167.

12. Ibid., p. 176.

13. Marimar Benitez, 'A Glance at the Art of Puerto Rico', in *Puerto Rico: Five Hundred Years*, p. 31.

14. Benitez, p. 30, and Asela Rodriguez de Laguna, 'The Puerto Rican Literary Heritage', also in *Puerto Rico: Five Hundred Years*, pp. 51–2.

15. Kalman, *Abe Fortas*, pp. 176–7.

16. In March 1969, Casals was offered, but declined, first refusal on the purchase of the calle Méndez Vigo house for $42,000. See offer of 21 March 1969, PCW, File 8a.

17. H. L. Kirk, *Pablo Casals: A Biography*, London, Hutchinson, 1974, p. 485.

18. Casals to Schneider, 24 February 1956, ASLC.

19. Alexander Schneider, *Sasha: A Musician's Life*, New York, 1988, p. 172.

20. This concert was recorded and issued on disc by Philips (L77.408L).

21. Schneider to Casals, 17 September 1956, ASLC.

22. Casals to Schneider, 24 October 1956, ASLC.

23. Casals to Istomin, 7 November 1956, PCW.

24. This first movement of the Schubert Symphony was recorded by Columbia, and issued in December 1957 on disc ML 5236. See Columbia Masterworks contract digest, Pablo Casals and Festival Casals Inc., dated 12 February 1957, p. 29.

25. Kirk, *Pablo Casals*, pp. 494–5.
26. The *New York Times*, 17 April 1957.
27. Schneider, *Sasha*, pp. 174–5.
28. Marta Montañez to Schneider, 20 May 1957, PCW.
29. Kahn, *Joys and Sorrows*, p. 276, and see Marta Montañez to Schneider, 12 July 1957, PCW.
30. Marta Montañez to Schneider, 22 February 1957; see also Inés Muñoz Marín to Schneider, 23 January 1957, PCW.
31. Interview with Marta Casals Istomin, 'Song of the Birds: A Portrait of Pablo Casals', BBC TV, September 1991.
32. Interview, Marta Casals Istomin, 9 December 1991.
33. Interview, Marta Casals Istomin, BBC TV, September 1991.
34. Kirk, *Pablo Casals*, p. 498.
35. Casals–Metcalfe Divorce Decree, Mexico, 17 May 1957, PCW.
36. Interview with Jack Delano, 15 April 1992.
37. Kahn, *Joys and Sorrows*, p. 277.
38. The *New York Herald Tribune*, 6 August 1957.
39. Casals to Schneider, 2 August 1957, ASLC, and Schneider to Casals, 5 September 1957, PCW.
40. Casals to Schneider, 17 September 1957, PCW.
41. From documents in PCSS, Box 10 (i), and see Stanfield, 'Concours Pablo Casals', *The Strad*, December 1957, pp. 280–2.
42. Milly Stanfield, 'September in Switzerland', *Violins and Violinists*, November/December 1960.
43. Carol Easton, *Jacqueline du Pré: A Biography*, London, Hodder and Stoughton, 1989, p. 52.
44. Jacqueline du Pré to Casals, 10 December 1961, PCW. For du Pré's view of Casals, see also Christopher Nupen's television documentary, 'Jacqueline', filmed in 1967 and remade in 1982.
45. Casals to Schneider, 29 May 1959, PCW.
46. Tortelier to Casals, 10 July 1960, PCW.
47. H. T. Ma to Casals, 10 November 1961, PCW.
48. Casals to Schneider, 25 September 1959, PCW.
49. See PCSS, Box 8 (iii).
50. The young usher was Aníbal Ramírez, later to become curator of the Museo Pablo Casals in San Juan; interview 15 April 1992.
51. Enric Casals, *Pau Casals: dades biogràfiques inèdites, cartes intimes i records viscuts*, Barcelona, Editorial Pòrtic, 1979, p.139.
52. Interview, Enriquetta Casals Touron, 30 April 1990. The carillon has now been replaced by electronic bells, and hotel guests hear a recording of 'Song of the Birds' twice a day.
53. Manfred Clyne to Casals, 29 June 1964, PCW.
54. Quoted in Kirk, *Pablo Casals*, p. 504.
55. Kahn, *Joys and Sorrows*, p. 15.
56. Schneider, *Sasha*, pp. 184–5; Kahn, *Joys and Sorrows*, pp. 15–16.

57. For example, see Schneider to Casals, 9 January 1957, PCW.
58. Fournier to Schneider, 24 October 1973, PCW.
59. Schneider, *Sasha*, p. 139.
60. Sándor Végh reckoned the impulse that took Casals to Bonn came from his Swiss friend U. Bodmer, a wealthy patron of music and the owner of the largest collection of Beethoven manuscripts in private hands. Interview, Végh, 6 April 1990. Horszowski's recollection was given to James Methuen-Campbell.
61. Casals to Schneider, 9 January 1956, PCW.
62. Schneider to Casals, 7 March 1956, ASLC.
63. Irving Kolodin, 'The Big World of Don Pablo', *SR*, 31 December 1966.
64. United Nations Day Concert programme, 24 October 1958, PCW, File 12 (a).
65. Casals to Schneider, 7 October 1958, PCW.
66. Thirty-four years later, in autumn 1992, Marta Casals Istomin was herself appointed Director of the Manhattan School of Music.

CHAPTER 13: MUSIC AND THE FIGHT FOR PEACE, 1960–1973

1. Casals, in conversation with Albert Kahn in the late 1960s, see Albert E. Kahn, *Joys and Sorrows*, p. 301.
2. The Agrupación Catalana had also sought to nominate Casals for the 1957 Nobel Prize for Peace – which went to the Canadian, Lester Pearson – but were too slow. The president of the nominating committee, based in Lima, Peru, was Josep Camps, and the secretary, Victor Castells. See Camps to Schweitzer, 21 April 1957, PCSS, Boxes 6 (vii) and 10 (i).
3. See Harvey Sachs, 'Pablo Casals' in his own volume, *Virtuoso*, London, Thames and Hudson, 1982, p. 149.
4. Ibid., p. 150.
5. Lael Wertenbaker, draft notes for her May 1950 article in *Life*, PCSS, Box 8 (iv).
6. Interview, BBC Television, 'Song of the Birds', 1991.
7. Elise Kirk, *Music at the White House: A History of the American Spirit*, Urbana, University of Illinois Press, 1986, pp. 290–1.
8. C. David Heymann, *A Woman Named Jackie*, London, Heinemann, 1989, p. 269. Jacqueline Kennedy Onassis herself does not recall this: letter to author 18 March 1992.
9. Casals to Fortas, 24 September 1961, PCW, File 12a.
10. Ibid.
11. Confidential Memorandum, Abe Fortas to Pierre Salinger, 5 October 1961, Kennedy Library.
12. Fortas to Casals, 26 October 1961, PCW, File 12a.
13. Casals to Fortas, 28 October 1961, PCW, File 12a.
14. Theodore C. Sorensen, *Kennedy*, London, Hodder and Stoughton, 1965.
15. On Kennedy's policy in Puerto Rico and Latin America, see Arthur M.

Schlesinger, *A Thousand Days: John F. Kennedy in the White House*, London, André Deutsch, 1965, p. 656. On the strategic benefit of the democratic, Catholic Puerto Rican vote, see Theodore H. White, *The Making of the President*, 1960, London, 1962, pp. 350–65, and Appendix A, pp. 385–7.

16. Schlesinger, *A Thousand Days*, p. 632. At a subsequent dinner in the 'Casals' series, honouring Western Hemisphere Nobel laureates, Kennedy delivered one of the classic remarks of his presidency, saying he was entertaining 'the most extraordinary collection of talent, of human knowledge, that has ever been gathered together at the White House, with the possible exception of when Thomas Jefferson dined alone'.

17. From 'La Busqueda de la Excellencia', FLMM, Puerto Rico, 1991.

18. Hugh Sidey, *John F. Kennedy: Portrait of a President*, London, André Deutsch, 1963, p. 277.

19. Schneider, *Sasha: A Musician's Life*, New York, 1988, p. 182.

20. Laura Kalman, *Abe Fortas*, New Haven and London, Yale University Press, 1990, p. 177.

21. Fortas to Marta Casals, 31 October 1961, PCW.

22. The *New York Times*, 17 December 1961.

23. Casals to Kennedy, 6 January 1962, PCW. Dean Rusk and Adlai Stevenson both later visited Spain, and in February 1963 there was a rumour that Kennedy himself would meet Franco. Casals wrote in alarm to Fortas, who checked and discovered that the President had no such immediate plans. See Marta Casals to Fortas, 6 February 1963, and Fortas to Marta Casals, 12 February 1963, PCW.

24. Fortas to Casals, 8 September 1962, PCW.

25. Kahn, *Joys and Sorrows*, p. 286.

26. A full list is given in Enric Casals, *Pau Casals*, pp. 334–5.

27. The *New York Times*, 23 June 1962.

28. Eli Carmen, quoted in Schneider, *Sasha*, p. 183.

29. The recording, made by Columbia, was issued in Europe by Discophon in 1974, (S) 4267/8. *El Pessebre* was also recorded in 1962, by Dr Franchesci, and in 1967, by Dr Franchesci again and by WIPR. None of these recordings has been issued on compact disc.

30. See Casals to Schneider, 18 February 1962, PCW.

31. Fortas to Schneider, 19 February 1962.

32. Interview, Wilfred Stiff, 29 July 1992.

33. Boult to Casals, 30 September 1963, PCW.

34. Serkin to Casals, 20 November 1958, PCW.

35. See Tully Potter, 'The Man with the Endless Bow', *The Strad*, June 1992, pp. 548–52.

36. David Blum, *Casals and the Art of Interpretation*, Berkeley, University of California Press, 1977.

37. John H. Planer, 'Sentimentality in the Performance of Absolute Music:

Pablo Casals' Performance of Saraband from Johann Sebastian Bach's Suite No. 2 in D Minor for Unaccompanied Cello, S. 1008', *The Musical Quarterly*, vol. 73, no. 2, 1989, pp. 212–49.

38. Blum, *Casals and the Art of Interpretation*, p. 146.
39. From Alexander Schneider, 'Casals' Genius', *CBC Time*, 22–28 April 1951.
40. The Casals Master Class Series, in 'The Library of Master Performers', is available in an eight-video-cassette set from Homevideo Exclusive/Kroll Production Inc. (US) and Amati Video (UK).
41. Marta Casals to Milly Stanfield, 14 April 1967.
42. Milly Stanfield, 'Echoes of South-West Europe', *The Strad*, October 1966, p. 213.
43. *Time*, 12 August 1966.
44. Thomas Frost, ' "So beautiful . . . a simple little flower": Pablo Casals remembered by Thomas Frost', *High Fidelity*, July 1974, p. 79.
45. See 'Compact Discography', pp. 304–20.
46. See Frost to Abe Fortas, 9 March 1966, PCW.
47. I am grateful to José Alfaro for information on the recording of the Casals Festivals in Puerto Rico.
48. See Fortas memo, 26 February 1962. The recording was subsequently released a second time, again illegitimately, by Bellock Company in New York, and proceedings were again instituted.
49. Kalman, *Abe Fortas*, p. 293. In October 1968 Fortas was nominated, by Lyndon Johnson, to the post of Chief Justice, but after Judicial Committee hearings the President was forced to withdraw his nomination. Fortas resigned from the Supreme Court in May 1969 and returned to private practice.
50. Golda Meir to Casals, 23 October 1958, PCW.
51. Interview, Eugene Istomin, 7 December 1991.
52. Schneider to Marta Casals, 30 June 1972, PCW.
53. H. L. Kirk, *Pablo Casals: A Biography*, London, Hutchinson, 1974, p. 546.
54. Barry Farrell, 'Serenade to Ninety Years of Greatness', *Life*, vol. 61, no. 20, 11 November 1966, with photographs by Gjon Mili.
55. Interview, Amaryllis Fleming, 24 January 1992.
56. See the calculations by José Alfaro in 'Letters', *The Gramophone*, November 1976.
57. Schneider, *Sasha*, p. 188.
58. Interview, Rosa Cueto, 15 April 1992.
59. Harold Schonberg in the *New York Times*, 16 April 1970.
60. Interview, Sylvia Fuhrman, 20 April 1992, and see Sylvia Fuhrman, 'A Hymn to the UN is born', *Secretariat News*, May 1989, pp. 8–9.
61. Henry Raymond in the *New York Times*, 24 October 1971.
62. Casals to Schneider, 2 September 1972, PCW.
63. Blum, *Casals and the Art of Interpretation*, p. 49.

64. Marta Casals to H. L. Kirk, 12 September 1973, PCW.
65. Interview, Marta Casals Istomin, 1 October 1990.


EPILOGUE
  1. The *New York Times*, 24 October 1973.
  2. Eugene Ormandy to Schneider, 7 November 1973, PCW.
  3. Alan Rich, 'Don Pablo's Foundation', *New York*, 17 February 1975.
  4. The Casals Hall, Ochanomizu Square, Chiyoda, Tokyo.
  5. The *New York Times*, 4 February 1975.
  6. Hooper, *The Spaniards*, p. 255.
  7. Rostropovich, telegram to Marta Casals Istomin, 1 November 1979, PCW.

# Sources and Bibliography

MANUSCRIPT SOURCES

Pablo Casals archives, Casa Museu Pau Casals, San Salvador, Spain [PCSS].
Pablo Casals archives, private collection, Washington, DC [PCW].
Pablo Casals/The Casals Festival archives, Prades, France [PCP].
Secció de Música, Biblioteca Nacional de Catalunya, Barcelona.
Elizabeth Sprague Coolidge Foundation Collection, The Library of Congress, Washington, DC.
Ibbs and Tillett archives, London [file on Pablo Casals].
Instituto Español de Musicologia (Institució 'Milài Fontanals', Consell Superior d'Investigacions Cientifiques, Barcelona).
The Library of the Performing Arts, Lincoln Center, New York [files on Pablo Casals].
Museo Pablo Casals, San Juan, Puerto Rico.
Pamela Hind O'Malley [Prades study notebook].
The Fred and Rose Plaut archives, Yale Music Library, New Haven, Ct.
The Royal Archives, Windsor [The Journals of HRH Queen Victoria].
Alexander Schneider Papers, The Library of Congress, Washington, DC [ASLC].
Milly Stanfield ['Looking Back', privately circulated typescript].
Sir Donald Francis Tovey Papers, The Reid Music Library, University of Edinburgh.
R. C. Trevelyan Papers, The Wren Library, Trinity College, Cambridge.


PRINTED SOURCES

Alavedra, Juan, 'Casals and Kennedy', *Bulletin of the Instituto de Estudios Norteamericanos*, 13, Barcelona, Spring/Summer 1967.
*La Extraordinària Vida de Pablo Casals*, Barcelona, Edicions Proa, 1969.
*Pau Casals*, Spanish edn, Barcelona, Plaza y Janes, 1963. (Catalan edn, Barcelona, Aldos, 1962.)
*El Poema del Pessebre*, 3rd edn, Barcelona, Editorial Selecta, 1956.

Albet, Montserrat, 'Pau Casals: A Lifetime of Music', trans. by Jacqueline Hall, in *Pau Casals and his Museum*, Fundació Pau Casals, Sant Salvador–El Vendrell, 1986.

Alexanian, Diran, *Theoretical and Practical Treatise of the Violoncello/Traité théorétique et pratique du violoncelle*, with a preface by Pablo Casals, Paris, Salabert, 1922. (English parallel translation by Frederick Fairbanks.)
'La Technique et l'esthétique de Pablo Casals', *Le Monde Musical*, July 1921, pp. 230–4.

Alfaro, J. D., 'Pablo Casals: Activity in his 90s', *The Gramophone*, 54: 768, November 1976.

Alvin, Juliette, 'The logic of Casals's technique', *Musical Times*, 71, 1930, pp. 1078–9.

anon., *Five Hundred Years of Change and Continuity in Puerto Rico*, Institute for Puerto Rican Affairs, Washington, DC, 1991.

anon., *Casals Hall*, Shufunotomosha Auftakt, 1987 (a volume published to commemorate the auditorium, built by Shufunotomo Company in Ochanomizu Square, Tokyo, to mark the centenary of the birth of the founder of the Company, Takeyoshi Ishikawa).

anon., 'Concurso de Espluga de Francoli', in *Stadium*, 116, 14 August 1915, pp. 522–3.

anon., 'Im Exil von Prades wird Pablo Casals', *Die Woche*, Zurich, 20–26 July 1953.

anon., Marlboro Music: Programs 1951–1984, Marlboro Music School and Festival, Marlboro, Vermont, n.d.

anon., 'Pablo Casals and his violoncello by Matteo Goffriller', *Violins*, 10, October 1949, p. 262.

anon., *Pablo Casals: L'Homme, L'Artiste*, Geneva, Labor et Fides 19, 1956, Paris Librairie Protestante.

Applebaum, Samuel and Sada, 'Pablo Casals', in *The Way They Played*, Book 1, S. and S. Applebaum (eds), New Jersey, Paganiniana Publications Inc., 1972.

Arazi, Ishaq, 'Always Back to Bach: A Glimpse into the Career of Maurice Eisenberg, Cellist', *American String Teacher*, Spring 1968.

Balius i Juli, Ramon, 'Un Esportista dit Pau Casals', *Apunts d'educació física i medicina esportiva*, XX, 1983, pp. 205–10. (Translated in *The Olympic Review*, 1983.)

Barenboim, Daniel, *A Life in Music*, London, Weidenfeld and Nicolson, 1991.

Bauer, Harold, *His Book*, New York, W. W. Norton, 1948.

Blum, David, *Casals and the Art of Interpretation*, Berkeley, University of California Press, 1977.
*The Art of Quartet Playing*, London, Gollancz, 1986.

Boult, Adrian C., 'Casals as Conductor', *Music and Letters*, vol. IV, no. 2, April 1923.

Brenan, Gerald, *The Spanish Labyrinth*, 2nd edn, Cambridge, Cambridge University Press, 1950.

Bunting, C., and Pratt, D. C., *Cello Technique: 'from one note to the next'*, Cambridge, Cambridge University Press, 1987.

Campbell, Margaret, *The Great Cellists*, London, Gollancz, 1988.

Carr, Raymond, *Puerto Rico: A Colonial Experiment*, New York, New York University Press and the Twentieth Century Fund, 1984.

Casals, Enric, *Pau Casals: dades biogràfiques inèdites, cartes intimes i records viscuts*, Barcelona, Editorial Pòrtic, 1979.

Casals, Pablo, 'The Story of My Youth', *Ovation*, October 1983, reprinted from *Windsor Magazine*, November 1930, and *The Gramophone*, December 1932.

Casella, Alfredo, *Music in My Time*, trans. and ed. by Spencer Norton, Norman, Oklahoma, University of Oklahoma Press, 1955.

Cherniavsky, David, 'Casals' Approach to Teaching the Cello', *Etude*, June 1952. Also published as 'Casals's Teaching of the Cello', *Musical Times*, 92, September 1952, and in English and Italian in *Rivista Musicale Italiana*, April–June 1953.

Clapham, John, *Antonin Dvořák: Musician and Craftsman*, London, Faber and Faber, 1966.

Cláudio, Mário, *Guilhermina*, Porto, Imprensa Nacional/Casa da Moeda, 1986.

Conrad, Peter, 'The Conscience of the Artist', *Times Literary Supplement*, 267, 5 March 1976 (review of *Pablo Casals* by H. L. Kirk).

Conte, Arthur, *La Légende de Pablo Casals*, Perpignan, Editions Proa, 1950 (with six photographs by Gjon Mili).

Corredor, J. Ma., *Casals: Biographia Ilustrada*, Barcelona, Ediciones Destino, 1967.

*Conversations with Casals*, London, Hutchinson, 1956, translated by André Mangeot from the original French edition, *Conversations avec Casals*, Albin Michel, Paris, 1955, reissued with annotations by Jean-François Labie and Philippe Morin, Pluriel/Hachette, Paris, 1982.

'Las Memorias de Pablo Casals', as told to Thomas Dozier, *Life en Español*, 4 May, 18 May and 1 June 1959.

Cowling, Elizabeth, *The Cello*, London, Batsford, 1975.

Dale, S. S., 'Gaspar Cassadó', *The Strad*, October 1977, pp. 507–9.

De'ak, Stephen, *David Popper*, New Jersey, Paganiniana Publications, 1980.

Delbanco, Nicholas, *The Beaux Arts Trio*, London, Gollancz, 1985.

Dozier, Thomas, 'Las Memorias de Pablo Casals', *Life en Español*, 4 May, 18 May and 1 June 1959.

Dubal, David, *Conversations with Menuhin: A Celebration on his Seventy-fifth Birthday*, London, Gollancz, 1991.

Durgin, Cyrus, *Prades and the Casals Concert*, Boston, The Boston Globe Publishing Company, 1950.

Eastman, Max, 'The Greatness of Pablo Casals', *Etude*, April 1953.

Easton, Carol, *Jacqueline du Pré: A Biography*, London, Hodder and Stoughton, 1989.

Eisenberg, Maurice, 'Casals and the Bach Suites', *New York Times*, 10 October 1943.

'Casals at Eighty: A Tribute', *Violins and Violinists*, 18, January–February 1957, pp. 4–6.

*Cello Playing for Today*, 1957; 2nd edn, New Jersey, Lavender Press, 1966.

Eisenberg, Maurice, and Masters, Michael (eds), *J. S. Bach: Six Suites for Violoncello Solo*, with foreword by Pablo Casals, New Jersey, Paganiniana Publications, 1975.

Evenson, Norma, *Paris: A Century of Change, 1878–1978*, New Haven and London, Yale University Press, 1979.

Farrell, Barry, 'Serenade to Ninety Years of Greatness', *Life*, vol. 61, no. 20, 11 November 1966, with photographs by Gjon Mili.

Feuermann, E., 'Feuermann inveighs against "mechanical methods"', *Musical America*, 25 February 1940.

Fischer-Dieskau, Dietrich, *Echoes of a Lifetime*, trans. by Ruth Hein, London, Macmillan, 1989.

Flanner, Janet, 'Letter from Prades', The *New Yorker*, 17 June 1950.

Flesch, Carl, 'A Propos de Pablo Casals', *Le Monde Musical*, nos. 8–9, 1937.

Forsee, Aylesa, *Pablo Casals: Cellist for Freedom*, New York, Crowell & Co., 1965.

Frost, Thomas, 'So beautiful . . . a simple little flower: Pablo Casals remembered by Thomas Frost', *High Fidelity Magazine*, July 1974.

Gaisberg, Fred, *The Music Goes Round*, New York, Macmillan, 1942.

García Borrás, José, *Pablo Casals, Pelegrino En América: Tres Semanas con il Maestro*, Bolivar, Mexico, Talleres Graficos Victoria, 1957.

Gavoty, Bernard, *Les Grands Interprètes: Pablo Casals*, Geneva, Editions René Kister, 1955.

*Alfred Cortot*, Paris, Editions Buchet/Chastel (Collection 'Musique'), 1977.

Gianoli, Reine, 'Pablo Casals' in *Images Musicales*, 5, November 1945.

Ginsburg, Lev, *Pablo Casals*, Moscow, 1966.

*History of the Violoncello*, ed. Herbert R. Axelrod, trans. from Russian by Tanya Tchistyakova, New Jersey, Paganiniana Publications, Inc., 1983.

*Ysaÿe*, ed. Herbert R. Axelrod, trans. by X. M. Danko, New Jersey, Paganiniana Publications, Inc., 1980.

Goldsmith, Harris, 'Pablo Casals (1876–1973)', *High Fidelity Magazine*, July 1974.

Gollancz, Victor, *Journey Towards Music: A Memoir*, London, Gollancz, 1964.

Grierson, Mary, *Donald Francis Tovey: A Biography Based on Letters*, London, Oxford University Press, 1952.

Grottendieck, Germaine (comp.), *Homage à Pablo Casals: Connaissance de Roussillon*, a volume produced to mark the centenary of Casals' birth, Prades, 1976.

Gruppe, Paulo M., 'The Six Cello Suites of J. S. Bach', *American Teacher*, Winter 1972.

Henle, Fritz, *Casals*, New York, American Photographic Book Publishing, 1975; Spanish edn, Malaga, 1983.

Heymann, C. David, *A Woman Named Jackie*, London, Heinemann, 1989.

Hooper, John, *The Spaniards: A Portrait of the New Spain*, London, Viking, 1986.

Hughes, Robert, *Barcelona*, London, HarperCollins, 1992.

Istomin, Eugene, 'The Virtuoso and Chamber Music', *Music and Artists*, February/March 1968.

Itzkoff, Seymour W., *Emanuel Feuermann, Virtuoso: A Biography*, Alabama, University of Alabama Press, 1979.

Jackson, Gabriel, *A Concise History of the Spanish Civil War*, London, Thames and Hudson, 1974.

Jackson, Judith, 'The Master in Exile', *Sunday Times Magazine*, November 1972.

Johnson, Stephen, 'The Gramophone Collection: Schubert Quintet in C Major, D956', in *The Gramophone*, March 1991, pp. 1643–4.

Kahn, Albert E. (ed.), *Joys and Sorrows: Pablo Casals*, New York, Simon and Schuster, and London, Macdonald, 1970, reissued London, Eel Pie Publishing, 1981.

Kalman, Laura, *Abe Fortas*, New Haven and London, Yale University Press, 1990.

Katchen, Julius, 'The Miracle of Pablo Casals', *Music and Musicians*, 14, January 1961.

Kennedy, Michael, *Barbirolli: Conductor Laureate*, London, MacGibbon and Kee, 1971.

Kirk, Elise K., *Music at the White House: A History of the American Spirit*, Urbana, University of Illinois Press, 1986.

Kirk, H. L., *Pablo Casals: A Biography*, New York, Doubleday, and London, Hutchinson, 1974.

Kolodin, Irving, 'The Big World of Don Pablo', *SR*, 31 December 1966, pp. 43–7 and 59, with a discography by Richard Freed.

Littlehales, Lillian, *Pablo Casals*, New York, W. W. Norton, 1929; 2nd edn 1948; reissued Westport, Ct., Greenwood, 1970.

Lannon, Frances, and Preston, Paul (eds), *Elites and Power in Twentieth-Century Spain*, Oxford, Clarendon Press, 1990.

Llongueras, Juan Ramon, Juan, i María Carratelà, *Pau Casals*, Barcelona, Edicions de la Nova Revista, 1927.

Lloyd Webber, Julian, *Song of the Birds: Sayings, Stories and Impressions of Pablo Casals*, London, Robson Books, 1985.

Ludwig, Emil, 'Pablo Casals', in *Galeria de Retratos*, Madrid, Ediciones Aguilar, 1960.

MacDonald, Malcolm, *Schoenberg*, London, Master Musicians Series, Dent and Sons, 1976.

Menuhin, Yehudi, *Unfinished Journey*, London, MacDonald and Jane's, 1977.

Mitchell, David, *The Spanish Civil War*, London, Granada, 1982.

Montalbán, Manuel Vázquez, *Barcelonas*, trans. by Andy Robinson, London, Verso, 1992.

Moor, Paul, 'Casals at Prades', *Theatre Arts*, October 1950.

Moore, Gerald, *Am I Too Loud?: Memoirs of an Accompanist*, London, Hamish Hamilton, 1962.

Morris, Jan, *Spain*, London, Faber and Faber, 1964; rev. edn, 1979.

Müller-Blattau, Joseph Maria, *Casals*, Berlin, Rembrandt Verlag, 1964.

O'Malley, Pamela Hind, 'Casals and Intonation', *The Strad*, vol. 94, no. 1122, October 1983, pp. 378–9 (orig. pub. ESTA 'News and Views', April 1981).

'Casals as Teacher', *The R.C.M. Magazine*, vol. 46, 1950, pp. 99–100.

Pirani, Max, *Emanuel Moór*, London, P. R. Macmillan, 1959 (with a preface by Pablo Casals).

Planer, John H., 'Sentimentality in the Performance of Absolute Music: Pablo Casals's Performance of Saraband from Johann Sebastian Bach's Suite No. 2 in D Minor for Unaccompanied Cello, S. 1008', *The Musical Quarterly*, vol. 73, no. 2, 1989, pp. 212–48.

Pleeth, William, *Cello* (Yehudi Menuhin Music Guides), London, Macdonald, 1982.

Preston, Paul, *Salvador de Madariaga and the Quest for Liberty in Spain*, Taylorian Special Lecture, 3 November 1986, Oxford, Clarendon Press, 1987.

Puerto Rico Department of Education, *Pablo Casals en Puerto Rico, 1955–56* (Publicationes ser. 3, no. 106), San Juan, 1957.

Read, Oliver, and Welch, Walter L., *From Tin Foil to Stereo: Evolution of the Phonograph*, Indianapolis, Howard W. Sams, 1976.

Rearick, Charles, *Pleasures of the Belle Epoque: Entertainment and Festivity in Turn-of-the-Century France*, New Haven and London, Yale University Press, 1985.

Reid, Charles, *John Barbirolli*, New York, Taplinger, 1971.

Rich, Alan, 'Don Pablo's Foundation', *New York*, 17 February 1975.

Rubinstein, Arthur, *My Young Years*, London, Jonathan Cape, 1973.

*My Many Years*, London, Jonathan Cape, 1980.

Sachs, Harvey, 'Pablo Casals' in *Virtuoso*, ed. H. Sachs, London, Thames and Hudson, 1982.

Sainati, Edward, 'Pablo Casals Foundation', *The Strad*, vol. 94, no. 1122, October 1983, pp. 374–7.

Schang, F. C., 'At Eighty Pablo Casals is at Summit of Powers', *Musical America*, 15 January 1957.

Schneider, Alexander, *Sasha: A Musician's Life*, New York, privately published, 1988.

'Casals' Genius', in *CBC Time*, 22–28 April 1951, vol. 3, no. 40.

Schonberg, Harold C., *The Great Pianists*, New York, Simon and Schuster, 1963; London, Gollancz, 1981.

Shirakawa, Sam H., *The Devil's Music Master: The Tragic Life and Times of Wilhelm Furtwängler*, New York, Oxford University Press, 1992.

Snyder, Robert, 'Filming Casals: A Memoir', from *Intermezzo*, programme for 'Homage to Casals Concert', 24 December 1976.

Speyer, Edward, *My Life and Friends*, London, Cobden-Sanderson, 1937.

Stanfield, Milly B., *The Intermediate Cellist*, London, Oxford University Press, 1973.

'Casals at Ninety', *The Strad*, 921, January 1967, p. 339.

'Cello Days in Israel', *Musical Opinion*, December 1961.

'Concours Pablo Casals', *The Strad*, December 1957, pp. 280–2.

'Echoes of South-West Europe', *The Strad*, 918, October 1966, p. 213.

'Lessons by Example', *The Strad*, September 1950, pp. 162–4.

'Guilhermina Suggia: Obituary', *The Strad*, September 1950, pp. 154–5.

'September in Switzerland', *Violins and Violinists*, November/December 1960.

Stein, Erwin (ed.), *Arnold Schoenberg Letters*, London, Faber and Faber, 1964.

Straeten, Edmund S. J. van der, *History of the Violoncello, the Viol de Gamba, their Precursors and Collateral Instruments*, London, William Reeves, 1914.

Stricker, Noemi, *Pelerins du Monde*, Menton, Editions Aubanel, 1957.

Suggia, Guilhermina, 'The Violoncello', *Music and Letters*, vol. I, no. 2, April 1920.

'Violoncello Playing', *Music and Letters*, vol. II, no. 2, April 1921.

'A Violoncello Lesson: Casals' *Obiter Dicta*', *Music and Letters*, vol. II, no. 4, October 1921.

Tapper, Bernard, 'A Cellist in Exile', The *New Yorker*, 24 February 1962.

'Casals at 92', *The New Yorker*, 19 April 1969.

*Cellist in Exile: A Portrait of Pablo Casals*, New York, McGraw-Hill, 1962.

Thibaud, Jacques, *Un violon parle, souvenirs recueillis par Jean-Jacques Dorian*, Paris, Editions du Blé, 1947.

Thomas, Hugh, *The Spanish Civil War*, London, Hamish Hamilton, 1977.

Thomson, Virgil, 'Casals and the Matterhorn', *New York Herald Tribune*, n.d.

*Virgil Thomson*, London, Weidenfeld and Nicolson, 1967.

Thoresby, Christina, 'Bach Festival in Prades' *The Strad*, July 1950, p. 106.

Tortelier, Paul, 'Saraband', an interview with Tortelier in *The Economist*, 25 August 1990, pp. 81–2.

Tortelier, Paul, and Blum, David, *Paul Tortelier: A Self-Portrait*, London, Heinemann, 1984.

Trueta, Joseph, *The Spirit of Catalonia*, London, Oxford University Press, 1946.

Ulam, Adam B., *Russia's Failed Revolutions: From the Decembrists to the Dissidents*, London, Weidenfeld and Nicolson, 1981.

Valaitis, Vytas, *Casals*, New York, Grossman Photographic Books, 1966.

Vayo, J. Alvarez de, 'Pablo Casals – Freedom's Artist', *The Nation*, 17 June 1950.

Vives de Fabrigas, Elisa, *Pau Casals*, Barcelona, Rafael Dalmau, 1966.

von Tobel, R., *Pablo Casals*, Zurich, Erlenbach, 1941.

Wasielewski, Wilhelm Joseph von, *The Violoncello and its History*, London and New York, Novello, Ewen & Co., 1894.

Wordsworth, William (ed.), *Jacqueline du Pré: Impressions*, London, Granada, 1983.

Ysaÿe, Antoine, *Ysaÿe*, trans. Frank Clarkson, Great Missenden, Bucks, W. E. Hill and Sons, 1980.

FILM, TELEVISION AND RADIO

Casals Master Class Series ('The Library of Master Performers'), Amati Video/Homevideo Exclusives/Kroll Productions Inc. (eight video cassettes).

'Pablo Casals en Puerto Rico', Government of Puerto Rico (Archive of the Moving Image), 1956, narrated by Tómas Blancó (directed by Jack Delano).

'Conversation with Pablo Casals', NBC, 1958 (with Madeline Foley; directed by Jacques Barathier).

'Casals at Eighty-Eight', CBS, 1964 (Casals in conversation with Isaac Stern).

'Casals: A Portrait for Radio', Canadian Broadcasting, 1974 (produced by Glenn Gould).

'Master of the Cello', BBC TV: 'Omnibus', 1974 (directed by Rodney Greenberg).

'Music in Jerusalem', BBC TV: 'The Lively Arts', 1976 (directed by Paul Salinger).

'Allegro: Jacqueline du Pré and the Elgar Cello Concerto', Channel 4, London, 1982 (directed by Christopher Nupen).

'La Busqueda de la Excellencia' ['The Pursuit of Excellence'], Fundación Muñoz Marín, FLMM, Puerto Rico, 1991.

'Song of the Birds: A Portrait of Pablo Casals', BBC TV: 'Omnibus', 1991 (directed by Anna Benson Gyles).

INTERVIEWS

Macià Alavedra: 25 April 1990 (Barcelona).

José Alfaro: 9 October 1990, 20 April 1992 (New York).

Christopher Bunting: 10 October 1991 (London).

Rosa S. M. de Cueto Coll: 15 April 1992 (San Juan, Puerto Rico).

Jack Delano: 15 April 1992 (Rio Piedras, Puerto Rico).

Pablo and Helen Eisenberg: 5 December 1991 (Washington, DC).

Amaryllis Fleming: 24 January 1992 (London).

Sylvia Fuhrman: 20 April 1992 (New York).

Bernard Greenhouse: 17 April 1992 (New York).

Mercèdes Guarro i Tapis: 25 April 1990 (Barcelona); 24 May and 21 September 1991 (San Salvador, Spain).

Eugene Istomin: 2 October 1990, 7 and 9 December 1991 (Washington, DC); 23 October 1990 (London).

Marta Casals Istomin: 22 October 1987, 21 December 1989, 1 and 5 October 1990, 5 and 9 December 1991 (Washington, DC); 24 May 1991 (San Salvador, Spain).

Hélène Jeanbrau: 4 June 1991 (Prades).

H. L. Kirk: 12 May 1991, 19 April 1992 (New York).

Pamela Hind O'Malley: 8 November 1991 (Cambridge).

Jean-Pierre Marty: 6 March 1991 (London).

Aníbal Ramírez: 14–16 April 1992 (San Juan, Puerto Rico).

Alexander Schneider: 4 June 1991 (Prades); 17 April 1992 (New York).

Milly Stanfield: 15 December 1991 (New Jersey).

Enriquetta Casals Touron: 30 April 1990 (Prades).

Sándor Végh: 6 April 1990 (London).

# Compact Discography

This is both a compact discography and a discography of compact discs. The ambiguity is deliberate. Casals' recording career extended from 1915 until his death in 1973. Indeed he claimed to have made a recording – with the violinist Eugène Ysaÿe – as early as 1904, though this has not been traced. (See Judith Jackson, 'The Master in Exile', *The Sunday Times Magazine*, November 1972.) During these fifty-eight years he recorded hundreds of individual works, first on acoustic disc, then on 78 rpm and 33 rpm long-playing records. Since his death the CD revolution has occurred, and a substantial quantity of his music has been digitally re-mastered and reissued in this format. So far it represents a 'compact' and choice selection from the recorded archive, though competition between recording labels to release 'historic' performances makes it certain that the selection will increase rapidly. This discography is as complete a listing as possible of works performed, composed or conducted by Casals and available on compact disc at the date of publication.

Despite the large number of works that Casals did record, there are many that he did not. Like many musicians of his generation, Casals viewed recording as a distraction and a disturbance, and tried to avoid it. In any case he never thought recordings sounded much like the per-formances they represented. Given the quality of some of his acoustic and early electrical recordings, he was right. The consequence of his reluctance, however, is that there are important gaps in the material we have. There are no known recordings, for example, of his debut works, the Lalo and Saint-Saëns Cello Concertos. Casals did record the first two movements of the Haydn D Major Concerto (Op. 101), but the record-ing, in London in 1945, was cut short by his post-war boycott and has never been released. And, most conspicuously, despite his long patron-age of Emanuel Moór and Julius Röntgen, and the many occasions on which he performed their works, nothing is available on record. Happily, Casals' recording of the Tovey Cello Concerto was issued for the first time in early 1992.

The most complete and useful discography of recordings by Casals on vinyl disc is that compiled in 1973 by Teri Noel Towe for H. L. Kirk,

*Pablo Casals: A Biography* (London, Hutchinson, 1974), pp. 568–625. Mr Towe lists almost 200 separate works, and provides fully comprehensive reference data on each. There is also a vast and tantalizing 'hidden' archive of Casals' performances which were recorded but never commercially released. Almost everything Casals played or conducted after 1950 was taped, and hitherto unreleased material from the Prades, Puerto Rico and Marlboro Festivals is beginning to appear. In 1991 Sony Classical issued a series of recordings to commemorate the fortieth anniversary of the founding of the Marlboro Festival, among them several Casals performances which had not been previously heard.

Recordings below are listed alphabetically by composer. Performances which have appeared first on CD, are available only in that format, and are not listed by Towe, are marked with an asterisk. Where a performance of a work is available on more than one CD issue, it is indicated by (a), (b), etc. Where Casals recorded a work more than once, and with different artists, this is signalled by (i), (ii), etc. This list has been compiled from information on the discs themselves, from a sequence of Casals' artist contract cards compiled by Columbia Records, from Teri Noel Towe's discography cited above, from *Marlboro Music: Programs 1951–1984* (Marlboro, Vermont, n.d.) and from *The Classical Catalogue*, Master Edition No. 2 (London, 1992).

ACRONYMS

| | |
|---|---|
| ABBE | Abbey Recording Co. |
| AS | AS Discs |
| BIDD | Biddulph |
| CBS | CBS (Sony) |
| EMI | EMI Classics |
| MSCM | Music Memoria |
| LYR | Lyric (France) |
| PEAR | Pearl (Pavilion) |
| PHIL | Philips Classics |
| SCHW | Schwann |
| SONY | Sony Classical |
| STR | Stradivarius (Italy) |
| SYMP | Symposium |

ANON.

*El Cant dels Ocells* ('The Song of the Birds')
Medieval Catalan folk song; harmonized by Pablo Casals and orchestrated by Enrique Casals
Pablo Casals (cond.); Prades Festival Orchestra
CBS CD (*Pablo Casals Recital*) MPK 46724 (1991)*
Recorded at Prades, 1954

*Sant Marti del Canigou* ('Saint Martin du Canigou')
Catalan folk melody, orchestrated by Pablo Casals
Pablo Casals (cond.); Prades Festival Orchestra
CBS CD (*Pablo Casals Recital*) MPK 46724 (1991)*
Recorded at Prades, 1954

JOHANN SEBASTIAN BACH

*Brandenburg Concertos No. 1 in F Major, No. 2 in F Major and No. 3 in G Major*
Pablo Casals (cond.); Marlboro Festival Orchestra
CBS CD MPK 44835 (1988)
Recorded in Marlboro, Vermont, July 1964 (1 and 3); July 1965 (2)

*Brandenburg Concertos No. 4 in G Major, No. 5 in D Major and No. 6 in B Flat Major*
Pablo Casals (cond.); Marlboro Festival Orchestra
CBS CD MPK 44836 (1988)
Recorded in Marlboro, Vermont, July 1964

*English Suite No. 6 in D Minor*: Musette, arranged for cello and piano by Pollain
Pablo Casals (cello); Nikolai Mednikoff (piano)
BIDD LAB 017 (*Casals: the Victor Recordings*) (1990)
Recorded in New Jersey, 31 January 1928

*Sonata No. 1 in G Major for Viola da Gamba and Harpsichord*
(i) Pablo Casals (cello); Paul Baumgartner (piano)
SONY CD MPK 46445 (1990)
Recorded at Prades, June 1950

(ii) Pablo Casals (cello); Mieczyslaw Horszowski (piano)
*Casals Festivals at Prades*, Vol. II (Music & Arts Inc.) CD 689 (1991)
Recorded at Prades, 8 July 1956

*Sonata No. 2 in D Major and No. 3 in G Minor for Viola da Gamba and Harpsichord*
Pablo Casals (cello); Paul Baumgartner (piano)
Sony CD MPK 46445 (1990)
Recorded at Prades, June 1950

*Suites for Unaccompanied Cello*
No. 1 in G Major (recorded in Paris, 2 June 1938);
No. 2 in D Minor (recorded in London, 23 November 1936);
No. 3 in C Major (recorded in London, 23 November 1936);
No. 4 in E Flat Major (recorded in Paris, 13 June 1939);
No. 5 in C Minor (recorded in Paris, 13 June 1939);
No. 6 in D Major (recorded in Paris, 3 June 1938)
Pablo Casals (cello)
(a) EMI CHS 7 61027 2 PM6 (1989); (b) EMI CDH 7 63018-2 (No. 1: Prelude only, in '100 Golden Years of the Gramophone')

*Toccata, Adagio and Fugue in C Major*: 2nd movement, *Adagio*, arranged for cello and piano by Pablo Casals from the piano arrangement by Alexander Siloti
Pablo Casals (cello); Nikolai Mednikoff (piano)
(a) BIDD LAB 017 (*Casals, the Victor Recordings*) (1990); (b) MSCM MM 30428
Recorded in New Jersey, 28 February 1927


LUDWIG VAN BEETHOVEN

Overture to '*Egmont*' (Op. 84)
Pablo Casals (cond.); Marlboro Festival Orchestra
SONY CD SMK 46247 (1991)*
Marlboro Festival 40th Anniversary Series
Recorded in Marlboro, Vermont, 11 July 1970

*Minuet No. 2 in G Major*, from *Six Minuets for Piano*, arranged for cello and piano
Pablo Casals (cello); Otto Schulhof (piano)
PEAR GEMM CDS 9461 (1990)
Recorded in London, 7 March 1930

*Sonata in F Major for Horn and Piano* (Op. 17), arranged for cello and piano by the composer
Pablo Casals (cello); Mieczyslaw Horszowski (piano)
PHIL 462 105-2 PLC (1989)
Recorded at the Beethovenhaus, Bonn, September 1958

*Sonata No. 1 in F Major for Cello and Piano* (Op. 5, No. 1)
(i) Pablo Casals (cello); Mieczyslaw Horszowski (piano)
PEAR GEMM CDS 9461 (1990)
Recorded in Paris, 19–20 June 1939.

(ii) Pablo Casals (cello); Rudolf Serkin (piano)
CBS CD MPK 46725 (1990)
Recorded at Prades, June 1953

(iii) Pablo Casals (cello); Wilhelm Kempff (piano)
PHIL 420 077–2PLC (1988)
Recorded at Prades, July 1961

*Sonata No. 2 in G Minor for Cello and Piano* (Op. 5, No. 2)
(i) Pablo Casals (cello); Mieczyslaw Horszowski (piano)
PEAR GEMM CDS 9461 (1990)
Recorded in Paris, 20–21 June 1939

(ii) Pablo Casals (cello); Rudolf Serkin (piano)
SONY CD MPK 46725 (1990)
Recorded in Perpignan, summer 1951

(iii) Pablo Casals (cello); Mieczyslaw Horszowski (piano)
PHIL 462 105–2 PLC (1989)
Recorded in the Beethovenhaus, Bonn, September 1958

*Sonata No. 3 in A Major for Cello and Piano* (Op. 69)
(i) Pablo Casals (cello); Otto Schulhof (piano)
PEAR GEMM CDS 9461 (1990)
Recorded in London, 6–7 March 1930

(ii) Pablo Casals (cello); Rudolf Serkin (piano)
SONY CD MPK 45682 (1990)
Recorded at Prades, June 1953

*Sonata No. 4 in C Major for Cello and Piano* (Op. 102, No. 1)
(i) Pablo Casals (cello); Mieczyslaw Horszowski (piano)
PEAR GEMM CDS 9461 (1990)
Recorded in London, 26–27 November 1936

(ii) Pablo Casals (cello); Rudolf Serkin (piano)
SONY CD MPK 45682 (1990)
Recorded at Prades, June 1953

*Sonata No. 5 in D Major for Cello and Piano* (Op. 102, No. 2)
(i) Pablo Casals (cello); Mieczyslaw Horszowski (piano)
PEAR GEMM CDS 9461 (1990)
Recorded in Paris, 21–22 June 1939

(ii) Pablo Casals (cello); Rudolf Serkin (piano)
(a) *Casals Festivals at Prades*, Vol. I (Music & Arts Inc.) CD 688 (1991);
(b) SONY CD MPK 45682 (1990)
Recorded June 1953

(iii) Pablo Casals (cello); Mieczyslaw Horszowski (piano)
PHIL 426 105–2PLC (1989)
Recorded at the Beethovenhaus, Bonn, September 1958

*Symphony No. 1 in C Major* (Op. 21)
Pablo Casals (cond.); Marlboro Festival Orchestra
SONY CD SMK 45891 (1991)★
Marlboro Festival 40th Anniversary Series
Recorded in Marlboro, Vermont, 13 July 1969

*Symphony No. 2 in D Major* (Op. 36)
Pablo Casals (cond.); Marlboro Festival Orchestra
SONY CD SMK 46247 (1991)★
Marlboro Festival 40th Anniversary Series
Recorded in Marlboro, Vermont, 3 August 1969

*Symphony No. 4 in B Flat Major* (Op. 60)
Pablo Casals (cond.); Marlboro Festival Orchestra
SONY CD SMK 46246 (1991)★
Marlboro Festival 40th Anniversary Series
Recorded in Marlboro, Vermont, 27 July 1969

*Symphony No. 6 in F Major* (Op. 68)
Pablo Casals (cond.); Marlboro Festival Orchestra
SONY CD SMK 45891 (1991)★
Recorded in Marlboro, Vermont, 12 July 1969

*Symphony No. 7 in A Major* (Op. 92)
Pablo Casals (cond.); Marlboro Festival Orchestra
(a) SONY CD SMK 45893 (1991)★; (b) CBS MYK 37233 (1981,★ 1975)
Marlboro Festival 40th Anniversary series
Recorded in Marlboro, Vermont, 2 August 1969

*Symphony No. 8 in F Major* (Op. 93)
Pablo Casals (cond.); Marlboro Festival Orchestra
SONY CD SMK 45893 (1991)
Marlboro Festival 40th Anniversary Series
Recorded in Marlboro, Vermont, 14 July 1963

*Trio No. 3 in C Minor for Piano, Violin and Cello* (Op. 1, No. 3)
Hepzibah Menuhin (piano); Yehudi Menuhin (violin); Pablo Casals
(cello)
*Casals Festivals at Prades*, Vol. I (Music & Arts Inc.) CD 688 (1991)★
Recorded at Prades, 18 July 1959

*Trio No. 5 in D Major for Piano, Violin and Cello* (Op. 70, No. 1) ('Ghost')
(i) Rudolf Serkin (piano); Szymon Goldberg (violin); Pablo Casals (cello)
*Casals Festivals at Prades*, Vol. I (Music & Arts Inc.) CD 688 (1991)★
Recorded at Prades, 18 June 1954

(ii) Karl Engel (piano); Sándor Végh (violin); Pablo Casals (cello)
PHIL 420 855–2 PLC (1988)★
Recorded at Prades, July 1961

*Trio No. 6 in E Flat Major for Piano, Violin and Cello* (Op. 70, No. 2)
Rudolf Serkin (piano); Szymon Goldberg (violin); Pablo Casals (cello)
*Casals Festivals at Prades*, Vol. I (Music & Arts Inc.) CD 688 (1991)★
Recorded at Prades, 18 June 1954

*Trio No. 7 in B Flat Major for Piano, Violin and Cello* (Op. 97) ('Archduke')
(i) Alfred Cortot (piano); Jacques Thibaud (violin); Pablo Casals (cello)
Recorded in the Small Queen's Hall, London, 18–19 November 1928
(a) EMI CDH 7 61024 2 (1988); (b) EMI CHS 7 64057 2 (1991)

(ii) Mieczyslaw Horszowski (piano); Sándor Végh (violin); Pablo Casals
(cello)
PHIL 420 855–2 PLC (1988)
Recorded at the Beethovenhaus, Bonn, September 1958

Twelve Variations in G Major on 'See, the Conquering Hero Comes!',
from Handel's *Judas Maccabeus*, for Cello and Piano
Pablo Casals (cello); Rudolf Serkin (piano)
CBS CD MPK 46725 (1991)
Recorded in Perpignan, summer 1951

Twelve Variations in F Major on '*Ein Mädchen oder Weibchen*' from
Mozart's *Die Zauberflöte* (Op. 66)
Pablo Casals (cello); Rudolf Serkin (piano)
CBS CD (*Pablo Casals Recital*), MPK 46724 (1991)
Recorded in Perpignan, June 1951

Ten Variations in G Major for Piano, Violin and Cello (Op. 121a) on
'*Ich bin der Schneider Kakadu*'
Rudolf Serkin (piano); Szymon Goldberg (violin); Pablo Casals (cello)
*Casals Festivals at Prades*, Vol. I (Music & Arts Inc.) CD 688 (1991)★
Recorded at Prades, 18 June 1954

Seven Variations in E Flat Major for Cello and Piano, on '*Bei Männern, welche Liebe fühlen*' from Mozart's *Die Zauberflöte*
(i) Pablo Casals (cello); Alfred Cortot (piano)
EMI CHS 7 64057 2 (1991)
Recorded in the Large Queen's Hall, London, 21 June 1927

(ii) Pablo Casals (cello); Rudolf Serkin (piano)
CBS CD (*Pablo Casals Recital*), MPK 46724 (1991)
Recorded in Perpignan, June 1951

LUIGI BOCCHERINI

*Concerto in B Flat Major for Cello and Orchestra*
Pablo Casals (cello); Sir Landon Ronald (cond.); London Symphony Orchestra
PEAR GEMM CD 9349 (1989)
Recorded in London, 29 November 1936

*Sonata No. 6 in A Major for Cello and Piano: Adagio and Allegro*
Pablo Casals (cello); Blas Net (piano)
PEAR GEM CD 9363 (1989)
Recorded 16–17 June 1929

JOHANNES BRAHMS

*Double Concerto in A Minor for Violin, Cello and Orchestra* (Op. 102)
Jacques Thibaud (violin); Pablo Casals (cello); Alfred Cortot (cond.); Orquestra Pau Casals
(a) EMI CHS 7 64057 2 (1991); (b) PEAR GEMM CD 9363 (1989)
Recorded in Barcelona, 10–11 May 1929

*Sextet No. 1 in B Flat Major for Strings* (Op. 18)
(i) Isaac Stern, Alexander Schneider (violins); Milton Katims, Milton Thomas (violas); Pablo Casals, Madeline Foley (cellos)
CBS CD MPK 44851
Recorded at Prades, June 1952

(ii) Yehudi Menuhin, A. Gerecs (violins); K. Tuttle, E. Wallfisch (violas); Pablo Casals, Madeline Foley (cellos)
STR 10018 (1989)★
Recorded at Prades, July 1955

*Sonata No. 2 in F Major for Cello and Piano* (Op. 99)
Pablo Casals (cello); Mieczyslaw Horszowski (piano)
PEAR GEMM CD 9363 (1989)
Recorded in Europe, 28 November 1936

*Trio No. 1 in B Major for Piano, Violin and Cello* (Op. 8)
Eugene Istomin (piano); Yehudi Menuhin (violin); Pablo Casals (cello)
*Casals Festivals at Prades*, Vol. II (Music & Arts Inc.) CD 689 (1991)★
Recorded at Prades, 13 July 1955

*Trio No. 2 in C Major for Piano, Violin and Cello* (Op. 87)
Eugene Istomin (piano); Yehudi Menuhin (violin); Pablo Casals (cello)
(a) Capital Musica, *i protagonisti*, STR 10018 (1989)★; (b) *Casals Festivals at Prades*, Vol. II (Music & Arts Inc.) CD 689 (1991)★
Recorded at Prades, 13 July 1955

*Trio No. 3 in C Minor for Piano, Violin and Cello* (Op. 101)
Eugene Istomin (piano); Yehudi Menuhin (violin); Pablo Casals (cello)
*Casals Festivals at Prades*, Vol. I (Music & Arts Inc.) CDD 688 (1991)★
Recorded at Prades, 13 July 1955

*Trio in A Minor for Piano, Clarinet and Cello* (Op. 114)
Eugene Istomin (piano); David Oppenheim (clarinet); Pablo Casals (cello)
*Casals Festivals at Prades*, Vol. II (Music & Arts Inc.) CD 689 (1991)★
Recorded at Prades, 3 July 1955

*Variations on a Theme by Haydn* (Op. 56a)
Pablo Casals (cond.); Marlboro Festival Orchestra
SONY CD SMK 46247 (1991)
Marlboro Festival 40th Anniversary Series
Recorded in Marlboro, Vermont, 5 July 1969


MAX BRUCH

*Kol Nidrei* for cello and orchestra (Op. 47)
Pablo Casals (cello); Sir Landon Ronald (cond.); London Symphony Orchestra
(a) EMI CDH 7 63498 2 (1990); (b) PEAR GEMM CD 9349
Recorded at the Abbey Road Studios, London, 27 November 1936

Arranged for cello and piano
Pablo Casals (cello); Nikolai Mednikoff (piano)
BIDD LAB 017 (*Casals, the Victor Recordings*) (1990)★
Recorded in New Jersey, 31 January 1928

PABLO CASALS

*Sacred Choral Music*
(Nigra Sum; Tota pulchra es; Cançó a la Verge; Rosario; O vos Omnes;
Eucharistica; Recordare Virgo Mater; Oració a la Verge de Montserrat;
Salve Regina)
Escolania de Montserrat; Ireneu Segarra (dir.)
SCHW 313062 (1991)*
Recorded at the Abbey of Montserrat, Catalonia, 19–20 October 1987

(O vos Omnes)
Warwick St Mary's Collegiate Church Choir; S. Lole; C. Matthews
(dir.)
ABBE CDCA592

FRÉDÉRIC CHOPIN

*Nocturne in E Flat Major for Piano* (Op. 9, No. 2), arranged for cello and
piano by David Popper
Pablo Casals (cello); Nikolai Mednikoff (piano)
(a) BIDD LAB 017 (*Casals, the Victor Recordings*) (1990); (b) MSCM MM
30428
Recorded in New Jersey, 20 January 1926

*Prelude in D Flat Major for Piano* (Op. 28, No. 15), arranged for cello and
piano by Sieveking
Pablo Casals (cello); Nikolai Mednikoff (piano)
(a) BIDD LAB 017 (*Casals, the Victor Recordings*) (1990); (b) MSCM MM
30428
Recorded in New Jersey, 19 January 1926

FRANÇOIS COUPERIN

*Concert Pieces (Suite)*, arranged for cello and piano by Paul Bazelaire
Pablo Casals (cello); Mieczyslaw Horszowski (piano)
CBS CD (*Pablo Casals Recital*) MPK 46724 (1991)
Recorded at the White House, Washington, DC, 13 November 1961

CLAUDE DEBUSSY

*Petite Suite* for four hands on one piano: '*Menuet*', arranged for cello and
piano by Choisnel

Pablo Casals (cello); Nikolai Mednikoff (piano)
BIDD LAB 017 (*Casals, the Victor Recordings*) (1990)
Recorded in New Jersey, 4 January 1926

ANTONÍN DVOŘÁK

*Concerto in B Minor for Cello and Orchestra* (Op. 104)
Pablo Casals (cello); George Szell (cond.); Czech Philharmonic Orchestra
(a) EMI CDH 7 63498 2 (1990); (b) PEAR GEMM CD 9349 (1989);
(c) MSCM MM 30428
Recorded at the Deutsche Haus, Prague, April 1937

SIR EDWARD ELGAR

*Concerto in E Minor for Cello and Orchestra* (Op. 85)
Pablo Casals (cello); Sir Adrian Boult (cond.); BBC Symphony
Orchestra
EMI CDH 7 63498 2 (1990)
Recorded at the Abbey Road Studios, London, 14 October 1945

MANUEL DE FALLA

*Canciones Populares Espagñoles*: No. 5, 'Nana', arranged for cello and piano
Pablo Casals (cello); Eugene Istomin (piano)
CBS CD (*Pablo Casals recital*) MPK 46724 (1991)
Recorded at Prades, June 1953

GABRIEL FAURÉ

'*Après un rêve*', arranged for cello and piano by Pablo Casals
Pablo Casals (cello); Nikolai Mednikoff (piano)
(a) BIDD LAB 017 (*Casals, the Victor Recordings*) (1990); (b) MSCM MM
30428
Recorded in New Jersey, 5 January 1926

DAVID GODARD

*Jocelyn*: Berceuse, '*Cachés dans cet asile*', arranged for cello and piano
Pablo Casals (cello); Nikolai Mednikoff (piano)

(a) BIDD LAB 017 (*Casals, the Victor Recordings*) (1990); (b) MSCM MM 30428
Recorded in New Jersey, 20 January 1926

### ENRIQUE GRANADOS

*Danzas Españolas*: No. 5, '*Andaluza*', arranged for cello and piano by Pablo Casals
Pablo Casals (cello); Nikolai Mednikoff (piano)
BIDD LAB 017 (*Casals, the Victor Recordings*) (1990)
Recorded in New Jersey, 28 February 1928

*Goyescas*: 'Intermezzo', arranged for cello and piano by Gaspar Cassadó
Pablo Casals (cello); Nikolai Mednikoff (piano)
(a) BIDD LAB 017 (*Casals, the Victor Recordings*); (b) MSCM MM 30428
Recorded in New Jersey, 28 February 1927

### FRANZ JOSEPH HAYDN

*Sonata No. 1 in C Major for Violin and Viola: Tempo di Minuetto*, arranged for cello and piano by Alfredo Piatti
Pablo Casals (cello); Blas Net (piano)
PEAR GEMM CD 9363 (1989)
Recorded 21 June 1929

*Sonata No. 9 in D Major for Piano: Adagio*, arranged for cello and piano
Pablo Casals (cello); Eugene Istomin (piano)
CBS CD (*Pablo Casals Recital*) MPK 46724 (1991)
Recorded in Perpignan, summer 1951

*Trio No. 1 in G Major for Piano, Violin and Cello* (Op. 73, No. 2)
Alfred Cortot (piano); Jacques Thibaud (violin); Pablo Casals (cello)
(a) EMI CHS 7 64057 2 (1991); (b) BIDD LAB 028 (1991)
Recorded in the Large Queen's Hall, London, 20 June 1927

### PAUL JOSEPH HILLEMACHER

*Gavotte Tendre* for cello and piano
Pablo Casals (cello); Nikolai Mednikoff (piano)
BIDD LAB 017 (*Casals, the Victor Recordings*) (1990)
Recorded in New Jersey, 4 January 1926

FELIX MENDELSSOHN-BARTHOLDY

*Symphony No. 4 in A Major* (Op. 90) ('Italian')
Pablo Casals (cond.); Marlboro Festival Orchestra
SONY CD SMK 46251 (1991)
Marlboro Festival 40th Anniversary Series
Recorded in Marlboro, Vermont, 13 July 1963; 1965

*Trio No. 1 in D Minor for Piano, Violin and Cello* (Op. 49)
Alfred Cortot (piano); Jacques Thibaud (violin); Pablo Casals (cello)
(a) EMI CHS 7 64057 2 (1991); (b) BIDD LHW 002 (1990)
Recorded in the Large Queen's Hall, London, 20–21 July 1927


WOLFGANG AMADEUS MOZART

*Ch'io mi scordi di te? (Recitativo andantino), Non temer, amato bene (Rondo andante),* (K. 505), concert aria for mezzo-soprano and orchestra with keyboard obbligato
Collegium Musicum de Londres; Pablo Casals (cond.); Victoria de los Angeles (soprano)
*Les Années Casals,* LYR CD 102 (from the Archives of the Prades Festival) (n.d.)★
Recorded at Prades, 9 July 1953(?)

*Concerto No. 9 in E Flat Major for Piano and Orchestra* (K. 271)
Clara Haskill (piano); Pablo Casals (cond.); Prades Festival Orchestra
*Les Années Casals,* LYR CD 102 (Archives of the Prades Festival)★
Recorded at Prades, 19 June 1953

*Idomeneo, Re di Creta; 'Zeffiretti lusinghieri'* (K. 366, No. 19)
Victoria de Los Angeles (soprano); Collegium Musicum (London); Pablo Casals (cond.)
*Casals Festivals at Prades* (Music & Arts Inc.), Vol. II, CD 689 (1991)★
Recorded at Prades, 9 July 1959

*Quartet No. 2 in E Flat Major for Piano, Violin, Viola and Cello* (K. 493)
(i) Mieczyslaw Horszowski (piano); Yehudi Menuhin (violin); Ernst Wallfisch (viola); Pablo Casals (cello)
*Casals Festivals at Prades,* Vol. I (Music & Arts Inc.) CD 688 (1991)★
Recorded at Prades, 7 July 1956

(ii) William Kapell (piano); Arthur Grumiaux (violin); Milton Thomas (viola); Pablo Casals (cello)
*Casals Festivals at Prades,* Vol. II (Music & Arts Inc.) CD 689 (1991)★
Recorded at Prades, 1 June 1953

*Serenade in G Major* (K. 525) *'Eine kleine Nachtmusik'*
Pablo Casals (cond.); Marlboro Festival Orchestra
SONY CD 47295 (1992)
Recorded in Marlboro, Vermont, 16 July 1967

*Symphony No. 35 in D Major* (K. 385) ('Haffner')
Pablo Casals (cond.); Marlboro Festival Orchestra
SONY CD 47294 (1992)
Recorded in Marlboro, Vermont, 30 July 1967

*Symphony No. 40 in G Minor* (K. 550)
Pablo Casals (cond.); Marlboro Festival Orchestra
SONY CD 47294 (1992)
Recorded in Marlboro, Vermont, 6 July 1968

*Symphony No. 41 in C Major* (K. 551)
Pablo Casals (cond.); Marlboro Festival Orchestra
SONY CD 47294 (1992)
Recorded in Marlboro, Vermont, 15 July 1967

DAVID POPPER

*Mazurka in G Minor* (Op. 11, No. 3)
Pablo Casals (cello); Nikolai Mednikoff (piano)
BIDD LAB 017 (*Casals, the Victor Recordings*) (1990)
Recorded in New Jersey, 26 February 1928

*Danses Espagnoles* (Op. 54, No. 5) ('Vito')
Pablo Casals (cello); Nikolai Mednikoff (piano)
BIDD LAB 017 (*Casals, the Victor Recordings*) (1990)
Recorded in New Jersey, 31 January 1928

ANTON RUBINSTEIN

*Melody in F Major for Piano* (Op. 3, No. 1), arranged for cello and piano
by David Popper
Pablo Casals (cello); Nikolai Mednikoff (piano)
(a) BIDD LAB 017 (*Casals, the Victor Recordings*) (1990); (b) MSCM MM
30428
Recorded in New Jersey, 20 January 1926

CAMILLE SAINT-SAËNS

*Le Carnaval des Animaux* for orchestra and two pianos: No. 13, '*Le Cygne*', arranged for cello and piano
Pablo Casals (cello); Nikolai Mednikoff (piano)
(a) BIDD LAB 017 (*Casals, the Victor Recordings*) (1990); (b) MSCM MM 30428 .
Recorded in New Jersey, 5 January 1926

FRANZ PETER SCHUBERT

*Moments Musicals* (Op. 94: No. 3 in F Minor)
Arranged for cello and piano by Hugo Becker
Pablo Casals (cello); Nikolai Mednikoff (piano)
(a) BIDD LAB 017 (*Casals, the Victor Recordings*) (1990); (b) MSCM MM 30428
Recorded in New Jersey, 4 January 1926

*Quintet in C Major for Two Violins, Viola and Two Cellos* (Op. 163, D. 956)
(i) Isaac Stern, Alexander Schneider (violins); Milton Katims (viola); Pablo Casals and Paul Tortelier (cellos)
CBS CD MPK 44853
Recorded at Prades, June 1952

(ii) Sándor Végh, Sándor Zöldy (violins); George Janzer (viola); Pablo Casals and Paul Szabo (cellos)
PHIL 420 077–2PLC (1988)
Recorded at Prades, July 1961

*Symphony No. 5 in B Flat Major* (D. 485)
Pablo Casals (cond.); Marlboro Festival Orchestra
SONY CD SMK 46246 (1991)*
Marlboro Festival 40th Anniversary Series
Recorded in Marlboro, Vermont, 1970

*Symphony No. 8 in B Minor* (D. 759) ('Unfinished')
Pablo Casals (cond.); Marlboro Festival Orchestra
SONY CD 47297 (1992)
Recorded in Marlboro, Vermont, 13 July 1968

*Trio No. 1 in B Flat Major for Piano, Violin and Cello* (Op. 99, D. 898)
Alfred Cortot (piano); Jacques Thibaud (violin); Pablo Casals (cello)
(a) EMI CDH 7 61024 2 (1988); (b) EMI CHS 7 64057 2 (1991)
Recorded in the Kingsway Hall, London, 5–6 July 1926

ROBERT SCHUMANN

*Abendlied* for piano, four hands (Op. 85, No. 12) arranged for cello and piano
Pablo Casals (cello); Nikolai Mednikoff (piano)
BIDD LAB 017 (*Casals, the Victor Recordings*) (1990)
Recorded in New Jersey, 4 January 1926

*Adagio and Allegro in A Flat Major* for French horn and piano (Op. 70), arranged for cello and piano
Pablo Casals (cello); Clifford Curzon (piano)
*Hommage à Pablo Casals*, AS 350 (1989)★
Recorded at Prades, 195?

*Symphony No. 2 in C Major* (Op. 61)
Pablo Casals (cond.); Marlboro Festival Orchestra
SONY CD 47297 (1992)★
Recorded in Marlboro, Vermont, 18 July 1970

*Trio No. 1 in D Minor for Piano, Violin and Cello* (Op. 63)
Alfred Cortot (piano); Jacques Thibaud (violin); Pablo Casals (cello)
(a) EMI CDS 7 64057 2 (1991); (b) BIDD LHW 004 (1991)
Recorded in the Small Queen's Hall, London, 15 and 18 November, and 3 December 1928

*Trio No. 2 in F Major for Piano, Violin and Cello* (Op. 80)
Eugene Istomin (piano); Yehudi Menuhin (violin): Pablo Casals (cello)
(a) *Hommage à Pablo Casals*, AS 350 (1989); (b) *Casals Festivals at Prades*, Vol. II (Music & Arts Inc.) CD 689 (1991)★
Recorded at Prades, 4 July 1956

*Trio No. 3 in G Minor for Piano, Violin and Cello* (Op. 110)
Rudolf Serkin (piano); Sándor Végh (violin); Pablo Casals (cello)
(a) *Hommage à Pablo Casals*, AS 350 (1989); (b) *Casals Festival at Prades*, Vol. I (Music & Arts Inc.) CD 688 (1991)★
Recorded at Prades, 11 July 1956

GIOVANNI SGAMBATI

*Serenata Napoletana* for violin and piano (Op. 24, No. 2), arranged for cello and piano by Bouman
Pablo Casals (cello); Nikolai Mednikoff (piano)
BIDD LAB 017 (*Casals, the Victor Recordings*) (1990)★
Recorded in New Jersey, 1 February 1928

DONALD FRANCIS TOVEY

*Cello Concerto in C Major* (Op. 40)
Pablo Casals (cello); Sir Adrian Boult (cond.); BBC Symphony
Orchestra
SYMP 1115 (1992)*
Recorded in the Queen's Hall, London, 17 November 1937


RICHARD WAGNER

*Die Meistersinger von Nürnberg*, Act III: '*Morgenlich leuchtend im rosigen
Schein*' ('*Preislied*'), arranged for cello and piano by August Wilhelmj
Pablo Casals (cello); Nikolai Mednikoff (piano)
(a) BIDD LAB 017 (*Casals, the Victor Recordings*) (1990); (b) MSCM MM
30428
Recorded in New Jersey, 19 January 1926

*Tannhäuser*, Act III, Scene 2: '*O du mein holder Abendstern*', arranged for
cello and piano
Pablo Casals (cello); Nikolai Mednikoff (piano)
(a) BIDD LAB 017 (*Casals, the Victor Recordings*) (1990); (b) MSCM MM
30428
Recorded in New Jersey, 4 January 1926

# Index

(Pablo Casals = PC)